# OXFORD CLASSICAL MONOGRAPHS

*Published under the supervision of a Committee of
the Faculty of Classics in the University of Oxford*

The aim of the Oxford Classical Monograph series (which replaces the Oxford Classical and Philosophical Monographs) is to publish books based on the best theses on Greek and Latin literature, ancient history, and ancient philosophy examined by the Faculty Board of Classics.

# Almsgiving in the Later Roman Empire

*Christian Promotion and Practice (313–450)*

RICHARD FINN OP

OXFORD
UNIVERSITY PRESS

# OXFORD

**UNIVERSITY PRESS**

Great Clarendon Street, Oxford OX2 6DP

Oxford University Press is a department of the University of Oxford.
It furthers the University's objective of excellence in research, scholarship,
and education by publishing worldwide in

Oxford New York

Auckland Cape Town Dar es Salaam Hong Kong Karachi
Kuala Lumpur Madrid Melbourne Mexico City Nairobi
New Delhi Shanghai Taipei Toronto

With offices in

Argentina Austria Brazil Chile Czech Republic France Greece
Guatemala Hungary Italy Japan Poland Portugal Singapore
South Korea Switzerland Thailand Turkey Ukraine Vietnam

Oxford is a registered trade mark of Oxford University Press
in the UK and in certain other countries

Published in the United States
by Oxford University Press Inc., New York

British Library Cataloguing in Publication Data

Data available

Library of Congress Cataloging in Publication Data

Data available

Typeset by SPI Publisher Services, Pondicherry, India
Printed in Great Britain
on acid-free paper by
Biddles Ltd., King's Lynn, Norfolk

ISBN 0–19–928360–5   978–0–19–928360–6

1 3 5 7 9 10 8 6 4 2

# Acknowledgements

My thanks are due to a great many people whose teaching, aid, and encouragement have been invaluable in the writing of this book. Eric Griffiths taught me how to read, and tried to make me think, when I first went to university at St Catherine's Cambridge. Euan Bowie, Robin Osborne, Stephen Harrison, Christopher Taylor, and Greg Woolf equipped me to read and question classical texts in Latin and Greek when I was an undergraduate at Corpus, Oxford. Lionel Wickham, Eamon Duffy, and Jonathan Riley-Smith guided my first steps in church history at Jesus, Cambridge. A host of teachers at Blackfriars over the years, including Brian Davies OP, Fergus Kerr OP, Herbert McCabe OP, Paul Parvis, Timothy Radcliffe OP, Roger Ruston, and Simon Tugwell OP have all left their mark. Margaret Atkins has long been the source of gentle wisdom in matters academic as in much else. Other Dominican brethren and sisters, friends, and family have sustained me by their kindness. My D.Phil. examiners, Gillian Clark and Fergus Millar, provided the essential comments which allowed me to turn a thesis into what I hope is a readable book. I should also record my gratitude to the Arts and Humanities Research Board which funded the research. My greatest debt is of course to the two scholars who supervised the thesis: Averil Cameron and Peter Garnsey. Both have been a constant source of inspiration, support, constructive criticism, and guidance. Without their belief in what I was doing, I would have never seen the project through to its completion. Their generosity has been exemplary. Stubborn errors remain my own.

# Contents

# Abbreviations

| | |
|---|---|
| *AE* | *L'Année épigraphique* |
| *Ap. Const.* | *Apostolic Constitutions* |
| *BCH* | *Bulletin de Correspondance Hellénique* |
| *BCTH* | *Bulletin Archéologique du Comité des Travaux Historiques et Scientifiques* |
| *CIL* | *Corpus Inscriptionum Latinarum* |
| CCSL | Corpus Christianorum Scriptorum Latinorum |
| CSEL | Corpus Scriptorum Ecclesiasticorum Latinorum |
| *DACL* | *Dictionnaire d'archéologie chrétienne et de liturgie* |
| *En. in Ps.* | *Enarrationes in Psalmos* |
| GCS | Die griechischen christlichen Schriftsteller |
| GNO | Gregorii Nysseni Opera |
| *HTR* | *Harvard Theological Review* |
| *ICUR* | *Inscriptiones christianae urbis Romae*, ed. Degrassi |
| *ILCV* | *Inscriptiones Latinae Christianae Veteres*, ed. E. Diehl |
| *JAOS* | *Journal of the American Oriental Society* |
| *JECS* | *Journal of Early Christian Studies* |
| *JEH* | *Journal of Ecclesiastical History* |
| *JThS* | *Journal of Theological Studies* |
| OCA | Orientalia Christiana Analecta |
| OSA | Œuvres de saint Augustin |
| OOSA | Opera Omnia di Sant' Ambrogio |
| PG | Patrologia Graeca, ed. J.-P. Migne |
| PL | Patrologia Latina, ed. J.-P. Migne |
| PO | Patrologia Orientalis |
| *RB* | *Revue Bénédictine* |
| SC | Sources chrétiennes |
| *Serm.* | *Sermon* |

| | |
|---|---|
| *TS* | *Theological Studies* |
| *VC* | *Vigiliae Christianae* |
| *WSAT 3* | *The Works of Saint Augustine, A Translation for the 21st Century*, ed. J. Rotelle OSA, part 3, *Sermons*, tr E. Hill OP, i–xi (New York, 1990–7). |
| *ZAC* | *Zeitschrift für antikes Christentum.* |

# 1

## Introduction

### THE *SENTENCES OF SEXTUS*

At the close of the fourth century an aristocratic Christian, Avita, wife of the Roman senator Turcius Apronianus, was persuaded by her formidable aunt, the Elder Melania, to practise a greater asceticism and piety.[1] To this end she demanded suitable reading. Rufinus of Aquileia, a monk and scholar whose literary work already enjoyed Melania's patronage, was engaged to translate from Greek into Latin the *Sentences of Sextus*, a compilation of moral maxims long popular among the faithful in the Eastern part of the empire.[2] The work had been composed at some point before the mid-third century; for Origen had written of the *Sentences* as being widely known and respected by the Christians of his day.[3] The Latin translation testifies to the continued and widespread regard for this particular work of moral literature on the part of Christians in the late empire, some of whom attributed the collection to the early martyr and bishop of Rome, Xystus. Rufinus praised the text for its brevity, clarity, and force, such that the 'saying contained in a single line might suffice to

---

[1] C. Pietri and L. Pietri, *Prosopographie chrétienne du Bas-Empire*, ii *Prosopographie de l'Italie chrétienne (313–604)*, i (Rome, 1999), 228–9.

[2] Paulinus of Nola recommended Rufinus as Melania's 'companion on the spiritual journey', a man 'possessing a rich knowledge of both rhetoric and theology in Greek just as much as in Latin'. *Ep.* 28. 5, in W. Hartel (ed.) *Sancti Pontii Meropii Paulini Nolani Epistulae*, CSEL 29 (Vienna, 1894), 246.

[3] Origen, *Contra Celsum* 8. 30, ed. M. Borret, *Origène, Contre Celse*, 5 vols, SC 132, 136, 147, 150, 227 (Paris, 1967–76), iv. 238; *Commentary on Matthew's Gospel* 15. 3, ed. E. Klostermann, *Origenes Matthäuserklärung*, GCS 40 (Leipzig, 1935), 354.

perfect one's whole life'.[4] Others were to translate the Greek original into Syriac, Armenian, and Coptic.[5] Rufinus ensured the work's further diffusion in the Latin West. Jerome was to comment some fifteen years later on its wide circulation 'through many provinces'.[6]

Behind Rufinus' choice of this particular work lay a more general demand. Avita had asked for something that was not too difficult, but which she would profit from reading.[7] The translation indicates the demand for edifying moral literature in Christian circles, where it was thought neither desirable nor possible to meet this demand from existing pagan works. Avita and Melania, like others in the period, desired a distinctively Christian education in virtue. Rufinus indeed presented the work to the readers as a handbook (an *encheiridion* or *anulus*) of Christian morals. Yet the *Sentences of Sextus* in fact derive from an earlier pagan collection or collections of maxims, which 'a Christian compiler has edited, carefully revised and modified', a process evident from the large number of maxims from the *Sentences* also found in a pagan gnomic collection, the *Sayings of Pythagoras*.[8] Jerome noted the work's diffusion with displeasure: he castigated Rufinus, his former friend, for picking a work which contained 'nothing of Christ' and falsely ascribing it to a Christian martyr; to call it a handbook was 'mad'. Thus, the *Sentences* indicate the great extent to which Christianity was able to adopt, and adapt, an existing moral language for its own purposes, but also the controversial nature of that project.

The *Sentences of Sextus* reveal that these purposes included an education in the meaning and value of almsgiving—the gift of

---

[4] Rufinus, *Sentences of Sextus*, preface, in M. Simonetti (ed.), *Tyrannii Rufini Opera*, CCSL 20 (Turnhout, 1961), 259. Translations are my own unless otherwise stated.

[5] For the Syriac context, cf. S. Brock, 'From Antagonism to Assimilation: Syrian Attitudes to Greek Learning', in N. Garsoïan, T. Mathews, and R. Thompson (eds.), *East of Byzantium: Syria and Armenia in the Formative Period* (Washington, DC, 1982), 27.

[6] Jerome, *Commentary on Jeremiah* 4. 41. 4, ed. S. Reiter, *Sancti Hieronymi Presbyteri Opera: In Hieremiam Prophetam Libri Sex*, CCSL 74 (Turnhout 1960), 211.

[7] Rufinus, *Sentences*, preface, CCSL 20. 259.

[8] H. Chadwick, *The Sentences of Sextus: A Contribution to the History of Early Christian Ethics* (Cambridge, 1959), 138. On gnomic literature generally in the classical world, cf. T. Morgan, *Literate Education in the Hellenistic and Roman Worlds* (Cambridge, 1998), 120–44.

money, food, or clothing to the very poor—as an activity which met with God's blessing when rightly motivated, even though the gift itself might appear too small to excite the praise given in classical culture to a large and public benefaction: 'God greatly favours the person who gives food to someone in need from the bottom of his heart, even though the gift is small'.[9] Who counts as needy is not specified, but is partly determined in the context of the Greek original by another saying in which almsgiving to destitute beggars (in Greek the πτωχοί) is praised and linked to the practice of periodic fasting: 'It is also a fine practice to fast so as to feed a beggar'.[10] A maxim which echoes Proverbs 21: 13 ('Whoever stops his ears so as not to hear the poor, will also cry out himself, but will go unheard') promotes almsgiving as a necessary condition for success in prayer: 'God does not listen to the plea of one who does not himself listen to the plea of those in need'.[11] These maxims are not found in the *Sayings of Pythagoras*, though some are echoed in an earlier Jewish text from the Hellenistic period, the *Sentences of Pseudo-Phocylides*, part of which was incorporated, probably in the mid-second century, into a Christian version of the *Sibylline Oracles*.[12]

The maxims, therefore, raise questions about the place of almsgiving in the ethic professed by late antique Christians. To what extent was almsgiving a distinctive feature of Christian ethics in comparison with the *mores* articulated by pagan texts? Is this almsgiving to be distinguished by the type or range of practices advocated, or by the meanings which attach to the practices through the discourse surrounding them, a distinctive promotion or exhortation to almsgiving in Christian communities? How important in that discourse were the motives supposed to inspire the donor? The *Sentences of Sextus* indicate continuity in the advocacy of almsgiving between the early and late empire, but did this advocacy also change? What did it achieve? In his work for Avita, a married woman and mother, Rufinus asserted the value of the *Sentences* for those seeking

[9] Chadwick, *Sentences*, l. 379, pp. 54 and 55.
[10] Ibid., l. 267, pp. 42 and 43.
[11] Ibid., l. 217, pp. 36 and 37.
[12] *Sibylline Oracles* 2. 78–90, ed. J. Geffcken, *Die Oracula Sibyllina*, GCS 8 (Leipzig 1902), 30–1.

'perfection'. In the Gospels (Matthew 19: 21) Christ had instructed the rich man that, if he wished to be perfect, he should sell his possessions and give the proceeds to the poor. What place, then, did almsgiving have in Christians' pursuit of sanctity as a form of asceticism open to married as well as to virginal and widowed Christians, and which might be either a partial or complete fulfilment of the dominical command?

Paul Veyne long ago warned that we must 'distinguish carefully between the ethic that a society practises . . . and the ethic that this society professes. The two ethics usually have little in common.'[13] A gap between the two ethics in the area of almsgiving was certainly recognized in late antiquity and used as a point of attack by Christian preachers on the purses of their congregation. 'For who has become any readier to give alms as a result of these talks?' Chrysostom complained. 'Who has thrown out their money?'[14] Yet between profession and practice there is often far more than simply a gap, the slippage between an ideal and the actual. To profess an ethic is to do more than to assert it or even to exhort others to its practice. It may serve to construct, reinforce, or alter, the meaning of that practice. For 'the same form of behaviour may have many different meanings according to the local context', and one such context or element in that context is what is said about what is done.[15] Then again the ideal may belong to an ideology, the advocacy of which may serve vested interests. Exhortation to give may exert a pressure to conform on reluctant donors, but may also construct and offer to more or less willing donors an opportunity through which their actions win prestige. What, then, was the relation between the ethic professed and that practised in the case of alms? In the same way that we cannot isolate a practice from the discourse in which it is embedded, one practice may also alter the nature of other practices: how did Christian almsgiving disturb traditional patterns of public benefaction? What impact did almsgiving have in this and other ways on the later Roman Empire? These are the questions which I seek to answer in this book.

[13] Paul Veyne, *Bread and Circuses*, abridged O. Murray and tr. B. Pearce (London 1990), 25.

[14] John Chrysostom, *Homilies on Matthew* 88, PG 58. 779.

[15] D. Cheal, *The Gift Economy* (London and New York, 1988), 3.

It might be objected that many of these questions can receive no adequate answer, because in seeking to relate practices to the meanings attached to those practices we require a knowledge of meanings which is simply unavailable. Ramsay MacMullen has argued with respect to the Christian adoption of gestures, rites, and symbols found in pagan worship that 'adequately self-revealing moments in our sources are too few to support much generalization about what any given act meant to the participant'.[16] The meaning of an action, however, is not determined arbitrarily by a private mental act of the agent. The probable meaning of almsgiving on a given occasion can often be reconstructed from our written sources, texts which played a crucial role in assigning or inscribing the meaning or meanings of almsgiving within the culture of the period. Yet before turning to these texts and the practices whose meaning they shaped, it is sensible to begin by looking at the cities of the empire, in particular the poor who lived within them or flocked to them in times of famine, and the Christian churches which these cities contained, so that we have a context in which to place both words and deeds.

## SETTING THE SCENE: CHRISTIANS IN THE LATE ROMAN EMPIRE

The severity and duration of the persecutions suffered by the churches in the early fourth century had varied greatly from region to region, but persecution had targeted, at least initially, the hierarchy and institutional life of the church rather than the Christian population *per se.* In many places churches were demolished; the sacred texts were seized and burnt; liturgical vessels were confiscated; particular pressure was brought to bear on bishops and other senior clerics to offer sacrifice, or at least to betray where the scriptures had been hidden.[17] Some had fled their dioceses; not a few caved in to the

---

[16] R. MacMullen, *Christianity and Paganism in the Fourth to Eighth Centuries* (New Haven, Conn., and London, 1997), 149.

[17] Eusebius of Caesarea, *On the Martyrs of Palestine*, preface, ed E. Schwartz, *Über die Märtyrer in Palaestina*, Eusebius Werke ii/2, GCS 6/2 (Berlin 1999), 907. On the different stages of the persecution, when and where imperial edicts were enforced,

authorities.[18] An Egyptian martyrology tells how in AD 304 Satrius Arrianus, the *praeses* in the Thebaid, sought to persuade the physician Coluthus to sacrifice by praising Apollonius, bishop of Siout (Lycopolis), and Plutarchus, bishop of Sbeht, for their good sense in complying with the imperial edicts.[19] Basil related how churches had been destroyed in Cappadocia, Christians had been imprisoned, and how the wealthy had left their homes at Caesarea; but the bishop had to admit with disapproval that many Christians were sitting happily in the audience for the horse- and chariot-races held there in honour of the war god Mars when the former centurion, and would-be martyr, Gordius entered the arena, gave himself up to the authorities, and stole the show.[20] A great many must have followed the advice which they offered Gordius: 'Deny the faith only in what you say, but keep it, as you wish, in your heart.'[21] Although many apostasized at the time, like the crowd of men, women, and children who were observed waiting to sacrifice at Antioch by the deacon Romanus, persecution did little to reduce the great number of Christians in the empire.[22] Any estimate is speculative, but Keith Hopkins has nonetheless followed Adolf Harnack in putting the Christian population by the early fourth century at some six million, or a tenth of the total population within the empire. Others have plumped for five million.[23] Christians were to be found throughout the empire, though

and on the number of martyrs who gave themselves up to the authorities, cf. G. E. M. De Ste. Croix, 'Aspects of the "Great" Persecution', *HTR* 47 (1954), 75–113; T. D. Barnes, 'Constantine and Christianity: Ancient Evidence and Modern Interpretations', *ZAC* 2 (1998), 274–94.

[18] Eusebius of Caesarea, *On the Martyrs* 1. 3, GCS 6/2. 908.

[19] *Martyrdom of S. Coluthus* 90 R ii–90 V I, in E. A. E. Reymond and J. W. B. Barns, *Four Martyrdoms from the Pierpoint Morgan Coptic Codices* (Oxford, 1973), 147. Reymond and Barns defend the historical reliability of this trial scene in their introduction, ibid. 9–11.

[20] Basil of Caesarea, *On the Martyr Gordius* 2 and 3, PG 31. 496A and 497A. The bishop told his congregation that there were still people alive who had heard the martyr's confession of faith.

[21] Ibid. 6, PG 31. 501D.

[22] Eusebius, *On the Martyrs* 2. 1, GCS 6/2. 909.

[23] K. Hopkins, 'Early Christian Number and its Implications', *JECS* 6 (1998), 185–226, at 191–2; H. A. Drake, *Constantine and the Bishops: The Politics of Intolerance* (Baltimore and London, 2000), 73 and 495–6 n. 2. For the view that the number of Christians is often under-estimated, cf. P. J. Heather and D. Moncur, *Politics, Philosophy and Empire in the Fourth Century Select Orations of Themistius* (Liverpool, 2001), 58.

their numbers might vary widely from city to city, region to region, and would continue to vary sharply, even as they rose, in the next 150 years. By 350 Christianity was already to be found in areas of North Africa remote from the great cities and in rural Phrygia.[24] Yet David Mattingly has pointed out that, whereas 'hundreds of bishoprics' were 'established in *Africa, Byzacena, Numidia,* and in the Maureta-nian provinces' by the late fourth century, Tripolitania had only five even in 397.[25] Christianity in northern Italy was mainly limited before 350 to towns on or near the eastern seaboard. The next three decades probably saw expansion into further towns, but study of sermons by Italian bishops of the late fourth century has suggested that urban paganism was not easily dislodged or eroded.[26]

Adherence to the old civic cults drew strength in many places from the latter's role in the construction of civic pride and status, a role attested until the late third century by the images of gods and temples on provincial coinage, like that of Zeus Marnas and his temple, the *Marneion,* at Gaza.[27] That role was still to be seen in the fourth century in the honour attached to local priesthoods. We should not dismiss out of hand the statement in the *Life of Porphyry* that, Gaza, a city of some 20,000 or more people, still had only 280 Christians when Porphyry became its bishop in around 395, or his later admis-sion that the pagans still formed a decade later the majority of the

---

[24] W. H. C. Frend, 'Town and Countryside in Early Christianity', in D. Baker (ed.), *Studies in Church History,* 16 (Oxford, 1979), 26–7, 36, and 39. Frend's assertion in an earlier article that in the 'fourth century the monks and holy men were the chief agents of the final rout of traditional paganism in the countryside' is now accepted only for a small minority of regions. Idem, 'The Winning of the Countryside', *JEH* 18 (London, 1967), 1–14, at 7.

[25] D. J. Mattingly, *Tripolitania* (London, 1995), 210.

[26] For expansion, cf. M. Humphries, *Communities of the Blessed: Social Environ-ment and Religious Change in Northern Italy, AD 200–400* (Oxford, 1999), 96 and 175. For the continuing strength of urban paganism, cf. R. Lizzi, *Vescovi e strutture ecclesiastiche nella città tardoantica (L'Italia annonaria nel IV-V secolo d.C.)* (Como, 1989), 68–9.

[27] On such images in general on Greek imperial coins, cf. A. Burnett, M. Amandry, and I. Carradice, *Roman Provincial Coinage,* ii/1 (London and Paris, 1999), 33. For images of Marnas on coins at Gaza, cf. G. F. Hill, *Catalogue of the Greek Coins of Palestine (Galilee, Samaria, and Judaea)* (London, 1914), pp. lxvi–lxxix; and C. Augé, 'Les Monnaies antiques de Gaza', in J.-B. Humbert (ed.), *Gaza méditerranéenne: Histoire et archéologie en Palestine* (Paris, 2000), 70–2, at 72.

city's rich elite.[28] The author of the *Life* would not include those whom he considered members of heretical churches, such as Marcionites or Arians;[29] and the larger number of Christians who lived three kilometres away in the port of Maioumas were governed by a bishop of their own;[30] there is nothing implausible in a figure of some 300 Christians belonging to the church which controlled the city's principal basilicas and martyr's shrine. In such a city the religious affiliation of the local elite was a powerful force in keeping others from becoming Christian. This can be deduced from the snatches of conversation which Augustine wove into one of his sermons on the psalms: people could gossip that if a certain nobleman were to become Christian, no one would remain a pagan.[31] Such figures, Augustine observed, were like the walls surrounding and defending the 'city of disbelief'.

The outbreak in the early fourth century of the Donatist and Meletian schisms at Carthage and Alexandria, with their subsequent wider development and persistence in North Africa and Egypt, revealed how far persecution had weakened church life by making it prone to fissure.[32] Persecution weakened lines of authority within local church communities and bonds of inter-communion between such communities. The Christological and Trinitarian controversies

[28] Mark the Deacon, *Life of Porphyry* 19 and 63, in *Marc le Diacre, Vie de Porphyre, évêque de Gaza*, ed. H. Grégoire and M.-A. Kugener (Paris, 1930), 16 and 50. For the dating of Porphyry's election and a brief defence of the historicity of this event, cf. C. Rapp's introduction to her selected translations from the *Life* in T. Head, *Medieval Hagiography: An Anthology* (New York and London, 2001), 54–6. For Gaza's likely population, cf. R. Van Dam, 'From Paganism to Christianity at Late Antique Gaza', *Viator*, 16 (1985), 7.

[29] For evidence of Arian congregations who met for worship in the homes of their wealthier members, cf. H. O. Maier, 'Religious Dissent, Heresy and Households in Late Antiquity', *VC* 49 (1995), 51. Nicene Christians had likewise worshipped in private houses during the years when Arianism was in the ascendancy. Cf. Synesius, *Ep.* 66, in A. Garzya and D. Roques (eds.), *Synésios de Cyrène, Correspondance*, 3 vols. (Paris, 2000), 3. 179.

[30] Mark the Deacon, *Life* 58, in Grégoire and Kugener, *Vie*, 47. Mark attributes the larger size of the Christian church at Maioumas to the number of Egyptian wine merchants based in the port.

[31] Augustine, *En. in Ps.* 54. 13, in D. Dekkers and J. Fraipont, *Sancti Aurelii Augustini Enarrationes in Psalmos* li–c, CCSL 39 (Turnhout, 1956), 666.

[32] For the possible link between Apollonius' apostasy and the Meletian schism, cf. J. Barns and H. Chadwick, 'A Letter Ascribed to Peter of Alexandria', *JThS* (Oct. 1973), at 449.

of the fourth century would foment further, bitter, division. Unity was reasserted in such circumstances by celebrating the martyrs who had kept the faith. It is true that the cult of the martyrs long predated the fourth century: Eusebius of Caesarea included in his *Church History* an account of the second-century martyrdom of St Polycarp, which told how the surviving Christians of Smyrna had secured his remains in a suitable location where they would gather to celebrate the anniversary of his death.[33] In some places earlier Christians had raised monuments over the martyrs' graves: Gaius, an opponent of Montanism in the early third century, could write of monuments at the Vatican and on the road to Ostia which were dedicated to the memory of the apostles Peter and Paul as founders of the Roman church.[34] Yet the veneration of the martyrs now reached new heights; and what Delehaye once saw as a result of natural enthusiasm let loose in an hour of triumph may be, rather, a response to partial disarray, indicative of the need for a local cult analogous to that through which pagans were able to reinforce their common, civic, identity.[35] Numerous *martyria* (martyrs' shrines) were constructed, some of which would emerge as major centres of Christian pilgrimage. Constantine led the way: he decreed that the burial places of the martyrs were to be given or returned to the churches; he financed the construction at Rome of the huge basilica over St Peter's tomb in the Vatican necropolis; and at his new capital of Constantinople, dedicated to the 'God of the martyrs', he constructed several *martyria*, one of which was a shrine to a local saint, Mocius, executed under Diocletian or Licinius.[36] The destruction wrought by persecution was to be transmuted into glorious triumph. Peter Brown has observed that by the late fourth and fifth centuries the cult of the martyrs was changing the 'importance accorded to the areas of the living and . . . of the dead in most late-antique towns'. Where Antony had

---

[33] Eusebius, *Ecclesiastical History* 4. 15. 43–4, ed. G. Bardy, *Eusèbe de Césarée: Histoire ecclésiastique*, 4 vols., SC 31, 41, 55, and 73 (Paris, 1952–60), i. 189.

[34] Ibid. 2. 25. 6–7, SC 31. 92–3.

[35] H. Delehaye, *Les Origines du culte des martyrs* (Brussels, 1912), 52. For the esteem in which a local martyr was held, cf. Basil, *On the Martyr Gordius* 2, PG 31. 493B.

[36] Eusebius, *Life of Constantine* 2. 40 and 3. 48, ed. F. Winkelmann, *Über das Leben des Kaisers Konstantin*, Eusebius Werke i/1, 2nd edn. (Berlin, 1991), 65 and 104. Cf. T. D. Barnes, *Constantine and Eusebius* (Cambridge, Mass., 1981), 222.

been said to found a city in the desert, bishops 'now founded cities in the cemetery'.[37]

The fourth and early fifth centuries saw the establishment of many new bishoprics. Mark Humphries believes that, when the Christians of Vercelli elected Eusebius as their bishop not long before 355, Eusebius was in fact their first bishop, and that numerous towns in the region, like Bergamo and Tortona, were to gain bishops in the second half of the fourth century.[38] Ambrose, writing to the church of Vercelli in 396 or 397, described the bishop as the one 'in whom the life of all was formed'.[39] Christianity's presence, its social visibility and impact, might change dramatically when a bishop was first established in a city, and that establishment was not determined only by strength of numbers. The *Histories of the Monks of Upper Egypt*, a text written probably in the final decade of the fourth century, purports to tell what happened when, in around the mid-fourth century, a bishop was first established at Philae, a garrison city and centre of pagan cult on the far southern frontier of Roman Egypt.[40] A few Christians already inhabited the town, and were served on Saturdays and Sundays by a priest from the neighbouring city of Aswan. Their social presence and visibility in the city may be considered minimal. The *Histories* related only that they were 'badly mistreated by those who worship idols'. But a visiting dignitary and official, a Christian called Macedonius, discovered this state of affairs; he petitioned Athanasius, the patriarch of Alexandria, for a bishop to be sent to the city; and found himself appointed to the job.[41] On his return to Philae he apparently gave away his wealth, probably in alms; he tricked his way into one of the city's pagan shrines, and destroyed the cult statue it contained.[42] The drama does not end there. The two sons of the pagan priest in charge of the shrine flee from their father only to become the new bishop's priest and deacon.

[37] P. Brown, *The Cult of the Saints: Its Rise and Function in Latin Christianity* (London, 1981), 7–8.

[38] Humphries, *Communities*, 93 and 173–5.

[39] Ambrose, *Ep. Extra Coll.* 14. 46, ed. M. Zelzer, in G. Banterle, *Lettere*, 3 vols., OOSA 19–21 (Milan and Rome, 1988), iii. 286.

[40] *Histories of the Monks of Upper Egypt and the Life of Onnophrius by Paphnutius*, ed. T. Vivian (Kalamazoo, 1993), 53 and 66.

[41] Paphnutius, *Histories* 29–30, in Vivian, *Histories*, 85–6.

[42] Paphnutius, *Histories* 31, in Vivian, *Histories*, 87.

The pagan priest is himself converted to Christianity, gives away *his* wealth, and provides the first church in the city.[43] The story ends with the mass conversion of the city's pagan inhabitants.[44] As that ending suggests, the tale cannot be taken at face value: there were still pagans at Philae in the mid-sixth century.[45] Nonetheless, the *Histories* suggest something of the impact created by the arrival in a small city of a new bishop from the governing classes. They record, even as they exaggerate, the violence to the old order which might follow such an event, the wave of conversions it might trigger. The *Histories* show the disturbance within families as different generations gave their allegiance to one or other cult, though they also suggest how a family may negotiate changes in religion, displaying in a new religion the standing previously displayed in another. The work suggests the place which almsgiving might occupy in the story of conversion. It certainly tells us how the author (a monk) at the end of the fourth century *thought* almsgiving should feature in that story, as the mark of a saintly bishop and as a characteristic of conversion separating pagan from Christian. The tale helps us to think about the growing Christian population in better ways than just counting bodies.

The wealth of the different urban churches varied widely depending on the number and social standing of their members. It may also be variously understood: what the churches possessed, and might receive from regular income, differed from what they might command on occasion by eliciting further donations from their richer members, and by use of the bishop's own possessions. Few figures exist and, where they do, prove difficult to interpret. In around AD 400 Mark the Deacon was able to take forty-three *nomismata*, presumably gold pieces, from the surplus income of the tiny church at Gaza to finance Bishop Porphyry's mission to Constantinople, income which came in part from land owned by the church in the surrounding district and farmed by tenants.[46] We cannot tell what proportion of the surplus this represents, nor what levels of income and expenditure lay behind it. The church incomes recorded under

[43] Paphnutius, *Histories* 32–51, in Vivian, *Histories*, 87–95.
[44] Paphnutius, *Histories* 51, in Vivian, *Histories*, 95–6.
[45] Vivian, *Histories*, 60–2.
[46] Mark the Deacon, *Life* 22 and 34, in Grégoire and Kugener, *Vie*, 19 and 29.

Justinian vary, with rare exceptions, between less than two and thirty pounds of gold. Krause has argued on the basis of these sums that only a few dozen recipients of alms could be supported by smaller churches and several hundred in the larger sees.[47] Yet A. H. M. Jones read these figures as giving only the bishops' 'stipends', or share of total income, excluding 'offerings or the endowments of independent parishes and charitable institutions'.[48] What the absence of statistics cannot occlude is the social significance of the wealth at some bishops' disposal by the opening of the fourth century. When the bishop of Thumis, Phileas, was tried at Alexandria in around 305, the prefect Clodius Culcianus spoke of the wealth at the bishop's command such that he could 'feed and provide for' not only himself but the 'entire city'.[49] Whatever the exaggeration here, and however such wealth originated, the prefect offered to spare Phileas, and called on him to spare himself, because of his standing as a civic benefactor. It is possible that Culcianus was alluding to the bishop's duty to distribute alms to the poor. Were he to sacrifice, he would then be free to go about his charitable business.

The *Histories of the Monks of Upper Egypt* allows us to glimpse the importance of gaining a dedicated church building or complex within the city. The construction or dedication of a basilica gave the community who worshipped within it a more public and distinct identity, a place outside which Christians could be encountered as such by their pagan neighbours, so that the creation of new churches should be numbered among the technologies of Christian identity. Inscriptions testify to the multiple benefactions by clergy and laity of widely differing amounts which often paid for a church's construction and decoration; they show such work to be an exercise in the joint construction, and confident affirmation, of Christian identity in the aftermath of persecution.[50] Where a church already existed, the

---

[47] J.-U. Krause, *Witwen und Waisen im Römischen Reich*, 4 vols. (Stuttgart, 1994–5), iv. 25.

[48] A. H. M. Jones, *The Decline of the Ancient World* (London and New York, 1966), 262.

[49] *The Acts of Phileas* 11, in H. Musurillo (ed.), *The Acts of the Christian Martyrs* (Oxford, 1972), 342.

[50] J. P. Caillet, *L'Évergétisme monumental chrétien en Italie et à ses marges* (Rome, 1993), 427, 432, 461–2; Humphries, *Communities*, 74–9.

fourth and early fifth centuries saw in many places either its enlargement, the construction of a further church, or both. At Geneva a church and baptistery was built in the mid-fourth century on the site of the present cathedral, only to be substantially enlarged in the early years of the fifth century into an ecclesiastical complex covering some 7,000 m$^2$ with halls, in which the faithful could be instructed and the bishop could meet with his guests, as well with as smaller rooms for accommodation and storage.[51] Christian emperors displayed the generosity shown by pagan predecessors to pagan temples. Constantine in some measure made funds available for church building; he encouraged bishops to apply to provincial governors for help in the matter.[52] Later emperors and members of the imperial family continued to act on occasion as benefactors, especially in the Holy Land. Eudoxia, the wife of Arcadius, was said to have given Porphyry in 402 two hundred pounds of gold for the new church and pilgrim hostel or *xenon* at Gaza, where each traveller was to be fed and sheltered for up to three days.[53] She later sent in addition thirty-two marble columns.[54] Such buildings celebrated imperial patronage of the Christian religion, and the new church at Gaza was named the *Eudoxiana*, but the bishops in particular enhanced their status through new churches.[55] The sixth-century *Chronicle of Edessa* records the building of a church in the city in 312–13 as initially the work of its bishop Quona, later to be completed by his successor.[56] Epigraphy conveyed much the same message to contemporaries: a Greek inscription of AD 359 high on the wall of a baptistery at Nisibis proclaims the role of Vologaeses, the city's third bishop, and of a presbyter, Akepsumas, in the baptistery's construction.[57] Bishops gained more than simply a founder's or benefactor's honour: they

---

[51] F. Glaser, *Frühes Christentum im Alpenraum* (Regensburg, 1997), 49.

[52] Eusebius, *Life of Constantine* 2. 45–6, in Winkelmann, *Über das Leben*, 66–8. For modern scholars who accept Eusebius on this point, cf. Barnes, *Constantine and Eusebius*, 210 n. 9; and F. Millar, *The Roman Near East, 31 BC–AD 337* (Cambridge, Mass., and London, 1993), 212.

[53] Mark the Deacon, *Life* 53, in Grégoire and Kugener, *Vie*, 44.

[54] Mark the Deacon, *Life* 84, in Grégoire and Kugener, *Vie*, 66.

[55] *Mark the Deacon*, Life 92, in Grégoire and Kugener, *Vie*, 71.

[56] Millar, *Roman Near East*, 465.

[57] F. Sarre and E. Herzfeld, *Archäologische Reise im Euphrat-und-Tigris-Gebiet*, ii (Berlin, 1920), 337.

gained impressive stages on which the celebration of the liturgy further articulated their authority—such as the rite of baptism on Easter night. And all these church complexes created a public space where the bishop with his clergy could interact, and be seen to interact, with the very poor who crowded round the doors and porticoes. They created a public stage for the bishop's almsgiving.

The Christian population, therefore, was not only growing in numbers, but increasingly asserting itself within the cities and towns of the empire. The many new basilicas displayed the wealth, standing, and prestige of these communities with a bishop at their head. Beyond the towns, the countryside was not a wholly separate world. An urban centre had its wider territory. Origen had spoken in the third century of some itinerant preachers who visited 'not only cities but even villages and farms' and these were probably settlements within the civic hinterland.[58] Clergy in the fourth century continued something very like this practice.[59] Wealthy Christians with town houses owned distant estates, as St Basil's father owned a house at Neocaesarea and vast estates at Annesi and elsewhere. A Spanish church council of perhaps around AD 365 legislated to prevent such landowners from inviting Jews to bless their fields.[60] The urban church might itself own properties in the countryside: the Alexandrian church received income from lands in Cyrenaica.[61] The church at Hippo apparently controlled *coloni* or peasant farmers;[62] rural workers like these formed part of the Christian congregation in the surrounding district.[63] Town and country were linked for Christians by travellers in either direction, whether pilgrims seeking out monks, or monks entering the towns to sell their produce and champion the cause of orthodoxy. To what extent the countryside remained mission territory varied from one province to another, but in Egypt at least monks played an important role in disseminating

[58] Origen, *Contra Celsum* 3. 9, SC 136. 30.

[59] Humphries, *Communities*, 146.

[60] Canon 49 of Elvira, in J. Suberbiola Martinez, *Nuevos concilios Hispano-Romanos de los siglos III y IV: La coleccion de Elvira* (Malaga, 1987), 121. Jesus Suberbiola Martinez argues that the so-called 'Canons of Elvira' comprise legislation from a series of church councils. Ibid. 80 for his discussion of canon 49.

[61] Synesius, *Ep.* 66, in Garzya and Roques, *Synésios*, iii. 183.

[62] Augustine, *Ep.* 10*6, ed. J. Divjak, *Lettres* 1*–29*, OSA 46b (Paris, 1987), 176.

[63] *Ep.* 20* 20, OSA 46b, 322.

Christianity within rural areas. They might further the growth and practice of Christianity by peaceful means, as when Pachomius built a church at Pbow for the local villagers outside the monastery there, or by actively destroying pagan cult centres, as when Shenoute vandalized the temple statues in the village of Pnueit, fifteen miles north of his monastery at Sohag.[64]

The growth of monasticism, and of eremitical as opposed to coenobitic monasticism in particular, is hard to quantify and plot. It appears that there were several thousand semi-anchoretic monks at Nitria by the late fourth century.[65] We can chart the rapid rise of Pachomian coenobitic monasticism in Upper Egypt from the foundation of Tabennesi sometime in the years 320–3 to the existence of eight other male monasteries under Pachomius' rule by the time of his death in 346, when the two largest probably each contained a thousand or more monks.[66] The growth of monasteries during the fourth century in northern Syria can be partially reconstructed from Theodoret's *Historia religiosa*. We cannot quantify, however, the rising number of ascetics who by the late fourth century were living alone or in small communities, whether in Cappadocia, or ringing great cities such as Antioch, and who are known from the writings of Basil and Theodoret. We can assess something of their impact on popular piety by looking, for example, at what Theodoret reveals of his mother's contact with the monks around Antioch. She was recommended as a young woman to visit one, Peter, in order to be cured of an eye infection. She later sent the young Theodoret to receive the monk's weekly blessing at the tomb which Peter occupied, and she would use the monk's belt to treat family illnesses.[67] A famous monk, whose abode articulated the renunciation of this world's pleasures, was to be revered as a channel of divine healing and his favour cultivated. Christian ascetic practice and piety were in general

---

[64] J. Goehring, 'The World Engaged: The Social and Economic World of Early Egyptian Monasticism' in J. Goehring, C. W. Hedrick, J. T. Sanders, and H. D. Betz (eds.), *Gnosticism and the Early Christian World* (Sonoma, Calif., 1990), 136 and 140.

[65] D. Chitty, *The Desert a City* (London and Oxford, 1966), 30–1.

[66] P. Rousseau, *Pachomius: The Making of a Community in Fourth-Century Egypt* (Berkeley, Calif., and London, 1985), 74.

[67] Theodoret, *Historia religiosa* 9. 4–8 and 15, ed. P. Canivet and A. Leroy-Molinghen, *Théodoret de Cyr, Histoire des moines de Syrie*, 2 vols., SC 234 and 257 (Paris, 1977 and 1979), i. 414–22 and 434.

much altered in the fourth century by the rising fame of monasticism in all its forms. Athanasius wrote that the 'life of Antony provides monks with a fitting model of asceticism';[68] and the success of his *Life*, in popularizing as a pattern of sanctity Antony's withdrawal from direct participation in civic affairs and urban church communities, was a significant factor in the growing dissatisfaction among Christians with the older custom of *syneisaktism*, whereby an ascetic man and woman lived in the same household and provided for each other's needs. A model of peaceful reconciliation between once warring sexes increasingly gave way to a model of heroic separation. But the symbolic marking and enforcing of boundaries between the sexes was accompanied by the crossing of boundaries between rich and poor. As we shall see, monks would prove important as both beneficiaries and distributors of alms.

The expression of episcopal authority in the new urban church architecture was in part a response to the difficulties faced by bishops who sought to promote and give clear definition to what they believed was orthodox Christianity. Heretical and other movements prominent in the second and third centuries, and in the church history of that period, had not disappeared by the fourth and fifth centuries. Marcionites and Montanists, for example, continued to claim a Christian identity to the wrath of 'orthodox' Christians. In 310 a Marcionite bishop, Asclepius, was burnt to death on the same pyre as a young ascetic whom Eusebius recognized as a fellow member of the Catholic Church.[69] Montanism was still thought sufficiently dangerous in the second half of the fourth century for someone to pen a polemical dialogue, the *Dialexis*, purporting to relate a debate held between a Montanist and an orthodox Catholic.[70] Apocryphal literature composed in earlier centuries circulated widely. Boundaries between Jews, Christians, and pagans were not always neat and tidy, though powerful churchmen were eager to distance their own Christianity from what they saw as foreign or idolatrous. Jerome asserted that there were people in the Eastern

---

[68] Athanasius, *Life of Antony*, preface, 3, in G. Bartelink (ed.), *Vie d'Antoine*, SC 400 (Paris, 1994), 126.

[69] Eusebius, *On the Martyrs* 10. 2–3, GCS 6/2. 930–1.

[70] *Dialogo tra un Montanista e un Ortodosso*, ed. A. M. Berruto Martone (Bologna, 1999), 12 and 19.

Empire who thought of themselves as Jewish and Christian, but he himself denied that one could be both.[71] Augustine sought to dissuade those who saw themselves as Catholics from 'visiting idols'.[72] Basil of Caesarea was concerned at 'Christians joining non-Christian feasts in temples' around AD 375.[73] Robert Markus has argued that 'the image of a society neatly divided into "Christian" and "pagan" is the creation of late fourth-century Christians, and has been too readily taken at face value by modern historians' when studying earlier periods,[74] but that creation of a divided society was a highly significant act. As another scholar has stated, the fourth century was 'particularly rich in the proliferation of technologies for the production of self and other'.[75]

The wider 'Church' to which local churches saw themselves as belonging was both a mental construct and a set of social practices with shared rules governing the practices and membership of the institution. There was, however, only partial agreement in the fourth century over what the rules were and who were the members in this 'vast network of interrelating communities'.[76] In a period of fierce theological controversy those who called themselves Christian frequently owed allegiance to rival bishops, as Donatist and Catholic Christians did in many cities of Roman North Africa, or fought for control of different church buildings, as Nicene and Arian Christians competed for the Milanese basilicas in 385–6.[77] It cannot have been easy for many to know which bishop should claim their allegiance; bishops, on the other hand, found it hard to know whom to admit to or exclude from communion. A theologian such as Augustine understood the Church not only as those church communities united by

[71] Jerome, *Ep.* 112. 13, in I. Hilberg (ed.) *Sancti Hieronymi Epistulae*, 3 vols., CSEL 54–6, 2nd edn. (Vienna, 1996), ii. 381–2, and cited D. Boyarin, *Dying for God* (Stanford, Calif., 1999), 17. Cf. S. G. Wilson, *Related Strangers: Jews and Christians, 70–170 CE* (Minneapolis, 1995), 155–9.

[72] Augustine, *En. in Ps.* 88. 2. 14, CCSL 39. 1244.

[73] MacMullen, *Christianity and Paganism*, 163 n. 9.

[74] R. Markus, *The End of Ancient Christianity* (Cambridge, 1990), 28, quoted in Boyarin, *Dying*, 16.

[75] Boyarin, *Dying*, 18.

[76] C. White, *Christian Friendship in the Fourth Century* (Cambridge, 1992), 5.

[77] On this struggle, cf. N. McLynn, *Ambrose of Milan: Church and Court in a Christian Capital* (Berkeley, Los Angeles, and Oxford, 1994), 170–96.

bonds of mutual recognition and orthodoxy, but all those incorporated into the Mystical Body of Christ. The bishop of Hippo thus numbered Abraham and the Old Testament Prophets among the Church's members.[78] The historian cannot speak in the same way. I shall speak of the 'Church' to name an institution which transcended local urban churches and which was realized in letters of recommendation or mutual communion between churches, the functioning of regional synods and attendance at ecumenical councils, and so on. This requires me to distinguish on occasion between, for example, the *Catholic* Church or the *Donatist* Church of North Africa.

We may not assume that in such a ferment all the members of a given Christian group or church shared the same beliefs about the charitable practices they adopted, although the principle of 'orthodoxy' commonly held by contemporaries—that there was a correct set of beliefs which together constituted, or gave dogmatic form to, the Christian faith—means that we may expect some consistency or efforts to achieve it. The historian's extant sources are biased towards the beliefs of the learned clergy and the lay people for whom they often wrote. Lack of evidence concerning Marcionite and other gnosticizing churches has led me to exclude them from this study, but otherwise this book is concerned with almsgiving in all the different church communities found in late Roman cities. Homogeneity of practice and belief will not be assumed until shown.

## SETTING THE SCENE: THE POOR IN THE LATE ROMAN EMPIRE

Salvian noted in the fifth century that 'there is no single form of poverty shared by all those who number among the poor'.[79] He distinguished among the poor, for example, between those who lacked 'food but not clothes' and 'the many who lacked not clothing

---

[78] Augustine, *Serm.* 4. 11, in S. Lambot (ed.) *Sancti Aurelii Augustini Sermones de Vetere Testamento* i–l, CCSL 41 (Turnhout 1961), 28.

[79] Salvian, *Four Books of Timothy to the Church* 4. 21, ed. G. Lagarrigue, *Salvien de Marseille, Œuvres*, 2 vols., SC 176 and 220 (Paris, 1971 and 1975), i. 324.

but shelter'.[80] In such a society the poor did not form a single, distinct, social group or class.[81] The Graeco-Roman world distinguished between *paupertas*, poverty as relatively straitened circumstances (though relative to what varied widely); *egestas*, poverty as material deprivation; and *mendicitas*, the absolute destitution of the person forced to beg.[82] Involuntary and voluntary poverty usually implied dependence on others, concerned social as well as economic standing, but we should not under-estimate the gulf separating the relative poverty and the dependence of a client on his patron from the absolute poverty of beggars dependent on their donors. Poverty, furthermore, could be either a temporary or permanent condition; and the economic poverty experienced as hardship by many citizens of the empire is to be distinguished from the lack of freedom and the insecurity from violence experienced by slaves, such as the woman whipped by her owner until she revealed the whereabouts of her runaway daughter in a convent.[83]

A great many found themselves trapped in utter destitution, without home or savings, without a family to support them, unable to find sufficient work to feed and support themselves. In rural districts a few might join the bands of robbers who preyed on travellers.[84] Those who were citizens of the cities in which they lived might hope to benefit from the occasional benefactions of the rich, but those who could not claim citizenship were excluded even from this assistance. The urban destitute were to be found begging in public thoroughfares or wherever else they might hope to attract alms, at the city gates, at the entrances to baths, churches, and palaces. Libanius in *Oration* 7 portrays the naked and half-naked beggars, some crippled, sitting and standing in the cold at Antioch, probably near the entrance to the baths, who cry out for alms in the hope of receiving a piece of bread or an *obol* from the passers-by.[85] It was a fate which

---

[80] Ibid. 4. 22, SC 176. 324.

[81] M. Prell, *Sozialökonomische Untersuchungen zur Armut in antiken Rom: Von den Gracchen bis Kaiser Diokletian* (Stuttgart, 1997), 64.

[82] Ibid. 58. For a detailed discussion of the language of poverty in late Roman Latin literature, cf. V. Neri, *I marginali nell'occidente tardoantico* (Bari, 1998), 33–52.

[83] Theodoret, *Historia religiosa* 9. 12, SC 234. 428.

[84] Neri, *I marginali*, 369–71.

[85] Libanius, *Or.* 7. 1–2, in R. Foerster, *Libanii Opera*, 12 vols. (Leipzig, 1903–23), i. 2, 373–4.

awaited in particular the sick, the aged, the crippled, the blind, or otherwise disabled. The monk Hypatios found peasants weak from hunger or disease lying in the road whom he brought into his monastery.[86] At Jerusalem in the late fourth century Porphyry, the future bishop of Gaza, found a young man, Barochas, lying danger-ously ill in the street, whom he rescued, nursed back to health, and kept on as a household servant.[87] The anchorite Julian Saba was famed for healing a cripple whom he found begging at the palace gates in Antioch.[88] Jerome excited pity in readers by painting the vivid scene of a cripple scarcely able to drag himself along, and of a blind man stretching out his hand and crying for alms when there was no one to hear his cry for help.[89] The Alexandrian scholar Eulogius came across a beggar without hands or feet who was found accosting people in the marketplace, and whom Eulogius took home as a (not wholly willing) companion in the ascetic life.[90] The women supported in a Christian hospital at Alexandria, whom Palladius describes as 'mutilated' and having 'disfigured faces', were probably victims of leprosy.[91] As Valerio Neri has pointed out, the high proportion of sick and disabled beggars in Christian texts of the period cannot be explained solely in terms of biblical stereotyping, but reflects one facet of late antique poverty.[92]

By no means every beggar was ill or crippled: John Chrysostom spoke of beggars who approached and accosted people at home and in the streets;[93] some caught the attention of the crowd by making a spectacle of themselves;[94] and many were successful in gaining alms, whether from pagans or Christians; but we should not over-estimate or otherwise mistake that success. Chrysostom, for example, also allows us to hear the reasons or excuses which people gave for

[86] Callinicus, *Life of Hypatios* 4. 6 and 9. 4, ed. G. Bartelink, *Vie d'Hypatios*, SC 177 (Paris, 1971), 86 and 104.

[87] Mark the Deacon, *Life of Porphyry* 14, in Grégoire and Kugener, *Vie*, 13.

[88] Theodoret, *Historia religiosa* 2. 19, SC 234. 238.

[89] Jerome, *Ep.* 66. 5, CSEL 54. 652.

[90] Palladius, *Lausiac History* 21, in G. Bartelink (ed.), *Palladio, La storia Lausiaca* (Milan, 1974), 106.

[91] Palladius, *Lausiac History* 6, in Bartelink, *La storia Lausiaca*, 36.

[92] Neri, *I marginali*, 54.

[93] Chrysostom, *Homilies on Matthew* 35. 3 and 35. 5, PG 57. 409 and 411.

[94] *Homilies on 1 Corinthians* 21. 5, PG 61. 177.

refusing to aid young and apparently healthy beggars: they were thought to be avoiding work or to be runaway slaves.[95] Basil likewise suggests that beggars trod a tightrope between appearing too well-dressed to need alms, as a result of clothes they had been given, or so ill-clad in 'rotting rags' as to excite only disgust.[96] The practice of deliberately blinding children to increase their value as beggars may indicate both the alms to be won in this way and the difficulty of winning alms in other ways.[97] Beggars were frequently exposed to severe hunger and malnourishment: a preacher might speak of a poor man so hungry he could barely speak, or insolent because goaded by the last stages of hunger.[98] The destitute frequently lacked shelter and clothing. Basil of Caesarea reproached those who had more shoes than they needed when others went barefoot.[99] The orthodox interlocutor of the *Dialexis* claimed to have frequently come across women so poor they could not afford a piece of cloth with which to cover their heads in prayer.[100] The destitute were often exposed to the cold. Chrysostom sought to stir up pity in his congregation at Constantinople by describing how 'the temperature drops below freezing and the poor man lies prostrate on the pavement in his rags, all but dead from the cold, his teeth chattering'.[101] Zeno, bishop of Verona in the late fourth century, reminded his readers how the death of the poor through hunger, cold, and exploitation was a fact of daily life.[102] The diet of the very poor (largely of bread, with restricted access to cooked foods or meat) and their living conditions (many of them sleeping rough in the shelter of public porticoes) have been studied with respect to the Greek-speaking Eastern Empire by Evelyne Patlagean.[103] Beggars were also

---

[95] *Homilies on Matthew* 35. 3, PG 57. 409.

[96] Basil, *On Detachment*, PG 31. 556.

[97] Chrysostom, *Homilies on 1 Corinthians* 21. 5, PG 61. 177.

[98] Basil, *On Detachment*, PG 31. 553–6.

[99] *I Shall Knock Down My Barns*, 7, in Y. Courtonne, *Saint Basile: Homélies sur la richesse* (Paris, 1935), 35 (PG 31. 277A).

[100] *Dialexis* 5. 7–8, in Berruto Martone, *Dialogo*, 88.

[101] Chrysostom, *Homilies on Hebrews* 11. 3, PG 63. 94.

[102] Zeno, *Tractates* 2. 1. 19, in B. Löfstedt (ed.), *Zenonis Veronensis Tractatus*, CCSL 22 (Turnhout, 1971), 149.

[103] E. Patlagean, *Pauvreté économique et pauvreté sociale à Byzance 4e–7e siècles* (Paris, 1977), 44–53 (diet), 53–67 (living conditions), 95–101.

exposed to the possible violence of those whom they accosted. Basil, once again, berated the wealthy for punching beggars.[104] It might not be long in such circumstances before illness set in, and we should assume that the destitute were at high risk of early death on the streets.[105]

Late Roman society contained a great many others who were not destitute, but who lived at risk of destitution, those who may be termed the conjunctural or episodic poor.[106] To use ancient Greek categories, such people were numbered among the πένητες the poor whose slender income, from farmed small-holdings or other labour, usually enabled them to survive without begging; but they were at risk of becoming 'beggars', πτωχοί.[107] For some, rural farmers and labourers, destitution could be advanced by crop failure, by the exhaustion of stores before crops could be harvested. Basil evoked the pitiful sight of farm-workers sitting idle in the fields, staring at their wives and children, and feeling with their fingers for dry grass to pick.[108] Vermin might also spoil the stored grain: grubs threatened to ruin all the grain which Hypatios had stored in the monastery at Rouphinianes outside Constantinople.[109] Winter was often a time of shortage. Such people whose lives remain largely invisible to us, because they rarely appear in our extant sources, can be seen when they crowd into the cities during severe food shortages to seek help from the bishop or from the monasteries, like those who flocked in the winter to Rouphinianes.[110] But farmers were also at risk of impoverishment through debt and the inability to repay debts, like the poor man in Southern Egypt who sought out Abba Aaron when his creditor had threatened to seize his vineyard.[111] The *Life of Porphyry* recounts how a tenant farmer in one village attacked

[104] Basil, *On the Wealthy* 6, in Courtonne, *Homélies*, 61 (PG 31. 296C).

[105] Patlagean, *Pauvreté*, 95–101 (life expectancy) and 101–12 (vulnerability to disease).

[106] These terms are borrowed from A. Parkin, 'Poverty in the Early Roman Empire: Ancient and Modern Conceptions and Constructs', (PhD. thesis (Cambridge, 2001).

[107] Patlagean, *Pauvreté*, 26; cf. G. Hamel, *Poverty and Charity in Roman Palestine: First Three Centuries C.E.* (Berkeley, Calif., and Oxford, 1990), 168–70.

[108] Basil, *In Time of Hunger* 2, PG 31. 308B.

[109] Callinicus, *Life of Hypatios* 20, SC 177. 134.

[110] Callinicus, *Life of Hypatios* 31. 5, SC 177. 206.

[111] Paphnutius, *Histories* 109, in Vivian, *Histories*, 125–6.

Barochas, now acting as agent for the bishop of Gaza, when Barochas refused to give him further time with which to pay what he owed to the church. Such violence, in which the farmer was joined by other villagers, may reveal the belief that pagans in authority would shield the perpetrators from justice, but is also a measure of the desperation inspired by conjunctural poverty.[112] For poverty of this kind normally exposed villagers to violence. Theodoret allows us to glimpse the bullying to which villagers in Lebanon were exposed when the tax-collectors arrived.[113] Violence of another kind might hit the rural poor near the borders of the empire. Raiders would swoop down on undefended settlements to seize goods and livestock, but also to capture children who would be sold on into slavery. At Hippo members of Augustine's congregation bought captives to release as they passed through the port.[114] According to Synesius the raiders who swept down on Cyrenaïca, and from whom the rural peasants sought protection, were themselves 'commanded by hunger'.[115]

Many people in the cities also lived close to destitution, like the orphaned girl whom Porphyry found when he climbed across the roofs at Gaza to escape lynching from a pagan mob. The girl lived at home with her elderly and paralysed grandmother, presumably a widow, and she worked to support them both.[116] The house and the food which the girl provides for her visitors show that the women are not destitute, but their state is said to be one of destitution (πτωχεία), and they later accept a generous daily alms from the bishop of four *miliaresia*, both indications of their relative poverty. As the story suggests, episodic poverty threatened wherever illness and death weakened a household's ability to gain an adequate income. In a society where some 40 per cent of children had lost their father by the time they were 14 or 15 a great many such widows and orphans were to be found among the *penetes* at risk of destitution.[117]

---

[112] Mark the Deacon, *Life of Porphyry* 22, in Grégoire and Kugener, *Vie*, 19.

[113] Theodoret, *Historia religiosa* 17. 2–3, SC 257. 36–40.

[114] Augustine, *Ep.* 10*. 2–3 and 7, OSA 46b. 168–70 and 178–80.

[115] Synesius, *Ep.* 104, in Garzya and Roques, *Synésios*, iii. 233.

[116] Mark the Deacon, *Life of Porphyry* 97–100, in Grégoire and Kugener, *Vie*, 74–7.

[117] Krause, *Witwen und Waisen*, iii. 9. On the high number of children who lost their father before puberty and even higher number who lost their father before the age of 25, cf. R. P. Saller, *Patriarchy, Property and Death in the Roman Family* (Cambridge, 1994), 189.

Widows, whether young with a large family, or elderly and sick without family, were in many cases householders with inadequate support from a dowry, any testamentary bequest, or whatever badly paid work they or their children might find. Unless they could rely on richer relatives, they were vulnerable to impoverishment through taxation.[118] Orphans might have their own inheritance, but this was easily exhausted in the absence of a breadwinner by funeral costs and inherited debt.[119] The number of widows in Graeco-Roman society at any one time has been estimated by one scholar to have been as high as perhaps one-third of the adult female population,[120] and while Anneliese Parkin's more recent study of poverty in the early empire has argued against such a high figure, she has concluded that women generally made up a disproportionate percentage of the conjunctural poor.[121] The plight of widows and orphans was a commonplace of Christian discourse in late antiquity, as was the duty to relieve this plight through almsgiving. Such topoi reflected the genuine and widespread needs of widows and orphans in the late empire, though Parkin has contested Krause's further claim that women and children who in fact fell into abject poverty may have comprised the single biggest group among the abject or 'structural' poor.[122]

It is not clear to what extent conjunctural poverty in late antique cities was a product of change in economic fortunes, seasonal and other periodic unemployment, and the risks of industrial injury attendant on jobs open to the free poor. It is likely that these were all factors impinging to some extent on those who worked in the construction industry, docks, and maritime trade. *The Life of Porphyry* shows that labourers were hired by the bishop to build the new church on the site of the former *Marneion* at Gaza.[123] The work took several years, but was not necessarily carried out all year round, and in any case, on completion of the project the labourers would have

[118] Krause, *Witwen und Waisen*, ii. 52–5 (dowries); ii. 97–8 (the frequent absence of other means of support); ii. 159–60 (employment), ii. 224–5 (taxes).

[119] Ibid. iii. 130 and 145.

[120] '... der Anteil der Witwen an der weiblichen erwachsenen Bevölkerung lag bei ca. 30%'. Krause, *Witwen und Waisen*, ii. 1.

[121] Parkin, *Poverty*, 99–101 and 172.

[122] Krause, *Witwen und Waisen*, ii. 252; Parkin, *Poverty*, 41–2.

[123] Mark the Deacon, *Life of Porphyry* 83, in Grégoire and Kugener, *Vie*, 66.

been laid off, and we cannot tell with what success they would have then found other work. Chrysostom preached on how builders, farmers, and shippers were in greatest need of workers during the summer. In a winter sermon on almsgiving, the implication was that such workers were at risk of descent into destitution each time seasonal work dried up.[124]

Some will have profited from petty crime.[125] Valerio Neri has drawn attention to Egyptian evidence from the early empire for much petty theft by the poor, of animals, foodstuffs, clothing, and small sums of money, from neighbours or others not far removed from them in economic and social standing.[126] Debt drove some among the *penetes* to sell children into slavery. Basil preached eloquently on the agony facing a father forced by poverty to decide which of his sons to sell. He is not described as being wholly destitute, for he has a house, 'bits of furniture and articles of clothing', but the household is clearly on the edge of destitution for these are 'the kind of belongings you expect of the very poor (*ptochoi*), all worth just a few *obols*'.[127] Basil may well be reworking a literary topos, rather than relating a case known to him personally, yet the practice is known from other sources. Of the one hundred and twenty or so captives destined for the slave trade and liberated from the ships and docks at Hippo in *c*.428, Augustine informed Alypius that five or six had been sold by their families.[128] We cannot say what percentage of the population were destitute and wholly dependent on alms for their survival, or how many lived close to the edge of destitution,[129] but it is possible that the majority of the population outside Rome lived for shorter or longer periods near the edge, and under threat, of 'absolute poverty'.[130]

Preachers and others in the period sometimes included among the poor those holy men and women who had voluntarily renounced

[124] Chrysostom, *On Almsgiving* 1, PG 51. 261.
[125] For a detailed discussion of theft in the late Latin West, cf. Neri, *I marginali*, 279–365.
[126] Ibid. 328.
[127] Basil, *I Shall Knock Down my Barns* 4, in Courtonne, *Homélies*, 25 (PG 31. 268C).
[128] Augustine, *Ep.* 10*. 7, OSA 46b. 178.
[129] Prell, *Sozialökonomische Untersuchungen*, 72.
[130] Ibid. 66–7.

their possessions and so become dependent on alms, whether as solitaries or members of coenobitic monastic communities.[131] Augustine, in a sermon probably designed to encourage almsgiving by his congregation at Hippo to a monastery, identified those who had renounced their possessions and distributed them among the poor, so as to serve God unfettered as the 'least' spoken of by Christ in Matthew's Gospel (Matt. 25: 40).[132] In around 400 a wealthy deaconess had stumbled by accident on the small community of monks near the *martyrium* at Rouphinianes, and supplied them with the necessary food to survive.[133] Such ascetics came from a wide range of social backgrounds and endeavoured to adopt a diet and physical conditions similar to those in involuntary poverty, but their influence as holy men and women made them unlike the poor already mentioned.[134] They feature in this book both as recipients of alms and distributors.

Promoters of almsgiving also spoke at times of giving alms to those members of the clergy whose duties precluded them from earning a living. John Chrysostom preached that: 'alms are given only to those too weak to support themselves by the work of their own hands or to teachers, and those wholly taken up with the business of teaching'.[135] But writers and preachers more frequently distinguished between gifts for the upkeep of the clergy and alms for the poor; I am not concerned with gifts to the clergy except in so far as these gifts were redistributed to the poor.


## PREVIOUS SCHOLARSHIP

The history of almsgiving in the Early Church has itself a history. Much nineteenth-century scholarship was coloured by the theological suppositions and prejudices of its writers, whose questions

---

[131] Chrysostom, *Homilies on 1 Timothy* 14, PG 62. 574.
[132] Augustine, *Serm.* 113. 1, PL 38. 648.
[133] Callinicus, *Life of Hypatios* 8. 14–17, SC 177. 102–4.
[134] For the resemblances and differences between voluntary and involuntary forms of poverty in the later empire, cf. Patlagean, *Pauvreté*, 47 and 62–4.
[135] Chrysostom, *Homilies on 2 Thessalonians* 5. 2, PG 62. 494.

were shaped by a debate in political philosophy on the effect of charitable giving. For charity was attacked by some as contrary to the beneficial working of the market (where hunger sharpened the appetite of the poor to work), and by others as impotent to relieve the misery in which the poor were engulfed. A by-product of the debate was renewed interest in the charitable practices of the Early Church, which led to the publication in 1853 of Étienne Chastel's *Études historiques sur l'influence de la charité.* The book drew on sermons, treatises, saints' *Lives,* church orders, civil and ecclesiastical legislation, to defend the efficacy of charitable assistance by a study of those actions, from the first to the sixth century, which Chastel believed to be an expression of Christian charity. Certain assumptions both vitiated the work and would influence the approach taken by later writers. A dim view of paganism, as destructive of that sympathy which he considered the natural precondition of charitable assistance, led the author to a rapid dismissal of pagan almsgiving.[136] The belief that what was required under the Jewish Law was necessarily motivated by servile obedience, whereas true generosity was spontaneous, precluded serious consideration of Jewish almsgiving.[137] Later writers would likewise treat Christian almsgiving in isolation from pagan and Jewish practices. Regard for the literal veracity of the Bible, and for the Church Fathers as authoritative guides to the practices of a universal Church, fostered a naiveté with respect to rhetoric and an over-confident generalization from what was said in one place, and at one time, to what was done everywhere at different times. This encouraged Chastel to believe, on the one hand, that the pre-Constantinian churches were so many 'oases' offering close mutual support and relief from all the evils of deprivation.[138] On the other hand, it led him to consider the exhortation to almsgiving in fourth-century sermons as indicative of worsening poverty in the post-Constantinian Church, where the development of hostels and hospitals therefore witnessed to a cooling of that 'charitable spirit' by which individuals had previously cared for their neighbours.[139] These reading habits were to have a long

---

[136] E. Chastel, *Études historiques sur l'influence de la charité* (Paris, 1853), 4.
[137] Ibid. 19–20.  [138] Ibid. 120.
[139] Ibid. 175–6, 263–4, 281–2.

history.[140] Above all, by regarding the practices he reviewed as so many instantiations of a single virtue of charity which transcended the immediate culture where it found expression, Chastel was necessarily inattentive to how these practices served in the redefinition of classical virtues, as the latter were shaped by the discourse in which almsgiving gained significance. His further understanding of charity as essentially selfless precluded study of how these redefined virtues found a place in the construction of, and competition for, honour and authority.

Many of Chastel's judgements were accepted by Gerhard Uhlhorn, whose *Die christliche Liebestätigkeit in der alten Kirche* was published in Stuttgart in 1882 and translated into English a year later. But Uhlhorn, who studied the same six centuries and used many of the same sources, introduced further theological assumptions. Thus he accepted Chastel's contrast between the pre- and post-Constantinian Church, but further argued that the bishops elaborated and stressed the doctrine of redemptive almsgiving (the teaching that almsgiving atones for post-baptismal sin) to exhort a lukewarm laity. In this way, he argued, they made what was previously understood as a free expression of faith and love into a meritorious work. The care of the poor once shared by the congregation became the exclusive preserve either of the bishop with his assistants or of the monks. A distorting myth of initial novelty and purity was now accompanied by a Lutheran theology of faith in opposition to works. The picture of the two contrasted Churches (early and late, pure and impure) continued to minimize regional and chronological differences, to read the epigraphic evidence of sixth-century Gaul, for example, as illustrative of the same practices and mentality described by the sermons of the Cappadocian Fathers in the fourth and fifth centuries.

This image of Christian almsgiving at its best when undefiled by external influence could not last. Christian practice has to be understood against a background of 'the spirit of classical beneficence', which Christians inherited in civic culture but also sought to transform.[141] It has also to be seen in the context of a Jewish tradition of

---

[140] For a modern view that sees exhortation to alms as a measure of the institutional church's failure to provide sufficient alms, cf. Krause, *Witwen und Waisen*, iv. 45.

[141] A. R. Hands, *Charities and Social Aid in Greece and Rome* (London, 1968), 14.

almsgiving on which the early Christians had drawn, and which continued to develop in late antiquity. These two traditions of pagan benefaction and Jewish almsgiving were rightly contrasted by scholars in the last century. Heinrik Bolkestein showed how in the Graeco-Roman world of the early imperial period, unlike Ancient Israel, almsgiving did not count as a virtuous activity expressive of generosity or *philanthropia*, nor as a form of public benefaction.[142] Christian almsgiving could then be seen as in essential continuity with the Jewish, as opposed to the pagan, tradition: the 'teaching of the Christian authors followed Jewish precedent in several areas where pagan practice was decidedly different', above all, with respect to the principal *motives* for giving.[143] These shared motives included belief in the value of redemptive almsgiving, as that was promoted in the Septuagint texts of Proverbs, Daniel, and Sirach, and developed in the writings of the Apostolic Fathers.[144] William Countryman and Roman Garrison, two scholars who did much to examine the continuities between Jewish and Early Christian thought, also theorized about the function of almsgiving in mitigating social divisions between rich and poor within the early Christian communities, to present almsgiving as a 'cement of unity' binding communities internally with bonds of mutual service.[145]

Less attention was paid to Christian almsgiving in the late empire, or to the relationship between pagan benefaction and Christian almsgiving, other than to point out some of the differences between these two.[146] Boniface Ramsey could state in 1982 that there had been until then 'no study that touches exclusively upon the theme of almsgiving in the Western Church in the age of its greatest Fathers'.[147] Ramsey partly remedied this 'lacuna' in an article describing various 'themes', which together comprised the 'view of almsgiving' common to the major writers in the period: the identification of Christ and the

---

[142] H. Bolkestein, *Wohltätigkeit und Armenpflege im Vorchristlichen Altertum* (Utrecht, 1939), 101.

[143] L. W. Countryman, *The Rich Christian in the Church of the Early Empire: Contradictions and Accommodations* (New York, 1980), 103.

[144] R. Garrison, *Redemptive Almsgiving in Early Christianity* (Sheffield, 1993).

[145] Countryman, *Rich Christian*, 118.

[146] Patlagean, *Pauvreté*, 190.

[147] B. Ramsey, 'Almsgiving in the Latin Church: The Late Fourth and Early Fifth Centuries', *ThS* 43 (1982), 226.

poor; the exercise of moderation in almsgiving; the obligation on all to give to the needy, even to those who had sinned; the merit of almsgiving in atoning for post-baptismal sins; the value of alms in securing the intercession of the poor; the importance of right intention if one's gifts are to bear spiritual fruit. This was a major advance on previous scholarship, although the account was by no means exhaustive. Ramsey's survey neglected the circulation in the later empire of earlier Christian literature in which almsgiving featured and the movement of texts between East and West evidenced in Rufinus's translation of the *Sentences of Sextus*. There was no attempt to relate ideas to the practice of almsgiving in the period, nor to set themes in their rhetorical context, to study their place in preaching and exhortation.

Since Ramsey's article much more has been written on the churches of the late empire, and much of the best scholarship has focused on late Roman Italy.[148] Our knowledge of almsgiving at Rome in particular owes much to the work over many years of Charles Pietri in studying the broader issues of wealth, poverty, and euergetism, as well as his meticulous study of the Roman church between 312 and 440.[149] Jill Harries has studied almsgiving and the disposal of wealth among the Christian senatorial elite of the late fourth and early fifth century.[150] She has shown the extent to which the earlier ascetics praised in the literary sources by Jerome and Paulinus of Nola for their generosity towards the poor and their renunciation of wealth, women such as the elder Melania, Paula, and Albina, nonetheless ensured that their property was not alienated but handed down within the family in accordance with traditional practice. Harries has observed that Pammachius and Paulinus, who both practised a more radical dispossession, appear to have had no immediate family who might expect to inherit. This conservatism

---

[148] e.g. C. Truzzi, *Zeno, Gaudenzio e Cromazio: Testi e contenuti della predicazione cristiana per le chiese di Verona, Brescia e Aquileia (360–410 ca.)* (Brescia, 1985); Lizzi, *Vescovi e strutture*.

[149] C. Pietri, 'Les Pauvres et la pauvreté dans l'Italie de l'Empire chrétien (IVe siècle)', in *Miscellanea Historiae Ecclesiasticae*, 6, Bibliothèque de la Revue d'histoire ecclésiastique, 67 (Brussels, 1983), 267–300; 'Evergétisme et richesses ecclésiastiques dans l'Italie du IVe à la fin du Ve siècle: L'Exemple romain', *Ktema*, 3 (1978), 317–37.

[150] J. Harries, '*Treasure in Heaven*: Property and Inheritance among Senators of Late Rome', in E. M. Craik (ed.), *Marriage and Property* (Aberdeen, 1984), 54–70.

Harries contrasts with the stance of 'the next generation', in particular the younger Melania and her husband Pinianus, who were 'to reject the conventions on property'.[151] The extent of their rejection is measured by the opposition they encountered among their respective families. Yet both generations are shown to have turned away from public honours to display a traditional munificence in charitable works, building projects, and almsgiving that 'were also an extension of the Church's benefactions to its flock in the cities on every social level'.[152] Harries, therefore, identified a gap between theory and practice, but did not comment on why Jerome presented his patrons and pupils, or Paulinus his friends, in what now appear over-simple terms. She did not attempt to address the intended impact of discourse on practice. Nor was senatorial practice related to an understanding of character and virtue.

Peter Brown's discussion in *Power and Persuasion* of how eloquence, especially episcopal eloquence, gave authority and exercised influence in late antiquity has been a major influence on how current scholars approach Christian discourse on almsgiving.[153] Peter Brown inspired an as yet unpublished study by Michael De Vinne, which examines the portrayal of the poor in sermons by bishops.[154] Close readings reveal how these texts gave the very poor a new visibility in the cities by describing them as actors, athletes, and gladiators, in language borrowed from the games, shows, and gladiatorial contests opposed by the bishops. De Vinne notes the bishops' description of those receiving alms as recipients of benefactions, but also patrons of their donors. These texts, he argues, facilitated the emergence of the bishops as major patrons or 'megapatrons'.[155] Susan Holman has published a detailed study of six sermons concerning almsgiving by the Cappadocian Fathers, Basil of Caesarea, Gregory of Nazianzen, and Gregory of Nyssa.[156] Her close reading aims to explore 'how

[151] Ibid. 65.

[152] Ibid. 68.

[153] P. Brown, *Power and Persuasion in Late Antiquity: Towards a Christian Ethic* (Madison, Wisc., 1992).

[154] M. De Vinne, 'The Advocacy of Empty Bellies: Episcopal Representation of the Poor in the Late Roman Empire', Ph.D. thesis (Stanford, 1995).

[155] Ibid. 116.

[156] S. R. Holman, *The Hungry are Dying: Beggars and Bishops in Roman Cappadocia* (Oxford, 2001).

theological language was used to effect' the shift identified by Peter Brown in *Power and Persuasion* 'of the interdependent social network' as 'Christian discussion of philanthropy... redefined the criteria for receiving welfare'.[157] Most recently, Peter Brown has himself contributed a volume on the subject of how Christian almsgiving in the later empire affected the relationships between the clergy and surrounding society, in particular how the bishop emerged as a 'governor of the poor'.[158] Yet, when all is said and done, there has not been a general work on Christian almsgiving since the comprehensive, but theologically skewed books by Chastel and Uhlhorn in the nineteenth century.

This review of earlier scholarship reveals a patchwork of studies, most of which have split in two what the earliest scholars had brought together: the studies deal either with ideas as distinct from practices (Countryman, Garrison, Ramsey) or with practices as largely distinct from ideas (Krause); some turn a spotlight on only one area of the empire (Patlagean, Pietri, Truzzi, Lizzi, and Holman). Bolkestein, who was concerned with the relation of discourse to practice in the area of benefaction and almsgiving, though of enduring value for his insistence upon the distinctions to be made between classical euergetism and alms, largely confined himself to the period before the rise of Christianity; he offers little further help to the student of late antiquity. Where the Christian rhetoric of almsgiving is occasionally related to practice in the later empire, it is seen as deceptive (Harries) or an indicator of failure; Krause in this respect echoes Uhlhorn. This means that in studying Christian almsgiving in the later empire, and the discourse which shaped its meaning and practice, we are left with particularly urgent questions: about the status of discourse on almsgiving in late antiquity, its prominence and functions, intended or otherwise; about the place of almsgiving in a virtue ethic; about the impact of almsgiving as a significant set of practices for power relations.

Though it remains in general true to state that in 'their moral and social teaching Christians came very near to pagans',[159] it will emerge

---

[157] Holman, *The Hungry are Dying*, 18–19.

[158] P. Brown, *Poverty and Leadership in the Later Roman Empire* (Hanover and London, 2002), 79.

[159] Averil Cameron, *Christianity and the Rhetoric of Empire* (Berkeley, Calif., 1991), 40.

that Christian almsgiving was distinctive in comparison with the pagan culture it competed with, where that distinction involves the range of practices but, more importantly, the meaning of those practices. It will appear that, while episcopal almsgiving was limited in extent, scholars should not be misled by those limits in assessing how much help was given to the poor by other forms of Christian almsgiving. Nor should scholars be so concerned with the quantity of alms distributed that they under-estimate the significance of Christian almsgiving for its practitioners. In looking at how Christian discourse on almsgiving altered a moral philosophy of the virtues and gave meaning to practices, it will be possible to show how Christian almsgiving entered the negotiation of authority in ways far more complex and interesting than any simple picture of increased episcopal patronage. Although patronage is an important feature of late antique society influenced by almsgiving, it will appear that almsgiving is important for status and leadership in ways not always caught, nor aptly described, in terms of patrons and their clients. Oswyn Murray, in his introduction to the English translation of *Le Pain et le cirque* by Paul Veyne, lists among the things a 'different and perhaps less interesting historian might have written' a discussion of 'how the Christian conception of the gift...disrupted the pagan system by its different conception of the function and consequences of the gift'.[160] On a less disparaging note, Murray admitted to a desire 'to know what succeeded the Imperial form of euergetism, and how it developed or was replaced in the early Christian and Byzantine periods'.[161] To study Christian almsgiving is to offer at least partial answers to these important questions.

---

[160] Veyne, *Bread and Circuses*, p. xviii.
[161] Ibid., p. xxi.

# 2

## Episcopal Almsgiving

The presbyter Uranius wrote after his bishop's death at Nola in 431 that Meropius Pontius Paulinus had, on his conversion to Christ, 'opened his granaries to the poor' (*aperuit horrea sua pauperibus*) and 'opened up his store-rooms to all-comers'. For the bishop 'thought it a small thing to support those closest to him, if he did not also summon from every part those whom he might feed and clothe'.[1] The author echoes the account of Joseph opening all the granaries of Egypt at Genesis 41: 56 as translated by Jerome (*aperuitque Ioseph universa horrea*).[2] This allusion to a famed prototype of Christ, later made explicit, allows Paulinus' gift of alms on renouncing a political career to function within the text as a proof of his conversion or conformity to Christ by so acting. In presenting the gift as an act directed beyond the boundaries of Paulinus' immediate circle, Uranius demonstrates what he has asserted a few lines earlier: the saint's care for 'all' or for the 'many' now manifest in his 'daily prayers for us'. Past almsgiving is used to construct a posthumous spiritual authority.

The passage is one of several in the letter which locate the practices of almsgiving in specific contexts. First, Paulinus gives away his wealth in copious alms, food, and clothing, on adopting the life of an ascetic withdrawn from public affairs. Quantities are not given but the context of renunciation implies the dispersal of substantial wealth. Second, Uranius relates that the saint freed many captives

---

[1] Uranius, *De obitu Paulini* 6, PL 53. 862C.

[2] *Genesis (Liber ab Hieronymo ex hebraico translatus)* 41. 56 in R. Gryson, B. Fischer, J. Gribomont, H. F. D. Sparks, W. Thiele, and R. Weber (eds.), *Biblia Sacra Iuxta Vulgatam Versionem* (Stuttgart, 1994), 62.

and redeemed many from debt, specifying further types of almsgiving not tied to the initial act of renunciation.[3] Third, the bishop purchases and distributes to the poor some time before his death clothes worth forty gold *solidi*. Fourth, the cost of this episcopal charity is met by a donation of fifty *solidi*, sent by either a bishop or that bishop's brother. The man is said to be a 'clarissimus vir', a member of the senatorial class, and his donation is evidence of large gifts by those who had not abandoned public life and wealth to be distributed at a martyr's shrine, here that of Felix at Nola.[4] Almsgiving takes a variety of shapes within the different lives of bishops and their clerics, ascetics, or lay men and women. The next two chapters, therefore, describe the various practices of Christian almsgiving, and seek answers to the following questions. (i) Which were the principal forms in which Christians gave alms to the poor? (ii) Who were the principal beneficiaries and what benefits did they receive? (iii) What were the major centres and occasions that attracted almsgiving? And (iv) how did these practices change? The present chapter looks at the institutional almsgiving overseen by bishops, how they both raised and distributed alms. Chapter 3 traces the various patterns of almsgiving practised by ascetics or monks, gifts by individual lay men and women, and finally examines the almsgiving practised by the imperial family.

## THE SOURCES OF ALMS DISTRIBUTED BY THE BISHOPS

Eusebius in his *Martyrs of Palestine* described a former soldier turned ascetic, Seleucus, as caring for the destitute like a 'guardian' or 'bishop' (ἐπίσκοπος).[5] The simile shows how central almsgiving was to the image of a bishop in the early fourth century, but in his

[3] Uranius, *De obitu* 6, PL 53. 862C.

[4] Ibid. 3, PL 53. 861B. The donor belonged to the aristocratic governing class, but was not himself a holder of high office. On the expansion of the clarissimate in the 4th cent, and corresponding growth in titles of higher standing than *clarissimus*, cf. Jones, *The Later Roman Empire*, i. 527–30.

[5] Eusebius, *On the Martyrs* 11. 22, GCS 6/2. 943.

treatise on the bishop's office John Chrysostom noted that the bishop's duties towards the poor were not simply a matter of speedily distributing alms, but of first acquiring alms to distribute, 'collecting together the church's riches through the good will of the flock he rules over'.[6] One reason for exhortation to almsgiving was obviously the bishop's duty to move his flock to provide adequate resources for the church's charity. Where the *De obitu Paulini* shows the spiritual authority accruing through the bishop's distribution of alms, Chrysostom reveals how that authority depended on the prior good will of others whose generosity might be withheld. Episcopal almsgiving not only served in the construction of authority, but required a continual renegotiation of authority through persuasive oratory. In this a bishop might be aided by his clergy. The *Apostolic Church Order*, probably composed in Egypt *c.* 300 and translated into Latin at some point before the fifth century, speaks of the hortatory role of the deacons in winning alms: they are to be 'good at persuading others to acts done in secret, compelling the well-off among the brethren to open their hands'.[7]

Large donations by wealthy individuals, both in the donor's lifetime and at their death in bequests, were one source of episcopal funds. Sozomen recounted that many Christians in Cyprus gave bishop Epiphanius of Salamis donations of alms both in their lifetime and at their death, because he could be relied upon to spend the money in accord with their intentions.[8] The comment suggests the popular desire to give alms, and the wish of donors to control the uses to which their gifts were put. It is probable on the basis of evidence from Carthage that the bishop and his clergy were expected to distribute such large gifts openly, and to publicize the donor's name. The *Gesta apud Zenophilum* reveals an expectation in the early fourth century that a donation by a wealthy Carthaginian, Lucilla, had it been distributed, would have been accompanied by the

[6] Chrysostom, *De sacerdotio* 3. 12, in *Jean Chrysostome, Sur le sacerdoce*, ed. A.-M. Malingrey, SC 272 (Paris, 1980), 208.

[7] *Apostolic Church Order* 23, in J. W. Bickell (ed.), *Geschichte des Kirchenrechts* (Frankfurt, 1843), 107–32 at 125–6.

[8] Sozomen, *Ecclesiastical History* 7. 27, in J. Bidez and G. Hansen (eds.), *Sozomenus Kirchengeschichte*, 2nd edn. (Berlin, 1995), 342.

proclamation 'Lucilla gives you this from her own belongings'.[9] Bishop and donor would share the honour associated with the donation. What was said of Epiphanius explains why almsgiving might confer an exceptional moral authority on a bishop: a good reputation attracted further alms, which, once distributed, enhanced the cleric's reputation to win even greater funds for disbursement.

The same remark, however, also betrays an anxiety that not every bishop was so honest with gifts of this kind. The practice exposed the bishop and his clergy to charges of misappropriation, and a generous donor to charges of bribery. This was what happened to Lucilla and the deacon (later bishop) Silvanus, who found himself branded as a 'thief of what belonged to the poor'.[10] Caecilian's supporters alleged that the 400 *folles* given as alms by Lucilla were a bribe to purchase support from the clergy for her candidate, Majorinus, in a forthcoming episcopal election. The money was said never to have reached the poor.[11] The need to avoid charges of maladministration may lie behind the stipulation in an Egyptian church order, the *Canons of Hippolytus*, that gifts of alms were to be distributed to the poor by night-fall. Where there was more than enough to meet immediate needs, the rest was to be given out on the next day or, at the latest, on third day.[12]

These large gifts were stimulated partly by the literary portrayal of almsgiving held up for emulation in the hagiographic and apocryphal literature read in the period, in which spectacular healing miracles by a bishop or apostle might lead to large donations of alms by characters portrayed as civic notables. A fourth-century fictional work of Christian hagiography, the *Life of Abercius*, relates how the supposed second-century bishop of Hierapolis cured a blind woman, Phrygella, the mother of the local city magnate. Phrygella vows in gratitude, like a latter-day Zacchaeus, to 'bequeath half my wealth to

---

[9] *Gesta apud Zenophilum Consularem* 18 and 20, in J.-L. Maier, *Le Dossier de Donatisme*, 2 vols. (Berlin, 1987 and 1989), i. 237–8.

[10] Ibid. 6, in Maier, *Dossier*, i. 223.

[11] Ibid. 17, 18, and 20, in Maier, *Dossier*, i. 235–8. Optatus described Majorinus as Lucilla's 'servant' (*domesticus*), in *Against the Donatists* 1. 19. 4, ed. M. Labrousse, *Optat de Milève, Traité contre les Donatistes*, 2 vols., SC 412 and 413 (Paris, 1995 and 1996), i. 214.

[12] Canon 32 in *Les canons d'Hippolyte*, ed. R.-G. Coquin, PO 31. 2 (Paris, 1966), 405.

the destitute' ($\tau o \hat{\imath} s$ $\pi \tau \omega \chi o \hat{\imath} s$).[13] The fictional episode is partly modelled on, exaggerates, and serves to inspire actual gifts of alms by fourth-century readers. Literature stimulated in this way the imitation at different social levels of gifts made fashionable by trend-setting members of the elite, figures such as the former Augustus Vetranio, who was said to have practised almsgiving and supported church leaders in the mid-fourth century during his retirement from public life at Prusa in Bithynia.[14] But how, apart from such gifts, did bishops collect or otherwise gain their charitable resources? And where they relied on more than one method, which was the most important?

Chastel wrote that 'tithes, first fruits, gifts offered at the altar, regular or special collections, legacies, the bequest of things either outright or with certain restrictions, landed or other property: these were the principal sources of income provided by charity'.[15] This verdict must be revised. Tithes, as will be shown, were not a significant source of income for alms at this period. Nor were first fruits, if by the term is meant a gift distinct from other offerings. Chastel also ignores the likely role of imperial subventions and the possibility that a bishop would contribute to church alms from his own wealth. In any case, the historian should not assume the existence of a single standard pattern carried over in both East and West from the Early Church: not every church gained its resources in the same way. We know, for example, that the Alexandrian church, unlike most in the period, received alms from a burgeoning number of Egyptian monasteries (see below).

## Special collections

Evidence from the Carthaginian and Antiochene churches in the third century suggests that the bishop had by then the right and

---

[13] *The Life of Abercius* 20 and 22, in *S. Abercii Vita*, ed. T. Nissen (Leipzig, 1912), 17 and 18.

[14] *Chronicon paschale*, PG 92. 729. Eng. tr. in M. Whitby and M. Whitby, *Chronicon Paschale 284–628 AD* (Liverpool, 1989), 30.

[15] 'Dîmes, prémices, offrandes à l'autel, collectes régulières ou occasionelles, legs, donations partielles out totales, mobilières ou immobilières: telles étaient les principales ressources fournies par la charité.' Chastel, *Études*, 243.

duty to hold a special collection for gaining alms when need arose. Cyprian's correspondence during the persecutions of the mid-third century reveals that after the detention of Christians in Numidia Cyprian sent to the bishops there 100,000 sesterces for the prisoners' ransom, which had been collected from among the clergy and laity of Carthage itself and from bishops over other dioceses who happened to be in the city at the time.[16] Cyprian told how 'everyone gave freely and generously' to the fund (*collatio*), but as he also promised a list of the individual donors, either there was a general collection in which some gave far more than others, or only the wealthier members of the church were approached. As described in Cyprian's letter, the gift articulated and strengthened the bond uniting the different bishops and churches in Christ, while the collection itself expresses the unity of the Carthaginian church assembled around and subordinate to its bishop: the money had been 'taken here in the church over which I rule by God's favour' by means of a 'collection among the clergy and people present before me'. Raising alms in this way is understood and advanced as an activity constitutive of both unity and proper hierarchical differentiation in the Christian community. Another letter, written when Cyprian was in hiding, speaks of a small sum of money (*summula*) raised and distributed among the clergy of Carthage for them to hand out to the needy in his absence.[17] Cyprian did not specify how the money was realized; it is not improbable that this, too, came from a special collection.

A Latin translation from the late fourth century of the *Didascalia*, an Antiochene church order dating from the first half of the third century and no longer extant in its Greek original, demonstrates a similar provision for a special 'collecta' to meet sudden shortfalls in alms, if other sources failed due to the refusal by the bishop of gifts which he deemed to be the fruits of injustice.[18] The provision was

---

[16] Cyprian, *Ep.* 62. 3, in *Sancti Cypriani Episcopi Epistulae*, ed. G. F. Diercks, CCSL 3B–D, 3 vols. (Turnhout, 1994, 1996, and 1999), ii. 387.

[17] *Ep.* 5. 1, CCSL 3B. 27.

[18] *Didascalia Apostolorum* 4. 8, in F.-X. Funk (ed.), *Didascalia et Constitutiones Apostolorum*, 2 vols. (Paderborn, 1905), i. 228. For the date of the *Didascalia*, cf. M. Metzger, *Les Constitutions apostoliques*, 3 vols., SC 320, 329, 336 (Paris, 1985–7), i. 16. For the date of the Latin tr., cf. Funk, *Didascalia*, i, p. viii.

retained in the *Apostolic Constitutions*, compiled from the *Didascalia* and other ecclesiastical texts in the Antiochene area around 380.[19] Gifts by notorious sinners were not welcome and the *Apostolic Constitutions* provided a long list of those whose trades tainted their prospective offerings.[20] What this meant in practice is less than clear. Neither church order is a record of actual practice, but both set out a lasting ideal of right practice.[21] The *Apostolic Constitutions* suggests that the ban on improper donations was hard to enforce when belief in redemptive almsgiving encouraged precisely sinners to give, and when there was a real fear in the Christian community that strict enforcement of the ban would lead to a shortfall in alms. The text specifically addresses this fear: 'you may say that it is precisely these people [the notorious sinners] who give alms, and if we do not accept their offerings, from what source will the widows get our help and the needy among the people be fed?'[22]

It is more likely, therefore, that a special collection would be held to meet an emergency, like the ransom of captives, than in the conditions imagined above by the church orders. It is true that in Roman North Africa Augustine rebuked his congregation at Hippo when he lacked funds to distribute to the needy.[23] But this was not necessarily in the context of a special collection and is better understood in the context of encouraging the congregation to put more in the regular collection discussed below. The provisions in the *Didascalia* and *Apostolic Constitutions* demonstrate, however, the difficulty facing bishops. Their authority required the successful collection of alms, which was likely to be furthered by preaching the redemptive value of almsgiving, but that authority was also vulnerable to attack on the grounds of collusion with the wicked.

---

[19] *Ap. Const.*, 4. 8. 4, SC. 329. 184.

[20] Ibid. 4. 6. 5, SC 329. 178 and 180.

[21] On church orders as 'living literature' with idealizing tendencies and a tendency of editorial adaptation to contemporary practices, cf. P. F. Bradshaw, 'Ancient Church Orders: A Continuing Enigma', in G. Austin OP (ed.), *Fountain of Life* (Washington, DC, 1991), 3–22, esp. 13–19.

[22] *Ap. Const.* 4. 8. 1, SC 329. 184.

[23] Possidius, *Life of Augustine* 24. 14 and 17, in C. Mohrmann, A. A. R. Bastiaensen, L. Canali, and C. Carena (eds.), *Vita di Cipriano, Vita di Ambrogio, Vita di Agostino* (Milan, 1975), 194.

## Regular giving

It is extremely difficult to establish the forms by which Christians made regular gifts of alms to the urban churches, and whether any standard form came to predominate in the later empire. This is in large part because gifts by the faithful are variously described by church orders, councils, preachers, and writers, so that we must judge where that variety reflects distinct types of giving rather than different ways of speaking about the same realities. Nor does this language necessarily map neatly onto distinctions which a historian might wish to make between an organized collection and donations to a poor-box, or between collections devoted solely to almsgiving and offertory collections used for purposes which included almsgiving. Authors (for reasons examined in a later chapter) described almsgiving by church-goers in terms derived from both Old and New Testaments which may be read literally or metaphorically.

The limited evidence from the second century does not indicate the existence in the West at that time of a single standard pattern of regular collections held solely to finance episcopal almsgiving, as is shown by comparing the writings of Tertullian and Justin Martyr in this respect. Tertullian's *Apology* of 197 parades the voluntary contributions made by Christians at Carthage, where 'on one day a month or when they wish each person contributes a modest sum in alms' to a fund which Tertullian terms a 'sort of chest' (*arcae genus*), a term usually interpreted as alluding to an actual poor-box in which coins were dropped.[24] The passage has been taken to mean that alms were 'collected once a month on a voluntary basis'.[25] This is not an improbable reading, but it is not the only interpretation of the text: a contribution placed monthly *or otherwise* in an alms-chest is not identical with a monthly collection. Justin Martyr's earlier account of the Sunday Eucharist in one Roman church community of the mid-second century speaks of a voluntary collection (τὸ συλλεγόμενον) from the 'well-off' presented to the head of the Eucharistic assembly to use himself in assisting the needy, a detail which points to the

---

[24] Tertullian, *Apology* 39, in *Tertulliani Opera*, ed. D. Dekkers, CCSL 1 (Turnhout, 1954), 150–1.
[25] E. Osborn, *Tertullian, First Theologian of the West* (Cambridge, 1997), 68.

conjunction between ecclesial leadership and service of the poor to be found in later episcopal almsgiving.[26] Whether the collection took the form of money, food, or both is uncertain. Uhlhorn, unduly influenced by Tertullian, took Justin as referring to a monthly collection, yet the context makes a weekly collection more probable.[27] No standard pattern may be deduced from these early authors.

Such evidence as there is for the third century onwards points towards a collection in many places at the weekly *synaxis*. To this end there was an alms-box in the church variously named the 'corban' (after the Temple treasury in Jerusalem so named in Matthew 27: 6 and alluded to by Christ in Mark 7: 11), 'gazum', 'gazophylacium', and at least on one occasion the 'chariot' or 'quadriga'. Yet certainty is often precluded by the degree to which almsgiving is couched in biblical terms deriving both from the episode of the widow's mite thrown into the Temple treasury (Luke 21: 1–4 and Mark 12: 41–4) and the call of Christ to store up treasure in heaven (Matthew 6: 19–20, Luke 12: 33–4). In some places, but not all, this regular collection was for the clergy as well as the poor.

Commodian's *Instructions*, dated by most modern scholars to the third century but possibly later,[28] use verse to deliver a simple moral message and condemn 'barren Christians': 'you do no [good] works and put no offering in the treasury'.[29] How are we to relate these two clauses? It may be that the Christian puts his or her money in the treasury *so to speak* by good works, or that they do good works by putting money in an alms-chest known as the 'treasury' or 'gazum'. Commodian later reminds those who are poor but in good health that they should emulate the example of the widow in the Gospel and put some of what their work has won for them 'into the treasury'.[30] So, every Christian with something to spare, not only the wealthy

---

[26] Justin Martyr, *First Apology* 67, in M. Marcovich (ed.), *Iustini Martyris Apologiae Pro Christianis* (Berlin and New York, 1994), 130. Earlier in the same work Justin presents the Christians as turning away from greed to 'pool what we have and share it with every one in need'; cf. *First Apology* 14, in Marcovich, *Iustini Apologiae*, 52.

[27] Uhlhorn, *Christian Charity*, 142.

[28] A. Di Berardino (ed.), *Patrology* (Westminster, Md., 1986), iv. 259.

[29] Commodian, *Instructions* 2. 10 in J. Martin (ed.), *Commodiani Carmina*, CCSL 128 (Turnhout, 1960), 49.

[30] Ibid. 2. 27, CCSL 128. 65.

individual but also the poor person (or *penes*), was expected to give alms, an expectation with implications for how much was raised from general collections.[31] Chrysostom cited the episode of the widow's mite in extending the duty of almsgiving even to those *penetes* who were themselves the recipients of alms (for the significance of which see below).[32] But we cannot tell whether Commodian's 'treasury' was a literal poor-box or metaphor.

It is likewise impossible to determine from the text whether Ambrose envisaged placing alms in a box, when, after a passage in which he had expounded the mystical sense of the widow's mite, he told widows that Jesus was observing their gifts for the poor: 'The Lord is watching you, I say that Jesus is watching, when you go up to the treasury (*gazophylacium*) and think to give alms to the needy from the proceeds of your good works.'[33]

In his *De opere et eleemosynis* Cyprian attacks a rich woman at the Sunday Eucharist, who has overlooked the *corban*. She takes part of the sacrifice provided by the poor, but has come 'without an offering': 'Do you who are wealthy and rich think you are celebrating the Eucharist, when you totally disregard the *corban*, coming to the Eucharist without an offering and taking part of the sacrifice offered by the poor person?'[34] Cyprian bids her, and so his readers, recall the example of the widow who placed her two last coins in the treasury (*gazophylacium*). It is possible that the wealthy woman is castigated simply for her failure to give alms during the week, but it is more likely that she has failed to place an offering in the church poor-box.

Book 3 of the *Didascalia*, to judge by the Latin translation, advocated the practice of regular collections to be given to the bishop 'as a good administrator' (*dispensator*) for redistribution to the needy.[35] Book 2 indicates that this collection was supposed to happen at the Eucharist, if the 'strangers' referred to in the following passage

---

[31] Augustine, *Serm.* 39. 6, CCSL 41. 492.

[32] Chrysostom, *Homilies on Matthew* 52, PG 38. 523; *Homilies on Hebrews* 1, PG 63. 20.

[33] Ambrose, *De viduis* 5. 32, in F. Gori (ed.), *Verginità e Vedovanza*, 2 vols., OOSA 14/1 and 2 (Milan and Rome, 1989), i. 244–318 at 274.

[34] Cyprian, *De opere et eleemosynis* 15, ed. M. Poirier, *Cyprien de Carthage, La Bienfaisance et les aumônes*, SC 440 (Paris, 1999), 118. For Poirier's discussion of what 'corban' means in this context cf. idem, *Bienfaisance*, SC 440. 178–82.

[35] *Didascalia* 3. 4. 2, Funk, *Didascalia*, i. 186.

are understood to include the destitute (a reading supported by the fifth-century *Life of the Man of God* from Edessa, in which inmates of the hospital, who at death are buried in a pauper's grave, are referred to as 'strangers'[36]). The Latin *Didascalia* enjoins:

you are to love and honour the Lord with all your strength and regularly on each occasion present Him with his sacrificial offerings. Do not keep away from the church, and when you have received the Eucharistic sacrifice, take and share all that has come into your hands with the strangers; for it is collected by the bishop for the care of all the strangers.[37]

It is instructive to see how the redactor of the *Apostolic Constitutions* has altered the *Didascalia* in this respect. Book 3 of the *Apostolic Constitutions* stresses that the people's offering of alms consists of 'voluntary contributions' (ἑκούσια), where that word is taken from the *Septuagint* account of the various offerings made to God.[38] The section in book 2 which corresponds to the above passage from the *Didascalia* does not repeat the account of the bishop's role at this point, but instructs the donor to visit the church and 'present to the Lord your voluntary contributions', that is, the fruit of their labour. It goes on to urge that the donor 'share one, two or five coins with the strangers by throwing what you can into the *corban*'.[39] The alterations strongly suggest that the regular collection in the Antiochene churches associated with the *Apostolic Constitutions* was placed in an alms-box given the name 'corban'. They do not, however, imply a reduced role for the bishop: earlier in book 2 it is said that his task is to distribute the 'offerings volunteered for the poor' (the *penetes*).[40]

By the fifth century *gazophylacium* is clearly used in some places to name a church alms-box. A sermon once attributed to John Chrysostom on Matthew 6: 13 voices the objections of those who

---

[36] A. Amiaud, *La Légende syriaque de saint Alexis l'homme de dieu*, Bibliothèque de l'École des Hautes Études, 79 (Paris, 1889), 7–8.

[37] *Didascalia*, 2. 36. 4, Funk, *Didascalia*, i. 122.

[38] *Ap. Const.* 3. 4. 2–3, SC 329. 126. Cf. Deut. 12: 6 and Lev. 23: 38, in *Septuaginta, Vetus Testamentum Graecum Auctoritate Academiae Scientiarum Gottingensis Editum*, iii/2. *Deuteronomium*, ed. J. W. Wevers (Göttingen, 1977), 175, and ii/2. *Leviticus*, ed. J. W. Wevers (Göttingen, 1986), 256.

[39] *Ap. Const.* 2. 36. 8, SC 320. 260.

[40] *Ap. Const.* 2. 25. 2, SC 320. 228.

argue that it is impossible to give alms to the poor (τοῖς πένησιν 'without being seen, either by presenting alms to the priests or by throwing alms into the *gazophylacium*'.[41] The sermon's date is unknown, but its assertion that *xenodocheia* are now to be found throughout the inhabited world suggests a date no earlier than the late fourth century. Another homily to which Chrysostom's name was falsely attached encourages people to put even a few coins into the '*gazophylacium* of the widows and orphans'.[42] This suggests that in some churches collections of alms for the poor were distinct from collections for the clergy.

A sermon on almsgiving attributed to Paulinus of Nola, *De gazophylacio*, almost certainly preached within the period covered here, attests to the continuing importance of collecting voluntary alms at church. Paulinus condemned those who 'overlook the table placed by the Lord in the church for the poor' and who either 'regard it with contempt' or walk past 'tight-fisted' (*aridis manibus*).[43] But the word which gives the sermon its title does not appear in the text and that title may not be original.

It is impossible to know when exactly *gazophylacium* acquired the sense attested in these final examples. The entry for the Greek word in Lampe's *Lexicon*, where the first sense listed is 'offertory-box', cites Origen's *Commentary on John's Gospel*, but there and elsewhere in extant works Origen uses the word only to refer to the Temple treasury in Jerusalem and explains its use to an unfamiliar readership as 'a place for coins donated in honour of God and to provide relief for the poor', an explanation which the most recent editor believes Origen took from rabbinic sources.[44]

Some fourth- and fifth-century authors do not make clear whether *gazophylacium* refers to an alms-box or fund intended *only for the poor* or to a fund for gifts intended for wider purposes, a problem arising from the consideration in late antiquity, noted in Chapter 1, that gifts to the clergy were a form of alms. Nor is it always manifest whether the word refers to a box or strong-room for the storage of

---

[41] Pseudo-Chrysostom, *On Matthew* 6. 13, PG 59. 571.

[42] *De eleemosyna*, PG 60. 749.

[43] Paulinus of Nola, *Ep.* 34, CSEL 29. 303.

[44] Origen, *Commentary on John* 19. 7. 43, in C. Blanc (ed.), *Origène, Commentaire sur S. Jean*, 5 vols., SC 120, 157, 222, 290, and 385 (Paris, 1966–92), iv. 72–4.

valuables.[45] These difficulties may be illustrated by two sermons in which Chrysostom urges the congregation to make their house a church by setting money aside every Sunday for later almsgiving. In one he says: 'make your house a church, the box a treasury (γαζοφυλάκιον). Become a keeper of sacred funds, a self-appointed administrator for the poor. The treasury is a sign of this task even now. But while the symbol is still there, the actual practice is nowhere to be found.'[46] In the other he exhorts: 'let each house become a church with the sacred funds set aside within it. For the treasuries (γαζοφυλάκια) located there are symbols for these things.'[47] These passages might imply that while there is a place within the churches spoken of as the γαζοφυλάκιον, so named because gifts of alms were once stored there, it has now lost its original function and been turned into a store for church plate. But we should not be misled by the rhetoric, which here plays down the alms given in order to spur on the faithful to greater generosity. Alms in these churches were stored in a distinct place. Chrysostom encourages donations by encouraging the congregation to see themselves at home as participating in or mirroring the work of the bishop as guardian and distributor of church-funded alms. The rhetoric thereby suggests the honour attaching to the bishop's role in this regard.

Augustine certainly used the Latin loan-word *gazophylacium* to refer to a common fund to which the congregation contributed at Hippo for the support of the monastic clergy and bishop. He urged them not to make private gifts to the brethren, but give to the fund: 'think of the treasury (*Gazophylacium attendite*) and we will all have something'.[48] The clergy at Hippo had adopted voluntary and monastic poverty under Augustine's direction and he considered contributions to their upkeep as alms. This is seen in a sermon where Augustine explained the meaning of *gazophylacium* in Matthew 27: 6 as the chest belonging to God, 'where they kept the collection which was sent to relieve the needs of God's servants'.[49] Gifts to the clergy are reckoned as alms inasmuch as they relieve indigence.

[45] e.g. Ps-Athanasius, *Against Arius* 28, PG 28. 484D–485A.

[46] John Chrysostom, *Homilies on 1 Corinthians* 43, PG 61. 368–9.

[47] *De eleemosynis* 4, PG 51. 266.

[48] Augustine, *Serm.* 356, in C. Lambot, *S. Augustini Aurelii Sermones Selecti Duodeviginti* (Utrecht, 1950), 140.

[49] *En in Ps. 63* 11, CCSL 39. 814.

It is in this context that we should interpret a passage in Possidius' *Life of Augustine*, which recounts the saint's occasional preaching to his congregation on 'the neglect by the faithful of the treasury and the sacristy where the 'necessaries for the altar' were placed.[50] Augustine upbraided the laity for their failure to contribute sufficiently to the alms-box from which the clergy, but also the poor, were supported. Possidius explained that 'Augustine, who always had the poor in mind, provided for them from the same funds which served himself and all who lived with him, that is, the revenues from church property and the offerings of the faithful.'[51] This in turn aids interpretation of a canon found in a Gallic code of *c.*475, where 'offerings from brethren who are in disagreement' could not be accepted 'either in the treasury or the sacristy'.[52] The *gazophylacium* is here an alms fund, but probably not one earmarked solely for the destitute. Finally, we may note what appears to be a unique reference by Augustine to an alms-box as the 'chariot': the preacher closed his sermon with an exhortation for gifts for the beggars to be made 'ad quadrigam'.[53] The image of the chariot recalls Elijah's ascent into heaven, suggestive of the power of alms to raise the donor to heaven.

To sum up this section on regular giving, the textual evidence is too patchy and its rhetorical language too ambiguous for the historian to be certain of how regular gifts of alms for distribution by the bishop were made by the faithful in most churches. On the other hand, there is ample evidence to demonstrate that regular collections for this purpose were held, in many cases weekly, to which all with anything to spare were expected to contribute freely according to their means, but these collections did not follow a single standard pattern. Some collections for the poor were to benefit the voluntarily poor among the monks and clergy as well as the involuntarily poor. Nonetheless, almsgiving was an integral part of attending worship. And the rhetorical language which often occludes practical details is suggestive of the theological importance inherent in almsgiving of this kind, which is presented through the imagery of the 'treasury' as a form of spiritual savings.

---

[50] Possidius, *Life* 24. 17, in Mohrmann *et al.*, *Vita*, 194.

[51] Ibid. 23. 1, in Mohrmann *et al.*, *Vita*, 188.

[52] *Statuta ecclesiae antiqua*, canon 49, in C. Munier (ed.), *Concilia Galliae A.314–A.506*, CCSL 148 (Turnhout, 1963), 174.

[53] Augustine, *Serm.* 66. 5, PL 38. 433.

## Collections at set times of the year

Pope Leo's sermons establish the existence at Rome in the mid-fifth century of collections for alms (*collectae* or *collationes*) 'at different times', which Dolle plausibly interpreted as meaning at set periods of the year.[54] These may have supplemented more frequent regular collections. The only period Leo specifies are the days from 6 to 12 July, the days on which the *Ludi Apollinares* had formerly been held.[55] The sermons exhort the faithful to bring their gifts to the churches in their 'region', presumably one of the seven into which the city had been divided by Pope Fabian. They are all preached in advance of the 'first day of the collections' or day of the 'first collection'.[56] Leo presents the collections as established by the Apostles, which, while highly improbable, indicates they were no new invention in his own day.[57] Charles Pietri has argued that the collections were held in the periods of extended fasting and that is a reasonable assumption given the traditional link between almsgiving and fasting attested at Carthage by Tertullian in the early third century and advocated at Rome itself by the *Shepherd of Hermas* some fifty years or more before that.[58] This pattern of collections, however, cannot be extended with confidence to other churches. Chapter 4 will show that exhortation to almsgiving by preachers increased at set times such as Lent. Augustine closed a sermon perhaps delivered on the Sunday after Easter by urging his congregation: 'so, let us see if you can gladden the poor today'.[59] This strongly suggests a collection

---

[54] The sermons must date to different years, which in most cases cannot be ascertained, but the fourth has been dated with good reason to 444. Cf. *Léon le Grand, Sermons*, ed. R. Dolle, 4 vols., SC 22bis, 49bis, 74, 200 (Paris, 1964–73), ii. 48. n. 2. The phrase 'diversis temporibus' occurs in Leo, *Sermon on the Collections* 6, SC 49bis. 60.

[55] Ibid., SC 49bis. 8.

[56] Leo, *Sermon on the Collections* 2 and 4, SC 49bis. 30–2 and 42.

[57] Ibid., SC 49bis. 61.

[58] C. Pietri, 'Les Pauvres et la pauvreté', 299. Tertullian, *On Fasting* 13, ed. A. Reifferscheid and G. Wissowa, in *Tertulliani Opera*, CCSL 2 (Turnhout, 1964), 1272; *Shepherd of Hermas*, Similitude 5. 3. 7, in R. Joly (ed.), *Pasteur*, SC 53 (Paris, 1958), 230–2.

[59] Augustine, *Serm.* 376A, PL 39. 1671. For the conjectured date, cf. E. Hill OP (tr.), *The Works of Saint Augustine: A Translation for the 21st Century*, ed. J. Rotelle

was to be taken, but increased exhortation need not always imply additional collections.

## First fruits, tithes, and offerings

By the fifth century the language of tithing and first fruits was extensively deployed within the churches in connection with episcopal almsgiving, both as a form of advocacy in sermons and as part of the wider appropriation and reinterpretation by Christians of the Old Testament laws. It is far from easy to ascertain what practices underlie and are inscribed in this discourse. However, patient study of how different texts use the language of tithes and first fruits shows that urban churches before the late fifth century did not require and rarely received offerings of tithes (δεκάται or *decimae*), while offerings of first fruits (ἀπαρχαί or *primitiae*) did not usually constitute a set of gifts distinct from the offertory gifts (προσφοραί or *oblationes*) for the altar, though gifts of produce probably increased at harvest time. Tithes and first fruits could not, therefore, serve as major sources of episcopal alms distinct from the offertory gifts, part of which supported the clergy and part of which were distributed to the poor.

With respect to the Early Church, collections of first fruits and tithes are not attested in the writings of Justin and Tertullian. Irenaeus and Cyprian made the point that Christians differed from the Israelites in not giving a tithe.[60] With respect to the later empire, it is sometimes stated that Jerome advocated tithing as an Old Testament requirement still in force: Leclercq wrote that in Jerome's *Commentary on Malachi* 'we find the assertion that the prescriptions

---

OSA, part 3, *Sermons*, i–xi (New York, 1990–7), 10. 350. n. 1. This series of translated sermons is hereafter referred to as *WSAT* 3, followed by the volume number and page number.

[60] Irenaeus, *Adversus Haereses* 4. 18. 2, in A. Rousseau, B. Hemmerdinger, L. Doutreleau, and C. Mercier (eds.), *Irénée de Lyons: Contre les hérésies, Livre IV*, 2 vols., SC 100 (Paris, 1965), ii. 598; Cyprian, *De ecclesiae catholicae unitate* 26, in M. Bévenot SJ (ed.), *Cyprian, De Lapsis* and *De Ecclesiae Catholicae Unitate* (Oxford, 1971), 96.

of the Old Law concerning tithes are still in force'.[61] This is misleading: the passage cited by Leclercq shows that the Old Testament legislation has been swallowed up in Christ's commandment to sell everything and give to the poor:

What I have said about tithes and first fruits, which were given by the people in ancient times to the priests and Levites, you should take as also applicable to people in the Church, who are ordered not simply to give tithes and first-fruits, but also to sell all they have, give to the poor and follow the Lord, their Saviour.[62]

Jerome advocates something less formal than a tithe: 'If we are not willing to do this, let us at least imitate the start made by the Jews, so as to give some part of the total to the poor and offer to the priests and Levites the honour due to them.' Both the clergy and the poor deserve financial support, but this is not a call for the payment of tithes. Jerome does not envisage distinct sources of revenue for the clergy and for the poor. His letter to Nepotianus, a short treatise on clerical duties, is also open to misinterpretation. He writes: 'if I am God's portion, and a strand of his inheritance, I take no portion with the other tribes, but like a priest and Levite I live on tithes, and while serving at the altar I am supported by the offering for the altar, having food and clothing, and with this I shall be content . . .'[63] This might mean that Jerome, or the ideal priest of the treatise, was dependent on tithes, but it should be taken as teaching that the cleric, as Jerome states, is dependent on a share of the offertory: the reference to tithes is an Old Testament allusion to be taken metaphorically.

Augustine in one sermon contrasts Old Testament practice with Christ's call to go beyond the righteousness of the scribes and Pharisees, and then blames his congregation for giving far less in alms than a tithe.[64] Elsewhere Augustine uses that call in Matthew 5: 20 to suggest that, if the Pharisees give a tenth, his hearers should give at

[61] H. Leclercq, 'Dîme', in *DACL*, ed. F. Cabrol and H. Leclercq, iv (Paris, 1921), 997. See also his remark that Augustine affirmed the duty of giving tithes 'mais avec moins d'insistance que saint Jérôme', ibid. 998.

[62] Jerome, *Commentary on Malachi* ad 3. 10, in *S. Hieronymi Presbyteri Opera*, i. 6, ed. M. Adriaen, CCSL 76A (Turnhout, 1970), 935.

[63] *Ep.* 52. 5, in Labourt, *Lettres*, ii. 178.

[64] Augustine, *Serm.* 9. 19, CCSL 41. 144–5.

least double in alms.[65] In one place where he seems to advocate tithes, the context reveals a more complex picture in which we see him contrasting Jewish and Christian practices to urge some increase in the amount his congregation give as alms:

Take off some part of your income. Do you want a tenth part of things? Take off a tenth, however little it may come to. For Scripture says, because the Pharisees used to give tithes, 'I fast twice a week, I give tithes on all I own' (Luke 18: 12) And what does the Lord say? 'Unless your righteousness abounds more than that of the scribes and Pharisees, you will not enter the kingdom of heaven' (Matthew 5: 20). Yet the man you are to excel in righteousness gives a tenth part, whereas you do not even give one part in a thousand.[66]

Although Augustine thinks laymen and women should give away in alms at least one-tenth of what they own, this is not a tithe to the church in the sense that the laity were later required to give tithes.[67] The disposal of one-tenth of one's income or wealth in alms is a practice which Augustine thinks few observe. He states in a letter that, while it would be good if many Christians were giving a tithe of their earnings to the poor, extremely few actually do so.[68] It is in this context that we should understand his inclusion in a late work, the *Speculum*, of the biblical injunctions on tithing.[69] So, while Jerome and Augustine both appear on occasion to promote tithing, as regular gifts to the clergy (Jerome) or gifts to the poor (Augustine), they do not do so in the same sense and in neither case are we dealing with a levy of tithes in the sense of a set contribution expected of all the laity to be given to the church and then redistributed to various beneficiaries.

Chrysostom preached in a similar vein to Augustine on the scandal that prevailed when Christians failed to show in almsgiving even the generosity shown by the Jews under the Old Covenant, whose tithes had gone to help the widows, orphans, and strangers. He depicts

[65] *Serm.* 359A, *RB* 49 (1937), 270. See also *Quaestiones Evangeliorum* 2. 34. 2, ed. A. Mutzenbecher, CCSL 44B (Turnhout, 1980), 85.

[66] *En. in Ps.* 146. 17, in *S. Aurelii Augustini Enarrationes in Psalmos* CI–CL, ed. D. Dekkers and J. Fraipont, CCSL 40 (Turnhout, 1956), 2135.

[67] For a very similar passage, see also *Serm.* 85. 5, PL 38. 522.

[68] *Ep.* 36. 4. 7, in A. Goldbacher (ed.), *S. Aurelii Augustini Hipponensis Episcopi Epistulae*, 5 vols., CSEL 34 (1–2), 44, 57, and 58 (Prague, 1895–1923), ii. 36.

[69] *Speculum* 23, ed F. Weihrich, CSEL 12 (Vienna, 1887), 149.

someone as marvelling that a certain individual actually gave tithes:
'someone was telling me about someone else he admired, how "that
man gives tithes" '.[70] Giving a tithe, though not wholly unknown, was
obviously a rarity. Elsewhere Chrysostom reckoned that the Jews gave
up to a third or half their goods away in various tithes, whereas
Christians frequently give less than a tenth.[71]

Firm evidence in sermons for the promotion of paying tithes to
churches in the Western Empire, and thus some indication of likely
practice in those churches, only begins with any certainty with
Caesarius (bishop of Arles from *c.*502 to 543). There are a few sermons
once attributed to Ambrose or Augustine which advocate paying
tithes in the strict sense, but they are not now ascribed to these authors
and a number are now attributed to Caesarius.[72] Jean Gaudemet's
opinion that tithing 'was known in Gaul from the third century', even
when qualified by the avowal that 'it was often only a question of
suggesting a desirable amount rather than an individually set levy'
(*une prestation nettement individualisée*), exaggerates the extent to
which tithes were either promoted or collected, while a citation
following this statement from one of the sermons falsely attributed
to Ambrose suggests a likely source of Gaudemet's anachronistic
reading of the issue.[73] It is against this background that we should
evaluate a decretal noted by Gratian and once attributed to Pope
Boniface (418–22). This supposedly determines how Roman church
revenues, described as 'oblationes et decimae', are to be divided, but
does not appear in the early collections of papal judgements and
should not be considered genuine.[74] Even if it were authentic, the
phrase should not be taken as refering to two distinct types of gift.

---

[70] Chrysostom, *Homilies on Ephesians* 4, PG 62. 36.

[71] *Homilies on Matthew* 64, PG 58. 615.

[72] An example of a sermon of this kind once attributed to Augustine, but now
thought to be by Caesarius, is *De reddendis decimis*, in *S. Caesarii Arelatensis
Sermones*, ed. D. Morin, CCSL 103 (Turnhout, 1953), 142–7. Examples of sermons
once attributed to Ambrose, but with a content and style unlike Ambrose, are *De
sancta quadragesima* VIII, PL 17. 651–4 and the Lenten sermon which follows it in the
*Patrologia Latina*, PL 17. 654–6.

[73] J. Gaudemet, *L'Église dans l'empire romain (IVe–Ve siècle), Histoire du droit et des
institutions de l'Église en Occident*, ed. G. Le Bras and J. Gaudemet, iii (Paris, 1958),
292.

[74] Pseudo-Boniface, PL 20. 790. The letter is marked as spurious in the *Regesta
Pontificum Romanorum*, ed. P. Jaffé and W. Wattenbach, 2nd edn. (Leipzig, 1885), i. 54.

We may now assess the evidence from the Syrian church orders. The present text of the earliest extant order, the *Didache* (variously dated to the mid-first and mid-second century) requires first fruits (ἀπαρχή) to be offered from the various foodstuffs in one's possession to the 'prophet' or, in his absence, to the poor.[75] It is generally accepted that the passage itself is an interpolation, while the specific mention of the poor as recipients of first fruits in the absence of the prophets is a further interpolation within the first.[76] Both, however, are usually held to be early.[77] The *Didascalia* laid down in book 2 that the former tithes and first fruits offered by the Israelites to the Levites were now the 'prosphorae' offered by the bishops to God, while the Levites are replaced by the clergy, widows, and orphans.[78] Book 4 stated that 'the Levites' gifts, first fruits and sacrificial offerings' were to serve as the normal source for funds for the bishops addressed in this section of the work and for their episcopal alms.[79] The *Apostolic Constitutions* incorporated these passages.[80] Elsewhere, in book 7, the *Apostolic Constitutions* contained a redaction of the *Didache* in which it distinguished between first fruits, or certain first fruits to be given to the clergy, and tithes to be given to the needy widows, orphans, and strangers.[81] Book 8 further distinguished between first fruits for the senior clergy (bishop, presbyter, and deacons) and tithes for the lower clergy, virgins, widows, and other people in need.[82]

What sense can be made of this material? First, although Metzger has claimed that the different passages are inconsistent, the *Didascalia* and *Apostolic Constitutions* can be read as observing a fairly consistent distinction between tithes for almsgiving and first fruits for maintenance of the clergy.[83] However, this need not imply the existence of separate collections in the Syrian churches of the third

---

[75] *Didache* 13. 3–7, in W. Rordorf and A. Tuilier (eds.), *La Doctrine des douze Apôtres (Didachè)*, SC 248bis (Paris, 1998), 190.
[76] J. P. Audet, *La Didachè, Instructions des Apôtres* (Paris, 1958), 110, 457–8.
[77] Ibid. 120.
[78] *Didascalia* 2. 26, in Funk, *Didascalia*, i. 102.
[79] *Didascalia* 4. 8, in Funk, *Didascalia*, i. 228.
[80] *Ap. Const.*, 2. 26 and 4. 8. 4, SC 320. 236 and SC 329. 184.
[81] Ibid. 7. 29, SC 336. 60.
[82] Ibid. 8. 30, SC 336. 234.
[83] Metzger, *Constitutions*, SC 329. 107 n. 408.

and late fourth centuries, but might only indicate distinct names for those shares of the general revenue earmarked for different purposes. To decide which of these alternatives is more likely we must consider other evidence from the period. Two canons from the Council of Gangra in 343 deal with the proper control of 'offerings' (καρποφορίαν), but do not distinguish between tithes, first fruits, and other types of gift.[84] Chrysostom's sermons, an indeterminate number of which date from his residence in Antioch not long after the supposed compilation of the *Apostolic Constitutions*, lend no weight to the view that tithes were exacted or collected for almsgiving. This leads to the conclusion that, although some voluntary tithes may have been received (on which more below), what governs the language of the authors and redactors of the Syrian church orders, and so both the reference to and distinction between first fruits and tithes, is the need to interpret and commandeer for the Church the prescriptions of the Mosaic Law. The ideal enshrined within the text does not at this point map directly onto actual practice. Yet this rhetoric in turn influenced practice and encouraged voluntary tithing.

We cannot assume that practice in Egypt during the period was the same as that in the Syrian churches. Ewa Wipszycka has argued for an obligation to give first fruits of agricultural produce from the fourth to the eighth century.[85] Two Egyptian church orders must be examined. The *Canons of Hippolytus*, recently dated to between 325 and 381, legislate for how a priest should receive offerings of first fruits, but say nothing of tithes. An otherwise weak argument from silence has greater weight in this instance when the editor has detected in the canons an inclination 'to put back in force certain Old Testament prescripts'.[86] This points to the non-existence of widespread compulsory tithing. Canon 36 requires the bishop to accept gifts of 'first fruits' and to bless the donor.[87] But this need not imply two distinct types of gift to the church: first fruits and other offerings.

[84] Canons 7 and 8, in P.-P. Joannou (ed.), *Discipline générale antique*, 2 vols. (Rome, 1962–3), i. 92. For a discussion of other canons at Gangra, cf. P. Garnsey and C. Humfress, *The Evolution of the Late Antique World* (Cambridge, 2001), 193–5.

[85] E. Wipszycka, *Les Ressources et les activités économiques des églises en Égypte du IVe au VIIIe siècle* (Brussels, 1972), 70.

[86] Coquin, *Canons*, 320.

[87] Ibid. 409–11.

The *Canons of Athanasius*, which Wipszycka has dated to somewhere between 350 and 450,[88] lay down in canon 14 that 'tithes and first fruits' are to be accepted on behalf of the poor, but in canon 82 it appears that only what is left of the 'first fruits and tithes' over and above the portions set aside for the clergy and the sick is to be given by the bishop to the poor.[89] What is significant here is that the offerings of whatever kind made by the faithful are simply amassed and divided according to need, with the clergy and the sick enjoying a claim ahead of the poor. The language at this point of 'tithes and first fruits' once again names the general offerings made by the faithful. Canon 83, however, requires the clergy, from the bishop down to the doorkeepers, as well as the laity, to give tithes.[90] This implies either that the clergy should both receive and give a tithe, which appears odd but not impossible if the 'tithe' here means 'alms', or that poor clerics were entitled to receive, while more prosperous clerics were expected to give. Whichever reading is correct, canon 83 looks like a polemical attempt to encourage the specific practice of tithing and indicates a late date for this stipulation. Brakke's assertion, citing this canon, that Christians in fourth-century Egypt 'both lay and clergy, were expected to tithe' is over-confident.[91] Wipszycka correctly judged concerning Egypt that 'tithing continued to exist as a voluntary gift by exceptionally devout Christians'.[92] That judgement holds good throughout the late Roman Empire.

The above account of general practice does not exclude, therefore, individual gifts of 'first fruits' or 'tithes' as alms to monks. In book 21 of Cassian's *Conferences* Abba Theonas describes a group of such donors eagerly presenting their gifts of 'tithes or first fruits' (*decimas vel primitias*) to Abba John in his capacity as monastic almoner, whereupon John thanks them for their generosity. In book 14 a peasant, who always gives 'first fruits and tithes' from his crops to the church where he worships, appears one day at the monastery with

---

[88] Wipszycka, *Ressources*, 15–16.

[89] Canons 14 and 82, *The Canons of Athanasius of Alexandria*, ed. W. Riedel and W. E. Crum (London, 1904), 26 and 50.

[90] Canon 83, ibid. 50.

[91] D. Brakke, *Athanasius and the Politics of Asceticism* (Oxford, 1995), 191.

[92] Wipszycka, *Ressources*, 72.

'first fruits' for Abba John.[93] In both cases these are voluntary gifts of produce, over and above the offerings to the local church, intended either as alms for the monks or for redistribution by them. Likewise, a letter by the monk Isidore of Pelusium shows him thanking a wealthy *clarissimus* of the city, Herminos, for 'offering the first fruits and tithes from the produce of your estate'.[94]

This interpretation of the evidence has stressed the adoption of the biblical language of tithing by those seeking to persuade the faithful to greater generosity in almsgiving. The *Life of Severinus* composed by Eugippius in the early sixth century presented the holy man as sending out letters to the different communities in late fifth-century Noricum, where Roman control was fast collapsing, for 'tithes' with which to feed the poor.[95] It also portrays the citizens of Lauriacum eventually providing their tithe, despite food shortages, after the saint had miraculously averted the threat of blight.[96] This biblical language with which earlier Christians had described their ordinary gifts to the Church was easily adapted to new ends. The language was an important weapon in fund-raising, though it might take an apparent miracle to underwrite its authority.

## Imperial gifts to the churches

A grant of Constantine ensured that each year the Alexandrian church received grain from the state for redistribution to widows and possibly others among the poor. Athanasius was later accused of abusing it for his own interest.[97] The emperor made similar grants to a wide number of churches which significantly swelled their

---

[93] Cassian, *Conferences* 14. 7 and 21. 1, in *Jean Cassien: Conférences*, ed. E. Pichery, 3 vols., SC 42, 54, 64 (Paris, 1955–9), ii. 188 and iii. 76.

[94] There are two different ways of referring to the letters of Isidore of Pelusium: (i) as they are numbered by their most recent editor and commentator, Évieux; (ii) as they were numbered by Migne, who groups them into collections. For ease of reference I use Évieux's numbering but then give the Migne number afterwards. Isidore, *Ep.* 317, Migne, Ep. 1. 317, PG 78. 365C.

[95] Eugippius, *Life of Severinus* 17. 4, in P. Régerat (ed.), *Eugippe, Vie de saint Séverin*, SC 374 (Paris, 1991), 226–7.

[96] Ibid. 18. 1–2, SC 374. 228–30.

[97] Athanasius, *Apologia secunda (contra Arianos)* 18. 2, in H.-G. Opitz, *Athanasius Werke*, ii/1 (Berlin and Leipzig, 1935), 100; Socrates, *Ecclesiastical History* 2. 17, in

revenues. Eusebius praised Constantine for his almsgiving to the 'outcasts and to pitiful beggars in the marketplaces' in providing them with clothing as well as money or essential food.[98] It is wholly unlikely that these were direct acts of almsgiving, and Eusebius should be taken as referring to specific gifts made to the churches for their distribution, possibly the same gifts later recorded in the *Vita Constantini* of estates, grain allowances ($\sigma\iota\tau o\delta o\sigma\acute{\iota}a$), and clothing.[99] The emphasis in each case on the clothing involved suggests as much.[100]

Roland Delmaire has reasonably interpreted the *Vita* in the light of a report in Theophanes' *Chronicle* that Constantine sent grain to the churches in each city during a period of widespread food shortages, which Delmaire dates to between 328 and 330, though the relevant chronicle entry is reckoned as 331/2 by recent English translators.[101] Delmaire has further argued convincingly on the basis of other passages (in Sozomen, the *Chronicon Paschale*, etc.) first that the grants were to every city and not only the capitals and other major cities. Second, he argues that they represented part of the tax levied in the cities and, third, that they were maintained under Constantine, increased under Constantius, repealed by Julian, and restored at a lower rate, one-third of the previous sum, by Jovian. If Delmaire is correct, not only were church revenues greatly augmented by these grants in the form of grain, but churches were aided in proportion to the size of the city and so to the likely numbers of clergy and people in need.

We certainly know from Libanius that at Antioch there was a frequent levy of some kind on businesses in the late fourth century for 'relief of the destitute' ($\tau o\grave{\upsilon}s$ $\pi\tau\omega\chi o\grave{\upsilon}s$), but this, the pagan orator

G. Hansen (ed.), *Sokrates Kirchengeschichte* (Berlin, 1995), 109; Sozomen, *Ecclesiastical History* 3. 9, in Bidez and Hansen, *Sozomenus*, 112.

[98] Eusebius, *De vita Constantini* 1. 43, in F. Winkelmann (ed.), *Über das Leben des Kaisers Konstantin*, Eusebius Werke i/1, 2nd edn. (Berlin, 1991), 38.

[99] Ibid. 4. 28, in Winkelmann, *Über das Leben*, 130.

[100] The view that Eusebius is recording the same gifts twice is not, however, discussed in the most recent commentary on the text. Cf. Averil Cameron and S. Hall, *Eusebius: Life of Constantine* (Oxford, 1999), 220, 324, and 331.

[101] Theophanes, *Chronographia*, ed. C. De Boor (Leipzig, 1883), 29. Eng. tr. in C. Mango and R. Scott, *The Chronicle of Theophanes Confessor* (Oxford, 1997), 48. R. Delmaire, *Largesses sacrées et res privata: L'Aerarium impérial et son administration du IVe au VIe siècle* (Rome, 1989), 648–9.

claimed, was 'both voluntary and supported with pleasure by those who paid'.[102] Petit has dated the oration to 392, at the end of Libanius' life, and argued that this is 'perhaps nothing other than begging on a more or less official footing' (*une mendicité plus ou moins officiellement organisé*).[103] If so, it does not belong in this section on imperial grants. But in a metropolis with a large Christian population by this date it is possible that the levy was distributed through the church.

## Divided revenues and the sale of property

Examination of the language of first fruits, tithes, and oblations, together with the reports of imperial subventions, leads to the conclusion that episcopal almsgiving was funded not only by large individual gifts to the church for this purpose and by collections in alms-boxes, but also by a proportion of the general revenues. The sources and extent of these revenues must have varied widely from diocese to diocese, as indicated in Chapter 1. Peter Brown has recently warned against exaggerating the landed wealth enjoyed even by the great metropolitan churches at this time compared with that held by others—and by the churches themselves in the sixth century.[104] Yet nor should we under-estimate the resources accrued from different sources, which increased greatly during the period. Nor should the paucity of figures blind us to what else we may learn about the claim of almsgiving to a share of general revenues. The Alexandrian church was exceptional, but serves as a good example of both points. It could count on contributions from other Egyptian dioceses and from the mid-fourth century began to amass estates in the nomes and elsewhere.[105] Synesius, consecrated bishop of Ptolemais in 412, praised in a letter to Theophilus of Alexandria another bishop in the Pentapolis, Dioscorus, for 'labouring

---

[102] Libanius, *Orations* 46. 21, in Foerster, *Libanii Opera*, iii. 389.
[103] P. Petit, *Libanius et la vie municipale à Antioche au IVe siècle après Jésus-Christ* (Paris, 1955), 96.
[104] Brown, *Poverty and Leadership*, 54.
[105] N. Russell, *Cyril of Alexandria* (London and New York, 2000), 10.

in the fields' of the destitute of Alexandria. Dioscorus made the most of any opportunity to 'win harvests from unproductive grounds'.[106] The same letter reveals a certain Lampronianos whose business affairs have been hampered by the loss of a contract in a shipwreck but who is waiting to sell crops at a good price and so realize the sum of 157 gold pieces which is 'money for the destitute' ($\tau \grave{a} \ \pi \tau \omega \chi \iota \kappa \grave{a} \ldots \chi \rho \acute{\eta} \mu a \tau a$).[107] Either by the early fifth century income from some Alexandrian estates in the Pentapolis was set aside for the poor, or revenues owed to the Alexandrian church were seen as belonging *in toto* to the poor, though in practice used for a number of purposes. The idea that whatever belonged to the church was in fact the property of the poor was certainly held by Bishop Rabbula at Edessa (see below). It was probably a major factor behind the increasing gifts of land to the churches. If the overall value of revenues available to the Alexandrian and other, far smaller, churches cannot be ascertained, we can ask how varied these purposes were, to what extent they would bite into the general revenues, thereby reducing whatever portion remained to aid the poor, and conversely whether the duty of episcopal almsgiving exercised a restraint on other forms of expenditure.

The Synod of Antioch in 341 stated that the bishop had authority over the church's property 'in order to distribute it to all those in need'.[108] Ambrose's comments on the importance of moderation in distributing alms as integral to the wise division of resources between various types of expenditure demonstrates that bishops in the later empire retained considerable theoretical freedom of manœuvre in what was spent.[109] Gaudemet believes that this discretionary power of the bishop featured throughout the period with which we are concerned.[110] While this is largely correct, some qualifications must be added to Gaudemet's verdict.

In Rome the estates and revenues donated by Constantine were in some cases reserved for particular uses, such as the maintenance of

---

[106] Synesius, *Ep.* 66, in Garzya and Roques, *Synésios*, iii. 183.

[107] Ibid. iii. 184.

[108] Joannou, *Discipline*, i. 125–6.

[109] Ambrose, *De officiis* 2. 21. 111, in M. Testard (ed.), *Saint Ambroise, Les Devoirs*, 2 vols. (Paris, 1984 and 1992), ii. 59.

[110] Gaudemet, *L'Église romaine*, 309.

lights, and were attached to particular churches and mausolea, the maintenance of which took priority over other uses. Pietri has argued that the Roman bishops had free use only of the remaining surpluses (and perhaps not even this in the case of churches closely linked with the imperial family) together with whatever was raised by the general collections.[111] He has further argued that the *tituli* which indicate the smaller urban and suburban churches at Rome, such as the *titulus Fasciolae*, imply legal provisions securing donations (whether income or plate) for the use of a particular foundation.[112]

Theoretical freedom meant little if prior claims in practice left little for the poor. In some instances the construction and decoration of new basilicas took much of the church's income. The link between generosity in episcopal almsgiving and restraint in building is shown by two portraits of Bishop Rabbula of Edessa. In the anonymous *Life of Rabbula* he is praised for extraordinary almsgiving throughout his life and for building no new churches as bishop, undertaking only one major repair.[113] In the *Life of the Man of God* the story is of sudden conversion to great almsgiving and the bishop's concomitant abandonment of building projects.[114] Both versions demonstrate the ease with which construction costs swallowed up available income. Lay donors from all social levels were contributors to church building and decoration, but J. P. Caillet has argued with respect to Italy that members of the aristocratic elite are found less frequently in this period than before as builders or decorators of complete churches in urban areas rather than on their great estates.[115] Many small gifts paid for mosaics, but not for building work.[116]

The bishop's clergy (presbyters and deacons together with their families, but perhaps also lectors and their dependants) who lacked sufficient family wealth or income from business might claim a further sizeable, though unquantifiable, portion of church revenues. Clergy numbers varied widely. The Alexandrian church in the early

---

[111] Pietri, 'Evergétisme et richesses ecclésiastiques', 327 and 332.

[112] Ibid. 328.

[113] *Life of Rabbula*, tr. G. Bickell, *Ausgewählte Schriften der syrischen Kirchenväter Aphraates, Rabbula und Isaak v. Ninivie* (Kempten, 1874), 155–211, at 194.

[114] Amiaud, *La Légende syriaque*, 9.

[115] Caillet, *L'Évergétisme monumental*, 424 and 459.

[116] Ibid. 461–2.

fourth century had twenty-three priests and thirty deacons.[117] A document of 439 from the Egyptian village of Karanis reveals twelve presbyters and five deacons.[118] The absence of much evidence for priests in Egypt engaging in economic life has led Bagnall to conclude that they were supported by church funds.[119] We cannot ascertain what proportion of Egyptian church revenues were used to maintain the clergy, nor safely generalize from what we find at Karanis to estimate the numbers and maintenance of the clergy elsewhere in the empire, but other evidence indicates that income spent in this way was a major restriction on almsgiving. The loss of potential alms is shown by Rabbula's attempts to limit clerical expenditure at Edessa. An extant canon legislates that all those 'who have become disciples of the Messiah shall not be covetous to possess more than their needs, but they shall distribute it to the poor', a stipulation which is plausibly interpreted to warn the clergy from claiming too much.[120] The *Life of Rabbula* presents the bishop teaching his clergy to consider that they receive a share of the goods belonging to the poor rather than think that the poor received a portion of the goods belonging to the clergy. They were not to demand more than personal necessity required.[121] The hortatory nature of the passage probably shows how easily revenues were diverted away from almsgiving, and how little control the bishop had in limiting this expenditure. It certainly reveals another area in which the ability to give alms depended on the prior oratory of the bishop; but Rabbula was also using the claims of almsgiving to increase his control over fractious clergy. The bishop's unquestionable duty to give alms from what was seen as the property of the poor gave him an advantage in any dispute over what was owed to the clergy, and bishops tended to disagree with their clergy over the use of revenues. Augustine's use of church property led to ill-will (*invidia*) on the part of his clergy at Hippo. He responded by

---

[117] A. Martin, *Athanase d'Alexandrie et l'église d'Égypte au IVe siècle (328–373)* (Rome, 1996), 180.

[118] R. Bagnall, *Egypt in Late Antiquity* (Princeton, 1993), 283.

[119] Ibid. 284.

[120] H. J. W. Drijvers, 'The Man of God of Edessa, Bishop Rabbula, and the Urban Poor: Church and Society in the Fifth Century', *JECS* 4 (1996), 241.

[121] Bickell, *Ausgewählte Schriften*, 194.

addressing the congregation on the subject and asserting that he would prefer to depend solely on collections and cede to the faithful the administration of the estates.[122] Oratory was clearly needed to deflect criticism of mismanagement. More importantly, we may detect in such disputes the strain internal to churches as they experienced claims that outstripped the resources available to meet them, when growth in numbers brought a concomitant need for further clergy, but also a high expectation that significant sums would be given in alms.

Looked-for revenues might fail to materialize. One of the *honorati* at Carthage with an estate at Hippo sent a contract making this over to the church and kept only the usufruct, then reneged on the agreement at a later date and offered instead 100 *solidi* for the poor.[123] Augustine sent back the contract and rejected the money. Anicia Falconia Proba made over the 'greater sum' of the annual revenues from estates she owned in Asia to the Roman church for use by 'clergy, the poor and monasteries'.[124] But Celestine's letter in 432 to Theodosius II reveals that the revenues were no longer arriving at the expected level, to the 'detriment of the poor'. The pope appealed to the emperor to intervene as though what had been set aside as 'alms for the poor' were his own property.[125]

In this context it is not surprising that holy bishops were praised for diverting to almsgiving part of the income which would otherwise have paid for their own household. When Chrysostom became bishop of Constantinople he examined the treasurer's accounts and on reaching the bishop's own expenses transferred additional funds to the hospital (νοσοκομεῖον).[126] Honoratus of Marseilles likewise praised Hilary of Arles for giving away whatever was surplus to his living requirements: 'when he had calculated his own living expenses, if there was anything surplus to his needs, he would earmark it for spending on charity'.[127] We cannot tell, however, whether the author

---

[122] Possidius, *Life of Augustine* 23. 2, in Mohrmann *et al.*, *Vita*, 188.

[123] Possidius, *Life of Augustine* 24. 4, in Mohrmann *et al.*, *Vita*, 190.

[124] Celestine, *Ep.* 23. 6, PL 50. 546

[125] Ibid., PL 50. 547.

[126] Palladius, *Life of John Chrysostom* 20, in *Palladii Dialogus de Vita S. Joannis Chrysostomi*, ed P. Coleman-Norton (Cambridge, 1928), 19.

[127] Honoratus, *Vita Hilarionis* 11, in P.-A. Jacob (ed.), *Honorat de Marseille: La Vie d'Hilaire d'Arles*, SC 404 (Paris, 1995), 114.

was describing a large and regular surplus or making the most of very little.

In the metropolitan churches, whose wealth from donations grew rapidly in the period, there still remained much to distribute. Chrysostom's sermons indicate that revenues provided a sizeable amount of episcopal alms. He complained of the time the clergy spent on managing the church's estates at the expense of teaching and their other spiritual duties, time that could be better spent if the laity were to assume direct responsibility at least for the provision, if not the distribution, of alms for the poor.[128] At Antioch the church apparently aided 3,000 widows and virgins, together with an unspecified number of prisoners and sick men and women, cripples, pilgrims or other travellers, those serving at the altar, and beggars.[129] He stressed the infrastructure required to produce and deliver this level of assistance: the fields, the properties, the mules with their drivers. Churches in smaller cities obviously would have had much less from their revenues to give away.

Revenues were sometimes swelled by the sale of church plate and other properties to raise alms, and such acts might excite the praise of hagiographers: Hilary of Arles, according to Honoratus, took 'whatever silver belonged to all the basilicas' and left only vessels of glass in order to ransom captives.[130] Yet, the opposition of local clergy to the sale of plate and other treasure by bishops, who were eager to redeem captives or otherwise distribute the proceeds to the poor, is attested on numerous occasions. Ambrose, in defending his right as bishop to break up the church's plate, admitted the hostility (*invidia*) he had faced as a result.[131] Possidius noted that Augustine's orders to melt down church plate to aid 'captives and a great many in need' met with disapproval.[132] Chrysostom faced charges of improperly alienating church properties for unspecified purposes: it was alleged that marble acquired by Nectarius for the decoration of the Anastasia church had instead been sold, as were a

---

[128] Chrysostom, *Homilies on Matthew* 85. 4, PG 58. 761–2.
[129] *Homilies on Matthew* 66, PG 58. 630.
[130] Honoratus, *Vita Hilarionis* 11, SC 404. 116.
[131] Ambrose, *De officiis* 2. 28. 136, in Testard, *Devoirs*, ii. 70.
[132] Possidius, *Life of Augustine* 24. 15–16 in Mohrmann *et al.*, *Vita*, 194.

number of treasures and the estate donated by a certain Thecla.[133] Rabbula was forced to abandon plans for the sale of gold and silver plate belonging to the church in face of opposition from his clergy.[134] Cyril of Alexandria sold a gold thread vestment, given by Constantine to Macarius, in order to relieve a famine, but he was criticized for so doing by Acacius of Caesarea.[135]

Various reasons were given for this opposition. At Edessa it was claimed that the vessels could not be sold, as they had been given to secure prayers for the dead. To judge by Ambrose's defence at Milan, the sale of treasures could be attacked for stripping the church of due ornament and for profaning what had previously been consecrated to divine service. To avoid the latter charge Ambrose argued that wherever possible the church should surrender plate which had not yet been consecrated for divine use and that it should be broken into small fragments.[136] Neil McLynn has suggested other reasons why Ambrose faced opposition for selling church treasures: his extension of the practice to finance new church building projects increased the bishop's own prestige while dismantling 'the legacy of Auxentius and Constantius, who had probably supplied many of the items involved'.[137] But sale of church plate and property for episcopal almsgiving might always excite opposition. Acacius, bishop of Amida, melted down 'both gold and silver treasures' in c.422 for funds with which to ransom and feed the starving Persian soldiers held captive by the Romans. But he first summoned together his clergy and had to defend the action at some length.[138] He won renown, as Socrates was to attest, but the episode further demonstrates the persuasive oratory needed by the bishop in securing alms and which was here directed not at the faithful but at the clergy.

Various measures were aimed at controlling alienation of church property. African synods stipulated that a bishop, wherever possible,

---

[133] Photius, *Library* 59, in R. Henry (ed.), *Photius, Bibliothèque*, 9 vols. (Paris, 1959–91), i. 53–4.
[134] Bickell, *Ausgewählte Schriften*, 178.
[135] Janes, *God and Gold*, 161.
[136] Ambrose, *De officiis*, 2. 28. 138 and 143, in Testard, *Devoirs*, ii. 71 and 74.
[137] McLynn, *Ambrose of Milan*, 56.
[138] Socrates, *Ecclesiastical History* 7. 21, in Hansen, *Sokrates*, 367.

was not to act in this regard without first involving fellow bishops in the decision-making process.[139] Pope Leo I wrote in a letter to the Sicilian bishops that no bishop was to 'give away, sell or exchange' any church property.[140] The bishops assembled at Chalcedon determined that every diocese was to have a treasurer (οἰκονόμος) to administer the church's property under the bishop's direction, so that no scandal might arise from the absence of any witness to what was distributed.[141] Other legislation discouraged the use by bishops of their relatives as managers of church properties. In the context outlined above, such legislation not only sought to prevent abuses, but to restrict the scope for false accusations of misconduct which undermined episcopal authority. Cyril of Alexandria asserted that bishops were grieved by demands to produce accounts for how they spent either the church's revenues or offerings from the people.[142]

## Personal wealth for episcopal alms

Sozomen, in the passage mentioned at the start of this chapter, reported that Epiphanius had given away his own wealth. He was not alone. Ambrose's biographer, Paulinus, passed over the bishop's controversial sale of church properties, but claimed that Ambrose had made over his gold and silver 'to the church or to the poor' on taking office. He then added that the bishop's estates were given to the church once provision had been made for his sister, a consecrated virgin, to receive the usufruct on which to live.[143] A gap of some years may lie between these two donations. Santo Mazzarino argued that Ambrose in fact retained his *patrimonium* until 386.[144] At the death of his brother Uranius Satyrus in 378 the bishop spoke of their

---

[139] Joannou, *Discipline*, i. 242 and 248.
[140] Leo, *Ep.* 17, PL 54. 705.
[141] Canon 26, in Joannou, *Discipline*, i. 89–90.
[142] Ibid. ii. 279–80.
[143] Paulinus of Milan, *Vita di S. Ambrogio*, ed. and tr. M. Pellegrino (Rome, 1961), 38.
[144] S. Mazzarino, *Storia sociale del vescovo Ambrogio* (Rome, 1989), 28. For the standard view cf. B. Ramsey OP, *Ambrose* (London and New York, 1997), 38.

having shared an 'undivided patrimony'.[145] In 386 Ambrose replied to the emperor's demands for a basilica: 'were you to demand something of mine, a farm, house, gold or silver, what was rightly mine, I would happily offer it'; yet nothing can be taken from the church.[146] The contrast suggests that Ambrose still retained legal ownership of the family estate. The convention of a bishop giving his wealth to the church allows the biographer, with hindsight, to tidy out of sight complications and protractions in handing it over. What matters here is the likelihood that some of Ambrose's wealth at least was distributed in alms. In the late 470s Constantius of Lyons likewise wrote of Germanus, bishop of Auxerre (d. 448), that his possessions (*substantia*) were given away to the poor after his consecration.[147]

There is no evidence, however, that this self-dispossession was standard practice on entering office. As suggested at the start of this chapter, it appears to belong, rather, with the adoption of an ascetic life. Many bishops had a family to keep. When the African bishop Chronopius was condemned by seventy others in *c*.368 or 369 he was wealthy enough to be fined fifty pounds of silver.[148] But those who retained their possessions might be expected to contribute from this wealth to their almsgiving. The poor might be considered to have some claim on that wealth, which perhaps explains why the emperor required Chronopius to dispense the fifty pounds of silver as poor relief.

In conclusion to this section on the sources of episcopal alms it may be said that no figures can be placed on the typical or standard sums at a bishop's command for almsgiving. This now appears, however, not as a fault of the historical record, but, rather, as a result of the degree to which funds were dependent on the size of the see, the personal circumstances, and the eloquence of the individual bishop. Augustine told Albina that he commanded at Hippo church

---

[145] Ambrose, *De excessu fratris* 1. 7 and 59, ed. O. Faller, in G. Banterle, *Le orazioni funebri*, OOSA 18 (Milan and Rome, 1985), 24–158, at 28 and 62.

[146] Ambrose, *Ep.* 75A (*Sermo contra Auxentium*), 5, OOSA 21. 116.

[147] Constantius of Lyons, *Life of Germanus* 2, in R. Borius (ed.), *Vie de saint Germain d'Auxerre*, SC 112 (Paris, 1965), 124.

[148] H. Chadwick, *Priscillian of Avila: The Occult and the Charismatic in the Early Church* (Oxford, 1976), 45.

property some twenty times the value of the patrimony he had given to the church at Thagaste on becoming a monk, and implied that the great African churches possessed far more.[149] Krause calculated that church revenues up until the reign of Justinian varied between two and thirty pounds of gold, a quarter of which may have been distributed in alms, and from this figure calculates the dozens or hundreds of likely beneficiaries. As is now apparent, this calculation fails to take into account the full range of sources from which episcopal almsgiving was funded.[150]

## RECIPIENTS OF EPISCOPAL ALMS

Many descriptions by contemporary sources of who received episcopal alms are extremely general, speaking simply of the 'poor' or 'needy' (*pauperes, indigentes,* οἱ πένητες, οἱ δεόμενοι) and of 'beggars' (οἱ πτωχοί). Others are also formulaic, adopting the scriptural language of 'widows and orphans'. Were these recipients always or usually Christian? Were the widows only or predominantly members of an order of widows? How poor were these poor? Were there criteria by which some were chosen and others passed over? What emerges in answer to these questions is a series of criteria by which some had a better claim than others or a prior claim to others.

Paul's Letter to the Galatians had urged the churches in Galatia to 'do good to all, but especially to those who belong to the household of faith' (6: 10). This was interpreted by Christian writers in the fourth century to mean that Christians had a greater responsibility to give alms to fellow Christians than to others, although they were not to limit their almsgiving only to church members. Ambrose in *De officiis* alluded to the text from Galatians in asserting that fellow Christians had a prior call on the Church's charity.[151] Jerome explained to Hebidia that it was not forbidden for Christians to give alms to Jews or pagans, but they were to give preferential

[149] Augustine, *Ep.* 126. 7, CSEL 44. 13.
[150] Krause, *Witwen und Waisen*, iv. 25.
[151] Ambrose, *De officiis* 1. 30. 148 in Testard, *Devoirs,* i. 166–7.

treatment to fellow Christians.[152] Christ, according to Matthew 5: 42, had commanded the disciples to 'give to the person who asks you' and it is instructive to observe how the editor of the *Apostolic Constitutions* reworked the gloss on this passage in the very much older *Didache*. For the author of the *Didache* the import of Christ's command is that, though one should attempt to identify a worthy recipient, one will be blessed by God even for giving alms to those whose need is merely feigned and whom God will punish for their deceit.[153] The issue is not whether they are Christian. Whereas the author of the *Apostolic Constitutions*, after affirming that it is 'right to give to all from what our own hard work has provided', adds that 'the saints are to be preferred'.[154] For him it is an issue about whether the recipients are Christians, for Christians have a prior claim. It seems that some Christians went further and thought it improper to give alms to pagans. In the *Histories of the Monks of Upper Egypt* Mark, a priest about to become bishop of Philae, confides to Athanasius that he has rejected requests for food aid from poor Nubian pagans. Athanasius quotes scripture to show that almsgiving to pagans is, after all, a laudable practice. We do not have to believe in the historicity of the episode to recognize that the text deploys the authority of the bishop of Alexandria to answer critics of such gifts to people beyond the household of faith.[155]

The theoretical extension of alms to non-Christians, however, was not without purchase on practice. Augustine spoke in a sermon on the Psalms of the many non-Christians who flocked to the church for temporal aid, which is not explicitly a reference to alms and might refer to the intercessory role of the bishop in mediating between provincials and imperial officials, but which probably includes reference to alms.[156] Gregory of Nyssa, in his funeral oration for St Basil, recounted his brother's feeding of the city's children during the famine of 369, whether Christian or not, though the fact

[152] Jerome, *Ep.* 120. 1, in Labourt, *Lettres*, vi. 124–5. Cf. also Jerome's *Commentary on Isaiah*, 16. 58, 6. 7, in M. Adraien, (ed.), *Commentariorum in Esaiam* xii–xviii, CCSL 73a (Turnhout, 1963), 666–7.

[153] *Didache* 1. 5, SC 248bis. 144 and 146.

[154] *Ap. Const.* 7. 2. 7, SC 336. 28.

[155] Paphnutius, *Histories* 61–3, in Vivian, *Histories*, 101–2.

[156] Augustine, *En. in Ps.* 46. 5, in *Sancti Augustini Enarrationes* i–l, ed D. Dekkers and J Fraipont, CCSL 38 (Turnhout, 1956), 532.

that Gregory picks out this fact for special mention indicates that it was probably common for Christians to limit their almsgiving to fellow Christians.[157] Nevertheless, the Emperor Julian admitted that Christians helped pagans as well as Christians in poverty.[158]

Jerome also applied moral criteria to determine who was worthy to receive alms. In his letter to Hebidia he glossed Galatians 6: 10: 'The fellow servant (*domesticus fidei*) is the one to whom you are joined by the practice of the same religion and whose sins have not separated him from the common life of the brethren.'[159] That raises the question of whether, if sin disqualifies someone from receiving alms in Jerome's view, excommunicated or penitent Christians could receive alms? There may have been divergent opinions on the matter. Ambrose taught that the clergy were not to refuse alms to the needy who were 'banned from the church' (*ab Ecclesia relegatis*).[160] Whether he was thinking of both types of separated Christians or only of penitents cannot be ascertained.

There was a widespread view that 'genuine' beggars were to be distinguished from false claimants. Basil taught that there was no spiritual value in giving alms to the unworthy and advocated distribution of gifts by an experienced official who could tell the genuine from the merely greedy.[161] Miracle stories warned that God would distinguish the genuine from the fake and punish the offenders. A story told how a beggar who feigned death so that his companion would gain additional money from the bishop for his 'burial' died in the act and the bishop refused to intercede for his recovery.[162] Sozomen states that the same story had reached him applied to two different bishops: it was presumably retold for its moral and not simply to enhance the reputation of the bishop concerned. It is significant that the beggar wanted too much. He had a claim on the bishop's alms, but a strictly limited claim. The

---

[157] Gregory of Nyssa, *Oration in Praise of his Brother Basil*, ed. O. Lendle, in G. Heil, J. P. Cavarnos, O. Lendle, and F. Mann (eds.), GNO 10/1 (Leiden, 1990), 124.

[158] Julian, *Ep.* 84a (formerly *Ep.* 49), J. Bidez and F. Cumont, *Iuliani Imperatoris epistulae et leges* (Paris and London, 1922), 114.

[159] Jerome, *Ep.* 120. 1, in Labourt, *Lettres*, vi. 125.

[160] Ambrose, *De officiis* 2. 16. 77 in Testard, *Devoirs*, ii. 43.

[161] Basil, *Ep.* 150. 3, in Y. Courtonne, *Saint Basile, Lettres*, 3 vols. (Paris, 1957–66), ii. 74–5.

[162] Sozomen, *Ecclesiastical History* 7. 27, in Bidez and Hansen, *Sozomenus*, 343–4.

story then finds an echo in the behaviour of the Roman matron condemned by Jerome for hitting an old woman who had already been given one coin, but then returned to receive a second.[163]

Ambrose complained about those who sought alms (*subsidia pauperum*) without good reason, when in good health and so able to seek work, and whose demands for more alms reduced what was available for the poor who had no other means of keeping themselves.[164] The distinction between those able to work or keep themselves by other means and those wholly reliant on alms gives one criterion by which the poor were identified as worthy recipients of alms. The different categories of recipients noted in the *Didascalia* and *Apostolic Constitutions* cover people either unable to work through age or sickness or unable by their work to keep a family: they get help 'on the grounds of being a young orphan, or of weakness in old age, of falling ill, or the high cost of feeding the children'.[165] John Chrysostom was suspicious of the distinction between real and fake beggars when used by individuals to excuse their refusal to give alms in the street—if someone went to the trouble of begging and faking extreme misery just to get a loaf of bread, that in itself was a sign of real need—but that suspicion does not imply that he ignored the distinction himself when it came to the distribution of episcopal alms under public scrutiny.[166]

## Widows

Krause has estimated that as many as one in three adult women in the towns were widows, often with young families.[167] In the big cities only a very small percentage of these women could have been the recipients of church aid. Within the Christian community there existed an 'order of widows' in which elderly women could be enrolled by the bishop and which allotted them a distinctive place

---

[163] Jerome, *Ep.* 22. 32, in Labourt, *Lettres*, i. 147.

[164] Ambrose, *De officiis* 2. 16. 76, in Testard, *Devoirs*, ii. 42–3.

[165] *Ap. Const.* 4. 3. 3, SC 329. 174.

[166] Chrysostom, *Homilies on 1 Corinthians* 21. 8, PG 61. 177.

[167] Krause, *Witwen und Waisen*, ii. 1 and idem, 'La Prise en charge des veuves par l'église dans l'antiquité tardive', in C. Lepelley (ed.), *La Fin de la cité antique et le début de la cité médiévale* (Bari 1996), 116.

in the church's public devotions. Paul had set 60 as the minimum age for such widows, although this age requirement was not universally observed. Krause has pointed out that, whereas the *Didascalia* dropped the minimum age for enrolment to 50, the *Apostolic Constitutions* sought to restore the Pauline figure of 60.[168] He shows that Ambrose in Milan observed this restriction. Widows in Cappadocia might be enrolled before the age of 60 at the bishop's discretion, because Basil told Amphilocus that remarriage for these younger widows did not incur the penalty of exclusion from communion, but his ruling suggests that enrolment before 60 was exceptional and thought hazardous.[169] Krause argues that while the church did not limit its aid to these enlisted widows, those on the lists were entitled to a certain regular dole which it was the bishop's duty to ensure they received, leaving other needy widows to receive a lesser hand-out depending on what if anything was available at the time.[170]

Krause's judgement seems largely correct, but it should be emphasized that a number of younger widows with dependent children also had a title and place on a list. The formula 'widows and orphans' refers not only to the elderly members of the widows' order and those children who had lost both parents, but also to younger widows in the community and their dependent children. Chrysostom's treatise on the nature of the priestly office of the bishop states that he is to 'be a father to orphans and take the place of a husband for their mother'.[171] One of the accusations that Athanasius levelled against George and his Arian sympathizers was that on their arrival in Alexandria 'they seized bread and houses belonging to the widows and orphans'.[172] The new arrivals apparently took for their own use the alms due to the widows and orphans and arranged for their eviction from the city.[173] It is probable that these widows and orphans belonged to family units living in the same houses. In theory

---

[168] Krause, 'La Prise en charge', 119–20.
[169] Basil, *Ep.* 199. 24, in Courtonne, *Lettres*, ii. 159.
[170] Krause, 'La Prise en charge', 120.
[171] Chrysostom, *De sacerdotio* 3. 1, SC 272. 104.
[172] Athanasius, *Apologia de fuga sua* 6, in *Apologie à l'empereur Constance, Apologie pour sa fuite*, ed. J.-M. Szymusiak (Paris, 1958), 139.
[173] On expulsions of women belonging to various factions in the Alexandrian church and denial of alms, cf. C. Haas, 'The Arians of Alexandria', *VC* 47 (1993), 234–45, esp. at 238 and 241.

the bishop's duty towards orphans extended beyond their immediate needs. The *Apostolic Constitutions*, for example, require the bishop to provide for those orphans who are not adopted by the rich. The bishop is to see that the orphaned boys acquire a trade and tools, while the girls find a husband.[174]

Chrysostom's treatise *De sacerdotio*, dated by Malingrey somewhere in the years 388–90, is an important source of information for the way in which episcopal almsgiving served the construction of authority: how the display of certain virtues, generosity (μεγαλοψυχία) and forbearance (ἀνεξικακία and μακροθυμία), made for the exercise of leadership (προστασία) by a bishop who became the patron (προστάτης) of widows in his care.[175] This will be further examined in Chapter 5. Here, concern falls on what a bishop was expected to do in the exercise of this care, and the problems that he might face in executing his duties.[176] These included the administrative oversight to ensure that those responsible for the widows received without serious interruption the necessary money, but also the selection of whom to enrol as a widow with the entitlement to a regular dole.[177] To choose badly, Chrysostom warned, was to acquire widows with a reputation for immorality. Not only are the immoral to be rejected, but all those who might be able to fend for themselves.[178] Chrysostom emphasized the degree to which a bishop frequently met with vociferous complaints and ingratitude from the enrolled widows. He spoke of their disruptive actions and even their propensity to steal.[179] This he put down in part to old age.[180] He added that the complaints were partly driven by hunger, and that the need to beg (from the church, if not others) caused them to behave impudently. He stressed the intelligence required to remove every pretext for complaint.[181] Elsewhere, in one of his sermons, Chrysostom states that 'to the multitude their

---

[174] *Ap. Const.* 4. 1–2, SC 329. 170–2.

[175] Chrysostom, *De sacerdotio* 3. 12, SC 272. 202–8.

[176] On the date of the treatise, cf. Malingrey, *Sacerdoce*, SC 272. 12–13.

[177] *De sacerdotio* 3. 12, SC 272. 200 and 202.

[178] Ibid. 202.

[179] For similar vocal behaviour, cf. *The Life of Abba Apphou* in F. Rossi, *I papiri copti del Museo Egizio di Torino*, in *Memorie delle Reale Accademia delle Scienze di Torino*, 37 (1886), ii. 87.

[180] Chrysostom, *De sacerdotio* 3. 12, SC 272. 204.

[181] Ibid. 3. 12, SC 272. 202 and 206.

plight appears despicable and inauspicious'.[182] This suggests first the low social level and extreme poverty of the women chosen. Second, it indicates the difficulty which even the large Antiochene church faced in maintaining regular and adequate supplies. Third, it indicates that what was distributed did not go far or last long.

Boniface Ramsey has remarked that the Fathers said little about receiving alms in their treatment of widows: 'In his treatise *On Widows* Ambrose makes no reference to them as the recipients of charity but rather as almsgivers... The same is true of Augustine's treatise *De Bono Viduitatis*...'[183] In part this reflects the hortatory nature of Ambrose's and Augustine's preaching and writing: they addressed the wealthy or financially secure widows, those with something to give. They were advocating widowhood as a virtuous condition in life to be retained by such women where possible. They could not, therefore, dwell on an inherently shameful aspect of this state. But the phenomenon Ramsey observes may also be due to the existence of too many eligible claimants among the poorer members of the congregation, who threatened to drain whatever resources the churches possessed for almsgiving. The writers chose not to stress what was owed to widows if the debt could not be honoured. Ramsey further observes that Ambrosiaster, commenting on 1 Timothy 5: 16, says that 'widows are often deprived of their ordinary means of support (namely spinning) by their relatives and hence are obliged to throw themselves upon the resources of the Church. The result is that the Church is overburdened and cannot adequately aid those who have no means of support at all.'

## Other privileged claimants

Consecrated virgins without other means of support were also privileged claimants because of their high standing in the Christian community. Mention has already been made of the virgins enrolled with the widows at Antioch.[184] It seems that bishops had occasionally enrolled a virgin among the order of widows to facilitate their

---

182  *Homilies on 1 Timothy* 13, PG 62. 566.
183  Ramsey, 'Almsgiving', 232 n. 34.
184  Chrysostom, *Homilies on Matthew* 66, PG 58. 630.

support, because Tertullian complained about a virgin in her late teens who was enrolled in this way and argued that some other mechanism should have been found by the bishop if she required help.[185] Establishing a daughter as a consecrated virgin became a way in which some sought to limit the ravages of poverty: St Basil observed that relatives attempted to have young girls not yet 17 enrolled as virgins in order to secure them 'something to live on' (τί βιωτικόν).[186] Another criterion by which some among the poor were given alms and not others was illness.[187] Gregory of Nyssa preached that 'the person who is poor and sick is destitute twice over' (ὁ πένης καὶ ἄρρωστος διπλοῦς ἐστι πτωχός).[188] This is reflected in the establishment of hospices or hospitals discussed below. Other favoured claimants already mentioned in the chapter were captives requiring ransom. Ambrose also allowed alms to be given to the suddenly impoverished, prosperous and aristocratic Christians who had fallen into relative poverty, perhaps through political disgrace. But this kind of expenditure could not be undertaken at the expense of the hungry.[189]

## Lists of episcopal recipients

It is already clear that in some places there was a list (*matricula* or κατάλογος) of those widows entitled to alms. Paul's Letter to Timothy set a precedent (1 Tim. 5) for inscribing the church's official widows on such lists, which was widely imitated. It is not clear whether only widows and virgins were enrolled in this way. Chrysostom spoke of the widows and virgins assisted by the Antiochene church as being in a κατάλογος.[190] Elsewhere he spoke of the poor who had been 'enrolled' or 'registered' (τῶν ἐγγεγραμμένων πενήτων).[191] These might be one and the same group: *penetes* does not suggest the destitute recipients of alms. Augustine, in a letter to Fabiola of late 422 or early 423,

185 Tertullian, *De virginibus velandis* 9, ed. E. Dekkers in CCSL 2. 1219.
186 Basil, *Ep.* 199. 18, in Courtonne, *Lettres*, ii. 156–7.
187 Chrysostom, *De sacerdotio* 3. 12, SC 272. 208.
188 Gregory of Nyssa, *De pauperibus amandis* 1, ed. Van Heck, in GNO 9. 98.
189 Ambrose, *De officiis*, 2. 15. 69, in Testard, *Devoirs*, ii. 40.
190 Chrysostom, *Homilies on Matthew* 66, PG 58. 630.
191 *Homilies on 1 Corinthians* 21, PG 61. 179.

recounted the early history of a wayward African bishop, Antoninus of Fussala, whose penniless parents had arrived with him at Hippo, presumably at around the turn of the century, when Antoninus was still a child, only to separate. Father and son had entered one of the monasteries, while the mother was placed 'on the list of the poor supported by the church'.[192] This might possibly suggest that only women could be listed in this way at Hippo, even though episcopal alms reached a wider group including the local monks, but it seems more likely that Augustine had an eye to the available accommodation, and to the boy's education. Clement at Alexandria had urged his congregation to show compassion by giving alms to all 'enrolled' Christians.[193]

Did every church have such a list? Instances of the word *matricula* itself are extremely rare in this period, but Augustine did not have to explain himself to Fabiola when recounting Antoninus' troubled history, and we may reasonably suppose that a similar list was known to her in Rome. The Younger Melania expected to 'be inscribed on the church list and fed among the beggars in accordance with the [divine] commandment' when she arrived from Rome in Jerusalem in the early fifth century.[194] The editor of the Greek text asserts that 'all the churches had such a "matricula"... and clerics, generally under the direction of an archdeacon, whose responsibility it was to care for the different categories of poor people registered as designated recipients' but this is to go beyond the available evidence and imply a bureaucracy that is unlikely to have existed except in the larger churches and cities.[195] Herrin, on the basis of Mark the Deacon's *Life of Porphyry*, has also stated that in the late fourth and early fifth century Bishop Porphyrius of Gaza 'drew up a register of those in need' who received '6 *obols* a week, a sum increased during the 40 days of Lent to 10'.[196] In this instance, though, the money is

[192] Augustine, *Ep.* 20\*. 2, OSA 46b. 294.

[193] Clement, *Quis dives salvetur?* 33, in *Clemens Alexandrinus*, ed. O Stählin, iii (Leipzig, 1909), 182.

[194] Gerontius, *Vita Melaniae iunioris* 35, in *Vie de sainte Mélanie*, ed. Denys Gorce, SC 90 (Paris, 1962), 194.

[195] Gorce, *Mélanie*, SC 90. 194 n. 1.

[196] J. Herrin, 'Ideals of Charity, Realities of Welfare: The Philanthropic Activity of the Byzantine Church', in R. Morris (ed.), *Church and People in Byzantium* (Birmingham, 1986), 154.

probably from Porphyry's own residual wealth, not church revenues, as the arrangement was made permanent in his will with funds set aside to finance it in future.

In conclusion to this section on recipients we can map out a series of priorities. The church's officially registered widows and orphans had first claim, together with those consecrated virgins who could not support themselves. After them, sick and elderly Christian beggars unable to work took priority. Theophilus, patriarch of Alexandria between 385 and 412, determined that gifts offered at the Eucharist, if surplus to immediate requirements, were to be distributed by the clergy for their own use and that of other baptized Christians but not that of the catechumens.[197] If Wipszycka is correct, these gifts took the form of blessed loaves of bread.[198] After this we should envisage competing claims. Captives and the suddenly impoverished had different special claims. Needy Christians not in good standing with the Church had probably a better claim than non-Christians. It is not clear, of course, how far any particular church's funds would stretch in meeting these various needs and it would be wrong to overlook the variations due to local circumstance: Epiphanius, for example, was said to help those who had been shipwrecked.[199] The numbers involved are rarely cited. At Rome, in an earlier period under Pope Cornelius, the church apparently supported 1,500 widows and needy people,[200] while I have already mentioned Chrysostom's figure of 3,000 widows and virgins supported by the Antiochene church together with further gifts to an unspecified number of the sick and poor (the lack of any number is a further indication that these recipients were not enrolled). In most places the numbers aided must have been far lower. Augustine makes clear that demand outstripped supply: he told the congregation at Hippo that so many were requesting alms each day that some had to remain unsatisfied 'because we do not have enough to give all something'.[201]

---

[197] Joannou, *Discipline*, ii. 269.
[198] Wipszycka, *Ressources*, 102.
[199] Sozomen, *Ecclesiastical History* 7. 27, in Bidez and Hansen, *Sozomenus*, 342.
[200] Eusebius, *Ecclesiastical History* 6. 43, SC 44. 156.
[201] Augustine, *Serm.* 355. 5, PL 39. 1572.

## THE BISHOP'S ASSISTANTS

The next two sections look at how church alms were distributed, by whom they were given out, when and in what form. In some places the bishop took an active role in the distribution. That is the implication of advice by Isidore of Pelusium to a bishop that he should avoid women's company except for special circumstances such as dispensing alms to the destitute.[202] The bishop normally exercised his duty towards the poor, however, with the help of his clergy. The *Apostolic Church Order* stipulated that the elders or priests were to be 'generous (εὐμεταδότους) to the brethren'.[203] Those most closely involved were the deacons, an *oikonomos* (or manager of church funds) in many places, and in some places various other officials in charge of hostels (see below). The canons of Gangra refer to the cleric put in charge of 'administering good works' (εἰς οἰκονομίαν εὐποιίας).[204] Sozomen mentions a deacon Marathonius, who under bishop Macedonius of Constantinople (341–8, 350–6) was a 'zealous general-manager of the poorhouses' (σπουδαῖος ἐπίτροπος πτωχείων).[205]

Offerings were not to be accepted or given out without the bishop's knowledge or permission. The *Apostolic Constitutions*, in the final section which Metzger believes to incorporate contemporary canonical material (8. 47. 1–85), states that the bishop controls the church's wealth, 'so as by his authority to distribute everything to the needy through his priests and deacons'.[206] Deacons are expected in the *Apostolic Constitutions* to 'visit all those in need' (ἐπισκέπτεσθαι πάντας τοὺς δεομένους ἐπισκέψεως and report on what they find to the bishop. In churches where there were deaconesses, it was they who were to visit the women.[207] But some texts also indicate a certain freedom of action in making small gifts: the so-called *Canons of Athanasius* allow the steward to act independently of the bishop in giving out alms of up to five *oipe*.[208]

---

[202] Isidore of Pelusium, *Ep.* 89 = Migne Ep. I. 89, PG 78. 244C.

[203] *Apostolic Church Order* 18, in Bickell, *Geschichte des Kirchenrechts*, 123.

[204] Canon 8, Joannou, *Discipline*, i. 92.

[205] Sozomen, *Ecclesiastical History* 4. 20, in Bidez and Hansen, *Sozomenus*, 170.

[206] *Ap. Const.* 8. 47. 41, SC 336. 288.

[207] Ibid. 3. 19, SC 329. 160–2.     [208] Wipszycka, *Ressources*, 138–9.

The insistence in canonical legislation and church orders on the need for the various assistants not to give alms independently of the bishop without his approval suggests that practice did not always live up to this ideal. This is significant, given that these regulations are not only concerned with accountability and efficiency, but also with the proper distribution of honour to those caring for the poor on behalf of the bishop. Deacons, like their bishop, could expect to gain honour from their role in episcopal almsgiving. The Latin translation of the *Apostolic Church Order* envisaged that as a result of their conscientious work with the poor the deacons would be 'regarded with all honour, respect and fear by the people'.[209] But this respect was not to undermine the bishop's status as the ultimate leader or father of the poor. It would seem that the church orders here present an ideal of co-operation and subordination when the reality was also inherently competitive.

## THE FORM OF EPISCOPAL ALMS: DAILY BREAD, COINS, AND CLOTHES

Chrysostom's concern, noted above, to provide money for those in charge of the enrolled widows suggests, though it does not prove, that the latter did not receive money themselves. On the other hand, both this passage and imperial legislation give reason to think that the great churches did not simply store all the produce from their estates and any offerings of produce for later distribution. An edict dated by Roland Delmaire to 346, but which deals with a law of Constantine (*Codex Theodosianus* 16. 2. 10) provides tax exemption from the *chrysargyron* for clerical income from shops and workshops 'destined for the poor'.[210] Delmaire regards a law of 343 (*C. Th.* 16. 2. 8) where there is an exemption *alimoniae causa* as an earlier example

---

[209] *Apostolic Church Order* (Latin tr.), 65, in E. Tidner, *Didascaliae Apostolorum Canonum Ecclesiasticorum Traditionis Apostolicae Versiones Latinae*, Texte und Unter-suchungen, 75 (Berlin, 1963), 107 and 109.

[210] Delmaire, *Largesses*, 363. For an alternative dating to 320, cf. P. R. Coleman-Norton, *Roman State and Christian Church: A Collection of Legal Documents to A.D. 535*, 3 vols. (London, 1966), i. 79–80.

of the same principle, with immunity from the same tax 'limited to purchases made in caring for the poor'.[211] Delmaire considers that Constantius restricted these privileges by a law of 359 (*C.Th.* 16. 2. 15), but what matters here is the glimpse afforded into the mechanism by which produce and goods were sold and money made available for charitable purposes. At Alexandria those with a claim to episcopal alms, the widows and others who 'did not go out in public' (ἀνέξοδοι), had jars for collecting oil and wine, while we may presume that they also received loaves of bread.[212] The quantities involved cannot be ascertained. Chrysostom's insistence that even 'someone whose sustenance depended on begging' should give what they could spare suggests that registered widows received more, though not much more, than the minimum which would keep them alive.[213]

It is possible that episcopal alms were distributed daily at the entrance to the church, but more likely that such alms were only distributed weekly on a Saturday or Sunday. The *Lausiac History* describes sick beggars at Ancyra crowding into the stoa or porch of the church to receive their 'daily sustenance' (τὴν ἐφήμερον τροφήν).[214] But as beggars received alms from private individuals in front of the church, often in the form of small coins, it is not clear what type of almsgiving is described at Ancyra. The Egyptian *Canons of Athanasius* specified that the bishop was to give alms on a Sunday, at Epiphany, Easter, and Pentecost.[215] This seems to refer both to ordinary distributions and others marking the great Christian festivals. Annick Martin has drawn attention to evidence showing that at Oxyrhynchus in the late fourth century the poor received alms on a Saturday evening at the church and that bishop Apphou left his monastery to visit them there on a Saturday and Sunday.[216] Uranius, the biographer of Paulinus met at the opening of this chapter, told how John, the

---

[211] Delmaire, *Largesses*, 362. The phrase, however, is ambiguous. For the alternative reading, that the exemption permits clerics to feed themselves and their family, cf. Martin, *Athanase*, 201.

[212] Athanasius, *Historia Arianorum* 13. 3, in Opitz, *Werke*, ii/1. 189.

[213] Chrysostom, *Homilies on Hebrews* 1, PG 63. 20.

[214] Palladius, *The Lausiac History* 68. 2, ed. G. Bartelink, *Palladio, La Storia Lausiaca* (Milan, 1974), 280.

[215] Canon 16 in Riedel and Crum, *Canons*, 26–7.

[216] Martin, *Athanase*, 722.

bishop of Naples at the time of Paulinus' death, 'paid' or 'rewarded' his clergy and the poor on the 'fifth day' or Thursday 'according to custom'.[217] As the day in question was Maundy Thursday, this was presumably a distribution linked to the Easter celebrations.[218] The *Life of Rabbula*, in accordance with a topos of hagiography, attributed to its hero foreknowledge of his approaching death, as a result of which he distributed in June the alms he normally gave out in December.[219]

Augustine spoke in a sermon on the anniversary of his episcopal consecration of the obligation to feed the poor on that day: 'today we have our fellow men, the poor, to feed and we must extend our compassion to them' (*pascendos habemus hodie compauperes nostros, et cum eis communicanda est humanitas*).[220] Edmund Hill OP has commented: 'it seems that bishops or at least this bishop regularly gave a feast to the poor on the anniversary of their ordination'.[221] The sermon is in fact less clear on this matter than Fr Hill suggests. The text urges generosity towards the poor, presented in terms of storing up treasure, while the bishop presents himself as feeding the people by exhorting them and drawing on his treasure of divine teaching. It is impossible to be certain whether behind the rhetoric lies a meal for the poor, a distribution of alms, or a special collection. The sermon was later adapted by Caesarius of Arles for his own use near Christmas: 'the Lord's birthday is at hand, we have our fellow men, the poor, to feed'.[222] So phrased, it suggests a collection on the anniversary of the bishop's consecration looking forward to a distribution of alms at Christmas. What is clear, however, is that in both versions of the sermon the bishop's concern for the poor, both directly in providing for them, and indirectly by exhorting the congregation to provide for them, serves on the day in question as a model of episcopal conduct, and allows Augustine to present

---

[217] 'remunerans omnes clericos atque pauperes': Uranius, *De obitu* 11, PL 53. 865B.

[218] For further evidence of the importance of giving food and drink at Easter, cf. Commodian, *Instructions* 2. 30, CCSL 128. 67.

[219] Bickell, *Ausgewählte Schriften*, 208.

[220] Augustine, *Serm.* 339. 4, in Lambot, *Sermones Selecti Duodeviginti*, 115.

[221] Hill, WSAT, 3/9. 290 n. 8.

[222] Caesarius of Arles, *Serm.* 231. 3, in G. Morin (ed.), *S. Caesarii Arelatensis Sermones Pars Altera*, CCSL 104 (Turnhout, 1953), 916.

himself as the leader whose words and deeds together secure the unity of the congregation. The message made possible by almsgiving and the preaching that surrounds it is that the bishop feeds his people, whether literally or metaphorically. In the quotation given above the unity which this engenders is articulated in Augustine's use of the first person plural, where 'we' might mean only the bishop but probably means the entire congregation, and through compounds which echo and reinforce the preposition 'cum', in particular the rare compound 'compauper' (its distinctive use by Augustine, who may have coined the word, is picked up and echoed by Possidius in his biography of the saint).[223]

Episcopal alms were not restricted to food. Some churches stored clothing to give out as need arose. An inventory from the church in the African town of Cirta dating from 303 listed '82 women's tunics, 38 capes, 16 men's tunics, 13 pairs of men's shoes, 47 pairs of women's shoes, 19 peasant clasps (*coplas rusticanas*)'.[224] It is hard to know what these were kept for unless they were part of a store for the needy. If they were sets of liturgical dress of some kind, we would not expect such different numbers for the different items. Scholars dispute why clothing for women was present in far greater quantity than clothing for men. MacMullen's suggestion that the gender imbalance reflects a similar imbalance among wealthy donors is implausible: it presupposes they donated what was surplus to the needs of their private wardrobe rather than of their household.[225] It is more likely to be an indication of the greater number of poor women in need of clothing. Much later, in the second half of the century, Basil informed the imperial official, the *Commentariensis*, how thieves had been apprehended for stealing from the church at Caesarea 'cheap clothes belonging to the destitute, who should rather have been clothed than stripped'.[226] This, too, suggests a store for distribution.

These stores indicate that the church complex of the basilica with its surrounding store rooms and apartments was the normal centre of distribution, though in a large metropolis district or parish

---

[223] Possidius, *Life of Augustine* 23. 1, in Mohrmann et al., *Vita*, 188.
[224] *Gesta apud Zenophilum* 3, in Maier, *Dossier*, i. 219.
[225] MacMullen, *Christianity and Paganism*, 164 n. 16.
[226] Basil, *Ep.* 286. 1, in Courtonne, *Lettres*, iii. 156.

churches rather than a single cathedral were used. This is evident in events at Alexandria, as related by Athanasius, when the Nicene clergy 'charged with the widows' care' attempted to feed both them and the 'needy' at other points in the city after the *dux* had handed over the churches to the Arians.[227] At Rome it is generally held that alms were distributed not in one place only, but in each of the seven districts that Pope Fabian had assigned to the different deacons.[228]

## CHURCH *XENODOCHEIA, NOSOKOMEIA*, AND *PTOCHOTROPHEIA*

The bishop might also be responsible for hostels or hospitals in the city, though control of such institutions was contested in the period. By the mid-fifth century they were sufficiently common to be included in legislation at Chalcedon, which stipulated that clerics who moved from one diocese to another were not to retain control or oversight of institutions in their former diocese whether these were '*martyria* or hostels for visitors or poor men' (μαρτυρίων ἢ πτωχείων ἢ ξενοδοχείων).[229] The dispute over who was to control these institutions is likely in some cases to originate in their foundation by private means on the part of wealthy clerics, rather than through the use of church funds, coupled with the patronage which such an act might confer on the founder with respect to the beneficiaries. The legislation indicates how this type of almsgiving approximated in form to the euergetism of those who built more traditional Christian monuments and so featured in the competition for the status conferred by an evolving euergetism, which is to be examined in Chapter 5. What, though, was the history of these institutions for the poor?

*Xenones* or guest-houses were not new in the fourth century, though we cannot presume that they usually catered for the very

---

[227] Athanasius, *Historia Arianorum* 61. 2, in Opitz, *Werke*, ii/1. 217.

[228] C. Pietri, *Roma christiana: Recherches sur l'Eglise de Rome, son organisation, sa politique, son idéologie de Miltiade à Sixte III (311–440)*, 2 vols. (Rome, 1976), i. 135.

[229] Joannou, *Discipline*, i. 77–8 (canon 10).

poor. Bishops and monks offered accommodation to visitors and pilgrims visiting the martyrs' shrines or travelling to the Holy Land, who in some cases came armed with letters of recommendation from their local bishop. The Synod of Antioch in 341 determined that no visitors were to be taken in and given assistance unless they had these 'letters of peace'.[230] The bishops at Chalcedon sought to ensure that poor and rich were not treated alike: they were to receive different types of letter: the poor are to get letters of peace, the rich letters of recommendation.[231] The importance of such hostels for pilgrims is seen in the *xenodochium* built at Hippo in the early fifth century next to a basilica for the martyrs at much the same time as the church itself was built.[232] Monasteries often had a *xenodochium* which functioned as the guest-house for visitors, though that Greek loan-word had not previously been current in Latin.[233]

The mid-fourth century provides the first evidence for hostels and hospitals probably dedicated to the care of the poor. Theophanes records that Constantine's gift of grain already mentioned in this chapter was for the clergy, widows, 'hostels and the poor' (ξενοδοχείοις πένησί), though it is possible that Theophanes' description, however interpreted, was anachronistic.[234] Gregory of Nyssa accused Aetius, a deacon at Antioch under bishop Leontius after 344, of pretending to practise medicine while seeking converts to his theological opinions among the 'outcasts' or 'good for nothings' (ἀπερριμένοι).[235] It is plausible, but not definite, that the deacon tended them in a *xenodocheion* or hospice under an equivalent name. Before 386 Antioch certainly had a 'hostel' (καταγώγιον) for beggars on the approach to the city', where the desperately sick could be seen.[236] What cannot be ascertained is how many institutions existed then in the city and by whom they were established.

[230] Ibid. i. 110 (canon 7).

[231] Ibid. i. 78–9 (canon 11).

[232] Augustine, *Serm.* 356, PL 39. 1578.

[233] *Tractatus in John* 97. 4, in *Sancti Aurelii Augustini In Iohannis Evangelium Tractatus*, ed D. Willems, CCSL 36 (Turnhout, 1954), 575.

[234] Theophanes, *Chronographia*, 29. Eng. tr in Mango and Scott, *Chronicle*, 48.

[235] Gregory of Nyssa, *Against Eunomius* 1. 42, ed. W. Jaeger, in GNO 1 (Leiden, 1960), 36.

[236] Chrysostom, *Ad Stagirum a daemone vexatum*, PG 47. 490.

Macedonius appointed his deacon Marathonius some time between 344 and 350 as an 'industrious superintendent of the poorhouses and monastic communities of men and women' at Constantinople.[237] It is possible that Macedonius was the founder of these charitable centres in the new capital from his own purse. Palladius related that Chrysostom examined the accounts of one hospital (νοσοκομεῖον) at Constantinople when he became bishop and founded two more.[238] This does not mean that only one hostel for the poor still existed when Chrysostom took office, but suggests that by 398 only one was under episcopal control.

Eustathius set one of his followers in charge of a hostel for the poor at Sebasteia some time after he became bishop there in 357.[239] Epiphanius in his *Panarion*, composed in the years 374–8, explained to his readers that this was a *xenodocheion*, 'which in Pontus is called a *ptochotropheion*', a hostel provided by 'the leaders of the churches' there for the 'incapacitated and crippled'.[240] Such centres were clearly still novel for Epiphanius' readership. Basil built a hostel for the destitute (πτωχοτροφεῖον), the famous *Basileiados*, just outside Caesarea in the early 370s.[241] The foundation, which was probably staffed by monks, is examined in Chapter 6. In Cappadocia there were a number of πτωχοτροφεῖα under the direction of the country bishops by 373.[242] According to Palladius, Ephraem, by now a deacon, set up a temporary hostel during a severe food shortage at Edessa in c.372–3 with some 300 beds in the porticoes.[243] The author has Ephraem describe himself as the ξενοδόχος or hostel manager who offers the starving ξενοδοχίαν or welcome. This seems to imply either that there was then no *xenodocheion* attached to the church in the city or, more likely, that it did not cater for the very poor. The

[237] Sozomen, *Ecclesiastical History* 4. 20.2., in Bidez and Hansen, *Sozomenus*, 170. For acceptance of Sozomen's dates, cf. S. Elm, '*Virgins of God': The Making of Asceticism in Late Antiquity* (Oxford, 1994), 112 n. 15.
[238] Palladius, *Life of John Chrysostom* 20, in Coleman-Norton, *Palladii Dialogus*, 32.
[239] Epiphanius of Salamis, *Panarion* 75. 1 in K. Holl (ed.), *Epiphanius, Panarion 65–80*, GCS (Berlin, 1985), 333.
[240] F. Williams, *The Panarion of Epiphanius of Salamis* 1 (Leiden, 1987), p. xvi.
[241] Basil, *Ep.* 176, in Courtonne, *Lettres*, ii. 113.
[242] Basil, *Ep.* 142, Courtonne, *Lettres*, ii. 65.
[243] Palladius, *Lausiac History* 40, in Bartelink, *Palladio*, 206–8.

*Lausiac History* also told how a monk famous for his care of the poor was an assiduous visitor in the fourth century to the prison and the hospital (νοσοκομεῖον) at Ancyra.[244] The same work offers a rare glimpse into arrangements inside one such hostel, the *ptocheion* at Alexandria, where in 388 under the administration of a presbyter, Macarius, it was occupied exclusively by lepers, women on an upper floor with the men on the ground floor beneath.[245]

A number of scholars led by Gilbert Dagron have argued that many of the above institutions were the product of a distinctive Eustathian programme of monastic foundations with a charitable purpose in urban or near-urban settings.[246] Eustathius certainly had great influence on Basil and Marathonius. Timothy Miller and Susanna Elm point out that some of the early founders were Arian or Homoiousian, and contend that the early foundations were a distinctive feature of Arian or Homoiousian Christianity.[247] This is far less likely. Dagron himself pointed out that Macedonius was only later labelled an Arian by Nicene Christians who read back a doctrinal split into the contest between Paul and Macedonius for the see of Constantinople after the death of bishop Alexander, while Macedonius was himself the target of Arian attacks.[248]

Whether or not the early foundations were Arian in character, what is significant is how many were founded by bishops, who appointed both the overseer and the monks who were to administer whatever care was provided. This pattern was to continue: at Edessa in the early fifth century bishop Rabbula used church properties to endow and refound an existing hostel or hospital, which may have been that established by Ephraem in 373 (see below). He also founded a separate hospital for women. The former was run by a deacon assisted by monks, the second by a deaconess with help from

---

[244] Palladius, *Lausiac History* 68. 2, in Bartelink, *Palladio*, 280.

[245] Palladius, *Lausiac History* 6, in Bartelink, *Palladio*, 34–6.

[246] Cf. G. Dagron, 'Les Moines et la ville: Le Monachisme à Constantinople jusqu'au Concile de Chalcédoine (451)', *Travaux et Mémoires*, 4 (1970), 252. Elm, *Virgins*, 125. T. S. Miller, *The Birth of the Hospital in the Byzantine Empire*, 2nd edn. (Baltimore and London, 1997), 78–9.

[247] Ibid. 76–88; Elm, *Virgins*, 212.

[248] G Dagron, *Naissance d'une capitale: Constantinople et ses institutions de 330 à 451* (Paris, 1974), 419–23, 439, and 442.

nuns.[249] Syriac canons, which Vööbus dated to the fifth century, state that *xenodocheia* were to be established in each town with an overseer appointed by the bishop from among 'the rank of monks'.[250] This collaboration between city clergy and monks or nuns may further account for some later disputes for control. Dagron has argued that at Constantinople Chrysostom was not so much the founder of several νοσοκομεῖα, as Palladius would have it, but the reformer of monastic hospitals now taken under episcopal control.[251] How a hospital founded by monks might feature in competition for status with a bishop will be considered in Chapter 5. Here it may be noted that where bishops employed monks some, such as Basil and Rabbula, also tended to the poor in person.[252] The founder's status was confirmed through personal involvement. It is also significant that a number of the early hospices established outside the city walls appear to have catered for lepers. At Edessa Rabbula built a third hospital outside the city specifically for them.

Even where founded by a bishop or other cleric many of the hostels were in part privately funded. The *Basileiados* was partly funded by a gift of land from the Emperor Valens according to Theodoret.[253] Basil provides evidence for hostels at Amaseia at least partly funded by private patrons: he petitioned a fiscal officer who was one such patron.[254] Ephraem's hospital at Edessa was financed through donations from the city's wealthy lay people. What is odd in this context is that the rich Edessenes are reported as saying that they had not given anything earlier for want of someone they could entrust with the job of poor-relief: 'There is no one we can entrust with the task of ministering to the hungry. For they are all out to make a profit from the situation.'[255] What does this imply about the city's bishop, Barsê (363–379), and his role, if any, with the holy

[249] Bickell, *Ausgewählte Schriften*, 205–6.

[250] A. Vööbus, *History of Asceticism in the Syrian Orient*, 3 vols. (Louvain, 1958–88), ii. 371.

[251] Dagron, *Naissance*, 511.

[252] Bickell, *Ausgewählte Schriften*, 206.

[253] Theodoret, *Ecclesiastical History* 4. 19, in L. Parmentier and G. Hansen (eds.), *Theodoret Kirchengeschichte*, 3rd edn. (Berlin, 1998), 245. This is accepted by Delmaire, *Largesses*, 624.

[254] Basil, *Ep.* 143, Courtonne, *Lettres*, ii. 65.

[255] Palladius, *Lausiac History*, 40, in Bartelink, *Palladio*, 208.

ascetic in the establishment of the hospital? It is known that Ephraem criticized members of the Edessene church for opposing Barsê, who was to be expelled from the city together with some of his senior clergy only months after Ephraem's foundation of the hospital and death.[256] The bishop's opposition to Arianism made him unpopular not only with the Emperor Valens but also with a sizeable number of rich Edessene Christians. They withheld their financial support from Barsê's charitable activities until won over by Ephraem. This refusal is a telling indication of how far charitable care of the poor and episcopal status were interlocked. The ascetic, though operating with the bishop's blessing, allowed them to give alms without being seen to accept the leadership of a figure they deemed heretical.

The conclusions from this section may be summarized by stating that hostels for the poor developed during the second half of the fourth century, beginning in the major cities of the Eastern Empire, from where the above examples come, and this development continued in the fifth century, not only in terms of the further geographical diffusion of hostels, but the establishment of more than one such hostel in the bigger cities (as at Antioch and Constantinople). They were sufficiently widespread and well-known to be imitated by Julian the Apostate in the early 360s. A letter of Julian shows him ordering the establishment of *xenodocheia* and grain distributions as part of a philanthropic programme designed to outshine the Christians.[257] Later Christian sources tell the same story: Gregory Nazianzen described Julian as founding 'inns... and hostelries (ξενῶνες), holy places (ἁγνευτήρια), houses of virgins, academies' and promoting 'philanthropy for those in need' as well as copying letters of recommendation.[258] Sozomen reported that Julian set up hostels for the relief of strangers and the poor (καταγωγίοι ξένων καὶ πτωχῶν).[259] This awareness on the part of Christians of the pagan emperor's competitive attempt to imitate

[256] J. B. Segal, *Edessa: 'The Blessed City'* (Oxford, 1970), 88 and 91.

[257] Julian, *Ep.* 84a (formerly *ep.* 49), Bidez and Cumont, *Epistulae*, 114. For Julian's concern to counter the Christian agapes cf. *Ep.* 89b. 305D, Bidez and Cumont, 146.

[258] Gregory Nazianzen, *Against Julian* (*Oration* 4) 110, in J. Bernardi (ed.), *Grégoire de Nazianze, Discours 4–5*, SC 309 (Paris 1983), 266–8.

[259] Sozomen, *Ecclesiastical History* 5. 16, in Bidez and Hansen, *Sozomenus*, 217.

Christian practice is likely in turn to have fostered the creation on their part of further hostels and hospitals. These institutions, because dependent in many cases on private funds and founders, or served by monks under their own leaders, were not always easy for the bishop to control and so featured more than once in competitions for honour. It will appear in the next chapter, however, that when hostels appear in the West during the early fifth century, their origins lie with private lay men and women.

## CONCLUSION

Almsgiving took specific forms in the Christian communities. The most prominent was that of episcopal almsgiving, the principal sources of which were the revenues from imperial subventions, church properties, and a proportion of the general offerings after the bishop and clergy had received their allowances and the costs of lights for the church and other types of maintenance had been met. A separate tithe was rarely given. These alms were the responsibility and gift of the bishop, whose eloquence was essential to their successful collection and whose moral authority was enhanced, but also opened up to criticism, through their distribution. The bishop usually retained a personal hand in this distribution which formed a bond of patronage or leadership with the principal beneficiaries, though he was aided by his deacons, and often by an *oikonomos* appointed for the purpose, so that others shared in this construction of leadership and might compete for the standing which it enhanced. The principal recipients of episcopal alms were the enrolled widows and their dependent children, together with the poorer virgins, whose enjoyment of a low but relatively secure dole helped to ensure their long-term survival on the edge of penury without falling into utter destitution. A varying number of destitute Christians and non-Christians, who were probably not enrolled and so had no title to alms, merely a claim to what was left, also benefited when and where there was enough to go round and so survived for a while longer. The recipients were not lifted out of poverty, but kept from starvation. Among the destitute, Christians had a better claim than others. Church alms were given in the form of staples, probably on a weekly basis, and on the great festivals of the Church year. This care was augmented in the period through the growing establishment of hospitals for the very ill and crippled. Assistance from the bishop formed a bond between him and the recipients to be further investigated in Chapter 5.

# 3

## Almsgiving by Monks and Lay Christians

### ASCETIC SELF-DISPOSSESSION AND MONASTIC ALMSGIVING

The fifth-century *Life of Alexander*, dated by Dagron to *c*.460,[1] celebrates a charismatic monk who at the start of the century had embraced voluntary poverty and distributed his wealth to the destitute before entering a monastery.[2] It was by then a common motif in hagiographic literature. The *Historia monachorum in Aegypto*, composed in Greek from earlier texts during the final years of the fourth century and revised in Latin by Rufinus shortly afterwards, portrayed Paphnutius as persuading a rich merchant, whose slaves had presented the monk with ten sacks of vegetables for the monastery, to go one step better and adopt the ascetic life. This the merchant did at once, ordering the slaves to distribute his remaining wealth to the poor.[3] In the *Histories of the Monks of Upper Egypt* a soldier who encounters a lion in the desert vows to become a monk if he escapes with his life. When the prayer is answered he sells his horse and other belongings to minister to the poor of the district before entering a monastic community.[4] The *Vita Hilarionis* told how the later bishop of Arles first became a monk in the early fifth century.

---

[1] Dagron, 'Les Moines et la ville', 231 n. 13.

[2] *Life of Alexander* 6, ed. E. De Stoop, *Vie d'Alexandre l'Acémète*, PO 6 (Paris, 1911), 661.

[3] *Historia monachorum in Aegypto* (Greek version) 14. 19–22, ed. A. J. Festugière OP (Brussels, 1971), 108–9; Latin version, 16. 3. 1–3. 4, in E. Schulz-Flügel (ed.), *Tyrannius Rufinus: Historia Monachorum sive De Vita Sanctorum Patrum* (Berlin, 1990), 345–6.

[4] Paphnutius, *Histories* 88, in Vivian, *Histories*, 115.

He received money from his brother in exchange for his share of the family estates. Hilary gave this away in alms 'either for the benefit of the destitute or for the comfort... of the monks'.[5] The *Life of Honoratus* presents the future bishop as fulfilling the dominical command to sell all and give to the poor (Matthew 19: 21) on becoming a monk at Lérins in the early fifth century. This in turn inspired others to make a similar gesture, entrusting him with the alms for redistribution.[6] For this purpose Honoratus had 'a great many agents in many places'.[7]

The literary topos of ascetic self-dispossession and almsgiving might be said to highlight rare extremes. We know that not every would-be monk saw fit to give away all he possessed on leaving the world. To judge from Cassian's *Institutes* some sought to hold on to at least some of their wealth with the justification that they would be able to distribute it charitably as monks.[8] Perhaps this was the practice of the ascetics described by the author of the *Consultationes Zacchaei et Apollonii*, who did not retreat into the desert but supplied the needy with what he termed 'a manageable, though not copious, sum' (*non profusum, sed tractabilem censum*).[9] Yet Cassian was concerned to eradicate this retention of wealth as an abuse: the complexities of actual practice were thus under pressure from an ideal recognized as worthy of pursuit, and almsgiving on ascetic self-dispossession was sufficiently common for Augustine to number and praise amongst the different kinds of vow renunciation of all one's possessions and their distribution to the poor on entry into a monastic community.[10]

In some cases it was the monastery which acted as the almsgiver on these occasions. Susanna Elm has noted that at the White monastery in Egypt Shenoute's successor, Besa, required entrants to give away all

    [5] Honoratus, *Vita Hilarionis* 6, SC 404. 102.
    [6] Hilary of Arles, *Life of Honoratus* 20, in S. Cavallin, *Vitae Sanctorum Honorati et Hilarii Episcoporum Arelatensium* (Lund, 1952), 64.
    [7] Hilary of Arles, *Life* 21, in Cavallin, *Vitae*, 65.
    [8] Cassian, *Institutes* 7. 16 in J.-C. Guy (ed.), *Jean Cassien: Institutions cénobitiques*, SC 109 (Paris, 1965), 312 and 314.
    [9] *Consultationes Zacchaei et Apollonii* 3. 3. 12, in J. L. Feiertag and W Steinmann (eds.), *Questions d'un païen à un Chrétien*, 2 vols., SC 401 and 402 (Paris, 1994), ii. 182–4.
    [10] Augustine, *En. in Ps.* 75. 16, CCSL 39. 1048.

their property to the monastery, but that a share of this was then given to the poor.[11] Basil was asked, at what date we cannot ascertain, to determine how a would-be ascetic should dispose of his goods in accordance with the dominical commands at Matthew 19: 21 and Luke 12: 33. His answer was that the aspirant might either redistribute (οἰκονομεῖν) his possessions himself, if competent, or entrust the task to those who possessed the necessary discretion (δοκιμασία). He did not recommend leaving this to relatives.[12] Relatives presumably did sometimes undertake this role in the late fourth century, but were suspected of sequestering what should have been given in alms. Other answers reveal why relatives might hold back goods (apart from the wish to preserve and improve family estates): the need to pay taxes incurred by the individual before their abandonment of the world. Basil advised a monastic community to pay such taxes only when the entrant had made a substantial gift to the community.[13] These answers, though not given as part of any systematic legislation for religious life, were collected, codified, and widely admired by Eastern monastic communities in the fifth century.[14]

The pattern of self-dispossession and almsgiving attracted alms from ordinary Christians for redistribution. The *Life of Hypatios* recounts that the holy monk was left a legacy by a *scholastikos*, comprising money and clothes: the former was at once distributed among the monasteries and the latter among the poor.[15] Voluntary poverty offered an apparent guarantee to donors that their gifts would not be misused. Alexander's followers made a point of giving to the destitute whatever surplus they acquired over and above the amount needed to feed them for a day.[16] Their fame lay in how little they stored, but many other monasteries were also active in almsgiving, both through redistributing part of the alms they had received and through use of revenues from their manual labour,

---

[11] Elm, *Virgins*, 301.
[12] Basil, *Regulae fusius tractatae* 9, PG 31. 941B–C.
[13] *Regulae brevius tractatae* 94 and 107, PG 31. 1148B–C and 1156B.
[14] Cf. P. Rousseau, *Basil of Caesarea* (Berkeley, Los Angeles, and Oxford, 1994), appendix II, pp. 354–9.
[15] Callinicus, *Life of Hypatios* 34. 1–6, SC 177. 220.
[16] *Life of Alexander* 27, PO 6. 678.

which for this reason appear to have been tax exempted.[17] Basil urged monks to carry out their work precisely with a view to the 'care of the needy' (ἡ ὑπηρεσία τῶν δεομένων) which it made possible.[18] Chrysostom presented the monks in one sermon 'collecting a large income for the needy'.[19] Here, too, the alms were given away in the form of food.[20] Rhetoric might exaggerate the amounts involved, but not falsify the practice. Basil's answers on how to practise the ascetic life recommended that the distribution should be the responsibility of a single brother and that others be discouraged from acting independently.[21] An episode in the Greek *Life of Simeon Stylites* indicates that Basil's stipulation was widely accepted as a rule, but not always observed, nor simply regarded as an ideal for each and every ascetic: Simeon took his daily portion of food each evening and secretly gave it to the poor until he was discovered by another monk who reported him to the archimandrite.[22] The author of the *vita* clearly saw a virtue in Simeon's transgression.

The practice of monks attracting alms for redistribution quickly became controversial. It compromised monastic withdrawal from secular business. It exposed monks in general, but solitaries in particular, to the temptation to hoard and to charges of avarice by others. A letter on the anchoretic life which came to be ascribed to Basil but is probably from a fourth- or fifth-century hermit strongly warned against acceptance of alms for redistribution precisely because it exposed an anchorite to the charge of being 'money-loving'.[23] Where the ascetic knew of destitute individuals in the vicinity, he was to instruct the donor to present his gifts directly to those in need. Jerome likewise attacked the practice of redistribution

---

[17] Chrysostom, *In Defence of Monks*, PG 47. 364.

[18] Basil, *Regulae fusius tractatae* 42, PG 31. 1025A.

[19] Chrysostom, *Homilies on Matthew* 68. 3, PG 58. 644.

[20] *Homilies on Matthew* 72. 4, PG 58. 671.

[21] Basil, *Regulae brevius tractatae* 91, 100, and 101, PG 31. 1145B, 1152B–C, and 1152C–1153A.

[22] Anon., *Life of Simeon Stylites* 6, tr. A. J. Festugière OP, *Antioche païenne et chrétienne* (Paris, 1959), 494.

[23] Basil, *Ep.* 42. 3, Courtonne, *Lettres*, i. 104. The arguments against Basil's authorship and support for a date in the 4th or 5th cent. can be found in E. Amand de Mendieta, 'L'Authenticité des lettres ascétiques 42 à 45 de la correspondance de saint Basile de Césarée', *Recherches de science religieuse*, 56/2 (1968), 241–64.

in the *Life of Hilarion*, the ascetic who rose to become the head of what appears to be a semi-anchoretic monastic community in Palestine. Jerome recounted how Orion, a wealthy layman, attempted to thank Hilarion for a miraculous cure by a large gift of alms. Hilarion steadfastly refused: 'you can distribute your own property best'.[24] In the *Life of Longinus*, a Coptic version of an earlier Greek text about the fifth-century monophysite head of the Ennaton monastery at Alexandria, Longinus rejects a large donation by a sea captain, who is instead instructed to give the sum to a person whom he will find at a certain spot in the city, and who turns out to be someone deeply in debt and on the verge of suicide.[25] Practices clashed as individuals gave monks gifts to distribute which the monks themselves tried to refuse. Melania and her husband Pinian attempted to give alms to the Egyptian monk Abba Hephestion. They wished him to accept 'a little gold' from their hand, presumably a gold coin or *solidus*. When he protested, Melania hid the gold piece in the monk's store of salt. But soon after the touring pilgrims took their leave, Abba Hephestion discovered the ruse played upon him and came in hot pursuit of his donors:

After they had crossed the river, the man of God ran toward them, holding the gold and shouting 'Why do I want this?' Holy Melania said to him, 'In order to give it to those in need.' He solemnly swore that he would not keep it nor give it away, chiefly because the place was a desert and none of the needy was able to come there. Because they could not persuade him to accept their gold, the holy man threw it into the river after a long discussion.[26]

The donors' determination is suggestive of the prominent place almsgiving held in their understanding of the ascetic life which they had adopted as wealthy members of the Roman elite. Abba Hephestion is equally determined not to be a recipient of their alms. In the context of a cell bereft of all property other than a mat and two storage baskets for salt and biscuits, his obstinacy measures his refusal

---

[24] Jerome, *Life of Hilarion* 18, PL 23. 36.

[25] Anon., *Life of Longinus* 28, in T. Orlandi and A. Campagnano (eds.), *Vite dei monaci Phif e Longino* (Milan, 1975), 77–9.

[26] Gerontius, *Vita Melaniae iunioris* 38, SC 90. 198, tr. E. A. Clark, *The Life of Melania the Younger*, Studies in Women and Religion, 14 (New York and Toronto, 1984), 53.

to hoard whatever exceeds his absolute need for food and shelter. Two ways for Christian men and women to be holy fail to mesh. Melania believes that the monk should redistribute the alms which she provides, a role which Hephestion says is impossible in the desert.

We can distinguish in the literary sources between the undoubted but controversial redistribution of alms by monks and their non-controversial ideal of distributing as alms part of what they produced by their own labours. Pachomius was said to have grown enough vegetables as a solitary ascetic to share with the poor of the nearby village, and to have entrusted his small-holding to another solitary monk when leaving 'because of the needs of the poor'.[27] The same source presented his first teacher in the monastic life as explaining how the surplus income from weaving and other crafts was given to the poor.[28] This charitable aspect to manual labour then justified, with citation of Proverbs 31: 20, the restriction of total fasting in Holy Week to just two days.[29] The *Life of Longinus* portrays its hero as making ropes in his cell which sailors bought as talismans onboard ship, so supplying an income from which the monk gave alms to the poor.[30] Another Coptic *Life* has Abba Timothy relate how, when he withdrew from his monastic community to live as a hermit, 'a number of people gave me work to do and I gave the money in charity to strangers'.[31] We may speculate that in these last two examples a reputation for holiness brought with it a business that might otherwise have gone elsewhere, that almsgiving to monks for the purposes of redistribution might take the more acceptable form of purchase or employment.

The ideal whereby individual monks gave alms from their surplus income seems to have extended to monastic communities. The *Historia monachorum* included the portrayal of a priest in the Arsinoite nome, Serapion, at the head of a large monastic federation comprising several houses, all of whose members gave a portion of their income, at harvest time especially, for distribution to the needy.

---

[27] *Bohairic Life of Pachomius* 8 and 10, in L. T. Lefort, *Les Vies coptes de saint Pachôme et de ses premiers successeurs* (Louvain, 1943), 83 and 84.

[28] *Bohairic Life* 10, in Lefort, *Les Vies*, 85.

[29] *Bohairic Life* 35 in Lefort, *Les Vies*, 106.

[30] Anon., *Life of Longinus* 19, in Orlandi and Campagnano, *Vite*, 67.

[31] Paphnutius, *Life of Omnophrius* 5, in Vivian, *Histories*, 147.

The author observed that such gifts were made by almost all Egyptian monks. Both the extant Greek and Latin texts claim that some of this was sent by boat to feed the poor of Alexandria, as there were otherwise not enough recipients in the immediate vicinity of the monasteries to benefit.[32] Only the details differ: the Greek states that the ships carried clothes as well as grain. Given that this chapter probably comes from a now lost work attributed by Sozomen to one Timothy, an 'administrator of the Alexandrian church' (*Historia ecclesiastica* 6. 29),[33] it is probable that the chapter reveals an important source for the episcopal alms distributed in the metropolis in the second half of the fourth century, though the figure given in the Greek text, whereby each monk gave 40 *modii*, does not furnish a reliable basis for calculations. Cassian told his readers that the Egyptian monks supplied alms won by their own labour far afield in Libya.[34] Elsewhere in Egypt, moral sayings to be memorized by monks and attributed to Abba Isaiah likewise encouraged almsgiving to individuals and manual labour to fund these small gifts, but discouraged the monk from keeping such charity secret from his superior.[35]

Scholars, however, have questioned the reality behind the picture found in these sources. Cassian claimed that the Egyptian monks did not depend on others for their food, unlike the practice he apparently found elsewhere, but Ewa Wipszycka has argued that the likely productivity of the monks, restricted by other duties, and the low retail value of typical monastic produce must have left Egyptian monasteries dependent on lay donations both for their own survival and for their charitable works.[36] If so, the distinction we have observed in the sources between accepting gifts for redistribution and almsgiving from one's own surplus hides a less immediate but

[32] Greek version: *Historia monachorum* 18, in Festugière, *Historia*, 114–15; Latin version, *Historia Monachorum* 18, in Schulz-Flügel, *Tyrannius Rufinus: Historia*, 349–50. For Rufinus' work as reviser, ibid. 46–8.

[33] Schulz-Flügel, *Tyrannius Rufinus: Historia*, 20–1.

[34] Cassian, *Institutes* 10. 22, SC 109. 420–2.

[35] Abba Isaiah, *Logoi* 5, 16. 9, 16. 26, 16. 55, 16. 95, 16. 133, ed. the monks of Solesmes, *Abbé Isaïe: Recueil ascétique*, Spiritualité Orientale, 7 (1970), 29, 128, 129, 132, 134, and 142.

[36] E. Wipszycka, *Études sur le christianisme dans l'Égypte de l'antiquité tardive* (Rome, 1996), 324.

nonetheless essential role for monasteries in the redistribution of wealth. A theological ideal of self-sufficient labour and the charitable distribution of a surplus given by God for this purpose will have partially obscured the economics of religious life. Wipszycka's analysis goes against much prima-facie evidence in the sources, and depends on assumptions about productivity and consumption which are hard to prove, but it is instructive in this regard that several texts which suggest the growing importance of monasteries during food shortages and famine do not suggest that such relief could easily be supplied from their own funds or stores. The *Historia monachorum* tells in both the extant Greek and Latin versions the miracle story of a monastery where the remaining few baskets of bread fed for some four months the women and children who came begging for alms.[37] The work sets out to impress its readers with tales of extraordinary virtue and sanctity: its value for the historian here lies not in the reported miracle as such, but in the pattern of conduct by beggars and monks which it presupposes, and in revealing the limited stores retained by the monastery. A rare insight into the collection of monastic alms in hagiography is offered by the *Life of Hypatios*, where the hero, the founder of a monastic community outside Constantinople, is warned by an angelic vision of approaching famine and so borrows money to buy large quantities of pulses and corn cheaply, ten days before the price unexpectedly rockets.[38] The same *vita* presents the monk as providing crucial help to the surrounding rural population in winter: 'when the entire countryside was ravaged by hunger, they depended on God and on him, in winter above all'.[39] Once again, rhetoric may exaggerate the extent of help provided, but the text reveals the seasonal importance of almsgiving, and how a monk could organize large-scale aid without a sufficient surplus to draw on. The *vita* gives a rare indication of numbers: Hypatios was at one point feeding on cooked beans some 500 people who assembled each day at the ninth hour.[40] The number is meant to impress the

---

[37] Greek version: *Historia monachorum* 8. 44–7, in Festugière, *Historia*, 63–5; Latin version, *Historia monachorum* 7. 12., in Schulz-Flügel, *Tyrannius Rufinus: Historia*, 300–1.

[38] Callinicus, *Life of Hypatios* 31. 3–4, SC 177. 205.

[39] Callinicus, *Life of Hypatios* 31. 5, SC 177. 206.

[40] Callinicus, *Life of Hypatios* 31. 6, SC 177. 206.

reader and was clearly exceptional. The precise sources of monastic almsgiving remain uncertain, and we must be wary of over-generalization in a period of varied practice; what is certain is that ascetic and monastic almsgiving of some kind was not only taken for granted by Christians of the period, it was integral to a theology of virtuous monastic labour.

The role of monks in hospitals founded or overseen by the local bishop has already been noted. In some places they also founded and ran similar institutions themselves. Theodoret, in his *Historia religiosa*, praised a monk, Limnaios, who since the start of the fifth century had founded a series of hostels (καταγώγια) for blind beggars funded by donations.[41] The *Life of Alexander* portrayed its hero as the founder of a *xenodocheion* for the poor at Antioch, who then exhorted wealthy Christians to provide the necessary funds.[42] It is not clear whether the monks Chrysostom portrayed tending the wounded, the crippled, and the blind belonged to such an independent institution or whether they were under church control.[43] But the Bohairic *Life of Pachomius* indicates that, in Egypt at least, one Pachomian tradition ran counter to this form of poor relief: it portrays Pachomius, while still a solitary living in close proximity to a village, as no longer attending to the sick in the village on the grounds that it was not a proper part of monastic life, but 'rather that of the clergy and Christian elders'.[44] It is not clear whether this should be seen as a defence by the author against criticism of monastic practice or as criticism by the author of clerical negligence.

The significance of this monastic and institutional almsgiving in terms of the virtues it was seen to exemplify, the consequences for the status of such monks, and its contribution to competition with local bishops is examined in Chapter 5. Here, it is necessary to recognize monastic alms as an important source of help for the destitute in urban as well as rural areas, in addition to the aid given by the bishop (and in the case of Alexandria as a likely source of the bishop's aid). Monastic aid for the destitute complemented episcopal aid aimed

---

[41] Theodoret, *Historia religiosa* 22. 7, SC 257. 132.
[42] *Life of Alexander* 39, PO 6. 688–9.
[43] Chrysostom, *Homilies on Matthew* 72. 4, PG 58. 671.
[44] *Bohairic Life* 9, in Lefort, *Les Vies*, 84.

first at the enrolled widows. It is true that to some extent monks attracted gifts of alms from individual lay men and women, which might otherwise have gone to the involuntary poor. The Bohairic *Life of Pachomius* includes the tale of a donor who gave the monks at Tabennêsi grain that he had originally intended to send to prisoners in the mines.[45] But this loss to the very poor was offset by alms from the sale of monastic goods. In other cases monks not only redistributed what they themselves possessed, but directed the poor with a suitable recommendation to well-disposed wealthy Christians.[46] Patlagean considers the monks as essential intermediaries in Palestine between donors and recipients.[47]

## ALMSGIVING BY LAY INDIVIDUALS

Individuals gave alms to the poor directly as well as to church collections. They did so at the doors of their home and especially at church entrances on their way to the Sunday *synaxis*. Chrysostom described the beggars 'glued to the church doors' (προσηλωμένοι ταῖς θύραις τοῦ ναοῦ) and thankful for an *obol* or waiting at the doors for gifts from the entrants.[48] He described someone entering the church as 'passing through the poor'.[49] Paulinus depicted a similar picture in the sermon *De gazophylacio*: 'many are waiting for you and hang on your arrival, looking round to see you. The prayers of all the needy and the entreaties of the weak depend on you for their success.'[50]

The *Life of the Man of God* portrays its hero at Edessa as 'standing at the church door with hand outstretched once evening had fallen to receive alms from those entering the church'.[51] The saint takes for

---

[45] *Bohairic Life* 39, in Lefort, *Les Vies*, 108.

[46] Callinicus, *Life of Hypatios* 11. 4, SC 177. 110.

[47] Patlagean, *Pauvreté*, 194.

[48] Chrysostom, *Homilies on 1 Corinthians* 30, PG 61. 254 and 255; *Homilies on 2 Timothy* 1, PG 62. 606.

[49] *Homilies on Matthew* 89, PG 58. 786.

[50] Paulinus of Nola, *Ep.* 34. 7, CSEL 29. 308–9.

[51] *Life of the Man of God*, in Amiaud, *La Légende*, 5.

himself only what he needs, his diet consisting of ten *menîn* of bread and two of vegetables, giving to others what was surplus to these requirements. Given that this was probably close to the minimum on which a man could survive, and that the saint did not accept alms during the day, this suggests that daily, private alms from church-goers, though small in themselves, were more than numerous enough for a number of the very poor to survive on. Chrysostom defended the poor widows and 'destitute' (ἀκτήμονας ἄνδρας) from the charge that they were only at church because of what they received in alms, by stating that if they had no desire to pray they could beg in the agora and the lanes.[52] Given the pressure of circumstance to which these recipients of private alms were subject, and without reducing religious motivations to economic forces, it must also be the case that they fared as well if not better by begging at church than elsewhere in the late antique city.

A letter of Jerome to a widow praised her husband, Nebridius, 'whose doors were besieged by swarming crowds of the poor and weak' because of his known generosity in almsgiving.[53] Typical gifts were small and took the form of money, food or, more rarely, clothing. Maximus of Turin speaks at one point of 'a few coppers' (*nummulos paucos*).[54] Chrysostom spoke of 'a loaf and a little money' given to those who sought alms presumably by going from door to door.[55] Augustine, turning from a literal to a metaphorical gift of alms, presented the latter as 'nothing taken from the store cupboards, nothing from a purse' (*nihil de apothecis, nihil de sacculo*), which implies that ordinary alms took the form of both food and money.[56]

Individuals were encouraged to give to beggars in the street, though it is clear from Chrysostom's sermons that wealthy individuals in the Antiochene church were reluctant to give alms to the beggars who accosted them on their travels across town.[57] Chrysostom chided them for their excuses, which are themselves

[52] Chrysostom, *Homilies on 1 Corinthians* 30, PG 61. 254–5.

[53] Jerome, *Ep.* 79. 2, in Labourt, *Lettres*, iv. 95.

[54] Maximus, *Serm.* 71, in *Maximi Episcopi Taurinensis Sermones*, ed. A. Mutzenbecher CCSL 23 (Turnhout, 1962), 298.

[55] Chrysostom, *Homilies on Matthew* 66. 3, PG 58. 629.

[56] Augustine, *Serm.* 208. 2, PL 38. 1045.

[57] Chrysostom, *Homilies on Matthew* 35. 7, PG 57. 412.

revealing. People said: 'I haven't got a servant with me now and I'm a long way from home'.[58] They said that they were too far from a money-changer. They claimed that the beggar 'has already received the church hand-out' (ἔχει τὸ κοινὸν τῆς 'Εκκλησίας).[59] Such excuses imply that church aid was not exhausted by the numbers of clergy, widows, and virgins, but did reach some of the destitute, that private alms often took the form of small change, and that the well-to-do were reluctant to give alms in person rather than through their servants, perhaps on account of the shame or social stigma involved in direct contact with the very poor. Donors may also have preferred to give in an ecclesial setting, where the gift was visible to other Christians and gained significance from its context.

Preachers sought to influence this private almsgiving. The individual was encouraged to show the same favouritism to fellow Christians in need as the institutional church: Jerome cited 1 Timothy to the wealthy widow Furia: 'Give to whoever asks you, but especially to those who belong to the household of faith.'[60] Chrysostom encouraged his congregation to set aside money for alms each Sunday in an alms-box kept at home for this purpose near where they stood to say their prayers, though it is not clear whether the money was to be handed on to the church or given out by the individuals themselves.[61] He also urged them to give alms whenever misfortune struck.[62] More typically, Maximus of Turin urged his congregation to give alms with greater generosity (*liberalitas*) during periods of fasting in, for example, the penitential season of Advent.[63] Augustine urged his congregation to give more in alms during Lent by making larger and more frequent gifts.[64] The *Apostolic Constitutions* expected the faithful to give in alms what they saved by fasting throughout the year on Wednesdays and Fridays.[65]

---

[58] *Homilies on Matthew* 35. 7, PG 57. 412.
[59] *Homilies on 1 Corinthians* 21. 11, PG 61. 179.
[60] Jerome, *Ep.* 54. 12, in Labourt, *Lettres*, iii. 35.
[61] Chrysostom, *Homilies on 1 Corinthians* 43, PG 61. 372.
[62] *Homilies on Thessalonians* 3, PG 62. 415.
[63] Maximus of Turin, *Sermons* 60–2, CCSL 23. 240–51.
[64] Augustine, *Serm.* 207. 1, PL 38. 1043; *Serm.* 208. 2, PL 38. 1045.
[65] *Ap. Const.* 5. 20. 18, SC 329. 284.

The sermons give a glimpse of the ordinary practices which preachers hoped many people, not only the wealthiest, would adopt. But on occasion they suggest other conventional forms of almsgiving to which the wealthy were more attracted and better placed to practise. These forms appear more frequently in the hagiographical and epistolary sources, the former because of their interest in the exceptional display of generosity, the latter because often written to people of considerable substance.

## Charitable largesse: distributions at pilgrimage centres

The scene of the Roman matron hitting an old woman observed by Jerome at St Peter's, already mentioned above, is an example of a wealthy donor choosing a martyr's shrine for distributing a large quantity of alms in person.[66] That pilgrims regularly gave alms at the basilica is possibly implied by the report of Ammianus Marcellinus that the praetor, Lampadius, summoned 'certain of the needy' (*quosdam egentes*), presumably beggars, from the Vatican to receive his extraordinary largesse in 365.[67] It is likely that distributing alms was a typical, though by no means universal, piety practised by pilgrims on arrival at their various destinations. Those with the wealth to travel also had wealth to disburse. A sermon, in which Chrysostom defends God's providence when affliction falls even on the virtuous, deals with the case of a pilgrim who is shipwrecked on route to a martyr's shrine while 'carrying alms for the poor' (πένησι χρήματα διακομίζων).[68] Rabbula distributed alms on his visit to the *martyrium* of Cosmas and Damian.[69] The church complex at Edessa, where the 'Man of God' stood and begged, contained a *martyrium*.[70] At Nola pilgrims attending the January festival in honour of Felix were encouraged by Paulinus to give alms

[66] Jerome, *Ep.* 22. 32, in Labourt, *Lettres*, i. 147.

[67] Ammianus Marcellinus, *Res Gestae* 27. 3. 6, in *Ammien Marcellin, Histoire*, ed. M.-A. Marié, v (Paris, 1984), 109. For the view that these were not beggars from the basilica, cf. A. Chastagnol, 'Observations sur le consulat suffect, et la préture du Bas-Empire', *Revue historique*, 219 (1958), 242 n. 2.

[68] Chrysostom, *Homilies on the Statues* 1, PG 49. 29.

[69] Bickell, *Ausgewählte Schriften*, 170.

[70] *Life of the Man of God*, in Amiaud, *La Légende*, 4–5 and 4 n. 2.

to the crowds and provide the rural poor with meat from animals they had dedicated as offerings for the saint.[71]

The church of the Holy Sepulchre in Jerusalem was particularly favoured as a place to distribute alms. Jerome recalled for Eustochium how Paula had distributed alms to the poor on her arrival in Jerusalem before travelling on to Bethlehem.[72] Rabbula distributed alms at Jerusalem on his visit to the holy places.[73] Pilgrims to the Holy Land were no doubt encouraged by what they visited on the way: the journey from Tyre to Caesarea in Palestine included by 333 a stop at the baths of the centurion Cornelius, 'who used to give much in alms'.[74] The *Itinerarium Burdigalense* in which the baths are noted has been described as a 'handbook for pilgrims'. It indicates here not simply what pilgrims were encouraged to see, but how they were to regard what they saw, the scriptural narrative into which the tourist attraction was fitted, and what was important in that narrative for their own religious edification—Cornelius' virtue as an almsgiver. The *De obitu Paulini* with which the previous chapter opened indicated the related practice of sending alms for distribution by others at famous shrines. Jerome's letter to a widow, Theodora, likewise reveals that her late husband, Licinius, sent money for this purpose to Jerusalem and Alexandria.[75]

## Charitable largesse: *agapes* and hostels

It had long been traditional to hold an *agape*, a meal to which the poor were invited together with members of the clergy, in obedience to the dominical command at Luke 14: 13. In the highly stratified society of the later empire such events, in which the more or less elite met their social inferiors in a supposed celebration of Christian fraternity, were subject to pressures which threatened to destroy

---

[71] D. Trout, *Paulinus of Nola* (Berkeley, Los Angeles, and London, 1999), 150.

[72] Jerome, *Ep.* 108. 10, Labourt, *Lettres*, v. 168.

[73] Bickell, *Ausgewählte Schriften*, 171.

[74] *Itinerarium Burdigalense*, 585, in P. Geyer and O. Cuntz, *Itineraria et Alia Geographica*, CCSL 175 (Turnhout, 1965), 13.

[75] Jerome, *Ep.* 75. 4, in Labourt, *Lettres*, iv. 36.

them or subvert their original meaning. These pressures are reflected in surviving legislation. Canon 11 of Gangra ordained that no one was to show contempt to those who held an *agape* or refuse to participate 'in order to disparage the event', which suggests that mixing with the poor in this way was considered by some an unacceptable humiliation.[76] Canon 27 of Laodicea decreed that the clergy invited to an *agape* were not to take part of the meal home with them, which is perhaps also an attempt to avoid social intercourse, while benefiting from the available food.[77]

The *Apostolic Constitutions* present an *agape* or δοχή (the word found in Luke's Gospel) as ideally a collaborative project, where the deacons identify the 'women in difficulty' (θλιβομένας) to be invited, and where the social pressures against such meetings are resolved through a careful grading of the gifts presented to those who attend: the bishop receives one type of gift and the priests and deacons, as a matter of honour, are to receive double what each of the women receive, a practice reminiscent of the grading of presents or *sportulae* according to the importance of the recipient, a principle the *Apostolic Constitutions* explicitly endorses: 'the laity are to grant each dignitary the appropriate honour through their gifts and respect in life'.[78] Jerome wrote of those at Rome who 'employ a herald' to summon the poor to an *agape*, suggesting how the institution might be used to trumpet the generosity and liberality of the donor.[79]

Paulinus' encouragement to the wealthy pilgrims at Nola to provide meals for the poor with meat from slaughtered animals suggests that the *agape* in the fourth century was linked in some places with the developing cult of the martyrs. Constantine had briefly referred to such meals in connection with the martyrs during his *Oration to the Saints*,[80] and in Roman North Africa these meals also seem to have been held on the occasion of martyrs' festivals: Faustus argued that Christians had turned pagan sacrifices into *agapes* and idols into martyrs. Augustine denied the derivation, but

---

[76] Joannou, *Discipline*, i. 93–4.

[77] Ibid. i. 141.

[78] *Ap. Const.* 2. 28. 1–5, SC 320. 244.

[79] Jerome, *Ep.* 22. 32, in Labourt, *Lettres*, i. 147.

[80] Constantine, *Oration to the Saints*, 12, tr. in M. Edwards, *Constantine and Christendom* (Liverpool, 2003), 29.

admitted that the meals often included meat as well as vegetables.[81] The food on these occasions therefore differed in kind from the staples normally provided as alms. There is scant evidence on which to generalize, but Latin Christians mirrored in this way, and so competed with, the distribution of sacrificial meats at pagan festivals. It is significant that when the Roman aristocrat Pammachius invited the poor at Rome to an *agape* on his wife's death it was held at the martyr's shrine of St Peter's.[82] The actual number of the poor invited is not stated, though Paulinus makes it sound as though the basilica was crowded with 'numberless' recipients. On this much-lauded occasion, three different forms of almsgiving coalesced: funerary alms, distribution of alms at *martyria*, and the *agape*.

Two sermons of Augustine may also point towards the continued provision of these charitable meals among other forms of almsgiving.[83] This depends on whether the phrase *agapas facere*, like the Greek ἀγάπας ποιεῖν, is taken to refer to the provision of an *agape* or to more general almsgiving.[84] It is difficult to draw firm conclusions from the limited evidence available, but it is possible that the *agape* was already in decline as a form of almsgiving at the outset of the period under study. Association with the popular cult of the martyrs did not stem this decline. Ambrose and Augustine both acted to end popular banquets on martyrs' festivals.

At the end of the fourth century a few Roman aristocrats could demonstrate their largesse towards the poor on an even greater scale. Jerome in 399 praised the virtues of Fabiola in founding a νοσοκομεῖον for the care of the gravely ill, crippled, and wounded.[85] Elsewhere, he praised Pammachius for founding a *xenodochium* where the needy were fed at Portus, one of the two main ports of Rome.[86] In fact, it appears that hospital and hostel were one and the same venture, in which both founders eventually co-operated to promote in the West an institution still largely confined to the

---

[81] Augustine, *Contra Faustum* 20. 4 and 20. 20, ed. J. Zycha, CSEL 25 (Prague, 1891), 538 and 560.
[82] Paulinus of Nola, *Ep.* 13. 3, CSEL 29. 86.
[83] Augustine, *Serm.* 178 and *Serm.* 259, PL 38. 962 and 1200–1.
[84] Cf. *Apophthegmata Patrum*, PG 65. 301C–D.
[85] Jerome, *Ep.* 77. 6, in Labourt, *Lettres*, iv. 45.
[86] *Ep.* 66. 11, in Labourt, *Lettres*, iii. 177.

Eastern churches.[87] Jerome hints at a certain rivalry for status between the two donors. Dagron records how in the East under Arcadius, one Florentius had his house turned at his death into a *gerokomeion* or hostel for the elderly, while Dexiokrates set up another under Theodosius II.[88] Yet, these private foundations by lay people remained relatively rare.

### Funerary alms

Individuals were encouraged to give alms as a way of gaining forgiveness of sins for the dead. The *Apostolic Constitutions* lists almsgiving together with the set days after the death on which the deceased was commemorated with prayers.[89] Chrysostom taught that while the Eucharistic sacrifice could not be offered for a dead catechumen, he or she might be aided by gifts of alms to the poor whose prayers for the dead would be heard by God.[90] He advocated the practice not only for catechumens, but for Christians in general, and urged the relatives of the dying to use their influence in this regard: 'whenever someone is about to die, the dying person's relative is to prepare the burial cloths and persuade the departing to leave something for the needy'.[91] Some at least heeded this message: they either left gifts of alms in their wills, requested on their deathbed that alms be distributed after their death, or gave alms for a dead relative. Ambrose's brother Satyrus instructed him to distribute as much money from their joint estate as Ambrose saw fit; Caesarius, the son of a Cappadocian bishop, gave his possessions to the poor as he lay dying.[92] Paulinus wrote that Pammachius had buried his wife 'with healing remedies and vital good works, that is, with gifts of

---

[87]   *Ep.* 77. 10, in Labourt, *Lettres*, iv. 50. Labourt's tr. sees this as a competition between Pammachius and his wife Paulina rather than an act by which Pammachius disposes of the money inherited from his wife. Pietri disregards any amalgamation of the two projects, *Roma cristiana*, i. 559 and 649.

[88]   G. Dagron, *Naissance*, 512.

[89]   *Ap. Const.* 8. 42. 5, SC 336. 258–60.

[90]   Chrysostom, *Homilies on Philippians*, 3, PG 62. 204.

[91]   *Homilies on John's Gospel* 85. 6, PG 59. 467–8.

[92]   Ambrose, *De excessu fratris* 1. 59–60, OOSA 18. 62 (the bishop further encouraged the practice at 2. 13, OOSA 18. 84); Basil, *Ep.* 32, Courtonne, *Lettres*, i. 74.

alms', summoning the poor to the basilica as the 'patrons of our souls deserving alms from the entire city of Rome'.[93] The nobleman left further money for the poor at his own death.[94] It has already been mentioned that Hypatios had been left a legacy by a *scholastikos* and that Rabbula changed the customary time of his annual almsgiving from December to June when he felt himself to be near death. He sent gifts to ascetic communities in and around Edessa as well as to Jerusalem.[95] However, these forms of funerary alms were sometimes disputed practices. Basil on occasion preached against deathbed gifts.[96] This was partly on the grounds that the mourners would not honour the dying person's wishes in this respect. His fears appear borne out by what he informed Sophronius had happened to Caesarius' goods, which were seized by members of the household and alleged creditors. Marcian's legislation of 455 allowed women to make bequests to churches, clerics, *martyria*, and to the poor, but the law was an attempt to clarify what had previously been contested.[97]

## Reluctance to give alms

Some sermons of the period reveal a reluctance on the part of private individuals to give alms in person to the needy rather than through the good offices of the bishop or via a respected holy man. Chrysostom attempted to change this preference: 'And what I have to say about alms, I'm not saying so that you bring them to me, but so that you yourself serve them out with your own hands.'[98] The reluctance may be in part the product of the long-standing encouragement evident in texts like the *Didascalia* and *Apostolic Constitutions* to give alms via the bishop rather than in person.[99] A homily on Paul's First Letter to Timothy directed at the enrolled widows suggests why

---

[93] Paulinus, *Ep.* 13. 11, CSEL 29. 92. Cf. Jerome, *Ep.* 66. 5, in Labourt, *Lettres*, iii. 170–2.
[94] Palladius, *Lausiac History* 62, in Bartelink, *Palladio*, 268.
[95] Callinicus, *Life of Hypatios* 34, SC 177. 220; Bickell, *Ausgewählte Schriften*, 208.
[96] Basil, *In Time of Hunger* 4, PG 31. 313B.
[97] Delmaire, *Largesses*, 612.
[98] Chrysostom, *Homilies on 1 Corinthians* 21. 6, PG 61. 179.
[99] *Ap. Const.* 3. 4. 2–3, SC 329. 126.

Chrysostom sought to alter traditional good practice in this respect: his belief in the greater virtue of direct giving, which required the donor to overcome repugnance at associating with those beneath her own social status: 'Do not give [alms] to the Church leaders for them to distribute. Administer them yourself, so that you enjoy the reward for your service as well as your expense. Give with your own hands...Become the distributor of your own possessions. The very love for your fellow human beings, the fear of God, appoints you to this office.'[100] Giving to the clergy what was destined for the poor not only avoided the shame of contact with the poor, it offered the chance to display one's generosity to other Christians. The preacher fiercely attacked this 'vanity'.[101]

## IMPERIAL ALMSGIVING

It has already been shown that Constantine and later Christian emperors gave grain to the bishops for distribution. But these subventions do not exhaust imperial almsgiving. To what extent was this any different from other forms of almsgiving by individuals to churches or directly to the poor?

In the *Vita Constantini* we are told that the emperor's agent on his behalf distributed alms of money and clothing to the destitute on the occasion of the synod at Jerusalem in 335.[102] Whether the agent distributed the money himself, or with the help of his servants, or merely passed on gifts to the church authorities, cannot be ascertained and nor can the sums involved. This may belong in part to the pattern of almsgiving at major shrine sites, but it should also be considered as an action which expressed the emperor's authority in a Christian key and perhaps presented him as a leader of the Christian churches. It is likely that similar important events in the life of the Church continued to attract imperial alms and that this particular expression of imperial generosity helped to legitimate the

---

[100] *Homilies on 1 Timothy,* 14. 3, PG 62. 574.
[101] *Homilies on Matthew* 15. PG 57. 235.
[102] Eusebius, *De vita Constantini* 4. 44, in Winkelmann, *Über das Leben,* 139.

emperor's considerable influence in these events. According to the *Chronicon paschale*, after the dedication of Hagia Sophia in Constantinople, a few days after the election of patriarch Eudoxius in 360, the Emperor Constantius made gifts to the poor orphans, widows, and *xenodocheia* of the capital. Imperial alms in otherwise conventional forms become distinctive in being associated with special events in the Church's life.

Optatus of Milevis portrayed Constantius as sending alms to Carthage for distribution to individual churches via his agents Paul and Macarius.[103] The men were in North Africa to direct the persecution of the Donatists. Unless the reported almsgiving is a fiction and figleaf to cover the less savoury activities of these two, it may be that the alms were intended as an incentive and palliative for submission to Catholic orthodoxy. It is said that Theodosius II sent large quantities of gold to the Jerusalem patriarchate for the benefit of the poor in 427/8, for which he was given in return the relics of the protomartyr Stephen. Theophanes related that the emperor acted 'in imitation of the blessed Pulcheria', but it may also be significant that the gift was made at a time of heightened tension with Persia.[104] It is possible that a traditional form of almsgiving, that recommended by Chrysostom in times of danger, takes on a distinctive imperial form when offered on behalf of the empire for its safety.

Women from the imperial family were reportedly prominent in almsgiving. Eusebius recounted Helena's gifts to the poor of clothing and money on her progress through the Eastern cities.[105] One should probably distinguish between those people who are said by Eusebius earlier in the passage to have approached her in person and the very poor who benefited from her almsgiving. Women from the imperial family seem to have specialized in founding hospitals and hostels. Eudocia, wife of Theodosius II, is said to have built a 'special *ptocheion* for epileptics with accommodations for four hundred persons. It was located at Phordisiis in Palestine, perhaps within the walls of Jerusalem.'[106] The Empress Eudocia-Athenais was said

---

[103] Optatus of Milevis, *Against the Donatists* 3. 3. 2, SC 413. 20.

[104] Theophanes, *Chronographia* 86, tr. in Mango and Scott, *Chronicle*, 135–6.

[105] Eusebius, *De vita Constantini* 3. 44, in Winkelmann, *Über das Leben*, 102.

[106] D. J. Constantelos, *Byzantine Philanthropy and Social Welfare* (New Brunswick, NJ, 1968), 263, with reference to Nicephorus Callistos Xanthopoulos, PG 146. 1240B.

to have built a *gerokomeion* in Jerusalem.[107] Likewise Theophanes' *Chronographia* relates that Pulcheria, sister of the Emperor Theodosius II, was a foundress of various hostels.[108] The Empress Flacilla, wife of Theodosius the Great, not only repaired hospitals, but was said to have visited them and nursed their inmates, even washing the occasional cup, despite the opposition she encountered at so doing.[109] Almsgiving by imperial women was an important element in the public virtue and devotion of the imperial family by which their rule was seen to reflect and be part of God's providential design for their subjects. It is in this context that we may understand the bold confidence of Germanus at Ravenna. His *Life* relates how the bishop retained the costly silverware, a 'most impressive silver vessel', in which Galla Placidia had sent food to him, returning in its place a wooden tray or platter, and reports the princess's pleasure in seeing her wealth thus transmitted to the poor.[110] For the bishop to presume upon a virtue was to acknowledge it. For Galla Placidia to ask for the return of her dinner plate would have been to deny a virtue she was expected to display. She instead set the wooden plate in a gold frame and displayed it as a relic.

## DISTINCTIVE PRACTICES?

How distinctive were these various practices by bishops, monks, Christian emperors, and ordinary church members in comparison with pagan practice? It would be a serious mistake to think that pagans in late antiquity did not give to people in desperate need. Augustine put the following rhetorical questions to his congregation: 'How many people appear to perform good works outside the Church? How many pagans even feed the hungry, clothe the naked, welcome the stranger, visit the sick, give solace to those in prison? How many do these things? ... How many good works are performed

---

[107] Constantelos, *Byzantine Philanthropy*, 225.

[108] Theophanes, *Chronographia*, 81.

[109] Theodoret, *Ecclesiastical History* 5. 19, in Parmentier and Hansen, *Kirchengeschichte*, 314.

[110] Constantius of Lyons, *Life of Germanus* 35, SC 112. 188.

by many heretics . . . ?'[111] Augustine thought such otherwise good acts were vitiated or wasted by being carried out outside the Church, the one place where they could feature in the economy of salvation, but he did not deny that they took place. The question is to know what specific practices lie behind the deliberate echo of Matthew 25: 35–6. To what extent did Christian and pagan almsgiving differ?

There had long been beggars dependent on pagan almsgiving by individuals in the cities of the empire. Seneca wrote of the *egentes* stretching out their hands on the Pons Sublicius.[112] Epictetus asked whether his pupils had ever seen a beggar who was not old, and described them shivering from the cold night and day, lying on the ground and 'eating only the bare minimum'.[113] This suggests that some at least of the disabled and elderly, who could not work and were not otherwise supported, might hope to survive by begging. Epictetus asked: 'Is a good person afraid that he will go without food? The blind do not go without food. The lame do not go without food. Will the good person go without food?'[114] Such texts at least suggest that almsgiving by individual pagans was widespread. When Libanius in *Oration* 7 portrays the naked and half-naked beggars, some crippled, sitting and standing in the cold at Antioch, probably near the entrance to the baths, who cry out for alms in the hope of receiving a piece of bread or an *obol* from the passers-by, there is no reason to think that they were begging only from Christians.[115] Such gifts were apparently motivated in large part by pity. Jerome admitted that pagans were moved to assist someone who had lost a hand or limb.[116] These accounts of beggars by pagan writers and of pagan almsgiving must qualify the invisibility of the very poor in the classical city alleged by Michael De Vinne.[117]

---

[111] Augustine, *En in Ps.* 83. 7, CCSL 39. 1151.

[112] Seneca, *De vita beata* 25. 1, ed L. D. Reynolds *L. Annaei Senecae Dialogorum Libri Duodecim* (Oxford, 1977), 192.

[113] Epictetus, *Discourses* 3. 26. 6, in J. Souihlé (ed.), *Épictète, Entretiens,* 4 vols. (Paris, 1943–65), iii. 115.

[114] Epictetus, *Discourses* 3. 26. 27.

[115] Libanius, *Or.* 7. 1–2, in Foerster, *Opera,* i/2. 373–4.

[116] Jerome, *Tractatus in Psalmos,* Ps. 134, ll. 164–74, ed. D. Morin, *Tratatus in Psalmos,* CCSL 78 (Turnhout, 1958), 288.

[117] De Vinne, *Advocacy,* 5.

Some philosophers had given away their possessions or made a living by begging themselves. Crates was famed for dropping his wealth into the sea. In Athens Diogenes the Cynic had gone about begging, because of his poverty, but no doubt also as a symbol of his freedom from empty desires for wealth or renown.[118] But self-dispossession was not linked for these men with almsgiving. Civic leaders and pagan emperors took various measures to alleviate poverty and food shortages for reasons of political stability, but also to gain status in a display of generosity. Not all need be discussed here. Those which continued in the late empire and which most closely resembled almsgiving were the *annonae*, imperial grants of grain to certain cities for the benefit of their citizens, and the purchase of grain by the emperor or local magnates during a time of shortage for resale to citizens at a lower price. Libanius described how the *curiales* at Antioch generously maintained the food supply for the city's population and through their gifts made up for the deficiencies of the harvest.[119] But these gifts were not alms inasmuch as they were not targeted at the poor, however much the latter may have benefited from them. In some places few did. At Oxyrhynchus in the late third century (the papyri date from the reigns of Claudius II and Aurelian) the monthly corn dole was limited to a maximum of 3,000 resident citizens of Oxyrhynchus, Rome, or Alexandria, chosen by lot, 900 others who had performed a public liturgy, and 100 individuals from outside the citizen body. They were each entitled to one *artaba* (five *modii*) of grain. The editor of the papyri has concluded on this evidence that 'the doles were not a provision for the very poor, but a perquisite of the already privileged middle classes of the cities, as in Rome'.[120]

Many pagan festivals included the distribution of sacrificial offerings to those present. Libanius accused those who had closed down the temples of murdering orphans, the infirm, and the elderly, who were thereby deprived of food.[121] But nothing suggests that the

---

[118] Diogenes Laertius, *Lives of Eminent Philosophers* 6. 49 and 57, in M. Marcovich, (ed.) *Diogenis Laertii Vitae Philosophorum*, 3 vols. (Stuttgart and Leipzig, 1999–2002), i. 405 and 411.

[119] Libanius, *Or.* 11. 134, in Foerster, *Opera*, i/1. 481.

[120] *The Oxyrhynchus Papyri*, ed. J. Rea, xl (London, 1972), 8.

[121] Libanius, *Or.* 30. 20, in Foerster, *Opera*, iii. 98.

poor were singled out as recipients of sacrificial offerings, and Libanius, who may be turning the Christian rhetoric of poor-relief against the Christians, is probably referring to gifts of alms by individuals as they visited the temples. There is little to suggest that the holders of priesthoods gave alms as a religious duty, nor that almsgiving featured in the negotiation and construction of their religious or social standing. It is true that Libanius described the temples as containing treasure which was 'a means of assistance to those in need'.[122] It is also true that inscriptions from Caria record the honourable actions of priests and priestesses in the Antonine period who gave unspecified help to the 'needy'.[123] But Ramsay MacMullen makes an unproven assumption when he regards the 'needy' so identified as the destitute, and makes an unsubstantiated generalization when this rare evidence serves as the basis for the claim that 'poor-relief suffered' as a result of legislation to close the temples.[124] Tertullian had contrasted what Christian charity (*misericordia*) gave in alms with what pagan piety (*religio*) gave to temples, an odd contrast if temples themselves distributed the gifts to the poor.[125]

Healing shrines often had hostels where sick pilgrims could shelter while visiting the temple complex. These may well have provided models for Christian *xenones*. But here, too, nothing suggests that there were pagan hostels which catered exclusively for the sick poor. On the contrary, there is evidence to suggest that some among the latter, such as lepers, found no place in the cities, their temples, or shrines, but were literally outcasts. Gregory of Nyssa reminded the faithful how such people 'are driven out from the cities, driven out from the public assemblies, from the festivals and public holidays'.[126] Episcopal institutional almsgiving as an expression of religious authority and of the unity of the Christian community, together with the almsgiving of the radical ascetics, and the foundation of *ptochotropheia*, were all practices distinguishing Christians from their pagan neighbours in the late imperial cities.

---

[122] Libanius, *Or.* 2. 30, in Foerster, *Opera*, i/1. 248.
[123] J. Hatzfeld, 'Inscriptions de Lagina en Carie', *BCH* 44 (1920), 74 and 87–90; idem, 'Inscriptions de Panamara', *BCH* 51 (1927), 92.
[124] MacMullen, *Christianity and Paganism*, 45.
[125] Tertullian, *Apology* 42. 8, CCSL 1. 157–8.
[126] Gregory of Nyssa, *De pauperibus amandis* 2, GNO 9. 111–27, at 117.

The Syriac *Life of Simeon Stylites* told how he and his brother Shemshi gave away their family wealth on becoming monks to monasteries and to the poor.[127] In this they too followed a second distinctive pattern of self-dispossession which won renown for its practitioners. Holy men and women not only gave away what they had, but in part by so doing attracted further alms for distribution. People brought alms to Simeon as thanks-offerings for cures and prayers answered.[128] The additional help which monasteries provided for the destitute beggars is a related form of almsgiving, which grew in importance throughout the period, though monasteries remained more numerous in the Eastern cities than in the West. Private individuals could and often no doubt did give in the street in much the same way as their pagan neighbours. But individual Christians were also able to give distinct shape and sense to their private alms by handing them out at church on Sundays or a *martyrion* visited on pilgrimage. Preachers sometimes claimed that their promotion of almsgiving was of little or no value in persuading their flock.[129] We can no more take this at face value than we can read the practices directly from their promotion by preachers. Promotion and practice interacted, as preachers like Chrysostom attempted not only to increase the amount given in alms, but to alter how people made their gifts.

Help for the very poor from these various sources was of particular importance at times of shortage. Theodoret speaks of agricultural labourers being forced to live on such hand-outs during a food shortage brought on by crop failure.[130] Whether all these practices represented a small but real improvement for the poor in the late empire, whether they fared better from Christian almsgiving than from pagan sacrificial and other euergetical practices, remains unproven and falls outside the scope of the present work. Some of what had once benefited the poorer citizens in a pagan funerary bequest with its *sportulae* and civic banquet may now have reached them in alms. The lot of those at the very bottom of the social pyramid, who were not citizens of the towns in which they lived, is

---

[127] *Life of Simeon Stylites* (Syriac), tr. F. Lent, *JAOS* 35 (1915), 117–18.
[128] Ibid. 160.
[129] Cf. Maximus of Turin, *Sermon* 42. 1 and 72. 3, CCSL 23. 169 and 302.
[130] Theodoret, *On Joel*, PG 81. 1637D.

most likely to have improved. It is significant that Basil described a beggar in one of his sermons as 'homeless and nowhere a citizen' (ἀνέστιος, ἄπολις).[131] To this extent Peter Garnsey and Caroline Humfress are right to say that 'Christian charity moved into a gap left by pagan systems of redistribution'.[132] But this new arrival did not simply fill a previously vacant space on the map. It partially redrew the map, so that food was distributed through different channels under different descriptions. And however that may be, change in how poor-relief was given had other consequences than simply altering the volume of aid delivered or extending the scope of those to whom it was delivered. The next chapter looks at how Christian practices were promoted by preachers and authors.

---

[131] Basil, *Look to Yourself* 6, ed. S. Y. Rudberg, *L'Homélie de Basile de Césarée sur le mot 'observe-toi toi même'* (Stockholm, 1962), 32.
[132] Garnsey and Humfress, *Evolution*, 127.

# 4

## The Promotion of Christian Almsgiving

The maxims on almsgiving in the *Sentences of Sextus* represent one element in the sustained promotion of almsgiving in the later empire by Christian writers, translators and copyists, preachers and spiritual guides in diverse works. By promotion is meant first the direct exhortation to give alms and the adoption of wider rhetorical strategies by which speakers and authors aimed to encourage almsgiving. Promotion in this sense concerns the Christian teaching of almsgiving. The meanings ascribed to almsgiving in this teaching and its place in an account of the virtues form the subject of Chapter 5. This chapter concerns the teaching's prevalence in different media, to ascertain whether it was widespread or was heavily promoted only by certain individuals or traditions, whether it was central or peripheral to an overarching image of the Christian life, and whether, as has been claimed, it received a new prominence in the preaching of the period. Such direct and deliberate promotion will be shown to be pervasive.

Yet, by promotion is also meant the unintended or incidental valorization of charitable practices resultant upon the favourable portrayal of almsgiving in the pursuit of other rhetorical objectives. Charles Taylor has stressed the 'constitutive dimension of language', one function of which is to create 'a common vantage point from which we survey the world together', a 'public space' where we share moral evaluations and establish social relations, 'the kind of footings we can be on with each other'.[1] Almsgiving was promoted in this sense as donor and beggar were repeatedly brought together through discourse into public gaze as the virtuous benefactor and worthy

[1] Charles Taylor, *Human Agency and Language, Philosophical Papers*, 1: (Cambridge 1985), 259, 263, 270, 271.

recipient. Promotion in both senses drew heavily on the scriptures and fostered a way of reading the sacred texts: Priscillian, or his early fifth-century editor, explained that where St Paul thanked those who were swift to give alms, he was 'exhorting others to this task'.[2] The present chapter examines the varying scope, nature, and importance of this promotion in the different types of Christian discourse in the period, which was not limited to contemporary works, but included older texts, such as the *Sentences*, still in wide circulation. It begins with those works judged to be less significant in terms of the size of audience they reached, and ends with the media judged most significant in these terms: saints' *Lives*, and sermons.

The different media involved do not correspond to discrete genres: a letter may serve as a treatise, a biblical commentary, or contain a set of canons. Athanasius's *Festal Letters* were sermons to be read out in Nicene churches across Egypt. A sermon may take the form of a homily on a liturgical reading, but a saint's *Life* may also be read out as a sermon. Clement of Alexandria's *Quis dives salvetur?* has been described as a 'homily treatise', which presumably means a published sermon on a theological topic rather than a scriptural commentary.[3] The taxonomy adopted here groups together works which more closely resemble each other than those in other groups. Analysis is further complicated by the way in which a work's significance might extend far beyond the circumstances of its original publication: letters and sermons were collected and transcribed for a new readership, while a treatise or commentary read by the small clerical elite influenced what they in turn preached to a far larger number.

## PROMOTION WITHOUT TEXTS

We know from the *Life of Hypatios* that almsgiving featured in the spiritual teaching or direction which that monk offered to his

---

[2] Priscillian, *Canons* 60, in G. Schepss, *Priscilliani quae supersunt*, CSEL 18 (Vienna, 1889), 134. On the possible identity of the 5th-cent. editor, cf. Chadwick, *Priscillian*, 59–60.

[3] D. Wyrka, 'Clement of Alexandria', in S Döpp and W. Geerlings (eds.), *Dictionary of Early Christian Literature*, tr. M. O'Connell (New York, 2000), 131.

visitors: 'To friends and visitors to the monastery he spoke about how they should live, by never losing their fear of God, keeping far from all injustice, always eager to enter the churches, and doing all in their power to give alms'[4] The hagiographer was keen to reveal the sanctity of the hero evident in his eloquence and its power to convert hearers: he related how: 'when they had received these admonitions, they would take their leave of him and go away better for it'.[5] The episode is indicative of the exhortation which urban lay people and officials in the East increasingly expected from spiritual teachers, whose partial withdrawal from civic life excited such visits. Exhortation gained its force in part from the obligation of gratitude incurred when requests for healing or other favours were answered through a holy man's intervention. The Syriac *Life of Simeon Stylites*, written shortly after 459, recounted for its readers how a military officer, who had been healed by the saint, gladly did 'whatever the saint commanded' on behalf of the poor.[6] A saint's petitions on behalf of the poor, for alms, debt relief, or the remission of taxes, gained additional force from stories of what befell those so foolish as to spurn them.[7]

## POETRY

Commodian's *Instructions* have featured in a previous chapter. Their popularity in the later empire is uncertain. Other poetry, however, of a more sophisticated style was composed in the late fourth and early fifth centuries which promoted almsgiving as a virtuous activity. Prudentius gave to 'Good Works' (*Operatio*) the task of defeating 'Greed' in his *Psychomachia*, and portrayed the virtue as having shed its former, burdensome, wealth in 'generous' gifts to the needy. The conquered vice is in turn stripped of its wealth, which is given as alms for the poor and the rescue of captives.[8]

---

[4] Callinicus, *Life of Hypatios* 27. 7, SC 177. 184.

[5] Callinicus, *Life of Hypatios* 27. 8, SC 177. 184.

[6] Lent, *Life of Simeon Stylites* (Syriac) 145.

[7] Ibid. 158–9.

[8] Prudentius, *Psychomachia* 573–603, ed M. P. Cunningham, *Aurelii Prudenti Clementis Carmina*, CCSL 126 (Turnhout, 1966), 170–1.

Almsgiving receives prominence of a different kind in his *Peristefanon*, with its vivid portrayal of the crippled and disfigured beggars supported by the Church whom the martyr Lawrence collects and presents to his Roman persecutor. The poet sharply contrasts their future glory with the fate awaiting the vicious who now enjoy power.[9] These works, probably composed before 408, 'provided devotional reading-matter for a cultured audience outside a church context'.[10] Anne-Marie Palmer has shown how their form made them attractive to a 'section of the Christianized circle of the Western aristocracy'.[11] They influenced a small but select group of readers.

## LETTERS

Letter writing among the elite occupied a complex place in classical society, where public and private concerns were interwoven, through intercession with powerful friends on behalf of clients, together with the publication of collected letters which brought honour to their authors and served in the transmission of elite culture. In church circles letters of friendship had developed by the late fourth century as pledges of intercommunion and as *fora* for theological discussion free from the invective which characterized polemical treatises. Letters of recommendation for travellers have been noted in an earlier chapter. Sebastian Brock has observed that the letter 'as a means of conveying exhortation and instruction is a genre well known from early Syriac literature'.[12]

The extant writings of Isidore of Pelusium, a monk living near the provincial capital of Augustmanis I in Egypt during the early fifth century, show how letters could directly promote almsgiving.[13] One letter criticizes the *hegemon* or *corrector* of the province, Cyrenios, for failing to give much in alms, and restates their redemptive power as

---

[9] *Peristefanon liber* 2. 145–52 and 265–76, CCSL 126. 262 and 266.
[10] A.-M. Palmer, *Prudentius on the Martyrs* (Oxford, 1989), 3 and 31.
[11] Ibid. 91.
[12] S. Brock, 'Ephrem's Letter to Publius', *Le Muséon*, 89 (1976), 262.
[13] For the authenticity of the letters and their correspondents, cf. P. Évieux, *Isidore de Péluse*, Théologie historique, 99 (Paris, 1995), 13.

'a ransom for you and propitiatory offering'.[14] Isidore appealed to scripture: another letter reminded Cyrenios of Christ's call to the rich young man in Matthew 19: 21 and warned him of the fate of Dives at Luke 16: 23.[15] An unnamed magistrate was attacked for his 'determination to make money at the expense of God and the destitute' ($\tau\grave{\eta}\nu$ $\kappa\alpha\tau\grave{\alpha}$ $\Theta\epsilon o\hat{\upsilon}$ $\kappa\alpha\grave{\iota}$ $\pi\tau\omega\chi\hat{\omega}\nu$ $\dot{\epsilon}\pi\iota\kappa\epsilon\rho\delta\hat{\eta}$ $\sigma\pi o\upsilon\delta\acute{\eta}\nu$), which P. Évieux has taken to mean stealing in some form from the Church and the 'funds for poor-relief'.[16] Isidore warned the bishop of Pelusium, Eusebius, to avoid future punishment by giving more alms: 'many Lazaruses surround you. Throw them a blaze of money, and you will inherit rest there with them.'[17] Eusebius was accused of diverting to building projects money meant for alms ($\pi\tau\omega\chi\iota\kappa o\hat{\iota}s$ $\delta\alpha\pi\alpha\nu\acute{\eta}\mu\alpha\sigma\iota\nu$).[18] The *oikonomos* of Pelusium, who had immediate responsibility under the bishop for distributing alms, was upbraided for misappropriating what belonged to the poor and accused of inverting the apostolic practice of selling one's own possessions to give to the poor: he took what was theirs to make it his.[19] Isidore took his campaign against Eusebius to other local bishops.[20] The letters confirm the *parrhesia* of the holy man in advocating almsgiving, to manifest his growing authority *vis-à-vis* the secular official and his competing authority *vis-à-vis* the bishop and diocesan clergy. In Charles Taylor's terms, these letters suggest both how Isidore's 'footing' made him a respected advocate of almsgiving and how that advocacy helped to establish this footing. Chapter 2 established the interrelationship of episcopal practice and rhetoric in constructing the bishop's spiritual authority. Isidore's letters further suggest how they also made a bishop vulnerable to attack, when that rhetoric could be turned against him.

Isidore's letters addressed a few individuals, but were preserved and read by a far wider audience of monks. It is unfortunately impossible to recover the process by which they first reached their

---

[14] Isidore, *Letter* 411 = Migne Ep I. 411, PG 78. 412A.

[15] *Letter* 420 = Migne Ep. I. 420, PG 78. 416. D–417A.

[16] *Letter* 490 = Migne Ep. I. 490, PG 78. 449A. Évieux, *Isidore*, 50.

[17] *Letter* 215 = Migne Ep. I. 215, PG 78. 317C–D.

[18] *Letter* 37 = Migne Ep. I. 37, PG 78. 205A–B.

[19] *Letter* 269 = Migne Ep. I. 269, PG 78. 341C–D.

[20] *Letter* 746 = Migne Ep. II. 246, PG 78. 684D–685C. For the recipient's identity, cf. Évieux, *Isidore*, 66.

wider audience, but Isidore's authoritative eloquence was later held up for imitation. Athanasius's *Life of Antony* likewise contains a model of epistolary good practice, where the great sanctity of the hero is reflected in the rank of the persons addressed: Athanasius relates that the hermit had sent a letter to the emperors in which 'he called on them to be generous and think of justice and the destitute' (φιλανθρώπους τε αὐτοὺς εἶναι ἠξίου καὶ φροντίζειν τοῦ δικαίου καὶ τῶν πτωχῶν).[21] The Syriac *Life of Simeon Stylites* composed a century later presented that saint responding to letters from kings (presumably though scribes or other intermediaries) by counselling them to help the poor.[22] In both cases the historicity of the correspondence is uncertain, and the *Life of Antony* may have served as a pattern for the *Life of Simeon*, but both episodes tell what was thought desirable and meritorious by author and readers.[23] The *vitae* point towards epistolary exhortation, but also validate and contribute to the impact made by this form of promotion.

Basil of Caesarea petitioned imperial officials to exempt hostels from taxation. This is not strictly speaking a case of exhortation to almsgiving, but the letters' incorporation among, and circulation with, Basil's collected letters would ensure their part in confirming a bishop's duty to act in this way.[24] Jerome used his biographical or eulogistic letters on Fabiola and Paula to promote generous almsgiving as part of complete self-dispossession.[25] These letters differed from Isidore's in being intended to influence an elite audience that extended beyond the immediate circle of the addressees. They were fed into a network where letters were quickly copied and disseminated.

Isidore's letters, however, indicate the central role of sermons in promotion. One shows the likely influence of Chrysostom's interpretative strategies: Isidore set out for bishop Asclepius a reading of Matthew 26: 6–13 and its coherence with Christ's other *dicta* on almsgiving (citing Matthew 5: 7, 9: 13; and 25: 40).[26] Isidore explained how Jesus acted to prevent the woman's humiliation, given

---

21 Athanasius, *Life of Antony* 81. 6, SC 400. 344.
22 Lent, *Life of Simeon Stylites* (Syriac) 135.
23 Cf. Bartelink, *Antoine,* SC. 400. 340–1 n. 2.
24 Basil, *Epp.* 142 and 143, in Courtonne, *Lettres,* ii. 64–5.
25 Jerome, *Epp.* 77 and 108, in Labourt, *Lettres,* iv. 39–52 and v. 159–201.
26 Isidore, *Letter* 588 = Migne Ep. II. 88, PG 78. 532A–C.

that she had already spent her money on the oil with which she anoints him. But, Isidore continued, if Christ had been asked beforehand what the woman should do with the money, he would have instructed her to give it away in alms. So, too, priests may receive gifts for the church, though they know that the money would be better spent as alms. The argument resembles that in Chrysostom's *Homily on Matthew's Gospel* 80: the same distinction is made between what is said to be good in the woman's case and what holds true as a general law, in order to deny that Jesus is making such a law. Isidore wrote of Jesus: 'If he had not approved the woman's action in this sense, he would have established a law requiring everyone to imitate her.' Chrysostom had written: 'You see, if he had been establishing a law, he would not have spoken with reference to the woman'.[27] Isidore wrote: 'So that if he had been asked before the ointment had been poured out, he would have ordered it to be sold and the proceeds given to the destitute.' Chrysostom had written: 'So that if someone were to ask him, had the woman not done this, he would not have given this answer.'[28] The letter implies a remembered familiarity with Chrysostom's reading of the episode. It shows how promotion in preaching was recycled within a short period after delivery to exercise a wide influence across some distance on readers of the published texts. Isidore, in adapting what was intended for a general congregation to address (initially) a single correspondent, offers insight into how promotional material was readily employed in the contentious affairs of the Christian community.

## BOOKS AND TREATISES

Few books or treatises wholly or partly devoted to promoting almsgiving existed in late antiquity in comparison with the large number on doctrinal matters, the production of which was stimulated by

---

[27] Chrysostom, *Homily on Matthew's Gospel* 80, PG 58. 726. Καίτοι εἰ ἐνομοθέται, οὐκ ἂν προσέθηκε τὴν γυναῖκα. Isidore: Εἰ δὲ μὴ τούτῳ τῷ νῷ ἀπεδέξατο τὸ γύναιον, ἐχρῆν νομοθετῆσαι πᾶσι μιμήσασθαι αὐτήν.

[28] Isidore: Ὥσπερ γὰρ εἰ πρὸ τοῦ ἐκχεῖν ἠρωτήθη, ἐκέλευσεν ἂν αὐτὸ πραθῆναι, καὶ δοθῆναι πτωχοῖς. Chrysostom: Ὥσπερ γὰρ εἴ τις αὐτὸν ἤρετο χωρὶς τοῦ ποιῆσαι τοῦτο τὴν γυναῖκα, οὐκ ἂν τοῦτο ἀπεφήνατο.

controversy and the format of which was suitable for private study and detailed treatment away from the public arena of the sermon. Books and treatises promoting alms were largely limited to two kinds: older works of edification still in circulation and a small number of controversial writings stimulated by Pelagian and ascetic currents of thought.

Among works of the first kind were the *Shepherd of Hermas*, a work originally composed to shape the *mores* of Christians at Rome in the mid-second century, and Clement of Alexandria's *Quis dives salvetur?*, a third-century work on almsgiving which in the first decade of the fourth century influenced Peter of Alexandria's sermon *On Wealth*.[29] Through a series of visions the *Shepherd* urged wealthy Christians to support the poor and thereby construct a strong church community or find themselves excluded from that community at the Second Coming of Christ. In late antiquity it was among the most widely read of all Christian texts outside the canon, and Jerome noted that it was read 'publicly' in some Greek churches, by which he presumably meant that it was read during the liturgy, though he went on to claim that it was all but unknown in Latin churches.[30] The continuing impact of Clement's work may be measured by a fifth-century Greek diatribe on wealth, which describes the *penetes* as more powerful than a hoplite army (στρατόπεδον ὁπλομάχων).[31] The phrase recalls Clement's description of the poor recipients of alms as 'an unarmed army' (στρατὸν ἄοπλον).[32] The graphic redescription of the poor contained in these texts will be discussed in Chapter 5. Equally important was the casting of the donor as a glorious commander. Promotion borrowed traditional images of success to raise the status of the advocated practice.

There was much continued interest among educated Latin Christians in Cyprian's writings. His *De opere et eleemosynis* was written in the mid-third century and was, as its title suggests, wholly

---

[29] B. Pearson and T. Vivian, *Two Coptic Homilies Attributed to Saint Peter of Alexandria: On Riches, On the Epiphany* (Rome, 1993), 27–8.

[30] Jerome, *De viris illustribus* 10, ed. A. Ceresa-Gastaldo, *Gerolamo, Gli uomini illustri* (Florence, 1988), 94–6.

[31] K.-H. Uthemann, 'Eine christliche Diatribe über Armut und Reichtum (CPG 4969): Handschriftliche Überlieferung und kritische Edition', *VC* 48 (1994), 235–90.

[32] Ibid. 268. Clement, *Quis dives?* 34, in Stählin, *Clemens*, 182.

concerned with the merits of almsgiving. The bishop of Carthage brought scripture to bear on those who supposedly feared that extensive almsgiving would impoverish their 'patrimony' or family wealth, and thereby located almsgiving within the Christian imitation of God's bountiful generosity. Almsgiving was cast in the language of honourable 'munera' or benefactions, a move the significance of which I shall explore in Chapter 5.[33] When Jerome wrote to Pammachius in 398 concerning the death two years before of the senator's wife, Paulina, he described Cyprian's *De opere* as a great or major work.[34] Michel Poirier has argued that the treatise was originally intended to stimulate giving to the bishop's poor-fund, but Jerome used it to promote a startling display of private funerary alms.[35] Promotion was not only recycled, but deployed to new ends. Almsgiving was also an important theme in several of Cyprian's other texts: the *Testimonia ad Quirinum* contains a catena of biblical precepts to give alms, and both the *De lapsis* and *De ecclesiae catholicae unitate* close with calls to almsgiving.[36] Continued interest in and high respect for these and Cyprian's other treatises, at least among North Africans, is indicated by the presence of all their titles on the so-called 'Cheltenham List', a list written in *c*.359–365 of works comprising the biblical canon and of the genuine works of Cyprian.[37] Augustine reminded his congregation of how the pleasure of reading Cyprian's works had contributed to this bishop's enduring fame.[38]

R. M. Ogilvie identified 'two possible reminiscences' of the *De opere* in Lactantius' *Divine Institutes*, although he did not believe that weight should be placed on them.[39] The *Divine Institutes*, written in the decade before 313 but later expanded, was an eloquent attack on paganism and a defence of Christianity. Lactantius, a rhetorician who

[33] Cyprian, *De opere et eleemosynis* 20–1, SC 440. 136.

[34] Jerome, *Ep.* 66. 5, in Labourt, *Lettres*, iii. 171–2.

[35] Poirier, *Bienfaisance*, SC 440. 58.

[36] Cyprian, *Testimonia ad Quirinum* 3. 1–2, ed. R. Weber, *Sancti Cypriani Episcopi Opera*, i, CCSL 3 (Turnhout, 1972), 80–8; *De lapsis* 35–6, *De ecclesiae catholicae unitate* 26–7, both in M. Bévenot SJ (ed.), *Cyprian, De Lapsis, and De Ecclesiae Catholicae Unitate* (Oxford, 1971), 53–4 and 97–9.

[37] G. W. Clarke (tr.), *The Letters of St. Cyprian of Carthage*, 4 vols. (New York, 1984), i. 8.

[38] Augustine, *Serm.* 310. 4, PL 38. 1414.

[39] R. M. Ogilvie, *The Library of Lactantius* (Oxford, 1978), 89.

had held posts at the imperial courts of both Diocletian and Constantine, and whose posthumous fame was acknowledged by Jerome, seemingly targeted the work at an educated pagan audience, but the book was read by many educated Christians in the fourth and fifth centuries.[40] It was certainly read with pleasure by the Spanish layman, Consentius, who told Augustine in 419 or later that he had little stomach for that kind of reading generally.[41] The author's pre-Nicene theology soon looked dated to theologians, but there is no reason to think this greatly diminished interest in his work. Augustine had read it within a few years of his conversion if not before.[42] Lactantius advocated the traditional Christian works of mercy in the context of a moral philosophy of the virtues (further discussed in Chapter 5), and in arguing for the moral superiority of Christianity criticized those who claimed to display *humanitas*, while refusing help to the destitute.[43] Promotion of this kind focused attention on almsgiving as a distinctive and exemplary Christian activity.

The years 344–5 saw the publication of Aphrahat's expanded *Demonstrations*, chapter 20 of which concerned the care of the poor. The Syriac work garnered a host of biblical texts in support of almsgiving, and called on the reader to 'encourage and persuade those who give, exhort all those who love the poor through these warnings'.[44] The collection of proof-texts, like that of Cyprian, served the preacher in need of authoritative quotations. The language of the *Demonstrations* limited its influence geographically, but there were many Syriac-speaking Christians within the Eastern Empire and it is

[40] Cf. Peter Garnsey's introduction to the new Eng. tr of the text, in A. Bowen and P. Garnsey, *Divine Institutes* (Liverpool, 2003), 1–54, esp. 3–4 (composition and fame), and 15 (audience).

[41] Augustine, *Ep.* 12*. 2, OSA 46b. 232. For the dating by Jules Wankenne, ibid. 488.

[42] Augustine cited Lactantius by name in the *City of God* 18. 23, ed. B. Dombart and A. Kalb, *Sancti Aurelii Augustini De Civitate Dei Libri XI–XXII*, CCSL 48 (Turnhout, 1955), 614. For Augustine's engagement with Lactantius, cf. P. Garnsey, 'Lactantius and Augustine', *Proceedings of the British Academy*, 114 (2002), 153–79; J. Doignon, 'Le Retentissement d'un exemple de la survie de Lactance', in J. Fontaine and M. Perrin (eds.), *Lactance et son temps, recherches actuelles* (Paris, 1978), 297–306.

[43] Lactantius, *Divine Institutes* 6. 11–12, in S. Brandt and G. Laubmann (eds.), *L. Caeli Firmiani Lactanti Opera Omnia*, i (Prague, 1890), 519–32.

[44] Aphrahat, *Demonstrations* 20, in M.-J. Pierre, *Aphraate le sage persan: Les Exposés*, SC 349 and 359, 2 vols. (Paris, 1988 and 1989), ii. 807.

a valuable, if oblique, indicator of almsgiving as a regular topic in sermons in Syriac-speaking churches. Nor is there any reason to think these churches idiosyncratic in this respect. Like Isidore's letters, the work points forward to the greater role of preaching. It also allows us to distinguish between promotional literature aimed at clerical formation and that aimed at the wider faithful.

It is in this context that we may place the church orders from earlier centuries, in particular the *Didache* and *Didascalia*, which continued to circulate in collections, to be translated and to be reworked in new compilations such as the *Apostolic Constitutions*. Paul Bradshaw has written of 'a succession of editors who shaped the stream of tradition'.[45] Three (the *Didascalia*, *Apostolic Church Order*, and *Apostolic Tradition*) were probably translated together into Latin in the late fourth century around 375.[46] We may conjecture that their editors and readers were mostly clerics.[47] In addition to the practices they stipulated (examined in Chapter 2) and the meanings they ascribed to them (discussed in Chapter 5), they contained direct exhortation to almsgiving.[48] The practice they promoted was that mediated by the 'beggar-loving' ($\varphi\iota\lambda\acute{o}\pi\tau\omega\chi o\varsigma$) bishop, but it is impossible to ascertain their impact, when so little is known of the part which they played in clerical formation or wider church life. It is possible that in the West Ambrose's *De officiis* was soon to eclipse these older works in the fifth century. The *De officiis* (*c.*388–9), discussed with Ambrose's other works in Chapter 6, certainly addressed a clerical audience and its defence of the controversial use of church treasures has already been noted in Chapter 2.

Ambrose promoted almsgiving for a different audience in the *De Tobia* (*c.*375–6) and the *De Nabuthae* (*c.*389).[49] Palanque's view that the two treatises are little more than sermons stitched together has been disputed recently: H. Savon has argued that 'if Ambrose has

---

[45] P. F. Bradshaw, *The Search for the Origins of Early Christian Worship* (London, 1992), 104.

[46] Bradshaw, 'Ancient Church Orders', 10–12.

[47] The late 5th-cent. *Statuta ecclesiae antiqua*, influenced by the *Apostolic Constitutions*, is now attributed to the Marseilles presbyter, Gennadius. Cf. U. Hamm, 'Gennadius of Marseilles', in Döpp and Geerlings, *Dictionary*, 248–9.

[48] e.g. *Apostolic Church Order* 14 in Bickell, *Geschichte des Kirchenrechts*, 118–19.

[49] Ambrose, *De Tobia* and *De Nabuthae*, ed. F. Gori, *Elia e il Digiuno, Naboth, Tobia*, OOSA 6 (Milan and Rome, 1985), 198–284 and 130–94.

reused sermon fragments here and there, he has integrated them so well into a new composition, controlled by the written word, that it is pretty much pointless to claim that one can gain even a rough idea of his preaching on the basis of these bits and pieces.[50] Yet, though more than restitched sermons, these texts nonetheless originated in sermons, both Ambrose's own and those of Basil, from which Ambrose borrowed extensively: they point to the greater importance of sermons in promotion. They are not treatises in the sense of controversial theological tracts, but polished works of eloquence to impress a court elite—with unknown results.

The late fourth and early fifth centuries saw a series of treatises which either excited controversy or took sides in existing controversies within the churches and which included promotion of almsgiving. They include a lost treatise or treatises by Vigilantius composed in or shortly before 404;[51] Jerome's riposte of 406, the *Against Vigilantius*;[52] Pelagius's *On the Christian Life*, to be dated to some point in the late fourth or early fifth century before 415;[53] two further works from much the same period, the *On Riches*, by the 'Pelagian Anonymous'[54] and the *Consultationes Zacchaei et Apollonii*; [55] and Salvian's *Four Books of Timothy to the Church*, which was probably written some time after 440.[56]

---

[50] 'Si Ambroise a ici et là réutilisé des fragments de sermons, il les a si bien intégrés dans un nouvel ensemble, où l'écrit domine, qu'il est assez vain de prétendre se faire une idée même approximative de sa prédiction à partir de ces lambeaux.' H. Savon, 'Ambroise prédicateur', *Connaissance des Pères de l'Église*, 74 (1999), 34–5.

[51] J. N. D. Kelly, *Jerome: His Life, Writings and Controversies* (London, 1975), 296.

[52] Ibid. 290.

[53] Pelagius, *On the Christian Life*, PL 40. 1031–46. Augustine cited this at Diospolis as a work of Pelagius, though Pelagius denied writing the cited passages. See *De gestis Pelagii* 6. 16, in C. F. Urba and J. Zycha (eds.), *Sancti Aurelii Augustini Opera* 8. 2, CSEL 42 (Prague, 1902), 69. For discussion of authorship, cf. B. R. Rees, *Pelagius, Life and Letters* (Woodbridge, 1998), 105–6.

[54] Pelagian Anonymous, *On Riches*, PLS 1. 1380–1418, Eng. tr. Rees, *Pelagius*, 171–211. The text belongs to the same milieu as the teachings on wealth condemned by Augustine c. 414. Cf. Rees, *Pelagius*, 173, and Augustine, *Ep.* 157. 23–39, PL 33. 686–92.

[55] M. Claussen, 'Pagan Rebellion and Christian Apologetics in Fourth Century Rome: The *Consultationes Zacchaei et Apollonii*', *JEH* 46 (1995), 601–2.

[56] Salvian, *Four Books*, SC 176. 138–344. For the *terminus post quem*, SC 176. 30. A slightly earlier date between 435 and 439 has also been advocated. Cf. J. Badewien, *Geschichtstheologie und Sozialkritik im Werk Salvians von Marseille* (Göttingen, 1980), 17.

We may distinguish between the text by Vigilantius and the others: Vigilantius attacked a particular practice, that of sending alms to Jerusalem rather than distributing them within one's own locality, whereas the others did not. Jerome's treatise rebutted Vigilantius on this and other matters. The other tracts promoted greater almsgiving among the good works necessary for salvation, and only attacked that almsgiving of whatever form which was seen to excuse the unjust retention of remaining wealth. Salvian's work demonstrates that the views on wealth expressed in the Pelagian tracts continued to be held and promoted in ascetic circles after Pelagius had been condemned.[57] Gennadius termed Salvian the 'teacher of bishops' and his influence on the Gallic church was by no means negligible.[58] However, if the *Four Books* were composed shortly before 450, which is by no means certain, they came too late to exercise any significant influence on the society considered in this study.

In conclusion to this section, promotion through books and treatises was not extensive, but nor was it insignificant in forming opinion among the literate. With the possible exception of Cyprian's writings, the texts reached only the few, but these included clerics whom these works educated and supplied with preaching materials, and others who had acquired a theological education, those drawn into Pelagian and ascetic circles, and those whose cultural education led them to enjoy Ambrose's Latin eloquence. Of greater importance, however, were the works considered next, the apocryphal *Acts* and saints' *Lives*.

## APOCRYPHAL *ACTS* AND SAINTS' *LIVES*

Almsgiving is a common feature of two types of Christian hagiographic literature read in the later empire: the saints' *Lives* increasingly composed in the period, but also the apocryphal *Acts* composed in the late second and early third centuries, which were

---

[57] Cf. Badewien, *Geschichtstheologie*, 176–99.

[58] Gennadius, *De viris illustribus* 68, in W. Herding (ed.), *Hieronymi De Viris Inlustribus Liber* (Leipzig, 1924), 99.

still being widely read, revised, and translated. The *Actus vercellenses* testify to the demand in the second half of the fourth century for a Latin *Acts of Peter* in what Gérard Poupon argues was a heterodox church or Manichaean group in North Africa.[59] The same century saw the *Acts of Thecla* produced in miniature codices which 'lent themselves well to the needs of pilgrim travel'.[60] One pilgrim, Egeria, related after her journey how she had read the *Acts of Thecla* on visiting her shrine at Seleucia and the 'writings of holy Thomas' at his *martyrium* in Edessa.[61] The verdict of A. F. Klijn that the *Acts of Thomas* 'were very poorly known in the Greek and Latin speaking world' is unduly pessimistic.[62]

The formation of a mid-fifth-century *Life of Thecla* from earlier *Acts of Paul and Thecla* indicates pressure to reshape older works. The various *Acts* were regarded with suspicion and denounced by Catholic leaders for what by the late fourth century was heretical teaching on doctrinal matters, but interpretative strategies allowed for their continued reading by orthodox Christians for purposes of moral edification. Filastrius of Brescia distinguished between what he took to be the original texts and heretical interpolations. The latter precluded acceptance of heretical doctrine, but the former provided valuable moral exempla.[63] Henry Chadwick has noted that Priscillian's *Third Tractate* 'skilfully and elegantly defends the right of instructed Christians to read apocryphal texts with discretion'.[64] These strategies meant that descriptions of almsgiving included in apocryphal texts for purposes other than direct advocacy

---

[59] G. Poupon, 'L'Origine africaine des *Acta Vercellenses*', in J. Bremmer (ed.), *The Apocryphal Acts of Peter* (Leuven, 1998), 192–9. Bremmer, Ibid. 19, further argues for a date post 359.

[60] S. J. Davis, *The Cult of Saint Thecla: A Tradition of Women's Piety in Late Antiquity* (Oxford, 2001), 146. For a 3rd- or 4th-cent miniature codex of the *Acts of Peter*, cf. C. Roberts, *Manuscript, Society and Belief in Early Christian Egypt* (London, 1977), 11. For a Coptic version of the *Acts of Peter* on papyrus from the 4th or 5th cent., cf. L. Vouaux (ed.), *Les Actes de Pierre* (Paris, 1922), 19. For Greek and Latin versions of the *Acts of John* from the late 4th century, cf. W. Schneemelcher (ed.), *New Testament Apocrypha*, 2 vols. (Cambridge and Louisville, 1990 and 1992), ii. 153–4.

[61] J. Wilkinson (tr.), *Egeria's Travels* 19 and 23 (Warminster, 1999), 132 and 141.

[62] A. F. J. Klijn, *The Acts of Thomas* (Leiden, 1962), 21.

[63] Chadwick, *Priscillian*, 24.

[64] Ibid. 64.

not only constituted indirect promotion, but were read by late antique Christians as a direct form of exhortation.

Among the apocryphal *Acts*, almsgiving is prominent in the *Acts of Peter* and *Acts of Thomas*, and appears in the *Acts of John*, *Acts of Andrew*, and *Acts of Paul and Thecla*. The texts display an exaggerated or narrow interest in large gifts by the nobility. In the *Acts of Peter* Marcellus promises a gold piece for every widow; the noble matron, whose son Peter has resurrected, brings 2,000 gold pieces for the 'virgins of Christ', while the boy brings 4,000.[65] One chapter later Peter accepts 10,000 gold pieces for 'Christ's servants' from a wealthy woman aptly named 'Chrysis' (or Goldy).[66] The *Acts of Paul and Thecla* tell how the heroine's protectress Tryphaena sent her much clothing and gold, so that she could leave it with Paul 'for the care of the destitute' ($\epsilon i s \ \delta \iota \alpha \kappa o \nu i \alpha \nu \ \tau \hat{\omega} \nu \ \pi \tau \omega \chi \hat{\omega} \nu$).[67] Promotion of this kind made almsgiving glamorous. In the *Acts of Thomas*, originally composed in Syriac but soon translated into Greek,[68] almsgiving is the main motif of the second, where Thomas promises to construct a palace for King Gundaphorus, but spends the money on the poor, so constructing a palace for him in heaven.[69]

These *Acts* frequently use almsgiving as a marker of the doctrinal orthodoxy recognized by their authors and redactors. Successful charity in the redacted *Acts of Peter* serves as a badge of orthodoxy. The senator Marcellus is presented as an extremely generous almsgiver towards widows and orphans while still an orthodox Christian, so that 'the poor called Marcellus their patron, and his house.... (the house) of pilgrims and of the poor'.[70] When lured into apostasy by Simon Magus, Marcellus renounces his former generosity. This is unlikely to be an oblique attack on any absence of almsgiving in actual heretical or Gnostic groups. What matters, as Magda Misset-Van de Weg notes, is that Marcellus' return to the

[65] *Acts of Peter* 19 and 29, in R. A. Lipsius and M. Bonnet (eds.), *Acta Apostolorum Apocrypha*, 2 vols. (Leipzig, 1891 and 1898), i. 66 and 79.

[66] *Acts of Peter* 30, in Lipsius and Bonnet, *Acta Apostolorum*, i. 79–81.

[67] *Acts of Paul and Thecla* 41, in Lipsius and Bonnet, *Acta Apocrypha*, i. 267.

[68] Klijn, *Acts of Thomas*, 13–14.

[69] *Acts of Thomas* 17–29, in M. Bonnet, ed. *Acta Philippi et Acta Thomae accedunt Acta Barnabae* (Leipzig, 1903), 124–46.

[70] *Acts of Peter* 8, tr. Schneemelcher, *New Testament Apocrypha*, ii. 294.

truth is marked by a return to his role as the widows' patron.[71] Likewise, when Peter restores Nicostratus to life, the boy both declares his new-found faith in Christ and brings the 4,000 gold pieces mentioned above.[72] Peter recovers Eubola's property on the strength of a miraculous vision: 'But Eubola having recovered all her property gave it for the care of the poor (*in ministerium pauperum*). She believed in the Lord Jesus Christ and so strengthened, despising and renouncing this world, she used to give to the widows and orphans and would clothe the poor until after a long time she was laid to rest.'[73] The intent to defraud the poor, the opposite of almsgiving, marks Simon as a heretic in this story. He asks Eubola for money 'for the maintenance of the poor' (*in administratione pauperum*) only to secrete the money in a cave.[74] As Misset-Van de Weg has observed, Simon's greed is contrasted with Peter's selflessness in handing over large gifts of alms to the church for the needy.[75] Almsgiving in the *Acts of Thomas* serves a similar literary function to distinguish the true man of God from a charlatan or sorcerer: Thomas's 'compassionate acts' ($\epsilon\dot{\upsilon}\sigma\pi\lambda\alpha\gamma\chi\nu\dot{\iota}\alpha\iota$) and cures, all performed without hope of reward, show that he is 'righteous or an apostle of the new God whom he preaches'.[76]

This symbolic meaning of almsgiving in the *Acta* read by Christians in the fourth century probably encouraged the accusations by Catholic and Arian bishops that their counterparts had misused church funds belonging to the poor. The charge that Athanasius was accused of misappropriating imperial alms was noted in the previous chapter.[77] He laid the same charge against his opponent: George and his Arian sympathizers were accused of seizing bread and houses in Alexandria belonging to the widows and orphans.[78] The symbolism

---

[71] M. Misset-Van de Weg, 'The Purpose of the Wondrous Works and Deeds in the *Acts of Peter*', in J. Bremmer (ed.), *The Apocryphal Acts of Peter* (Leuven, 1998), 97–110, 106.

[72] *Acts of Peter* 28–9, in Lipsius and Bonnet, *Acta Apocrypha*, i. 77–9.

[73] *Acts of Peter* 17, in Lipsius and Bonnet, *Acta Apocrypha*, i. 65.

[74] *Acts of Peter* 17, in Lipsius and Bonnet, *Acta Apocrypha*, i. 64.

[75] Misset-Van de Weg, 'Purpose', 98.

[76] *Acts of Thomas* 20, in Bonnet, *Acta Philippi et Acta Thomae*, 131.

[77] Athanasius, *Apologia secunda (contra Arianos)* 18. 2, in Opitz, *Werke*, ii/1. 100.

[78] Athanasius, *Apologia de fuga sua* 6 in Szymusiak, *Apologie*, 139.

also facilitated the exculpatory function of almsgiving in later *vitae* (see below).

Many saints' *Lives* are now lost, especially from what Gustave Bardy called the Arians' 'hagiographic workshops': the *Life of Lucian*, written after 330 and before the end of the century; the *Encomium of Eusebius of Emesa* by George of Laodicea, written before George's death in 360; or the *Life of Eusebius of Caesarea* composed by Acacius before 365.[79] Almsgiving, however, appears prominently and repeatedly as a praise-worthy activity in the third-century *Life of Cyprian*,[80] which continued to be widely read in the period, and appears with varying degrees of prominence in some twenty-one of the extant *vitae* of the fourth century and first half of the fifth century.

Ten date from the fourth century. They are: the *Life of Antony* by Athanasius (*c.*357[81]); the *Life of Pachomius* (347–400[82]); the Greek *Life of Abercius* (363–85[83]); the *Life of Macrina* by Gregory of Nyssa (soon after 379[84]); the same author's *Life of Gregory the Wonderworker*; the Latin *Life of Filastrius* written by Gaudentius of Brescia also in the late fourth century; the Greek *Life of Polycarp* by Pionius;[85] two Latin *vitae* by Jerome, the *Life of Malchus the Captive Monk* and *Life of Hilarion* (*c.*390–1[86]); and the *Life of Martin* by

---

[79] G. Bardy, *Recherches sur saint Lucien d'Antioche et son école* (Paris, 1936), 13. Cf. Buytaert, *L'Héritage littéraire*, 45.

[80] Pontius, *Life of Cyprian* 2. 6–7, 3. 6–10, 6. 4, 10. 2–4, and 13. 12, in C. Mohrmann *et al.*, *Vita*, 8, 12, 18, 26 and 36.

[81] The work was probably composed first in Greek, but was translated into Coptic soon afterwards. Bartelink has defended the contested but traditional ascription to Athanasius. Two Latin translations are known, the second *c.*375 by Evagrius. A Syriac version followed in the 5th or 6th cent. Bartelink, *Antoine*, SC 400. 27–35 and 99.

[82] J. E. Goehring, 'New Frontiers in Pachomian Studies', in B. A. Pearson and J. E. Goehring, *The Roots of Egyptian Christianity* (Philadelphia, 1986), 238. Bartelink believes the first Greek *Life* was composed *c.*400, idem, *Antoine*, SC 400. 39. It is not clear whether the work was originally in Coptic or Greek, but there were soon versions in both languages. Cf. P. Rousseau, *Pachomius: The Making of a Community in Fourth-Century Egypt* (London 1985), 37–48.

[83] D. Bundy, 'The *Life of Abercius*: Its Significance for Early Syriac Christianity', *The Second Century*, 7 (1989–90), 170.

[84] Gregory of Nyssa, *Life of Macrina*, GNO 8/1, ed. W. Jaeger, J. Cavarnos, and V. Woods Callahan (Leiden, 1952), 370–414.

[85] The text is found in J. B. Lightfoot (ed.), *The Apostolic Fathers*, ii/3 (London and New York, 1889), 433–65; for a date not earlier than the mid-4th cent. and not much after 400, see Lightfoot's introduction, 429.

[86] Kelly, *Jerome*, 170.

Sulpicius Severus, a first edition of which existed by 397.[87] The remaining eleven belong to the first half of the fifth century or soon afterwards. They are Paulinus' *Life of Ambrose* (412 or 422[88]); Palladius' Greek *Life of Chrysostom* (after 407); the *Life of Honoratus* by Hilary (430 or 431[89]); the Syriac *Legend of the Man of God* (436–49[90]) and *Life of Rabbula* (436–49[91]); the Greek *Life of Hypatios* by Callinicus (447–50[92]) and *Life of Thecla* (444–8[93]); the *Life of Apphou*;[94] the mid-fifth century Greek *Life of Syncletica*;[95] the *Life of Olympias*;[96] and the *Life of Porphyry* by Mark the Deacon.[97]

It is likely that the last three *Lives* listed above strictly belong outside the period covered by the present book, but they are a continuation of the same literary tradition. We may add to the list first the *Acta Archelai*, an anti-Manichaean work probably dating from the second quarter of the fourth century.[98] In this fictional tale the generosity to the poor of Marcellus, a leading citizen of an Eastern city named as Carchara, attracts the attention of Mani to a potential convert, as Simon Magus had been drawn to Marcellus in the *Acts of Peter*. The work's popularity is indicated by a Latin translation of the Greek text probably by 385 (which is now the

---

[87] *Sulpice Sévère, Vie de saint Martin*, ed. J. Fontaine, SC 133–5 (Paris, 1967–9), i. 17.

[88] B. Dümler, 'Paulinus of Milan', in Döpp and Geerlings, *Dictionary*, 468.

[89] Cavallin, *Vitae*, 14.

[90] Drijvers, 'Man of God of Edessa', 246.

[91] Ibid.

[92] Bartelink, *Vie d'Hypatios*, SC 177. 11–12.

[93] Davies, *Cult*, 41. Cf. G. Dagron, *Vie et miracles de sainte Thècle* (Brussels, 1978), 19.

[94] Its most recent Italian translator judges it to have been written not long after the events of 399–400 which it interprets. T. Orlandi, *Vite di monaci copti* (Rome, 1984), 53. For the plausibility of an original Greek rather than Coptic version, cf. T. Orlandi, 'Letteratura copta e cristianesimo nazionale egiziano', in A. Camplani (ed.), *L'Egitto cristiano: Aspetti e problemi in età tardo-antica* (Rome 1997), 51.

[95] E. Castelli, 'Pseudo-Athanasius: The Life and Activity of the Holy and Blessed Teacher Syncletica', in V. I. Wimbush (ed.), *Ascetic Behavior in Greco-Roman Antiquity* (Minneapolis 1990), 265.

[96] For a date after the mid-5th cent., cf. A.-M. Malingrey, *Jean Chrysostome, Lettres à Olympias, Vie anonyme d'Olympias*, SC 13bis (Paris, 1968), 396. For the view that the *vita* probably belongs in the early part of the mid-5th cent., cf. E. A. Clark, *Jerome, Chrysostom and Friends* (New York and Toronto, 1979), 120 n. 4.

[97] Rapp defends a date of initial composition during the 450s, in Head, *Medieval Hagiography*, 55.

[98] Hegemonius, *Acta Archelai*, ed. C. H. Beeson (Leipzig, 1906), pp. xv–xvi.

only complete extant version).[99] Second should be added a number of the short *Lives* found in the *Lausiac History* by Palladius (*c.*420)— stories of Macarius and the Rich Virgin (ch. 6), Pambo (ch. 10), Paesius and Isaias (ch. 14), Eulogius (ch. 21), Ephraem (ch. 40), Veneria (ch. 41), Philoromus (ch. 45), Olympias (ch. 56), Candida (ch. 57), the Younger Melania (ch. 61), Verus and Bosporia (ch. 66), Magna (ch. 67), the monk of Ancyra (ch. 68). Closely related to the above *Lives* are the two famous Greek funerary eulogies for Basil of Caesarea: Gregory of Nyssa's *Oration in Praise of his Brother Basil* (381) and Gregory Nazianzen's *In Praise of Basil (382).*[100]

Almsgiving is a characteristic activity in these texts largely in so far as it displays the character of the saint expressed in terms of the virtues and of the biblical models and texts which together form an authoritative matrix for the determination of virtuous action.[101] The meaning of the action (discussed in Chapter 5) is related rather than the specific circumstances of its performance, as seen in the example here from the *Life of Martin*:

> While he was still unbaptized, he behaved as someone who was a candidate for baptism by the good works which he performed: attending those in difficulty, aiding the wretched, feeding the needy, clothing the naked, retaining from his military salary nothing more than his daily ration. By this point far from deaf to the Gospel, he took no thought for the morrow.[102]

Allusions to Matthew 25: 35–6 and Matthew 6: 34 occlude any specifics of Martin's almsgiving. Fontaine has pointed out a similarity here with the Latin *Life of Antony*, where the Egyptian hermit 'used to give away... the proceeds from his labour to the needy, keeping only enough to pay for his bread'.[103] The modelling associates Martin with an agreed model of ascetic sanctity and the biblical allusions root this sanctity in fidelity to the Gospel.

---

[99] S. N. C. Lieu, 'Fact and Fiction in the *Acta Archelai*', in Peter Bryder (ed.), *Manichaean Studies*, i (Lund, 1988), 73.

[100] J. Bernardi, *Grégoire de Naziance, Discours 42–43*, SC 384 (Paris, 1992), 27–8.

[101] On portrayal of the holy man or woman, cf. Patricia Cox Miller, 'Strategies of Representation in Collective Biography: Constructing the Subject as Holy', in Tomas Hägg and Philip Rousseau (eds.), *Greek Biography and Panegyric in Late Antiquity* (Berkeley, Los Angeles, and London, 2000), 209–54.

[102] Sulpicius Severus, *Life of Martin* 2. 8, SC 133. 256.

[103] Fontaine, *Vie de saint Martin*, SC 134. 470 and n. 2.

This highly generalized redescription of almsgiving in biblical terms is also found in the *Life of Macrina*. A woman attracted to her community relates that Macrina had only one deposit box for wealth, 'treasure in heaven'.[104] Gregory informs us that she did not keep her portion of the family inheritance, but 'had everything distributed at the priest's hands in accordance with divine command'.[105] She 'didn't turn away people asking for something'.[106] Grain distributed during a famine miraculously does not diminish, although the author claims to pass over the story and furnishes no details.[107] All these are allusions to different forms of almsgiving drawing on biblical texts used by preachers in their promotion: Matthew 6: 19–20 was often cited in exhorting almsgiving. The divine command might be that of Christ at Matthew 5: 42 or 19: 21, both of which verses were taken to advocate almsgiving. The miracle of the unfailing grain supply associates Macrina with the widow of Zarephath.

The idealizing portrayal of almsgiving was a form of direct promotion to the extent that the saint was presented as a model for the readers' imitation: the 'argument from *Life* to action was always there'.[108] As the Divine Word had taken flesh in Christ, so the saint's life was itself understood as a word of exhortation addressed to the faithful. The author of the *Life of Alexander* told his readers that, if the saint himself kept silent, 'his life cried out with a loud voice and served unceasingly as a warning to those who disobeyed the commandments'.[109]

Almsgiving is not only present in the *Lives* as a form of implicit exhortation. In the *Lives* of Martin and Melania the Younger it also serves an exculpatory purpose. The blessing which Martin will receive from Christ for his compassion towards the beggar, when he tears his military cloak, a symbol of allegiance to the pagan emperor, more than covers up or outweighs the embarrassment of

---

[104] Gregory of Nyssa, *Life of Macrina*, ed. Jaeger *et al.*, GNO 8/1. 403.
[105] Ibid. 393.
[106] Ibid.
[107] Ibid. 413–14.
[108] Averil Cameron, *Christianity and the Rhetoric of Empire* (Berkeley, Calif., 1991), 147.
[109] *Life of Alexander* 44, PO 6. 692–3.

a bishop who once bore arms; and some bishops in Gaul had thought him too wild for episcopal office.[110] Almsgiving on a vast scale is the most important means by which Gerontius characterizes the holiness of Melania, and Elizabeth Clark has argued that the *vita*, by loudly asserting Melania's sanctity, seeks to validate the rejection by the monastic communities which she founded of the christological position adopted at Chalcedon.[111] So, too, it has been argued that in the *Lives* of the 'Man of God' and Rabbula, almsgiving reasserts the latter's sanctity not first and foremost for imitation, but over and against the absent figure of his successor at Edessa, bishop Ibas.[112] Direct and indirect promotion here shade into one another. On the other hand, explicit exhortation to almsgiving in saints' *Lives* was rare, and so was extended exposition of the Church's teaching on alms and wealth: these types of promotion were at odds with the narrative nature of the *Lives*. The *Life of Syncletica* is an exception to the rule in this respect, with its long central discourse on wealth and its later defence of almsgiving in the ascetic life.[113]

Apocryphal *Acts* and saints' *Lives* were not the only forms of hagiographic literature. Martyrs' *Acta*, usually without mention of almsgiving, continued to be read, their importance assured in some places by a place in liturgical commemoration.[114] But, in conclusion to this section, the Elder Melania was a great reader of saints' lives and she was by no means unique.[115] Translations give an indication of the immense popularity enjoyed by the *Life of Antony*, as do the passages in later *lives* modelled on a similar part of Athanasius' text.[116] A measure of these texts' significance for their readers is the enthusiasm with which Paulinus of Nola showed the *Life of Martin* by Sulpicius Severus to the Elder Melania and others in their circle.[117] Likewise, Augustine's *Confessions* not only shows the *Life of Antony* being read in the small monastery at Trier, but its profound impact

---

[110] Sulpicius Severus, *Life of Martin* 3. 3 and 9. 3–4, SC 133. 258 and 270–2.

[111] Clark, *Life of Melania*, 141–52.

[112] Drijvers, 'Man of God', 245–7.

[113] *Life of Syncletica* 73 and 75, in Castelli, 'Pseudo-Athanasius', 295–6 (Greek text, PG 28. 1529–32).

[114] Pressure to read martyrs' *Acta* was being strongly resisted at Rome in the mid-6th cent. Cf, Chadwick, *Priscillian*, 84.

[115] Clark, *Life*, 169.

[116] Bartelink, *Antoine*, SC 400. 68–9.          [117] Paulinus, *Ep.* 29. 14, CSEL 29. 261.

on the imperial officer who read it there one afternoon and on his comrade, both of whom, in an echo of Matthew 19: 21, resolved to 'leave their possessions behind' and follow God.[118] Promotion of this kind reached and moved a wide popular audience.

## SERMONS AND THEIR CENTRALITY IN CHRISTIAN TEACHING

Sermons were the most important way in which promoters of almsgiving advanced their cause. Preaching was regarded as the basic way in which Christian teaching, moral and doctrinal, was communicated to the faithful. In the *City of God* Augustine challenged the pagans to show where their gods assembled people to teach the necessity of preventing avarice in the way that Christians could point to churches for that purpose wherever the faith had spread.[119] He stressed the role of church attendance in teaching morality, and the place in that teaching of both readings from scripture and the preaching which accompanied them. At church Christians hear:

how virtuously they should live in this present world in order to merit, when this life is over, eternal life in bliss. Sacred Scripture and instruction in justice, given out from a raised pulpit in everyone's sight, reverberate through the church, where those who put it into practice hear something to their advantage and those who do not bring judgement on themselves.[120]

It may be objected, however, that Augustine presents an idealized account of how Christian teaching *should* be transmitted rather than a description of actual transmission. Scholars dubious of the impact of preaching have questioned how often preaching in fact took place, at whom it was targeted, and by whom it was heard and understood. These objections must be considered before proceeding further. Basil reminded his congregation of how they were *supposed* to respond by listening attentively and taking the message to heart: 'Listen with an

---

[118] Augustine, *Confessions* 8. 6. 15, ed. J. J. O'Donnell, 3 vols. (Oxford, 1992), i. 95.

[119] *City of God* 2. 6, in *Sancti Aurelii Augustini De Civitate Dei, libri I–X*, ed. B. Dombart and A. Kalb, CCSL 47 (Turnhout, 1955), 39.

[120] *City of God* 2. 28, CCSL 47. 63.

open mind, a docile heart, one simply accepting what I urge, impressed by the speaker, like wax when you press a seal into it.'[121] The presence of such a reminder, hoping to induce a greater docility, indicates that Augustine's idealized model of the church as a school of virtue is not to be taken at face value. Yet the preacher's appeal to an accepted model of docility nonetheless suggests the place of sermons in teaching.

It would be unwise to assume a single and unchanging standard practice with respect to preaching. Nautin concluded from comparing the length of Origen's sermons on the Old Testament and on the Gospels that on a Sunday in some third-century churches a short homily was given after each of the three readings.[122] Likewise Francis Van de Paverd has argued that at Antioch and elsewhere in the fourth and fifth centuries 'it was customary to deliver more than one homily during the mass', though it appears that only one sermon was preached in the daily Lenten services.[123] Augustine certainly preached regularly and frequently in his own diocese, as a visiting preacher at Carthage, and elsewhere. He normally preached twice weekly, on Saturdays and Sundays, but also on other days, such as feast days, and sometimes twice a day.[124] All this suggests a high level of preaching. It was part of the accepted duties of a bishop or the presbyter appointed in his place to preach regularly.[125] The *Life of Rabbula* speaks of 'daily exhortations' he gave to the monks.[126] Priests frequently preached in the churches of Alexandria.[127] Socrates related that at Caesarea and in Cyprus the bishops and priests explained the scriptures on Saturdays and Sundays 'in the evening at the lighting of the lamps'.[128]

[121] Basil, *In Time of Hunger* 1, PG 31. 305B.

[122] J. T. Lienhard SJ, 'Origen as Homilist', in D. G. Hunter (ed.), *Preaching in the Patristic Age: Studies in Honor of Walter J. Burghardt, S.J.* (New York, 1989), at 41.

[123] F. Van de Paverd, *St John Chrysostom, The Homilies on the Statues: An Introduction*, OCA 197 (Rome, 1991), 194.

[124] A. Trapé, *St. Augustine; Man, Pastor, Mystic*, tr. M. J. O'Connell (New York, 1986), 149.

[125] A. Olivar, 'Reflections on Problems Raised by Early Christian Preaching', in M. B. Cunningham and P. Allen (eds.), *Preacher and Audience: Studies in Early Christian and Byzantine Homiletics* (Leiden, 1998), 25.

[126] Bickell, *Ausgewählte Schriften*, 181.

[127] Martin, *Athanase*, 181.

[128] Socrates, *Ecclesiastical History* 5. 22. 55, in Hansen, *Sokrates*, 302.

A different objection might be that, however often the clergy preached, their message was heard and understood by only a fraction of the church's membership, either because only a tiny segment of the Christian population attended or because the majority who did attend could not understand what was said. Ramsay MacMullen has further objected that what was understood failed to address or concern the many women in the congregation: 'In the huge homiletic corpus they and their concerns hardly appear: the preacher addresses himself to the "brethren".'[129] He has claimed that this is 'what any skimming will confirm'.[130] Were preachers' comments on almsgiving aimed at partly or largely absent men and irrelevant to the many women supposedly ignored?

Preachers did complain that church attendance was patchy. Basil attacked the low attendance at a penitential service held at Caesarea when food shortages threatened.[131] There were often more women and children than men in the congregation: Augustine imagined a bearded man being mocked for his church attendance, described by the mockers as 'going where the widows and old ladies go'.[132] This might reflect an imbalance between the sexes in church membership, but is more likely to reflect different patterns of worship. Yet both men and women often crowded the Carthaginian churches: Aurelius had moved to segregate the sexes, who entered through different doors into different areas of the church.[133] Numbers fell during the Games: Augustine observed in 419 how few were present to hear him preach at the Restored Basilica.[134] Augustine began a sermon on the feast of St Lawrence by noting how few had turned up.[135] At Antioch attendance soared after the riots, when Chrysostom claimed that the church was full while the agora lay deserted.[136] Though numbers fluctuated, they rose on Sundays, for the great festivals, and in

---

[129] MacMullen, *Christianity and Paganism*, 7.

[130] Ibid. 165 n. 17.

[131] Basil of Caesarea, *In Time of Hunger* 3, PG 31. 309C.

[132] Augustine, *Serm.* 306B. 6 = Denis 18, in G. Morin (ed.), *Sermones post Maurinos reperti*, Miscelleanea Augustiniana, 1 (Rome, 1930), 96.

[133] *Serm.* 359B. 5 = Dolbeau 2. 5 in F. Dolbeau, *Vingt-Six Sermons au peuple d'Afrique* (Paris, 1996), 330.

[134] *Serm.* 19. 6, CCSL 41. 258.

[135] *Serm.* 303. 1, PL 38. 1393.

[136] Chrysostom, *Homilies on the Statues* 4. 1, PG 49. 59.

Lent.[137] At Rome this is indicated by use of the basilicas rather than the smaller *tituli* for the stational liturgy on those days.[138] Chrysostom was delighted by the crowd in church for the Christmas festivities, but admitted that he had waited long to see such numbers.[139] Elsewhere, with what rhetorical exaggeration is unclear, he complained about those who were scarcely seen in church from one year to the next.[140] At Hippo the congregation swelled for the Nativity, Easter, and the Ascension.[141] Augustine remarked there on the Sunday after Easter how 'everyone' was at church for the solemnity.[142] At Bulla Regia he compared the poor attendance on the feast of the Maccabees in 399 with the crowds expected at Easter.[143] Brottier's judgement on Chrysostom's congregation, that Christians were present above all for the Lenten homilies, for the major festivals of the liturgical year, and for the martyrs' feasts, may serve as a general verdict on patterns of church attendance.[144]

Evidence for patchy attendance does not lessen the importance of preaching as the only vehicle for instructing the many who were wholly or partially illiterate, and so had no access to letters, treatises, and written *Lives*. They may not have attended often, but when they did what they heard was crucial to their understanding of Christianity. Nor does it remove the significance of sermons for those, literate or illiterate, who frequently attended: Edmund Hill has inferred from Augustine's sermon 25 that it 'was preached to a congregation ... in the habit of attending every day'.[145] Those who *did* regularly hear sermons belonged to groups significant for the

---

[137] For Sunday attendance in North Africa, cf. Augustine, *Serm.* 68. 1 = MAI 126, in Morin, *Sermones*, 356.

[138] J. F. Baldovin, *The Urban Character of Christian Worship: The Origins, Development, and Meaning of Stational Liturgy* (Rome, 1987), 260–1.

[139] Chrysostom, *Sermon on Christmas Day*, PG 49. 351.

[140] *Homilies on 2 Corinthians* 2, PG 61. 401.

[141] M. Pellegrino, 'General Introduction', tr. M. J. O'Connell, in *WSAT* 3/1. 13–137, at 84.

[142] Augustine, *Serm.* 259. 6, PL 38. 1201.

[143] *Serm.* 301A. 8, Morin, *Sermones*, 88.

[144] L. Brottier, 'Le Prédicateur, émule du prophète ou rival de l'acteur? Jean Chrysostome: Un pasteur déchiré entre ses auditeurs et son Dieu', *Connaissance des Pères de l'Église*, 74 (1999), 8. For attendance at Alexandria in Lent and at Easter, cf. A. Martin, *Athanase*, 154–5.

[145] Hill, *WSAT* 3/2. 86 n. 1.

wider formation of opinion concerning almsgiving: candidates for baptism (the *competentes*) in Lent and neophytes at Easter, when attendance was compulsory and sermons were a main vehicle of Christian initiation; enrolled widows and virgins, monks and clerics, all of whom had either entitlements to church alms or duties of almsgiving.

It is sometimes argued that the poor and destitute were absent. Mary Cunningham and Pauline Allen have observed that 'it is striking that the poorest sectors of society, the indigent and beggars, are never addressed directly by preachers, suggesting that they remained outside the church doors and were regarded by both preacher and congregation only as objects of pity'.[146] There is certainly some evidence that the labouring poor did not always attend. In the *Histories of the Monks of Upper Egypt* fishermen tell Abba Aaron 'it is because of our poverty that we have not had the leisure to go to church on the Sabbath and on the Lord's day', a justification which the monk rejects with the reply that 'it is the duty of all Christians to go to the house of God first thing in the morning'.[147] This was clearly an ideal promoted by the text, not what always happened. We may also be dealing with an accepted ideal, not universal practice, when the *Apostolic Constitutions* instruct the deacons to find a place in the church for a 'beggar or low-born man or stranger' (πτωχὸς ἢ ἀγενὴς ἢ ξένος), while the deaconess is to greet the women in the same way, whether they were 'rich or poor' (πτωχαῖς ἤτοι πλουσίαις).[148] Yet it would be unsafe to conclude that the poor were usually or mainly absent. Not addressing the destitute may say more about their low status than their absence from the congregation. Pellegrino gathered evidence from Augustine's sermons to suggest that members of his congregation were mainly poor, though not so poor that they had no roof over their heads, but also 'differed among themselves in social status, education, and spiritual disposition'.[149] One sermon by Augustine, dated to around 420, talks of how 'all the beggars, the sore-infested, the cripples, the

---

[146] Cunningham and Allen, *Preacher and Audience*, 14. Cf. also De Vinne, *Advocacy*, 4.

[147] Paphnutius, *Histories* 121, in Vivian, *Histories*, 132.

[148] *Ap. Const.* 2.58. 6, SC 320. 323.

[149] Pellegrino, *WSAT* 3/1. 85.

rejects' identify with Lazarus on hearing the story of Dives and Lazarus in church. It imagines one such man's thoughts, 'a poor man in need, with scarcely enough to fend for himself or perhaps a beggar' on hearing the Gospel read in his presence and that of a well-dressed rich man.[150] In another sermon, on Psalm 51, Augustine surmises what a poor man thinks on hearing this psalm and looking at his 'own rags' (*pannos suos*) and then at the well-dressed rich man standing next to him in church.[151]

Study of contemporary sermons refutes the proposition that women and their concerns were not addressed by preachers, while we cannot show that women considered themselves excluded by an address to the congregation as 'brethren'. Augustine addressed a particular group of women, mothers, and widows, to rebuke them for their apparent interruption of their sons' 'good works'.[152] He proposed Susanna as a model of chastity, and advised wives under unjust suspicion of adultery to pray for their accusing husbands.[153] Women preparing for baptism were instructed not to take a husband who had a wife still living from a previous marriage. They were to endure patiently the misuse of their wealth by their husband, but not his marital infidelities. They were certainly not to imitate those infidelities.[154] In a sermon on the dangers of youth, Augustine (or perhaps an imitator) addressed the young women present after speaking about the temptations besetting the young men.[155] Chrysostom addressed the women in his congregation specifically in order to attack their supposed preoccupation with their appearance.[156] He reminded a congregation that his words on the dangers of youth were spoken as much to the women and girls as to the men.[157] He addressed the women to criticize what he saw as an

---

[150] Augustine, *Serm.* 20A. 9 = Lambot 24, CCSL 41. 273; For the date, cf. Hill, *WSAT* 3/2. 27 n. 1.

[151] *En. in Ps.* 51. 14, CCSL 39. 633.

[152] *Serm.* 72A. 3 = Denis 25, in Morin, *Sermones*, 158. Elsewhere he warned wives not to stand in the way of their husband's devotion to God, as manifested above all in the example of the martyrs: *Serm.* 159A. 9 ( = Mainz 42 = Dolbeau 13), in Dolbeau, *Vingt-Six Sermons*, 96.

[153] *Serm.* 343. 5, ed. C. Lambot, *RB* 66 (1956), 33.

[154] *Serm.* 392. 2, 4, and 5, PL 39. 1710–13.

[155] *Serm.* 391. 6, PL 39. 1709.

[156] Chrysostom, *Homilies on Matthew* 30, PG 57. 369–70.

[157] *Homilies on Matthew* 49, PG 58. 504.

insincere show of penitence, where fasting was not accompanied by a wider change of conduct.[158] They were not to laugh in church.[159] The women were castigated for spending on clothes and jewellery that detracted from almsgiving.[160]

On occasion the preacher's words were either drowned out by the hubbub in church or failed to carry to the aisles where the faithful crowded for lack of space: Augustine admitted in one sermon that this had been so the previous day, but he now returned to the theme of that day's sermon to make good the deficiency.[161] Chrysostom complained that people gossiped during the liturgy.[162] Yet, exhortation to almsgiving was not as difficult to comprehend as doctrinal arguments.

It might be objected that many ordinary Christians could not understand the Latin or Greek in which sermons were preached. Yet in North Africa Augustine could address the poor in Latin: 'Are you poor? Like Lazarus covered with sores, put your trust in him.'[163] He turned a Punic proverb into Latin 'because you do not all know Punic'.[164] Latin and Greek were the common vernaculars for a high proportion of urban congregations. At Antioch John Chrysostom drew attention on occasion to visitors in the congregation who did not speak Greek and appear to have been Syriac-speaking clergy from the countryside.[165] The passage suggests both that most of his congregation were Greek-speaking, and that Syriac speakers were served outside the city by a clergy fluent in that tongue. Some preachers could speak in Greek *and* Syriac: Eusebius of Emesa was fluent in both.[166] Libanius clearly thought Syriac speakers 'the lowest

---

[158] *Homilies on 2 Corinthians* 4, PG 61. 425.

[159] *Homilies on Hebrews* 15. 4, PG 63. 122.

[160] *Homilies on Matthew* 89. 4, PG 58. 786. For further evidence of the presence of women in the church at Antioch and Constantinople, cf. W. Mayer, 'Female Participation and the Late Fourth-Century Preacher's Audience', *Augustinianum*, 39/1 (1999), 139–47; on preachers' engagement with women's concerns, cf. A. Cunningham SSCM, 'Women and Preaching in the Patristic Age', in Hunter, *Preaching*, 58–64.

[161] Augustine, *Serm.* 68. 1 = MAI 126, in Morin, *Sermones*, 356.

[162] Chrysostom *Homilies on 2 Corinthians* 2, PG 61. 404.

[163] Augustine, *Serm.* 20A. 9 = Lambot 24, CCSL 41. 273.

[164] *Serm.* 167. 4, PL 38. 910.

[165] Chrysostom, *Homilies on the Statues* 19. 3, PG 49. 188–90. For discussion of the visitors' identity, cf. Van de Paverd, *St John Chrysostom*, 260–89.

[166] E. M. Buytaert, *L'Héritage littéraire d'Eusèbe d'Émèse*, Bibliothèque du Muséon, 24 (Louvain, 1949), 95.

of the low'.[167] They appear in his orations only once as the shopkeepers and *penetes* whose wooden bowls the craftsmen vie to mend.[168] Syriac sermons therefore offer some evidence for the accessibility of Christian preaching to the poor. Other tongues were also catered for on occasion. Chrysostom employed interpreters and clergy who spoke their language when arranging for regular preaching to the Goths at Constantinople.[169] In a Pachomian monastery one monk gave moral instruction to his brethren in Coptic, while another translated his words into Greek.[170] Finally, Western scholars, by virtue of their own linguistic and cultural education, may be inclined to overlook the volume of preaching from the period extant in Syriac and Coptic vernaculars.

Augustine's plain or conversational style as a preacher, with apostrophes and techniques borrowed from diatribe, his patience in explaining difficulties, the acclamations, applause, and other interruptions which greeted his preaching, together with his comments on the importance of clear instruction, strongly suggest that most in the congregation could follow him.[171] At one place Augustine states that members of the congregation are discussing his likely meaning during the sermon, those who have understood explaining to those who have not, and he retraces the argument 'in a more straightforward manner'.[172]

Having so far re-established the centrality of preaching in communicating episcopal teaching, though not yet the content of that teaching, we must note the importance of 'published' sermons, the transcripts and texts reworked by their authors for manuscript dissemination already indicated in the discussion of Isidore's letters. Interpolations in Peter of Alexandria's *On Wealth* show that the sermon continued to be read in Egypt in subsequent centuries.[173]

---

[167] A. F. Norman, *Antioch as a Centre of Hellenic Culture as Observed by Libanius* (Liverpool, 2000), 159 n. 45.

[168] Libanius, *Or.* 42. 31 in Foerster, *Opera*, iii. 323.

[169] Theodoret, *Ecclesiastical History* 5. 30, in Parmentier and Hansen, *Kirchengeschichte*, 330.

[170] *Epistulae Ammonis*, 4, ed. J. E. Goehring, *Letter of Ammon and Pachomian Monasticism* (Berlin, 1986), 127.

[171] Pellegrino, *WSAT* 3/1. 111; Augustine, *On Christian Instruction* 4. 25, in J. Martin (ed.), *Sancti Aurelii Augustini De Doctrina Christiana*, CCSL 32 (Turnhout, 1962), 133–4.

[172] Augustine, *Serm.* 23. 8, CCSL 41. 314.

[173] Pearson and Vivian, *Two Coptic Homilies*, 29.

Not only did publication extend the reach of sermons promoting almsgiving, on occasion it allowed that promotion to receive new prominence. Gaudentius included an exhortation to almsgiving as the right use of wealth in the preface to a collection of his sermons which he dedicated to Brescia's leading citizen, Benivolus.[174]

What place within this preaching did almsgiving occupy? The obvious way to proceed (not the only one, as will be explained below) is by empirical examination of extant sermons to ask in how many almsgiving figures as either the sole theme or as a major theme, though (i) the volume of extant material, even for the limited period under consideration, and (ii) the difficulties in attributing and dating late antique sermons, mean that any answer is provisional, indicating an order of magnitude rather than supplying exact numbers. We can assess with greater accuracy in how many sermons by selected preachers almsgiving figures, its significance as a theme, and its whereabouts in those sermons, as well as asking when such sermons may have been preached in the liturgical year, though we are hampered by the practice of later copyists, who (i) frequently excised material from individual sermons and (ii) created new sermons from a catena of passages extracted from a number of longer originals which may well have been preached at different times of the year.[175]

We should not assume that either the complete corpus of extant sermons, or the extant corpus of any one preacher, necessarily represent a typical sample of late antique sermons. We may presume that sermons on controversial doctrinal matters were more often kept and copied than sermons on less contentious moral teachings, due to the former's utility in combating perceived recurrences of earlier heresies. The development of doctrine, however, operated to weed out sermons and preachers judged unorthodox by the changed standards of subsequent generations, although some sermons now recognized as Arian survived through reascription to Nicene

---

[174] Gaudentius, *Praefatio*, in A. Glueck (ed.), *S. Gaudentii Episcopi Brixensis Tratatus*, CSEL 68 (Vienna and Leipzig, 1936), 7–8.

[175] For an example of the first practice, compare Augustine's *Sermon* 293A in Morin, *Sermones*, 223–6, with the longer form of the sermon, Dolbeau 3, in Dolbeau, *Vingt-Six Sermons*, 484–95. For an example of the second practice, Hill suggests Augustine, *Sermon* 97A = Casinensis 2. 114–15 in Morin, *Sermones*, 416–18. *WSAT* 3/11. 383 n. 1.

preachers.[176] A bias favoured the more polished, erudite, or literary sermons at the expense of the plain, both on the part of preachers themselves, in selecting those sermons of which they kept copies, and on the part of later collectors. Works by the famous were more likely to be kept than sermons by obscure preachers, although the latter's works might be misattributed to the former. The corpus may be further biased in favour of sermons on saints and martyrs, whose universal or widely celebrated feasts provided an additional incentive for preservation. It is also possible that the role of monks in the transmission of sermons may have acted to save a disproportionate number of sermons promoting asceticism. On these grounds the extant corpus probably under-represents the almsgiving promoted by preachers, but, as will be shown, this is not to say that almsgiving is rarely promoted in the corpus.

It is not obvious how best to classify the sermons in which almsgiving is promoted, nor which categories will be most revealing. It is not always clear which sermons belong where. The taxonomy employed here distinguishes between (1) sermons devoted essentially to the promotion of almsgiving; (2) sermons on wealth and poverty in which almsgiving is a major theme, but in which the preacher also tackles related issues of avarice and pride; (3) other sermons in which almsgiving is one of several important topics; (4) sermons in which almsgiving is promoted in conclusion to a sermon on some other topic, such as the need for repentance; and (5) sermons in which almsgiving is briefly promoted, as it were, in passing. A sermon does not necessarily belong in only one of these categories. Augustine's *Sermon* 60, for example, on why people accumulate wealth, has a chain of argument which concludes in the call to almsgiving. There are reasons to place it in categories (1) and (2): category (1) concerns the sermon's presumed purpose and not simply its contents, whereas category (2) is defined by contents. Likewise, the opening and closing sections of Augustine's *Sermon* 86 concern almsgiving, while the central section concerns avarice and extravagance. In this case

---

[176] e.g. two Easter sermons ascribed to Chrysostom in the MS tradition are possibly by 'Asterius', author of similar works, who may be the 4th-cent. sophist. Cf. J. Liébaert (ed.), *Deux Homélies anoméenes pour l'octave de Paques*, SC 146 (Paris, 1969).

Augustine ends by explicitly stating that he has given his congregation 'a sermon about almsgiving' (*de faciendis eleemosynis*).[177]

It might appear better to establish categories defined only by content, but this, too, is problematic. In *Sermon* 106, which is principally devoted to an interpretation of Luke 11: 41 (*Give Alms, and Behold, All Things are Clean for You*), and which is largely concerned with almsgiving by the Pharisees, Augustine only directly promotes Christian almsgiving briefly, before reinterpreting the verse in the light of its context: Jesus could not have meant that almsgiving by unbaptized Jews, with no faith in Christ, cleansed them from sin. Their alms are worthless. Jesus, Augustine argues, meant that they should give alms to the soul, feeding it with bread from heaven. Content alone does not indicate nor measure the direct promotion of Christian almsgiving, although the use of almsgiving as a metaphor is a form of indirect promotion. Hence the decision to select categories that concern purpose as well as content, while sermons are placed in only one category to avoid inflating the extent of promotion.

## The presentation of almsgiving in selected corpora

### Roman North Africa: Augustine

Counting Augustine's extant sermons is an art in itself and one still subject to new discoveries. In 1989 Dom Pierre-Patrick Verbraken noted '548 authentic sermons, complete or fragmentary', which in his judgement represented 'only one-tenth or even only one-fourteenth of all Augustine's sermons'.[178] This total did not include the *Enarrationes in Psalmos*, the *Tractates on John's Gospel*, nor the *Tractates on the First Letter of John*. In 1997 John Rotelle counted 546 sermons, to which he added twenty-one from the thirty sermons newly edited by Francois Dolbeau, making a total of 567. Promotion of almsgiving is found to a greater or lesser extent in 113 of these 567:

1. Ten sermons primarily devoted to the promotion of almsgiving (*Sermons* 61, 86, 113, 164A, 350B, 350C, 367, 388, 389, and 390), although it is probable that 350C is an 'abbreviated alternative

---

[177] Augustine, *Serm.* 86. 17, PL 38. 530.     [178] *WSAT* 3/1. 11.

version' of 350B 'possibly descending from a different stenographer', while two others, 367 and 388, are of disputed authenticity.[179] Of these ten, eight cannot be placed in the liturgical or calendar year. *Sermon* 86 is thought to have been delivered in winter, while *Sermon* 390, according to the manuscripts, was preached in Lent on the Saturday before Holy Week.[180]

2. Ten sermons in which almsgiving features as the right use of wealth in a treatment of riches and poverty (*Sermons* 14, 36, 39, 41, 42, 50, 60, 85, 107A, and 177), although it has been suggested that *Sermon* 42 is missing its original opening, in which case it might belong in section (3) below.[181] Of these ten, six cannot be placed in the year. *Sermon* 14, however, is thought to have been preached on a Sunday in early June; Augustine probably delivered *Sermon* 85 on a date between 19 and 24 June;[182] and it has been proposed that he gave *Sermon* 177 in May or June.[183] *Sermon* 60 is thought to have been preached at a similar time of year between the feasts of Ascension and Pentecost.[184]

3. Forty-five sermons in which almsgiving features as one important topic among others (*Sermons* 11, 18, 25, 25A, 32, 37, 53, 53A, 56, 58, 93, 103, 104, 105A, 113B, 114A, 114B = Dolbeau 5, 149, 164, 172, 178, 198 = Dolbeau 26, 205, 206, 207, 208, 209, 210, 211A, 217, 236, 239, 259, 299E, 302, 305A, 335C, 338, 339, 345, 352, 356, 358A, 359A, 399). Seventeen cannot be tied to any time of year, but eleven are thought to have been preached in Lent (*Sermons* 11, 56, 58, 205, 206, 207, 208, 209, 210, 211A, and 352) and three in the Easter season (236, 239, and 259).[185] Two were given on the feast of the Scillitan martyrs on 17 July (*Sermons* 37 and 299E), while two were given on 10 August, the feast of St Lawrence (*Sermons* 302 and 305A). Three

---

[179] *WSAT* 3/10. 117 n. 1.
[180] *WSAT* 3/3. 405 n. 1 and 3/10. 415 n. 1.
[181] *WSAT* 3/2. 236 n. 1.
[182] *WSAT* 3/3. 395 n. 1.
[183] *WSAT* 3/5. 288 n. 1.
[184] *WSAT* 3/3. 137 n. 1.
[185] There is a dispute as to whether *Sermons* 56 and 58 are Lenten or Easter sermons. Cf. Hill, *WSAT* 3/3. 106 n. 1. For the placing of *Sermons* 236 and 239 on the Tuesday of Easter week, cf. Hill, *WSAT* 3/7. 46 n. 1 and 3/7. 63 n. 1. For the delivery of *Sermon* 352 on the Saturday before the 2nd Sunday of Lent, cf. *WSAT* 3/10. 149 n. 1.

more were delivered in winter (*Sermon* 18 on a weekday, *Sermon* 53 on 21 January, and 114B = Dolbeau 5).[186]

4. Sixteen sermons in which the promotion of almsgiving features in conclusion to a text otherwise on different topics (*Sermons* 9, 47, 66, 91, 95, 99, 102, 114, 122, 123, 125A, 142, 261, 337, 357, and 376A). Nine cannot be dated to a given time or season of the year. Two were apparently delivered in winter (95, 125A).[187] One was delivered at Easter (376A), one on the Ascension (261), one on Wednesday 17 May, an ember day associated with fasting close to Pentecost.[188] Augustine is thought to have delivered *Sermon* 114 in the period from April to July.[189] Another was preached at the dedication of a church (337), whose building was a good work that led the preacher to recall other good works.

5. Thirty-two sermons in which almsgiving features, though only briefly and in passing (*Sermons* 15, 15A, 16A, 16B, 21, 22, 38, 45, 62, 72, 83, 87, 88, 90, 113A, 163B, 174, 204A, 229Z,[190] 296, 299A, 299D, 311, 313C, 313E, 346, 346A, 350A, 355, 359B = Dolbeau 2, 360B = Dolbeau 25, and 362). Only nine cannot be located at all in the church or calendar year. Two (296, 299A) were preached on the feast of Peter and Paul, 29 June. Two others date to May–June (15 and 360B = Dolbeau 25).[191] Three (*Sermons* 311, 313C, 313E) were preached on the feast of St Cyprian, 14 September. A further three (15A, 113A, 163B) were apparently preached in September, two on weekdays and *Sermon* 113A on a Sunday.[192] Four were preached during the winter (83, 204A, which is a sermon for Epiphany, 346A, 359B = Dolbeau 2, a sermon for St Vincent, and 362). One was probably preached at Easter (229Z). *Sermon* 45 is thought to be a Lenten homily.[193]

[186] *WSAT* 3/2. 86 n. 1, 3/3. 75 n. 1, 3/11. 115 n. 1.

[187] *WSAT* 3/4. 269 n. 9.

[188] *WSAT* 3/10. 189 n. 1.

[189] *WSAT* 3/4. 191 n. 1.

[190] C. Lambot, 'Une série pascale de sermons de saint Augustin sur les jours de la création', *RB* 79 (1969), 212 and 214. This is a fragment thought by some scholars to be from sermon 229V, but stated by Edmund Hill as belonging in greater likelihood to a separate sermon (Hill, *WSAT* 3/6. 341 n. 1).

[191] *WSAT* 3/1. 329 n. 1 and 3/11. 384 n. 1.

[192] *WSAT* 3/4. 182 n. 1 and 3/5. 186 n. 1.

[193] *WSAT* 3/2. 260 n. 1.

What may be gleaned from this information? First, the high level of promotion, present to a greater or lesser degree in one fifth of the sermons, makes the theme at least as prominent as, and arguably more prominent than, Augustine's promotion of asceticism in sermons and certainly more prominent than promotion of virginity and monastic life. Second, this promotion was a conventional feature of his winter and Lenten preaching, though not found in every winter or Lenten sermon, and a feature of sermons which he preached at designated times of fasting, such as the ember days around Pentecost. Such winter and Lenten exhortation to give alms coincided with a time of likely food shortages and high prices before the new harvest brought cheaper supplies onto the market.[194] Third, promotion reached the *competentes* and neophytes during Lent and Easter. Fourth, it was not limited at other times of the year to the faithful who attended regularly on weekdays.

## The Greek East: John Chrysostom

The circumstances in which the 900 extant sermons attributed to Chrysostom were delivered, the date and location of their delivery, and whether they were preached by John as a presbyter at Antioch or as bishop at Constantinople are rarely established with precision.[195] The *Homilies on Matthew's Gospel* were delivered at Antioch, for example, though little else is known of their place in the liturgical year. It has traditionally been thought that the *Homilies on John's Gospel* were delivered in the same city, but to a different audience, or on a different type of occasion, in part because they contain less moral teaching than the first series. Even where the occasion and setting are known, it remains uncertain to what extent the written texts reflect the spoken address. It has been decided here to select different groups within the corpus to facilitate comparison between different types of preaching: homilies on the Gospels and other New Testament texts; sermons on contemporary affairs; and catechetical sermons.

---

[194] P. Garnsey, *Famine and Food Supply in the Graeco-Roman World* (Cambridge, 1988), 24 and 54.

[195] For examples of such disputes, cf. W. Mayer, 'John Chrysostom: Extraordinary Preacher, Ordinary Audience', in Cunningham and Allen, *Preacher and Audience*, 108 n. 8.

**On the statues**

Shortly prior to Lent 387 Chrysostom commenced a series of sermons at Antioch, ending at Easter, in which he commented on the
aftermath of riots that had disturbed the city, when the imperial
statues had been toppled and dishonoured. Twenty-two extant
sermons are now held to belong to this series: twenty-one are
traditionally referred to as the *Homilies on the Statues*, and to these
should be added, according to Frans Van de Paverd, the sermon *Ad
illuminandos catechesis* 2.[196] For this reason it is included here as no.
22 and not with the catechetical sermons. Van de Paverd has drawn
up a revised table showing the likely day on which each sermon was
given. According to this table, three were preached before Lent
(*Sermons* 1–3), eighteen were delivered during Lent (in order of
delivery *Sermons* 5–8, 15, 16, 9–14, 17, 18, 20, 19, and 22). Most
were preached on weekday afternoons, but four or five were preached
on a Sunday (*Sermons* 1, 3, 18, 21, which was given on Easter Day,
and possibly *Sermon* 16).[197] One-third, eight, contain promotion of
almsgiving: two in which almsgiving is an important topic among
others (*Homilies* 1, 2); and six in which it is briefly promoted
(*Homilies* 3, 15, 16, 17, 20, 22). Of the eight, Van de Paverd assigns
six to a Saturday or Sunday, days when the Eucharist was celebrated,
the fast interrupted, and one sermon was delivered.[198] We have
already seen that attendance was probably higher on these days
than on weekdays. Elsewhere Chrysostom recounted how he had
often begun addresses on almsgiving 'on those days when we all
fasted' only to be interrupted by the onset of evening and this appears
to confirm the importance of Lenten preaching in promoting
generosity to the poor.[199] But other evidence is harder to interpret
as will be seen below.

**The catechetical sermons**

Twelve texts by Chrysostom have at various stages been
entitled catechetical sermons or baptismal instructions.[200] One,

---

[196] Van de Paverd, *St John Chrysostom*, 12 and 227–30.

[197] Ibid. 363–4.

[198] Ibid. 185 and 194.

[199] Chrysostom, *On Elijah and the Widow* 1, PG 51. 337.

[200] P. W. Harkins, *St John Chrysostom, Baptismal Instructions* (London, 1963),
8–15.

*Ad illuminandos catechesis* 2, has already been discussed. Of the remaining eleven examined here (and using Harkins's-titles), *Instructions* 1, 2, 9, 10, and 11 were given to the catechumens in Lent, the last on Maundy Thursday. *Instructions* 3 to 8 were delivered to the newly baptized in the days immediately after Easter. *Instruction* 3 was delivered on Easter morning. *Instruction* 8 is thought to have been delivered on the Saturday after Easter in 391.[201] Only two of the eleven contain unambiguous promotion: *Instruction* 7, where almsgiving is one important theme among others, and *Instruction* 1, where it is promoted in passing. The proportion of sermons promoting almsgiving seems low in comparison with the sermons *On the statues*. The present series, however, comprises incomplete groups of sermons which do not come from the same year. *Instructions* 1–8 were all given in the same year, but not the same year as *Instructions* 9–11.[202] Second, only *Instructions* 1 and 2 in the first group were delivered in Lent, while 3–8 came in Easter week. The absence of homilies in category 4, both in this series and the series on the statues, also seems unusual given other results. This is explained in part by Chrysostom's decision in more than one series to use the closing part of the sermons, usually devoted to moral exhortation, for a campaign against swearing oaths.

### Homilies on Matthew's Gospel
Of the ninety homilies in this series, over half, at least forty-eight, and perhaps as many as fifty-one, may be said to promote almsgiving: one (*Homily* 63) is a homily on poverty and wealth; almsgiving features as one important topic among others in nineteen (*Homilies* 15, 19, 20, 21, 31, 35, 48, 50, 52, 64, 66, 71, 77, 78, 79, 80, 85, 88, 89); there are ten homilies in which almsgiving is promoted in conclusion to a sermon on another topic (*Homilies* 4, 5, 33, 39, 41, 45, 46, 54, 74, 83); and some twenty-one in which almsgiving is briefly promoted (*Homilies* 3, 7, 8, 16*, 18, 22*, 23, 26, 27, 30, 37, 40*, 47, 49, 51, 57, 61, 65, 68, 72, 73).[203]

---

[201] Van de Paverd, *St John Chrysostom*, 290–1.        [202] Ibid.

[203] An asterisk indicates reference to almsgiving that may or may not amount to promotion depending on the criteria used.

That none of these sermons is devoted primarily to promotion of almsgiving and only one (*Homily* 63) may be described as essentially a homily on poverty and wealth, in which almsgiving features as the right use of wealth, is not surprising in a series which explicates the Gospel. What stands out is, first, the high number of homilies in which almsgiving is an important theme among others and, second, the large number of homilies in category 4, those which end with a call to almsgiving among other good works. The number of homilies which in fact end on this note is higher, since at least four (*Homilies* 48, 50, 52, 85) contain a sufficiently extensive degree of promotion for them to appear in category 3. The call to give alms is placed where it is given additional emphasis and is more likely to be remembered. This analysis may be compared with Chrysostomus Baur's assessment that in 'the ninety sermons on the Gospel of St Matthew, Chrysostom spoke forty times on almsgiving alone; he spoke some thirteen times on poverty, more than thirty times on avarice, and about twenty times against wrongly acquired and wrongly used wealth'.[204] Baur's categories slightly under-represent the promotion of almsgiving, but he also reveals the wider and supporting context for this promotion.

## Homilies on 1 Corinthians

Of the forty-four homilies in this series, generally thought to have been delivered at Antioch, just under half, twenty, include promotion: one (*Homily* 43) is essentially devoted to almsgiving; it is a major topic in eight (*Homilies* 10, 11, 13, 21, 27, 28, 30, 32); promotion of almsgiving among other good works forms the conclusion to two of these (13, 30) and talk of almsgiving ends a sermon on other topics in five others (*Homilies* 15, 20, 25, 35, 36); it is briefly promoted in a further six (*Homilies* 3, 9, 23, 39, 41, 44). The preacher consciously adapted St Paul's own practice, as Chrysostom described it in *Homily on 1 Corinthians* 43: it was when Paul had finished 'talking about doctrine' that he 'entered into issues more to do with morals' (εἰς τὸν ἠθικώτερον ἐμβαίνειν). St Paul at the end of 1 *Corinthians* 'sets everything else aside and proceeds straight to the most important good to be achieved, a discussion of alms'. But the apostle's normal practice, Chrysostom continues, was to conclude

---

[204] C. Bauer, *John Chrysostom and His Time* (London, 1959), i. 217.

the Epistles with a more general moral exhortation to almsgiving, self-control, gentleness, and patience.[205]

### Homilies on 2 Corinthians

Of the thirty homilies in this series ten, one-third, contain some promotion of almsgiving. It forms an important topic among others in five (*Homilies* 13, 16, 17, 19, 20), appears in the conclusion of a further two (*Homilies* 4, 30), and is briefly promoted in three (*Homilies* 1*, 12, 23).[206]

### Homilies on Philippians

It was long thought that all fifteen homilies in this series were delivered at Constantinople in 399, but Pauline Allen and Wendy Mayer have argued that two at least, sermons 1 and 9, were probably delivered in Antioch.[207] Almost two-thirds, nine, contain promotion of almsgiving: it is an important topic among others in three (*Homilies* 2, 6, 15), concludes a sermon in a further two (*Homilies* 1, 3), and is briefly promoted in four (*Homilies* 4, 8, 10, 12).

### Homilies on Hebrews

Of the thirty-four homilies in this series, just under half, fourteen, contain promotion of almsgiving: in three it counts as a major topic (*Homilies* 9, 11, 32); in seven it appears in the final section of moral exhortation (*Homilies* 1, 10, 13, 18, 24, 25, 31); it makes a brief appearance in a further four (*Homilies* 3, 28, 33, 34).

In addition to the exhortation to almsgiving contained within these different series of homilies, we must add at least two separate sermons of type 1 by Chrysostom: the *Sermon on Almsgiving* (PG 51. 261–72) and *On the Ten Virgins and Almsgiving* (PG 49. 291–300).[208] The evidence from Chrysostom's sermons broadly confirms the

---

[205] Chrysostom, *Homily on 1 Corinthians* 43. 1, PG 61. 367.

[206] An asterisk indicates reference to almsgiving that may or may not amount to promotion depending on the criteria used.

[207] P. Allen and W. Mayer, 'Chrysostom and the Preaching of Homilies in Series: A Re-examination of the Fifteen Homilies *In Epistulam ad Philippenses* (CPG 4432)', *VC* 49 (1995), 270–89.

[208] For confirmation of Chrysostom's authorship, cf. M. Aubineau, 'Un extrait retrouvé, chez Cosmas Indicopleustès, d'un *Discours sur l'aumône* de Jean Chrysostome (PL 49, 293)', *Bulletin de littérature ecclésiastique*, 80 (1979), 216.

picture of frequent promotion, often at times of high church attendance, offered by Augustine's sermons. It may be objected, however, that the two selected preachers, whose large corpora reduce, but cannot eliminate, the distortions caused by haphazard survival or loss, are nonetheless exceptional in their regard for the very poor. Chrysostom, it may be argued, is too well known for his insistent preaching on this matter to be taken as representative. It is necessary to answer these objections by study of further groups of sermons.

## Italy: Chromatius, Peter Chrysologus, and Leo

Some forty-one extant sermons or fragments from sermons are now attributed to Chromatius, the bishop of Aquileia from 387 to either 407 or 408.[209] Though many are truncated or have major lacunae (*Sermons* 8, 26, and 27) and others little more than short fragments (*Sermons* 7, 13, 18A, 20, 29, 34, 35, 36, 37, 38, and 39), promotion of almsgiving is found in a quarter, ten, as follows: two in which it is one important topic among others (*Sermons* 3, 23); four in which it concludes the piece (*Sermons* 1, 5, 11, 31); and four where promotion is very brief (*Sermons* 12, 24, 28, 35). According to the editors, R. Étaix and J. Lemarié, at least four sermons are likely to have been delivered during Lent (*Sermons* 11, 23, 24, 35); three were probably delivered in Eastertide (*Sermons* 1, 3, 31).

Of seven Lenten sermons by Peter Chrysologus, the bishop of Ravenna by 431, four promote almsgiving: two are devoted to almsgiving (*Sermons* 8, 9), and promotion comes as the conclusion to a further two (*Sermons* 7, 13).

Of the ninety-six extant sermons by Leo, bishop of Rome from 440 to 461, Claude Lepelley has found that forty are in large part given over to exhortations aimed at furthering almsgiving.[210] Eight of these were preached during the December fast, thirteen were Lenten homilies, four were preached at Pentecost, nine during the September fast, and six during the collections discussed in the previous chapter.

---

[209] R. Étaix and J. Lemarié (eds.), *Chromatii Aquileiensis Opera*, CCSL 9A (Turnhout, 1974), 3–180.

[210] C. Lepelley, 'Saint Léon le Grand et la cité romaine', *Revue des sciences religieuses*, 35 (1961), 134.

The evidence from these three Italian churches strongly confirms the importance of exhortation to almsgiving in Lent (often a time of scarcity) and in other penitential seasons. It also confirms the exposure of the *competentes* to this teaching as a core element in Christian conduct.

### Egypt: The Festal Letters *of Athanasius and Cyril of Alexandria*

The *Festal Letters* of Athanasius and Cyril of Alexandria have a particular value as works designed to open Lent with a summary account of its Christian import. Of the thirteen *Festal Letters* by Athanasius which have been preserved in their entirety, four exhort almsgiving in some way, whether explicitly, by calling for the distribution of alms to the poor, or implicitly by urging the people to be mindful of the poor.[211] Scholars have noted that exhortation to almsgiving is almost as frequent in them as the call to fasting.[212] Finally, the twenty-nine *Festal Letters* of Cyril delivered between 414 and 442 provide conclusive evidence that promotion of almsgiving was a major, conventional element of Lenten preaching.[213] All but one (*Sermon* 9) contain promotion of almsgiving expressed in terms of pity for and patronage of the poor, in particular the widows and orphans. In the great majority this exhortation features briefly, but decisively, in the sermon's closing section. Three (*Sermons* 11, 19, and 27) contain more extensive promotion.[214]

## Individual sermons by various authors

### *Sermons essentially devoted to the promotion of almsgiving*

Even a cursory survey of the extant works from the period reveals numerous other sermons, apart from those already listed above,

---

[211] Athanasius, *Festal Letters* 1, 4, 13, and 14, PG 26. 1366B, 1378B, 1418C, and 1422A.

[212] Brakke, *Athanasius*, 189.

[213] G. Munch-Labacher, 'Cyril of Alexandria', in Döpp and Geerlings, *Dictionary*, 155.

[214] Cyril of Alexandria, *Festal Letters*, PG 77. 401–982, and i–xvii, ed. W. H. Burns, *Cyrille d'Alexandre, Lettres Festales*, SC 372, 392, 434, 3 vols. (Paris, 1991–8).

which belong to category 1. They include two by Basil of Caesarea;[215] two by Gregory of Nyssa;[216] one by Gregory Nazianzen;[217] two by Gaudentius of Brescia;[218] one by Paulinus of Nola;[219] one by Peter Chrysologus;[220] one wrongly attributed in past centuries to Basil;[221] two likewise wrongly ascribed to Ambrose;[222] and some five wrongly ascribed to Chrysostom.[223] At least two more sermons have been constructed from other extant sermons.[224] These prefabricated sermons may well date to outside the period under examination, but show the continuing impact of older sermons from the period on clerical preaching and, where a sermon on almsgiving has been composed of extracts from sermons not originally dedicated to that purpose, show the later demand for dedicated sermons. There is also

---

[215] *I Shall Knock Down My Barns* (PG 31. 261–77), Courtonne, *Homélies*, 15–37, and *In Time of Hunger* (PG 31. 304–28).

[216] *De pauperibus amandis* 1 (*On Benefaction*) and *De pauperibus amandis* 2 (*On Matthew* 25: 40), GNO 9. 93–108 and 111–27.

[217] *On the Love We Owe the Poor* (Or. 14, PG 35. 857–909). Gregory explicitly opens the oration as being on this subject (τὸν περὶ φιλοπτωχίας λόγον). Almsgiving is revealed as the primary expression of this love in exhortation to hear the oration 'generously' (φιλοτίμως) 'so as to inherit the wealth of heaven' (ἵνα βασιλείαν πλουτήσητε), an apparent allusion to Matthew 6: 19–20: PG 35. 860A.

[218] Gaudentius, *Sermons* 13 and 18, CSEL 68. 114–24 and 151–63. *Sermon* 13 is a Christmas sermon. *Sermon* 18 is in letter format.

[219] *De gazophylacio* (*On the Almschest*), preserved as Paulinus, *Ep.* 33, CSEL 29. 303–12.

[220] Peter Chrysologus, *Sermon* 14, in A. Olivar, *Sancti Petri Chrysologi Collectio Sermonum*, CCSL 24 (Turnhout, 1975), 88–92.

[221] Pseudo-Basil, *On Mercy and Judgement* (PG 31. 1705–13).

[222] Pseudo-Ambrose, *Sermon on Luke* 12: 33 (Sermo 1 ex cod. sessoriano, PL 18. 109D–118B) and *Sermon Against Those Who Say that Possessions are Not to be Dispersed, But Their Fruits Used for Almsgiving* (Sermo 2 ex cod. sessoriano, PL 18. 119A–122A).

[223] *On the Ten Virgins and on Almsgiving* (PG 59. 527–32); *On Matthew* 6: 1–4 (PG 59. 571–4); *On Almsgiving* (PG 60. 707–12); *On Almsgiving* (PG 60. 747–52); and *On Almsgiving* (PG 62. 769–70). For the first two sermons a possible ascription to Severianus of Gabala has been suggested, though Zellinger and Montfaucon have denied the plausibility of the first. Cf. J. A. de Aldama, *Repertorium Pseudochrysostomicum* (Paris 1965), no. 341, p. 125; no. 307, p. 113; no. 296, p. 110; no. 380, p. 138; and no. 539, p. 201.

[224] *On Almsgiving* (PG 64. 433–44), created by stitching together fragments from the sermon *On Almsgiving* (PG 62. 769–70) already listed and *Sermon* 21 (PG 86. 424–52) falsely ascribed to Eusebius of Alexandria; *On Fasting and Almsgiving*, constructed from sermons of Chrysostom and clearly later than these. Despite its title it is wholly devoted to promoting almsgiving. Cf. de Aldama, *Repertorium*, no. 247, p. 90, and no. 217, p. 80.

an unedited manuscript sermon in Greek, *On Love of the Poor* (CPG 3983), ascribed in the tradition to Ephraem, but whose actual author is unknown.

## Sermons on wealth, fasting, and almsgiving

There are several sermons in which almsgiving features as a major theme in the context of a wider treatment of wealth (category 2). These include a sermon *On Wealth* by Peter of Alexandria; *On the Wealthy* by Basil;[225] two wrongly ascribed to Chrysostom;[226] and one *Diatribe on Wealth and Poverty.*[227] Others not wholly devoted to promoting almsgiving, nonetheless link promotion closely with other penitential acts. These include one wrongly ascribed to Ambrose and two to Chrysostom.[228] In this section may also belong the sermons, *On Fasting and Almsgiving* (CPG 4925) and *On Virginity and Almsgiving* (CPG 4985), and *On the Transfiguration and Almsgiving* (CPG 5009).[229] The last homily has been stitched together from extracts taken from genuine works by Chrysostom: *Homilies on John's Gospel* 39 and 23 and *Homily on Romans* 11.

These lists are obviously incomplete, but they demonstrate the wide extent of promotion in sermons, which is not restricted to a few figures at a limited time of year. It is not practical to attempt even a partial list of extant sermons in the remaining categories 3–5, although examples of these can be pointed out: the sermon *On the Blind Man Healed by Christ and on Zacchaeus* (PG 59. 599–610) would fall in category 3. It has been ascribed by some to Severianus, and is thought to have been delivered between Easter and

---

[225] Courtonne, *Homélies sur la richesse*, 40–71.

[226] *On Psalm 38. 7 and on Almsgiving* (PG 55. 559–64), to be dated later than Chrysostom, on whom it is dependent, and *On Riches and Poverty* (PG 63. 637–46), constructed from other sermons. Cf. Aldama, *Repertorium*, no. 444, p. 166, and no. 340, p. 125.

[227] CPG 4969. Cf. Uthemann, 'Eine christliche Diatribe', 235–90.

[228] Pseudo-Ambrose, *On Fasting and Almsgiving* (Sermo 40, PL 17. 682B–684B); Pseudo-Chrysostom, *On Penitence and Almsgiving* (PG 60. 699–706) and *On Almsgiving and Hospitality*. Cf. de Aldama, *Repertorium*, nos. 52 and 283, pp. 17 and 104–5.

[229] It has not been possible to examine these texts.

Pentecost.[230] Likewise, Zeno's *Tractatus de iustitia*, the outline for a longer sermon, belongs in this category.[231]

## An alternative method of assessment

Empirical analysis alone cannot prove that the promotion in the extant sermons detailed above is typical of the period. An alternative, literary, method of assessment both confirms the generally high level of exhortation to almsgiving in preaching and suggests the predominant appeal in that promotion to redemptive almsgiving. For promotion appears in late antique descriptions of preaching intended by the authors to be exemplary in different ways of that preaching. When Gregory of Nyssa recounted the skill of Gregory the Wonderworker in preaching the right message to each social group, he stated that Gregory taught the rich man not to consider himself the sovereign owner of his possessions, but only their administrator or distributor (οἰκονόμος).[232] Whether or not the third-century missionary actually preached in this way is uncertain, but the fourth-century panegyrist has him conform to current expectations that a preacher should address himself to the wealthy on the subject of their riches and to expectations of what that address should consist in.

The *Life of Antony* contains a lengthy discourse during which Antony briefly extols the value of the almsgiving practised by ascetics. At the end of the passage the reader is presented with a description of the monastic community inspired by his words to such charity.[233] The idealized picture of preaching by the holy man and the reception of this preaching is valuable for what the ideal says about popular expectation, which in turn suggests some kind of standard. This does not mean that Antony delivered this discourse as it stands, nor should we simply read the level of practice from the ensuing description, but it does mean that the gap which Veyne identified

---

[230] Aldama, *Repertorium*, no. 423, p. 155.

[231] Zeno, *De iustitia*, ed. B. Löfstedt, *Zenonis Veronensis Tratatus*, CCSL 22 (Turnhout, 1971), 145–50.

[232] Gregory of Nyssa, *Life of Gregory Thaumaturgus*, ed. G. Heil, GNO 10/1. 27, PG 46. 924A.

[233] Athanasius, *Life of Antony* 30. 2 and 44. 2, SC 400. 218 and 254.

between the profession of an ethic and its practice (see Chapter 1), was a gap which some believed could be bridged in ascetic withdrawal and monastic life. They sought to narrow the gap more generally among the faithful by promoting these models of perfection both in literature and in life.

A third example is offered by the *Life of Thecla*, which includes a supposed address or sermon by St Paul, based on Matthew 5: 7–12 and 1 Corinthians 7, in which he presents the Christian vision of the moral life. In this summary he advocates chastity and other virtues, but also insists on God's blessing for 'those who think to meet the needs of beggars and people in want, and who are seeking the same mercy from Almighty God'.[234] The final phrase shows both how almsgiving is typically understood as an expression of mercy on the part of those who give and as a way to win mercy as a sinner from God. It also echoes the way in which promoters of almsgiving cite or allude to Matthew 5: 7 in the extant corpus. Later in the text Thecla replays Paul's summary of the Christian Gospel to the apostle. She tells Paul of how 'I have learnt from you the value of prayer, fasting, and almsgiving'.[235] The traditional collocation of fasting, prayer, and almsgiving highlights a predominant, penitential, meaning of almsgiving.[236] These fictional texts suggest the place of almsgiving in the standard account of Christian life and confirm the centrality of promoting almsgiving as a core component of preaching.

## Direct and indirect promotion: rhetorical strategies in extant sermons

Sermons, not surprisingly, were the works in which explicit exhortation to almsgiving was most often found, and this explicit exhortation took many forms, both *with* quotation of clearly

---

[234] *Life of Thecla* 2, in Dagron, *Vie et miracles*, 178.

[235] *Life of Thecla* 26, in Dagron, *Vie et miracles*, 272.

[236] A.-M. La Bonnardière commented on the triad of prayer–fasting–alms in six sermons by Augustine for the opening of Lent in her article 'Pénitence et réconciliation des pénitents, d'après saint Augustin—I', *Revue des études augustiniennes*, 13 (1967), 46 n. 48.

supporting biblical verses[237] and *without* such quotation.[238] It was often couched in scriptural language, or alluded to scripture, relying on an accepted interpretation of certain passages: Chrysostom's call to 'buy oil' at the close of one sermon is an exhortation to almsgiving dependent on a particular reading of the parable of the foolish virgins.[239] The faithful were exhorted in circumlocutions or technical terms to 'works of mercy' (*opera misericordiae* or *opera iustitiae*), where these were understood to consist in, or include, almsgiving.[240] They were exhorted to 'good works' specified as almsgiving.[241] There was much exhortation to unspecified 'good works', but this has not been included here as promotion of almsgiving.

Deliberate promotion commonly took the form of favourable presentation and praise of almsgivers in the scriptures or those in the Bible who practised hospitality, figures such as Abraham, Job, the widow of Zarephath, Zacchaeus, Cornelius, and (less frequently) Tabitha;[242] the inclusion of almsgiving among the traits of the good or just individual;[243] inclusion of almsgiving and care of the poor among the virtues characteristic of monks;[244] stories in which almsgiving highlights the sanctity of the protagonist or his conversion;[245] the assertion that almsgiving ensured that prayers would be answered swiftly by giving them wings;[246] and the portrayal of heaven as a place where, unlike here, almsgiving is no longer needed.[247] To this may be

---

[237] Augustine, *Serm.* 198. 3, PL 38. 1025; *Serm.* 389. 6, ed. C. Lambot, *RB* (1948), 51–2.

[238] *Serm.* 208, PL 38. 1044–6; Chrysostom, *Homilies on Hebrews* 24. 3, PG 63. 236.

[239] Chrysostom, *Homilies on Matthew* 20. 6, PG 57. 294.

[240] Chromatius, *Sermons* 24. 3, 28. 2, and 35. 2, in Étaix and Lemarié, *Chromatii Opera*, 110, 130, and 159.

[241] Augustine, *Serm.* Dolbeau 16, in Dolbeau, *Vingt-Six Sermons*, 128.

[242] Augustine, *Serm.* Dolbeau 26. 20, in Dolbeau, *Vingt-Six Sermons*, 382–3; Chrysostom, *Homilies on Matthew* 83. 4, PG 58. 750; *Homilies on 1 Corinthians* 34. 6–7, PG 61. 295–6; *Homilies on 2 Corinthians* 19. 4, PG 61. 534.

[243] Augustine, *Serm.* 15. 9, CCSL 41. 200; Chrysostom, *Homilies on Matthew* 8. 4–5, PG 57. 87–8; *Homilies on Matthew* 23. 11, PG 57. 319.

[244] Chrysostom, *Homilies on Matthew* 68. 3, PG 58. 644 and 72. 4, PG 58. 671.

[245] Augustine, *Serm.* 178. 8, PL 38. 964; Chrysostom, *Homilies on Matthew* 30. 2, PG 57. 364 (Zacchaeus).

[246] Chrysostom, *Homilies on Matthew* 77. 6, PG 58. 710.

[247] Augustine, *Serm.* 299D. 7 = Denis 16 in Morin, *Sermones* 1. 80; *Serm.* 305A. 8 = Denis 13, Morin, *Sermones*, 1. 63; *Serm.* 358A. 2 = Morin 5, in Morin, *Sermones*, 1. 607; *Serm.* 362. 28, PL 39. 1631.

added the explicit condemnation of those who fail to give alms, both biblical figures such as Dives and others.[248] Condemnation, too, might be couched in the language of scripture, or allude to scripture, with a corresponding dependence on accepted readings: Chrysostom reproached his congregation for being unmoved at the sight of Christ as a naked stranger, for giving him at most a morsel of bread, a reference to almsgiving dependent on an accepted reading of Matthew 25: 35–42.[249] More rarely, Augustine promoted almsgiving indirectly and allusively, as when, on the feast of the Epiphany, he presented the Magi as urging and encouraging his congregation to imitate them by bringing gifts for the poor Christ.[250]

Preachers sometimes sought to promote almsgiving in a particular spirit (the examples are taken mainly from Chrysostom's homilies). The virtue in almsgiving depends on the intention involved: 'what is required, then, is not the mere giving of alms, but giving them as one should and to give them for this reason'.[251] It may be the reminder that almsgiving has a virtue only if given in a spirit of humility.[252] It should be practised only after reconciliation with one's enemies.[253] It is vitiated by a desire for earthly glory and contempt for the beneficiary.[254] It is worthless unless given in a spirit of charity.[255] This material is not concerned with the direct promotion of *greater* almsgiving. But repeated concern over the right kind of practice reinforces the centrality of the practice. Other forms of promotion were concerned to determine the *scope* of almsgiving, so that Chrysostom exhorted a congregation at Constantinople not to limit

---

[248] *Serm.* 178. 3, PL 38. 962; Chrysostom, *Homilies on Matthew* 27. 4, PG 57. 350 and 77. 4–5, PG 58. 707; *Homilies on 1 Corinthians* 34. 7, PG 61. 295; *Homilies on Philippians* 12. 3, PG 62. 274.

[249] *Homilies on Matthew* 7. 5, PG 57. 79.

[250] Augustine, *Serm.* 204A. 1, ed. R. Étaix, *RB* 98 (1988), 12. Cf. Hill, *WSAT* 3/6. 102 n. 3.

[251] Chrysostom, *Homilies on Matthew* 19. 1, PG 57. 275.

[252] *Homilies on Matthew* 15. 2, PG 57. 224–5.

[253] *Homilies on Matthew* 16. 9, PG 57. 251.

[254] *Homilies on 2 Corinthians* 13. 3–4, PG 61. 495; *Homilies on Matthew* 20. 4, PG 57. 291–2. In this second example, however, the preacher shows how God uses the very desires which lead people to sin in this way to draw them back to virtue. They can hope to win lasting glory in heaven.

[255] *Homilies on 1 Corinthians* 25. 4, PG 61. 212.

almsgiving to monks and ascetics, or the *manner* of almsgiving, to give in person and not through intermediaries.[256]

There was much other indirect promotion while pursuing various rhetorical objectives. Almsgiving might be used to describe other types of good work, such as forgiveness of injury.[257] Chrysostom presented God's gift of good things to those who do not seek them in the first instance, but who set their sights on the kingdom, as analogous to the way in which God rewards almsgiving with a glory in heaven which the giver must not seek on earth.[258] The assertion that Job's almsgiving had less merit than his continuing trust in God's providence at the loss of all his goods may be thought to valorize almsgiving even though faith is given greater value in contrast.[259] The condemnation of a man who thinks nothing of the envy which consumes him, but considers himself to be right before God on account of his fasting and limited almsgiving counts as a minor form of promotion to the extent that it keeps the topic before the congregation as a conventional element in the Christian life.[260]

Chrysostom recognized the value of indirect promotion. His *Homily on 2 Corinthians* 16 explained how St Paul avoids direct and immediate exhortation to give alms, but 'says this first, not what he wants, but something else instead, to reach the topic by a different route, so as not to reveal his true intention'.[261] He noted how Paul praises what had already been achieved to prepare the ground for exhortation and how the apostle sought to provoke 'emulation' in describing the almsgiving already demonstrated in the Macedonian churches. In the following homily he observed how Paul humours the Corinthians and avoids giving offence.[262] Elsewhere, he distinguished between the three different types of good example or persuasion in almsgiving to which St Paul appeals in the letter: the example of other Christians, the earlier example of the Corinthians themselves, and the example of Christ himself

---

[256] *Homilies on Hebrews* 10. 4, PG 63. 89.
[257] Augustine, *Serm.* 259. 4, PL 38. 1199.
[258] Chrysostom, *Homilies on Matthew* 22. 3, PG 57. 303.
[259] *Homilies on 2 Corinthians* 1. 6, PG 61. 389.
[260] *Homilies on Matthew* 40. 3, PG 57. 443.
[261] *Homilies on 2 Corinthians* 16. 2, PG 61. 513.
[262] *Homilies on 2 Corinthians* 17. 1, PG 61. 517.

in making himself poor to enrich others by his incarnation.[263] Examples promote good practice 'because man is an emulous creature'.[264] The preacher observed that the apostle advances both spiritual and temporal considerations in exhortation.[265] He noted the importance of Paul's metaphor of 'seed' in suggesting the great reward which almsgiving brought for a small or modest outlay.[266] We should expect a similar artfulness in Chrysostom's preaching and more widely among his contemporaries.

The most important element in the promotion by preachers was obviously the use and interpretation of biblical texts, which as God's word carried an irrefutable authority. Promoters had frequent recourse to favourable biblical texts, though each promoter did not necessarily use the same texts, or did not use particular texts as frequently as others, or did not use them in the same combination as others did. Augustine and many others made frequent appeal to Isaiah 58: 7 ('Break your bread to the hungry... clothe the naked'). Basil, by contrast, appears rarely to have cited this verse in his promotion of almsgiving.[267] Gregory Nazianzen's appeal to Ecclesiastes 11: 2 in his sermon *On the Love we Owe the Poor* is rarely found elsewhere.[268]

Almsgiving, unlike certain forms of asceticism, in particular the exaltation of virginity for women as a higher state than marriage, did not run contrary to particular biblical passages, but there were, nonetheless, problematic passages to be explained through close reading and what Elizabeth Clark has termed 'talking back', the use

---

[263] *Homilies on 2 Corinthians* 19. 1, PG 61. 529. The three forms of persuasion are introduced in the printed text by the phrase, Εἶδες σύνεσιν προαιρέσεως. Migne, however, notes a possible emendation to read παραινέσεως for the final word.

[264] Ibid.

[265] *Homilies on 2 Corinthians* 20. 1, PG 61. 535.

[266] Ibid.

[267] Augustine, *Serm.* 47. 25, CCSL 41. 599; *Serm.* 56. 11, ed. P. Verbraken, *RB* 68 (1958), 26–40, 33; *Serm.* 58. 10, ed. P. Verbraken, *Ecclesia Orans*, 1 (1984), 129–30; *Serm.* 62. 18, PL 38. 423; *Serm.* 217. 5 = Morin 3, in Morin, *Sermones*, 599; *Serm.* 299D. 7 = Denis 16, in Morin, *Sermones*, 80; *Serm.* 339. 6 = Frangipane 2, in Morin, *Sermones*, 196. The citation is sometimes adapted and worked into the surrounding text. cf. *Serm.* 15A. 5 = Denis 21, in Morin, *Sermones* 128; *Serm.* 93. 13, PL 38. 578; *Serm.* 104. 3 = Guelferb. 29, in Morin, *Sermones*, 545; *Serm.* 305A. 7 = Denis 13, in Morin, *Sermones*, 61–2. Basil, *I Shall Knock Down my Barns* 1, in Courtonne, *Homélies*, 17.

[268] Gregory Nazianzen, *On the Love we Owe the Poor*, PG 35. 885C.

of biblical citations to refute readings of other texts or to trump those texts.[269] Five passages in particular caused difficulty.

1. Matthew 26: 11. The insistence that in almsgiving one was giving to Christ in the person of the destitute, secured by Christ's words at Matthew 25: 40 ('whatever you do to the least of these you do to me'), had to be maintained despite his words at Matthew 26: 11 ('the poor you have always with you, but you do not always have me'). In the latter passage Jesus distinguished between himself and the poor to defend a woman who had spent on perfume for his feet money that might have been given in alms. Chrysostom's explanation as recalled by Isidore has already been mentioned. Elsewhere Chrysostom reminded his congregation first of Matthew 28: 20 ('I am with you always, even to the end of the world'), then of 'all the laws set down both in the Old and in the New Testament concerning almsgiving'. These he summed up by citing two verses from the New Testament (Luke 11: 41, Acts 10: 4) and one from both Old and New (Hosea 6: 6 and Matthew 9: 13). He further resolved the problem by reinterpreting Matthew 26: 11 as an incentive to almsgiving: we do not always have Christ with us when he is hungry, but only in this present life, for there will be no hunger in heaven for us to relieve.[270] Chromatius, on the other hand, resolved the problem by giving the anointing a number of symbolic meanings, one of which was that of virtuous almsgiving. The woman's hair represented her virtues, her perfume the 'works of mercy', by which he meant, above all, the gift of alms.[271]

2. 2 Thessalonians 3: 10. Almsgiving to those who had no gainful employment appeared contrary to St Paul's injunction that 'if any would not work, neither should he eat'. Chrysostom opposed to this the injunction a few verses later at 2 Thessalonians 3: 13 ('do not tire of doing what is right'), which he interpreted as a command to prompt almsgiving, and then sought to reconcile the apparent contradiction.[272] He differentiated between the audiences to which each verse was addressed, so that the first injunction was aimed at the

---

[269] E. A. Clark, *Reading Renunciation: Asceticism and Scripture in Early Christianity* (Princeton, 1999), 128–32.

[270] *Homilies on Matthew* 50. 4, PG 58. 510.

[271] Chromatius, *Sermon* 11. 5, in Étaix and Lemarié, *Chromatii Opera*, 51.

[272] Chrysostom, *Homilies on Matthew* 35. 4, PG 57. 409–10.

poor healthy enough to work, while the second was directed at potential benefactors.

3. 1 Corinthians 13: 3. St Paul's words, 'if I give all my goods to the feed the poor... but have not love, it is of no profit to me', were also problematic. Chrysostom asked how such total dispossession could fail to be loving. He set out different possible interpretations: either St Paul was imagining an impossible hypothetical for rhetorical effect or almsgiving was meant by God precisely to unite rich and poor through the bonds of fraternal charity and, therefore, had no virtue in the absence of that charity. But the preacher had then to reconcile what the apostle said here with Christ's assertion at Matthew 19: 21 that the rich young man should sell all his goods and give the proceeds to the poor in search of perfection. How could what was imperfect for Paul be advanced by Christ as a way to perfection? Chrysostom pointed out that the young man was not only told to give the proceeds to the poor: he had also to follow Christ and this was done in love of others.[273]

4. Luke 6: 30. A similar difficulty concerned the reconciliation of Christ's words at Luke 6: 30 ('Give to whoever asks from you') with the phrase cited by Augustine in his exposition of Psalm 103: 'Let your alms sweat in your hand until you find a just man to whom to give it'.[274] Augustine gives the impression that the second phrase came from the scriptures, but it is not to be identified with any known biblical passage or variant and rather resembles the advice in the *Didache* (1. 6), that Christians should let their alms or almsgiving make their hand sweat, until they know to whom they are giving, while it also echoes less closely a phrase exhorting almsgiving in the *Sibylline Oracles*.[275] It was clearly a saying of recognized authority within the churches. Augustine's strategy is to see the phrases as addressing different circumstances: the first dictates how the almsgiver should respond to requests made of him or her, whereas the second dictates how he is to seek out a recipient of unasked-for alms.

---

273 *Homilies on 1 Corinthians* 32. 5, PG 61. 271.
274 Augustine, *En. in Ps.* 103, s. 3. 10, CCSL 40. 1509.
275 S. L. Bridge, 'To Give or Not to Give? Deciphering the Saying of Didache 1. 6', *JECS* 5 (1997), 563 and 566.

5. Matthew 6: 1 and 6: 3–4. The difficulty caused by these verses was the apparent impossibility of fulfilling the command to practise almsgiving in secret: you might be seen putting the coins in the hands of the beggar, the clergy, or into the collection box. The strategy adopted by the unknown author of the *Sermon on Matthew* 6: 1–4, who articulated the fear that this might lead to a reduction in donations, was to allow the sense of 6: 2 with its reference to intention in almsgiving to interpret the surrounding verses in a non-literal sense, where, once again, it was the intention that was to count.[276]

The high number of biblical texts explicitly promoting almsgiving largely obviated the need for seeing almsgiving in biblical texts not obviously on this subject. Chromatius, however, was able to interpret the story of Cain and Abel so that the fat parts of Abel's offering stood for the 'works of mercy', thus given a sacrificial value.[277] Augustine in his extant corpus promotes almsgiving five times by appeal to Proverbs 22: 2 ('Rich and poor have met together and God makes rich and poor alike'). When Chrysostom explicated St Paul's comments in 1 Corinthians on the need for the rich to wait for the poor before celebrating a common Eucharist (1 Cor. 11: 33), he turned the verse into an intimation of the requirement on the part of the rich to give to the poor.[278] More widespread than this was the interpretation in favour of almsgiving of the distinction between the wise and foolish virgins of Matthew 25: 1–12. The oil possessed by the wise was the alms they had given. In Chrysostom's preaching this implied the greater value of almsgiving over virginity, a meaning certainly not intended by the original text.[279] Chrysostom made frequent appeal to the parable. Augustine, on the other hand, rarely or never alluded to the parable in this sense.

Alongside the appeal to biblical texts were other aids in promotion. Redescription of the poor (as brothers, as Christ himself) and the theological arguments for almsgiving are set out in Chapter 5. Here

---

[276] Ps.-Chrysostom, *On Matthew* 6: 1–4, PG 57. 572.

[277] Chromatius, *Sermon* 23. 2, in Étaix and Lemarié, *Chromatii Opera*, 105.

[278] Chrysostom, *Homilies on 1 Corinthians* 28. 2, PG 61. 234.

[279] *Homilies on Matthew* 47. 4, PG 58. 486, and 50. 4, PG 58. 510; cf. *Homilies on Matthew* 46. 4, PG 58. 481.

we may note first the importance of exciting compassion through graphic portrayal of the miseries of the poor, especially in winter. Chrysostom sought to stir up in this way the congregation at Constantinople: 'the temperature drops below freezing and the poor man lies prostrate on the pavement in his rags, all but dead from the cold, his teeth chattering. How he looks, how he is dressed, should exhort you.'[280] The same technique is found in a sermon ascribed to Chrysostom: 'the poor man enters your vestibule looking for alms, spends two hours there without receiving anything, and then you sometimes instruct your slave to throw him out'.[281]

Second, preachers responded to what they presented as the excuses and reasoning advanced by those who refused to give alms: the need to secure the well-being of one's children was answered by provision for their eternal happiness; the charge that beggars were fraudulent shirkers met with the response that no one would endure the humiliation of begging unless driven by necessity. Fear of impoverishment met with a reminder that wealth did not bring happiness and could not in any case be secured.

Third, preachers occasionally appealed to a Christian self-definition in which the faithful were called upon to give alms as an expression of their supposedly distinctive identity *vis-à-vis* their pagan neighbours: Augustine, in a sermon for New Year's Day thought to have been preached between 420 and 425, urged his congregation at Hippo Regius not to take part in the pagan festivities, but to maintain a distinctive identity through a different set of Christian practices: 'They give good luck presents; see to it that you give alms.'[282]

## An increasing promotion?

For Uhlhorn a sustained call to almsgiving was a feature of fourth-century churches after Constantine's conversion, one which indicated moral decline. He contrasted an idealized 'time of perfectly free gifts', when there was 'as yet no need of urgent exhortations to

---

[280] *Homilies on Hebrews* 11. 3, PG 63. 94.
[281] Ps.-Chrysostom, *On Almsgiving*, PG 60. 710.
[282] Augustine, *Serm.* 198. 2–3, PL 38. 1025. For the date, Hill, *WSAT* 3/6. 75 n. 1.

almsgiving', with the 'Post-Constantinian age', when preachers used 'every inducement to move their hearers to liberal alms'.[283] The dearth of sermons from before the mid-fourth century hampers an adequate assessment of the claim: no large corpus of sermons by any preacher from the early to mid-fourth century remains, and only one such corpus from the third century, that of Origen. But the apocryphal *Acts* offer limited indirect evidence for the view that promotion of almsgiving was a conventional feature of much earlier sermons. In chapter 35 of the *Acts of John*, thought to date from 'the second quarter of the second century',[284] the Apostle addresses the people of Ephesus to warn sinners of the doom awaiting them, including those who 'give nothing to the needy, although you have money put away'. He tells them how when they 'are burning in fire, begging for mercy' there will be no one to pity them.[285] Kurt Schäferdiek points out that this passage 'looks like a homiletic application of the pericope about the Rich Man and Lazarus' (Luke 16: 19–26).[286] The fictional account of an apostolic sermon reveals how the author interpreted the pericope and those Christian teachings likely to be conventional in contemporary sermons. Yves-Marie Duval has also drawn attention to how Pontius in his third-century *Life of Cyprian* presented that bishop as both acting at his baptism upon scriptural texts encouraging almsgiving and preaching on texts which the biographer had drawn from Cyprian's list of *testimonia* for almsgiving in the *Ad Quirinum* mentioned earlier. Thus, Duval has argued, Pontius indicates 'the place Scripture had held and would hold in Cyprian's conversion and apostolate'.[287] This allusive compliment suggests extensive preaching on almsgiving in Carthaginian church of that period. Given this evidence, the burden of proof should lie with those who argue for an increased level of promotion in the later empire.

---

[283] Uhlhorn, *Christian Charity*, 122–3.

[284] P. J. Lalleman, *The Acts of John* (Leuven, 1998), 270. Kurt Schäferdiek, on the other hand, argues for the 'first half of the third century', in Schneemelcher, *New Testament Apocrypha*, ii. 167.

[285] Schneemelcher, *New Testament Apocrypha*, ii. 178.

[286] Ibid. ii. 165.

[287] Y.-M. Duval, 'L'Écriture au service de la catéchèse', in J. Fontaine and C. Pietri (eds.), *Le Monde latin antique et la Bible* (Paris, 1985), 264.

## BIBLICAL COMMENTARIES

The late fourth and early fifth centuries saw the burgeoning production of biblical commentaries, on the Psalms especially.[288] They are placed last in this chapter and discussed only briefly, since they often originated in series of homilies, such as those by Chrysostom already examined, which were then reworked for publication, though it is not always possible for the modern scholar to determine which were composed in this way. These form a particularly influential subset of sermons. However composed, commentaries were used as guides by preachers, thereby influencing a much wider body than their immediate audience or readership, while they also circulated in monasteries and amongst influential lay Christians in the aristocratic elites as a form of spiritual reading and scripture study, where edification as well as exposition was expected. Eusebius of Caesarea's commentary on the Psalms was consulted by Theodoret and translated into Latin by Eusebius of Vercelli.[289] Jerome's *Commentary on Daniel*, dedicated to Pammachius and Marcella, was intended, at least in part, for dissemination within the influential circle of Roman ascetics to which these two belonged.

Promotion is found in many commentaries, such as the *Commentary on Matthew's Gospel* by Hilary of Poitiers, Jerome's *Commentary on Matthew*, and Ambrose's *Commentary on Luke's Gospel*. How much promotion depends in part on the style of commentary: a commentary containing much exhortation, such as Chrysostom's *Commentary on the Psalms* would contain more promotion than a simple exposition of the text, and not every commentary glossed each verse or set of verses. The matter raised by the verses might, for example, already have received adequate treatment in an earlier commentator or be discussed at a different part of the same commentary. Some, therefore, passed over verses on almsgiving in one place without comment, while other verses on the topic received attention elsewhere in the work. This can be seen in Hilary's

---

[288] Cf. M.-J. Rondeau, *Les Commentaires patristiques du Psautier (IIIe–Ve siècle)*, 2 vols., OCA 219 and 220 (1982 and 1985), i. 14 and 25.

[289] Ibid. i. 70–1.

*Commentary on Matthew* in how he treats verses 5: 40–2 and 6: 1–17.[290] Not surprisingly, most forms of promotion found in preaching are also found in commentaries: direct and explicit exhortation to give alms without citation of biblical texts;[291] the presentation of gifts to the poor as gifts to Christ, with allusion, implicit or explicit to Matthew 25: 40;[292] implicit calls to give alms, for example, in stating that they should pity and improve the plight of the poor;[293] condemnation of those who fail to give to the needy.[294]

## A DISTINCTIVE PROMOTION?

The chapter has shown how widely and persistently almsgiving was promoted in the Christian discourse of the later empire. To what extent was this distinctive in comparison with pagan discourse? Was the almsgiving by pagans noted in Chapter 3 encouraged by maxims similar to those found in the Christian *Sentences of Sextus* and which formed part of the education of those learning to read and write Greek? Teresa Morgan cites the saying 'Remember, being rich, to do good to the poor'.[295] The 'poor' in this saying, whom the rich are to aid with their benefactions, are the *penetes*.[296] Augustine's Punic proverb, mentioned earlier, ran: 'Plague is begging for a penny. Give her two and let her go away'.[297] Ancient Greek curses, the so-called *arai Bouzygeiai*, covered those who failed to give 'a coin for a beggar and a

---

[290] Hilary of Poitiers, *Commentary on Matthew*, ed. J. Doignon, *Hilaire de Poitiers, Sur Matthieu*, SC 254 and 258, 2 vols, (Paris, 1978 and 1979). The ascription and date are disputed, but the commentary has been accepted as Hilary's 'first published work' by Lionel Wickham in *Hilary of Poitiers, Conflicts of Conscience in the Fourth-Century Church* (Liverpool, 1997), p. xii.

[291] Chrysostom, *Commentary on Psalm 9*, PG 55. 122.

[292] *Commentary on Psalm 11. 4*, PG 55. 148–9.

[293] *Commentary on Psalm 9. 11*, PG 55. 139. Note that R. C. Hill follows the Hebrew numbering of the psalms in his Eng tr. and, with due warning, but without warrant, splits this homily in two, so that the passage in question features in his *Commentary on Psalm 10*.

[294] *Commentary on Psalm 44*, PG 55. 196.

[295] Morgan, *Literate Education*, 126.

[296] *P. Oxyrynchus* 3004, in P. J. Parsons (ed.), *The Oxyrhynchus Papyri*, xlii (London, 1974), 20.

[297] Augustine, *Serm.* 167. 4, PL 38. 910.

crust for a starving man'.[298] Such sayings encouraged occasional almsgiving at unspecified times to the poor in general. The Homeric poems were used at every stage of classical education, though the *Iliad* was more widely used than the *Odyssey* and only a very few studied what Ronald Hock terms the tertiary curriculum.[299] There, however, the *progymnasmata* (simple rhetorical exercises) included the use of maxims such as 'One should welcome a stranger when he arrives and send him on when he wishes to go' (*Odyssey* 15.–74).[300]

To these examples of direct promotion should be added examples of indirect promotion, the favourable portrayal of almsgiving for other ends, such as the description of the stranger and beggar under the protection of Zeus Xenios in *Odyssey* 14.[301] Morgan found four examples of this book by literary hands among the papyri, though none by schoolhands.[302] The Emperor Julian cited the Homeric texts to support his claim that pagan philosophy had long contained the same precepts as Christian scriptures. Yet Julian's polemic is an untrustworthy indicator of conventional readings; where direct promotion appears in Julian's letters, it is in imitation of Christian exhortation.[303]

Indirect promotion of almsgiving is found occasionally in literary portraits which circulated among the educated few. Diogenes Laertius told how Aristotle, questioned by pupils after giving alms (ἐλεημοσύνην) to a man they thought undeserving, had replied that he had taken pity on the man, not his character.[304] Aulus Gellius recounted how the magnate Herodes Atticus gave a beggar enough money to buy bread for thirty days despite being told that the man's claim to be a philosopher was bogus. He told his companions that they were giving the money 'not to a man, but as men'. He then related how

[298] Hands, *Charities*, 46.

[299] R. F. Hock, 'Homer in Greco-Roman Education', in D. R. MacDonald (ed.), *Mimesis and Intertextuality in Antiquity and Christianity* (Harrisburg, Pa., 2001), 63–4.

[300] Ibid. 72. The example is taken from Aphthonius's treatise, an early 4th-cent. work.

[301] Homer, *Od.* 14. 57–8.

[302] Morgan, *Literate Education*, 309, table 12.

[303] Julian, *Ep.* 84a (formerly *ep.* 49). 430B–C, in Bidez and Cumont, *Epistulae et leges*, 114. For Julian's concern to counter the Christian *agapes*, cf. *Ep.* 89b. 305D, in Bidez and Cumont, *Epistulae et leges*, 146.

[304] Diogenes Laertius, *Lives of the Philosophers* 5. 17, in Marcovich, *Vitae Philosophorum*, i. 316.

Musonius Rufus had replied to critics, after he had given a thousand sesterces to a beggar posing as a philosopher. When told that the man deserved nothing, he answered that he therefore deserved the money. The point was to show how little he valued his own wealth.[305]

Christian discourse was distinctive in the far greater extent of both its direct and indirect promotion of almsgiving. It was distinctive in that this promotion was specific in identifying in far greater detail those to be aided: above all, the widows and orphans within the community, but also the Christian poor before others. Unlike pagan discourse, it was specific about giving at set times and seasons. It showed a distinctive concern with how gifts were to be given and with the need to give *more*: the texts often play down actual or past gifts to stimulate increased giving. This characteristic concern both reflects the distinct types of almsgiving shown in Chapter 2 and the distinct meanings of almsgiving to be discussed in Chapter 5. Finally, Christian discourse on alms was distinctive in how it was voiced. Although the ethic of almsgiving was promoted in literature of many kinds, the extent to which it was articulated by religious leaders (bishops and holy men) finds no parallel among pagan priests or philosophers.

## CONCLUSION

Rita Lizzi has rightly stated that exhortation to almsgiving, together with the castigation of failure to give alms, may be defined as a *leitmotif* of pastoral preaching in the fourth and fifth centuries.[306] Direct and indirect promotion of almsgiving was a pervasive and highly distinctive feature of Christian discourse, both the official teaching or persuasive discourse of bishops and other authorities, and the popular discourse represented here by the apocryphal *Acta*, though the episcopal authorship and defence of much hagiography prevents any false dichotomy of 'official' and 'popular' works. In this

---

[305] Aulus Gellius, *Noctes Atticae*, 9. 2 ed. P. K. Marshall, 2 vols. (Oxford, 1990), i. 278–9.

[306] R. Lizzi, *Vescovi e strutture ecclesiastiche nella città tardoantica* (Como, 1989), 146.

promotion sermons played the most important role, not only as the main locus of non-controversial exhortation and other deliberate promotion by clerics, but also because of their far-reaching impact, as spoken addresses and published texts, on the different groups who comprised the Christian communities. This promotion was not the preserve of exceptional individuals, though sermons, like Augustine's *Sermon* 11, were copied, reused, and rewritten. Nor was it limited to rare occasions, when it would be heard only by a dedicated minority, but was a standard feature of Lenten addresses to the *competentes* and often in Sunday sermons. Not only were some sermons wholly devoted to almsgiving, but many more contained exhortation to give alms, in particular as a rousing conclusion. This exhortation was part of the bishop's duty as a preacher. It was part of his formation of those initiated into Christianity, his task in shaping their identity and conduct. Preaching on the topic increased at times of fasting and shortage (Lent, the ember days, and in winter). Chrysostom played on the twofold sense of *eleemosyne* as 'alms' and 'mercy' to remind his audience of their increased obligations in cold weather: 'It is always necessary to give sermons on almsgiving (περὶ τῆς ἐλεημοσύνης), since there is much we need to receive by way of mercy (πολλῆς ταύτης) from our Lord and Maker, especially in the present season, when the frost is sharp.'[307]

The main strategies of interpretation deployed in arguments for ascetic practices, above all the renunciation of marriage and abstinence from sexual relations within marriage, were also used to encourage almsgiving. Although individuals had their preferred citations and arguments, no significant differences have been identified between East and West, Greek or Latin authors. The promotional role of sermons is confirmed by evidence within other media: letters and *Lives*. Apocryphal *Acta* suggest this was nothing new. Popular hagiographic literature, some of which had been composed two centuries earlier, was a further influence upon the literate, for whom the saints were models of ideal action for imitation. Treatises were few and less significant in comparison, except in clerical formation, but reveal how almsgiving was caught up in fifth-century controversy over the means to salvation. Letters and *Lives* reveal that

---

[307] Chrysostom, *On Almsgiving* 1, PG 51. 261.

promotion was not limited to the diocesan clergy, but was advanced by monks and other ascetics to feature in the establishment of competing authorities. These different promoters encouraged alms-giving as an expression of Christian self-identity and orthodoxy, even though it was also practised by pagans and heretics.

Liebeschuetz is right to identify 'continuous moral pressure' on the wealthy to give to the poor, though we might add that this pressure extended to all sections of the Christian community above the bread line. His view that such pressure 'to some extent replaced the political pressure of the many on the few in the political city' is hard to assess.[308] The many retained the ability to riot at times of shortage. Their acclamations were sought by officials and emperors. It is in any case better not to think of Christian promotion as simply applying pressure on the wealthy. Bishops preached as they were expected to by the community of which they had charge, including the wealthy members of that community. As shown in Chapter 2, they were themselves the controllers and distributors of much wealth within that community in collaboration with wealthy lay men and women. Their words had their place in facilitating, increasing, shaping, and interpreting the flow of alms from the rich to the very poor.

This discourse drew extensively on biblical language and models to form the matrix in which practices held the meanings for Christians I shall consider in the next chapter. It changed how Christians perceived the world before their eyes. Augustine preached how: 'Often a beggar looking for a coin sings God's commands to you at the front door.'[309] It is unlikely that beggars at Hippo knew how to win alms from the devout by citing biblical verses. It is likely that the Christian donor was supposed to recognize an appeal to the Gospel in the beggar's act of asking. The hearing and reading of texts sustained a way of understanding how God spoke and acted to Christians in the everyday world.

---

[308] J. Liebeschuetz, *Barbarians and Bishops* (Oxford, 1990), 251.
[309] Augustine, *Serm.* 32. 23, CCSL 41. 409.

# 5

## The Meanings of Christian Almsgiving

The previous three chapters have established the forms of almsgiving practised by Christians in the late empire and their sustained, pervasive, and distinctive promotion in official and popular discourse. The present chapter establishes certain meanings which this discourse ascribed to practice, where ascription is both descriptive of a significance already inherent in the practice in its social context and constructive of that significance, shaping in reformulating the shared beliefs of church members about almsgiving. The chapter concerns first how the meaning of almsgiving was affected by some of the motives advanced for its practice; second, the redescription of the poor which ensued from its meaning as an exchange of gifts; third, the recharacterization of the donor and his or her virtues, which this exchange made possible; fourth, the characterization of donors' generosity in almsgiving as an expression of leadership or patronage of the poor; and, fifth, the effect of these ascribed meanings on urban Christian communities. In so doing, the chapter offers an enriched account of practice, for human actions and meanings are not wholly separable, where 'meanings...are ways of entering into social life, ways of being with each other'.[1]

The ascribed meanings may be far from simple, so that an intended act of expiation may also be an expression of generosity and an unintended title to honour, with consequences for the social standing of both donor and recipient, an expression respectively of power and dependency. The meanings ascribed to an act may vary with the status and identity of the donor, so that almsgiving means

---

[1] Herbert McCabe OP, *Law, Love and Language* (London and Sydney, 1968), 84.

one thing when practised by a bishop and something else when practised by his wife; it may mean one thing to those who regard both husband and wife as exemplary Christians, another to those who hold them dangerous heretics. Furthermore, the meaning of almsgiving was not necessarily determined only by the Christian discourse in which it featured. Christians were members of a wider society and some were readers of very different texts. Other and older patterns of thought and social interaction formed another part of the social context in which actions were significant for those who engaged in them, or observed them.

## RELIGIOUS MOTIVATIONS

Cyprian had taught the value of almsgiving 'according to God's command' (*secundum praeceptum Dei*);[2] and Ambrose termed Christ's call to sell one's possessions and give the money to the poor at Luke 18: 22 the 'misericordiae praeceptum' or 'command of mercy'.[3] Christians were to give alms out of obedience to this divine command which they found at certain points in the scriptures, as voiced by Christ and his apostle Paul in the New Testament,[4] and by the Old Testament prophets.[5] Later epigraphy reveals how this call was taken up: a fifth- or sixth-century epitaph at Aksaray in Cappadocia praised the deceased widow and deaconess, Maria, in language adapted from 1 Timothy 5: 9–10, for amongst other things her care of strangers and distribution of bread to the afflicted 'according to the words of the Apostle'.[6] The linguistic fidelity of the inscription to its biblical model paralleled Maria's obedience to God's word in

---

[2] Cyprian, *De opere* 8, SC 440. 98.

[3] Ambrose, *Commentary on Luke's Gospel* 8. 69, in G. Tissot, *Traité sur l'Évangile de S. Luc*, SC 45 and 52 (Paris, 1956 and 1958), ii. 130.

[4] Luke 11: 41, 12: 43, and 18: 22 = Matt. 19: 21 = Mark 10: 21. For Luke 11: 41 cited as the reason why the donor should give alms, cf Ambrose, *De Nabuthae* 2. 8, OOSA 6. 136.

[5] Isa. 58: 7.

[6] G. Jacopi, 'Esplorazioni e studi in Paflagonia e Cappadocia', *Bollettino del Reale Istituto di Archeologia e Storia dell'Arte*, 8 (Rome, 1938), 34.

almsgiving. Sustained promotion had determined this meaning of her acts for those who read her tombstone.

As stated in Chapter 4, Christians were also presented with a larger set of biblical passages, in which almsgiving featured as a virtuous activity rewarded in various ways by God's blessing, such as in the portrayal of the just man, Job, as a 'father of the poor' or the promise that 'sins are washed away through faith and almsgiving'.[7] They were to be further impressed by a third set of biblical texts which the promoters of almsgiving in the fourth and fifth centuries interpreted as bearing on almsgiving, including, for example, the parable of the wise and foolish virgins.[8] In all, promoters appealed to over one hundred different passages in the Old and New Testaments.[9]

The biblical texts gave a number of reasons why Christians should give alms: to ensure prosperity in this life (Proverbs 28: 27), as a matter of justice (Psalms 36: 21, 111: 9), as a means to win God's favour in general by securing the prayers of the poor (Sirach 35: 21), as a way to escape in particular the ever-present threat of death in a violent world (Tobit 4: 10), as expiation for sin (Daniel 4: 24, Sirach 3: 30, Tobit 12: 9), as a way to secure treasure in heaven (Matthew 6: 19–20, Luke 18: 22), as wealth lent to God to be repaid with interest of a spiritual kind (Proverbs 19: 17), as an act of kindness towards Christ in the person of the poor (Matthew 25: 31–46). These texts influenced almsgivers directly when read aloud in the Church's liturgy for all to hear or when read and consigned to memory by individuals. This chapter, however, looks more closely at the significance of certain passages as they were used by promoters, who influenced how they were heard, in selecting from them or weaving

---

[7] Job 29: 16 and Proverbs 15: 27 (LXX).

[8] Matthew 25: 1–13.

[9] The following is a list of the passages taken by commentators as referring to the good of almsgiving: Exod. 23: 15; Job 29: 15–16, 31: 17, 31: 20, 31: 32; Dan. 4: 24; Prov. 3: 3, 3: 27–8, 11: 25–6, 13: 8, 15: 27, 17: 5, 19: 7, 21: 13, 22: 2, 22: 9, 28: 27, 31: 20; 1 Kgs. 17; Isa. 1: 18, 58: 7; Hos. 6: 6, 10: 12; Sir. 3: 30, 4: 8, 29: 1–2, 29: 12, 35: 21; Ps. 36: 21, 40: 2, 41: 1, 111: 9; Tob. 4: 7–12, 4: 16–17, 12: 8–9; Matt. 5: 7, 5: 20, 5: 40, 5: 42, 6: 1, 6: 19–20, 6: 24, 6: 33, 7: 1–2, 10: 40–2, 13: 45, 19: 19, 19: 21–2, 25: 1–13, 25: 14, 25: 35–41, 26: 11; Mark. 2: 14, Luke 3: 11, 6: 30, 6: 34–8, 11: 41, 12: 16–21, 12: 33, 14: 13–14, 14: 33, 16: 9, 16: 20f, 18: 22, 19: 8, 21: 2–3; John 15: 4–6; Acts 2: 44–5, 3: 3–8, 4: 32, 4: 35, 6: 1–6, 9: 36, 9: 39, 10: 2, 10: 4–5, 10: 31, 1 Cor. 10: 24; 2 Cor. 8: 14, 9: 6–14; Phil. 4: 18; Jas 2: 19; Gal. 2: 10, 6: 10; 1 Tim. 6: 17–19; 1 John 3: 15; 1 Pet. 5: 7.

them together, so that one text interpreted another, or in explaining what lay behind biblical images and metaphors. Some verses, such as Proverbs 11: 25 ('Every generous soul is blessed'), were rarely used. Others were commonplace—above all Luke 16: 9 ('Make friends for yourselves of the Mammon of iniquity')—but open to various interpretations. I look at how these authoritative or received interpretations were taken up by members of the Christian community in the late empire and the meanings which they ascribed to almsgiving.

There is no point in duplicating here work already done by scholars to establish the full range of theological arguments for almsgiving advanced by promoters or their wider understanding of wealth. Roman Garrison and Boniface Ramsey have already established that almsgiving was uniformly presented as an activity enjoined on all Christians, rich and poor alike, which would be rewarded in the life to come both by facilitating entry into heaven and by a glory which would be theirs in heaven. Promoters in the fourth and fifth centuries all but universally advanced the view that almsgiving achieved this end as a means to redeem post-baptismal sins, although some preachers and writers, Lactantius and Basil in particular, made far less of this than others.[10] An appeal to self-interest was repeatedly advanced, and the texts most frequently cited included Proverbs 19: 17 and Luke 16: 9. The present chapter concerns only the interplay of certain elements in this wider picture.

## ALMSGIVING AS AN EXCHANGE OF GIFTS

Advocates of almsgiving as a means of expiation for post-baptismal sins commonly argued that the donor won forgiveness from God and other benefits through the prayers offered on their behalf by the

---

[10] Basil cites few of the biblical texts associated with redemptive almsgiving and those rarely, but appeals to the redemptive power of almsgiving during the food shortage at Caesarea in his homily *In Time of Hunger* 7, PG 31. 324C. For appeals to the redemptive value of almsgiving in Augustine's sermons, cf. *Serm.* 9. 17–18 and *Serm.* 42. 1 CCSL 41. 141–4 and 504; *Serm.* 259. 4, PL 38. 1199–1200; *Serm.* 261. 10, in C. Lambot, *S. Augustini Aurelii Sermones Selecti Duodeviginti* (Utrecht, 1950), 93–4; *Serm.* 352. 7, PL 39. 1557–8; *Serm.* 388, PL 39. 1700–1; *Serm.* 389. 5 in *RB* 58 (1948), 50.

grateful recipient. Christian discourse emphasized the high value of these prayers offered in return for alms. Clement of Alexandria urged the donor to

assemble an army for yourself, one without weapons or hostile intent, unstained by bloodshed and passion, made up of devout old men, God's beloved orphans, widows armed with meekness, men decked out in the jewellery of love. Use your money to acquire bodyguards like these to protect you body and soul, men who have God for their general, people through whom a sinking ship is buoyed up, steered only by the prayers of the saints; people through whom a disease is brought under control when at the height of its powers, banished by the laying on of hands; and through whom the attacking robbers are disarmed, stripped of their weapons by devout prayers; people through whom the violence of the demons is smashed, confuted and put to shame with strict orders.[11]

In the *Apostolic Constitutions* it is the bishop's responsibility in distributing gifts to the needy to 'tell them who the donor is, so that they may pray for him or her by name'.[12] Citations in close proximity of Daniel 4: 27 (LXX) and Proverbs 15: 27 make clear the underlying theology of redemptive almsgiving: the recipients were to pray for the forgiveness of the donor's sins.[13] Further on, the widows are to pray for the donor and for the whole church.[14] They are to pray for the donor even when he or she is unnamed.[15] The later Gallic canons, the *Statuta ecclesiae galliae*, likewise insisted that 'widows supported by Church alms' were bound to help the Church 'by their merits and prayers'.[16]

Ambrose has in this respect a revealing gloss on 2 Corinthians 8: 14 with its call to mutual aid:

'So that your abundant wealth addresses the need experienced by these people and their abundant wealth may address your need.' I think he is talking about roles here: that is, the people's prosperity should work well to meet the others' need of food and the spiritual wealth of those others

[11] Clement of Alexandria, *Quis dives?* 34, in Stählin, *Clemens*, iii. 182–3.
[12] *Ap. Const.* 3. 4. 2–3, SC 329. 126.
[13] *Ap. Const.* 3. 4. 6 and 7, SC 329. 126 and 128.
[14] *Ap. Const.* 3. 5. 2 and 3. 13. 2, SC 329. 128 and 148.
[15] *Ap. Const.* 3. 14. 1, SC 329. 150.
[16] *Statuta ecclesiae Galliae*, in Munier, *Concilia Galliae A.314–A.506*, 185.

should address the need of spiritual merit in the people and confer a favour on them.[17]

Where St Paul thought in terms of balancing out material goods over a period of time by communities whose fortunes might vary, Ambrose introduced an exchange of material for spiritual goods in each act of almsgiving. This is a necessary move only if the recipients may never know plenty, may never be in a position to repay the donors in kind.

The understanding of almsgiving as an exchange of goods under-lies the dramatic attempt by Pacianus to reform attitudes in his congregation. The fourth-century bishop of Barcelona not only complained that penitents were shirking their duties by failing to give alms and 'giving nothing to the poor', but ordered donors to 'seize the poor by the hand and plead with the widows'.[18] He urged donors to adopt the gestures of the recipients, to greet the poor as their benefactors, in a startling reversal of social expectations. The exhortation does not demonstrate an acceptance by bishop or con-gregation of any reversal in actual standing, but depends on their acceptance of the underlying exchange in which social position was modulated by mutual obligation and benefit. The rhetoric depends on a prior recognition that the recipient was no longer wholly without honour.

This revalorization of the poor recipient is also asserted in the *Apostolic Constitutions*, where the offering of a spiritual return by the recipient involved a particular change in how the poor are to be regarded: 'For [the poor person], considered as God's altar, will be honoured by God when he prays readily and unceasingly for his donors, not just lazily taking things, but, in so far as he is able, making a return for his gift through prayer.'[19] The poor become the altar on which the donor makes an offering.[20] Chrysostom used the same traditional image.[21] Almsgiving in this context took on

---

[17] Ambrose, *De officiis* I. 30. 153, in Testard, *Devoirs*, i. 170.
[18] Pacianus, *Sermo de paenitentibus* 10. 5 and 6, in *Pacien de Barcelone: Écrits*, ed. C. Granado, tr. C. Épitalon and M. Lestienne, SC 410 (Paris, 1995), 140.
[19] *Ap. Const.* 4. 3. 3, SC 329. 174.
[20] For earlier examples of this image, cf. C. Osiek, 'The Widow as Altar: The Rise and Fall of a Symbol', *The Second Century*, 3 (1983), 159–69.
[21] Chrysostom, *Homilies on 2 Corinthians* 20. 3, PG 61. 540.

the meaning or nature of prayer itself. This seems to be the underlying sense of the encouragement found in the so-called *Canons of
Athanasius*, when the rich are encouraged to make an offering for a
dead son by giving alms.[22] But what matters here is how almsgiving
as an exchange of gifts has consequences for the worth of the recipient and leads to a redescription of the poor. It offers a context in
which to make sense of the rhetorical claim advanced by Paulinus of
Nola that the poor whom Pammachius had fed were 'the patrons of
our souls'.[23]

## THE REDESCRIPTION OF THE POOR

Promotion of almsgiving as an exchange of valued gifts facilitated a
multiple redescription of the destitute. Augustine and Chrysostom in
particular redescribed the poor as gladiators, athletes and actors who
offered the wealthy a didactic spectacle in which the feminizing evils
of wealth are opposed to the masculine virtues of a Christ-like
poverty nobly endured.[24] This portrayal, however, should be placed
in a much wider redescription of the destitute in terms of: (1) being
active subjects rather than passive objects, with consequences for
further portrayal in terms of material rather than social conditions;
(2) an identification of the recipient with Christ; (3) a form of
friendship between donor and recipient; (4) a relationship between
the donor and those to whom he or she gave alms expressed in the
language of parent and offspring; (5) a fraternal relationship between
donor and recipient; and (6) a relationship in which both are fellow
servants of God.

The classical distinction between the poor ($\pi\acute{\epsilon}\nu\eta\tau\epsilon\varsigma$) and destitute
($\pi\tau\omega\chi o\acute{\iota}$) was not simply one of lesser or greater deprivation, but a
distinction between the poor yet active and the dependent poor,
passive recipients of what fate brought.[25] The meaning of almsgiving
as a redemptive activity winning the prayers of the $\pi\tau\omega\chi o\acute{\iota}$ turned the
previously passive, who as such had little value, into more valued

---

[22] *Canons of Athanasius* 84–5, in Riedel and Crum, *Canons*, 51.
[23] Paulinus, *Ep.* 13. 11, CSEL 29. 92.
[24] De Vinne, *Advocacy*, 48–83.     [25] Patlagean, *Pauvreté*, 26.

agents of redemption.[26] Chrysostom portrayed the poor as surgeons whose outstretched hands excised scars and healed wounds.[27] Blake Leyerle has written of Chrysostom's preaching that 'the very poor, who had previously been excluded from patron–client relations because they had nothing to contribute' were invested 'with a valuable commodity, namely, special access to God'.[28] But Chrysostom is not unusual or novel in this respect.

By the fourth century Christians and pagans increasingly spoke about the poor in different terms: pagans tended to remain faithful to an older, social, description given by the classical tradition; and Christians departed from this tradition under the influence of the biblical texts, rarely describing the poor in negative terms as the 'base' or 'ignoble' (ἄδοξοι, ταπεινοί), but more often using terms that spoke directly of the material want or plight to be addressed and referring to 'the needy' (οἱ δεόμενοι) and 'the afflicted' (οἱ θλιβόμενοι).[29] The needy were repeatedly identified with Christ, so that in giving alms the donors showed their love for Christ. Susan Holman has noted that the 'metaphor of Matthew 25, in which ministering to the poor is ministering to Christ, is a dominant theme throughout all three Cappadocians' writings on poverty relief'.[30] Yet, once again, this was far from novel or exceptional: Matthew 25: 35–46 is cited in promotion of almsgiving by Cyprian,[31] Clement,[32] Hilary of Poitiers,[33] Ambrose,[34] Chrysostom,[35]

---

[26] For the complex relations between a person's worth and their contribution to society in classical thought, cf. J. Rist, *Human Value* (Leiden, 1982), 15.

[27] Chrysostom, *Homilies on 1 Corinthians* 30. 7, PG 61. 255.

[28] B. Leyerle, 'John Chrysostom on Almsgiving and the Use of Money', *HTR* 87 (1994), 41.

[29] Patlagean, *Pauvreté*, 28. Patlagean's conclusions for the Greek East have been confirmed for 4th- and 5th-cent. Latin authors by Charles Pietri, 'Les Pauvres et la pauvreté', 277.

[30] S. Holman, 'The Entitled Poor: Human Rights Language in the Cappadocians', *Pro Ecclesia*, 9 (2000), 483.

[31] Cyprian, *De opere* 23, SC 440. 144–8.

[32] Clement, *Quis dives?* 13 and 30, in Stählin, *Clemens*, iii. 168 and 179–80.

[33] Hilary of Poitiers, *Commentary on Psalm 118* 14. 9, ed. M. Milhau, *Hilaire de Poitiers, Commentaire sur le psaume 118*, SC 344 and 347 (Paris, 1988), ii. 132 (PL 9. 593).

[34] Ambrose, *De Nabuthae* 14. 59, OOSA 6. 180; *De officiis* 2. 21. 107, in Testard, *Les Devoirs*, ii. 106–7.

[35] Chrysostom, *Homiles on Matthew* 4. 12, PG 57. 53; 35. 3, PG 57. 409; 50. 3, PG 58. 508; 85. 4, PG 58. 762; 88. 3, PG 58. 779; *Homilies on Ephesians* 24. 5, PG 62. 176.

Paulinus,[36] and Sulpicius Severus[37] among others. Augustine frequently cited the verses to this end.[38] Nor was the identification limited to citation of this passage.[39] Chrysostom urged his congregation to recall that their gifts were handed to Christ himself in order to encourage them to give alms directly rather than through the Church.[40]

Luke 16: 9, with its call to 'make friends using the Mammon of iniquity', was also commonly cited in promoting almsgiving.[41] The verse lent itself to a third form of redescription, in which the poor were portrayed as the new friends won through almsgiving. The prayers offered by the recipients of alms constituted a return allowing for this new relationship between rich and poor in a culture where 'belief in reciprocity' was 'a *sine qua non* of friendship'.[42] Jerome described Fabiola as summoning monks to whom she could give alms and so make friends using the Mammon of iniquity. He goes on to say that 'they came and became friends'.[43] Augustine preached: 'There are poor people here who have no shelters in which to welcome you. Make friends of them by using the Mammon of iniquity, that is, with the profits, which iniquity terms profits . . . Do not despise the poor who have nowhere they can return to, nowhere to go. They do have shelters; what's more they have eternal ones.'.[44]

[36] Paulinus, *Epp.* 1. 1 and 6, 5. 3, 13. 22, 32. 20, CSEL 29. 2, 5, 26, 103, 295.

[37] Sulpicius Severus, *Life of Martin* 3. 4, SC 133. 258.

[38] Augustine, *Serm.* 9. 21, *Serm.* 25. 8, and *Serm.* 38. 8 CCSL 41. 150, 339, and 484; *Serm.* 53A. 6 = Morin 11 in Morin, *Sermones*, 630.

[39] Paulinus, *Epp.* 13. 14, 23. 43, 34. 4, 42. 3, CSEL 29.96, 198, 306, 361. Jerome, *Ep.* 54. 12, in Labourt, *Lettres*, iii. 35.

[40] Chrysostom, *Homilies on 1 Timothy* 14, PG 62. 574.

[41] e.g. Tertullian, *De patientia* 7, ed. J.-C. Fredouille, *De la patience*, SC 310 (Paris, 1984), 86; Ambrose, *Commentary on Luke's Gospel* 7. 245, SC 52. 99; *De Helia* 20. 76, OOSA 6. 116; *De Nabuthae* 7. 36, OOSA 6. 156; Chrysostom, *Homilies on Matthew* 5. 5, PG 57. 60; Augustine, *Serm.* 14. 8 and *Serm.* 50. 6, CCSL 41. 189–90 and 627; *Serm.* 359A, in *RB* 49 (1937), 265, 266, 268, and 269; Paulinus, *Epp.* 13. 22, 14. 4, 32. 21, CSEL 29. 103, 110, 295; Pseudo-Rufinus, *On the Psalms* 65. 15, PL 21. 907B; Jerome, *Epp.* 54. 12, 71. 4, 79. 4, 108. 16, 118. 4, 123. 5, and 130. 7, in Labourt, *Lettres*, iii. 35, iv. 11–12 and 97–8, v. 179, vi. 92, vii. 79 and 173.

[42] White, *Christian Friendship*, 55.

[43] Jerome, *Ep.* 77. 11, in Labourt, *Lettres*, iv. 51.

[44] Augustine, *Serm.* 41. 6, CCSL 41. 500–1.

In fact, though preachers and writers often urged the faithful to 'make friends' through almsgiving who would welcome them into heaven, they rarely did so in terms which explicitly redescribed the poor as friends without further qualification. Jerome allows the historian to sense the resistance to this type of redescription. In the *Against Vigilantius* Jerome identifies the friends of *Luke* 16: 9 with the 'domesticos fidei', the phrase used by Paul at Galatians 6: 10 to describe Christians as fellow members of a single 'household of faith'. Only Christians who receive alms count here as friends. Not all who are poor qualify for friendship, only the poor in spirit.[45] Paulinus likewise uses Galatians 6: 10 to limit and interpret the friendship advocated in Luke 16: 9, when he assures Pammachius that as a result of his almsgiving he will have 'seed in Sion and household members in Jerusalem who in turn will welcome you into eternal habitations'.[46]

Clement of Alexandria had long before distanced the donor from immediate friendship with the poor by explaining that the donor was to give not only to friends, but also to his friends' friends. The donor gave to God's friends, though who these were among the poor was not for the donor to judge.[47] Cyril of Alexandria likewise explained Luke 16: 9 by distinguishing among the needy 'no small crowd of good, fair-minded people' who might perhaps escape detection on earth, but were not unknown to God: it was these who, when aided in this life, would return the favour in the next.[48] But he also urged his congregation to 'refresh' or 'win over' ($\dot{\alpha}\nu\alpha\kappa\tau\dot{\omega}\mu\epsilon\nu o\iota$, $\dot{\alpha}\nu\alpha\kappa\tau\eta\sigma\dot{\omega}\mu\epsilon\theta\alpha$) the widows and orphans,[49] the sick,[50] the maltreated,[51] a verb associated with winning friends and their good favour, and which he used to pick out the widows in particular.

Ambrose likewise made clear on several occasions that it was not the poor as such who became friends with the donor, but the saints

[45] Jerome, *Against Vigilantius* 14, PL 23. 350.

[46] Paulinus of Nola, *Ep.* 13. 16, CSEL 29. 97.

[47] Clement, *Quis dives?* 33, Stählin, *Clemens*, iii. 181.

[48] Cyril of Alexandria, *Paschal Homilies* 11. 6, in Burns, *Lettres festales*, ii. 286.

[49] *Paschal Homilies* 5. 8, 8. 6, 12. 6, 20. 4, 22. 4, 24. 4, 26. 4, and 28. 5, in Burns, *Lettres festales*, i. 328, ii. 112, iii. 78 and PG 77. 849B, 872D, 901A, 928C, 956C.

[50] *Paschal Homilies* 14. 2 and 30. 5, in Burns, *Lettres festales*, iii. 162 and PG 77. 981B.

[51] *Paschal Homilies* 6. 11, in Burns, *Lettres festales*, i. 398.

among whom were the Christian poor: '[the recipient] bestows more on you, who owes you your salvation: if you clothe the naked, you clothe yourself in righteousness; if you bring a traveller under your roof, if you support the person in need, he gains for you the friendship of the saints and eternal dwellings'.[52] The passage may be set beside part of Ambrose's commentary on Dives and the Parable of the Unjust Steward: 'We may observe that the same note of pity is struck in the parable above on the steward and present parable on the rich man. In the latter he teaches in truth that we must give to the poor, while perhaps in the former, it is to the saints, whom he terms friends and to whom he has granted dwelling places.'[53] The bishop had to undo the risk of indiscriminate friendship with the poor if his wealthy donors were not to be frightened off. Caroline White has observed that fourth-century Christians were reshaping and extending the classical pattern of friendship.[54] The passages above qualify White's verdict that Ambrose's ideas in this respect 'remained dominated by pagan thought' and are indicative of a wider conservatism.[55] Almsgiving featured in the developing Christian concept of friendship primarily as what friendship with God and his saints required of the rich. Yet occasional and controversial redescription of the poor attempted to bring the latter into a new form of friendship with their benefactors. Even Ambrose cited the classical proverb that 'Friends hold all things in common' to persuade his readers to generosity in the church. Ambrose argued, not so much that the church members were the friends of those whom they aided, but near relations (*cognati*) in the Body of Christ.[56]

As Job's alms made him a father to the poor, Christian discourse presented donor and recipient as parent and offspring. Basil convicted the rich young man of Matthew 19: 21 of failing to love his neighbour: had he clothed the naked and acted as a father to the orphans, he would not still retain considerable riches.[57] Elsewhere,

[52] Ambrose, *De officiis* 1. 11. 39, in Testard, *Devoirs*, i. 113. Testard notes the potential ambiguity of the *cum* clause, 'since' or 'though' at 231 n. 9.

[53] *Commentary on Luke's Gospel* 8. 20, SC 52. 108.

[54] White, *Christian Friendship*, 3–4.

[55] Ibid. 111.

[56] Ambrose, *De viduis* 1. 4, OOSA 14/1. 248.

[57] Basil, *On the Wealthy* 1, in Courtonne, *Homélies*, 41.

Basil sought to persuade the rich man to almsgiving by holding out the praise of being addressed as the 'father to countless children' on account of his alms.[58] Ambrose, drawing on Basil's sermons in the *De Nabuthae*, made the same point to present the donor as the 'father of orphaned children'.[59] Bishops in particular were presented as fathers of those to whom they gave alms. Gregory Nazianzen presented Athanasius as the father of the orphans at Alexandria.[60] The *Canons of Athanasius* not only specified that the bishop was to give alms every Sunday, but also that he was to 'know the poor and orphans as a father' in assembling them together to be fed and assured of food in future.[61] The *Life of Alexander* in the second half of the fifth century described Rabbula as 'nothing less than father of the widows and orphans'.[62] Alexander is portrayed in the same way as having 'cared for the destitute as a father'.[63]

Clement's *Quis dives salvetur?* offers an early example of the fifth type of redescription, the presentation of the poor as brothers, in so far as it likens those who fail to give alms to the loveless and murderous brother of 1 John 3: 15 ('He that loveth not his brother is a murderer').[64] The citation is almost unique in the promotion of almsgiving, but appeals to fraternal charity were widespread, unsurprisingly given the general use of 'brother' to designate a fellow Christian and less frequent use of the word to designate a fellow human being.[65] In the fourth century the appeal to fraternal charity and what is owed to a brother is one of the bases of Lactantius' moral reasoning in book 5 of the *Divine Institutes*, and hence part of his argumentation in favour of almsgiving.[66]

---

[58] *I Shall Knock Down My Barns* 3, in Courtonne, *Homélies*, 21.

[59] Ambrose, *De Nabuthae* 7. 36, OOSA 6. 158.

[60] Gregory Nazianzen, *Or.* 21. 10, ed. J. Mossay, *Grégoire de Naziance, Discours 20–30*, SC 270 (Paris, 1980), 132.

[61] *Canons of Athanasius* 16, in Riedel and Crum, *Canons*, 26–7.

[62] *Life of Alexander* 22, PO 6. 674.     [63] Ibid. 33, PO 6. 684.

[64] Clement, *Quis dives?* 37, in Stählin, *Clemens*, iii. 184.

[65] On this distinctive Christian usage, cf. H. Pétré, *Caritas, Étude sur le vocabulaire latin de la charité chrétienne* (Louvain, 1948), 104–40.

[66] Ibid. 127–9. Other examples of this redescription in promoting almsgiving include: *Ap. Const.* 7. 12. 5, SC 336. 41; Basil, *In Time of Hunger* 5, 6, 7 and 8, PG 31. 316B, 320D, 324C 325B–C; *I Shall Knock Down My Barns* 3, in Courtonne, *Homélies*, 23; Augustine, *Serm.* 36. 5, CCSL 41. 438; *Serm.* 107A. 2, RB 49 (1937), 273; Chromatius, *Serm.* 1. 7, CCSL 9A, 6.

The portrayal of donor and recipient as fellow servants of God (*conservi, σύνδουλοι*) is found in John Chrysostom's appeal for greater almsgiving by his congregation. They are to imagine what kind of behaviour they would expect of their own servants in delivering money to others in their household or on their estates, and then consider themselves as God's servants with a like task in sharing alms with the poor.[67] Paulinus used the term *conservus* of the poor to encourage alms to fellow Christians.[68] Ambrose, in a related move, described the poor man as *consors naturae* with the rich.[69] It is noticeable, however, that this form of redescription is less commonly found than the others so far established.

Promoters were not limited to these forms of redescribing the poor. Augustine, in particular, drew on the biblical injunction to store up treasure in heaven to characterize the destitute in his sermons as porters, cargo- or baggage-handlers (*laturarii*) who ensured that earthly goods given to them as alms were transformed into spiritual wealth.[70] The image, familiar to inhabitants of a busy port, again turned passive recipients into active agents. It was used by Peter Chrysologus, the bishop of another maritime centre, Ravenna.[71] Contrary to the views of Michael De Vinne, however, this is not to deploy an image which 'transforms the poor into deserving clients'. Not every workman and no servant is a favoured client.[72]

## THE CHARACTERIZATION OF THE DONOR

All these forms of redescription aided the campaign by clerics to remove the contempt frequently shown to recipients in classical society (see below) in an attempted remodelling of the donor's

---

[67] Chrysostom, *Homilies on Matthew* 35, PG 57. 412.

[68] Pétré, *Caritas*, 164.

[69] Ambrose, *De Nabuthae* 1. 2, 3. 12, and 8. 40, OOSA 6. 130, 138, and 162; *De officiis*, 1. 11. 38 and 3. 3. 16, in Testard, *Devoirs*, i. 113 and ii. 87.

[70] Augustine, *Serm.* 38. 9, CCSL 41. 485; *Serm.* 53A. 6 and *Serm.* 114A. 3–4, in Morin, *Sermones*, 630 and 235; *Serm.* 107A. 2, RB 49 (1937), 273; *Serm.* 389. 4, RB 58 (1948), 49.

[71] Peter Chrysologus, *Serm.* 7, CCSL 24. 54.

[72] De Vinne, *Advocacy,* 98.

attitudes and character as well as practice. Almsgiving was promoted
in the context of a character trait or virtue held central to Christianity, that of being 'a lover of the destitute' (φιλόπτωχος). The adjective
and its corresponding abstract noun are rarely attested in classical
usage, and the adjective is glossed as ecclesiastical by Liddell and
Scott.[73] Evidence for its usage by Christians before the fourth century
is provided by one or two fragments of Origen's writings.[74] In the
*Apostolic Constitutions,* when a bishop investigates the characters of
disputants who appear before him, this is one of the traits which is to
identify the virtuous Christian.[75] It is the virtue which shines out in
the countenance of Hypatios in his fifth-century *Life.*[76] It was one of
the principal virtues which Cyril of Alexandria urged the faithful to
show in Lenten almsgiving.[77]

A pity associated with contempt is to be replaced with a pity
associated with compassion or *misericordia.* Gregory Nazianzen
praised his sister Gorgonia for her εὐσπλανγχνία.[78] Pétré's normally
judicious account of the language of Christian charity in Latin
should be qualified at this point. She defined *misericordia* as charity
manifested towards the poor and rightly stated that Augustine frequently speaks of almsgiving as the *opera misericordiae.*[79] She also
stated, however, that what mattered most was not the affective aspect,
an emotional response to the sight of misfortune, but the person's
action in seeking to remedy misfortune.[80] It is more accurate to say
that Christian promoters of almsgiving sought to integrate emotion
and action, stressing right intention, motive, and manner of acting.
The quotation offered in support of Pétré's reading from Ambrose
makes just this point: 'your intention determines the name for what

[73] A rare exception is a citation by the grammarian Aelius Herodianus, *On
Universal Prosody,* in *Herodiani Technici Reliquiae,* ed. A. Lentz (Leipzig, 1867), 292.
[74] Origen, *Scholion on Luke 3. 10,* PG 17. 328D (dubious); Frg. XV *On 2 Samuel*
5. 6–8, in E. Klostermann (ed.), *Origenes Werke,* iii, revised P. Nautin (Berlin,
1983), 299.
[75] *Ap. Const.* 2.50. 1, SC 320. 294.
[76] Callinicus, *Life of Hypatios* 22. 2, SC 177. 140.
[77] Cyril of Alexandria, *Paschal Homilies* 15, 16, 25, and 30, in Burns, *Lettres festales,*
iii. 204 and 248, and PG 77. 912C and 981B.
[78] Gregory Nazianzen, *Or.* 8, PG 35. 804.
[79] Pétré, *Caritas,* 251.
[80] Ibid. 231.

you do' (*adfectus tuus nomen imponit operi tuo*).[81] So, too, does her quotation from Augustine's *City of God*: 'But what is mercy, if not a certain compassion in our heart towards another's wretchedness, on account of which, in so far as we can, we are bound to help them.'[82]

These character traits were part of a wider understanding of almsgiving as an expression on the part of the donor of highly respected virtues. The meaning of almsgiving as an exchange of gifts, and the relationships of paternal or fraternal charity both acknowledged in and established through almsgiving, meant that almsgiving could be advocated as expressing the virtue of mutual love or φιλαλληλία.[83] In particular, almsgiving was promoted as an expression of justice and generosity. Promoters of almsgiving frequently cited Psalm 111(112): 9 ('He has given funds; he gave to the poor; his righteousness remains').[84] Ambrose used the verse to link justice, pity, and almsgiving, asking the rhetorical question, 'What is justice if not showing pity?' (*Quae est iustitia nisi misericordia?*).[85] Augustine presented fasting, prayer, and almsgiving as required by justice, or as parts of justice.[86] Western churches in the fourth and fifth centuries were probably influenced in this respect by the variant reading of Matthew 6: 1: 'beware lest you do justice before men to be seen by them'.[87] Most important, however, was the understanding of almsgiving as an act of generosity, in what will appear by the end of the chapter as a redefinition by Christians of the classical virtues of *liberalitas* and *humanitas*.

[81] Ambrose, *De officiis* 1.30. 147, in Testard, *Devoirs*, i. 166.

[82] Augustine, *City of God* 9. 5, cited Pétré, *Caritas*, 232.

[83] Cyril of Alexandria, *Paschal Homilies* 17, 18, and 25, in Burns, *Lettres festales*, iii. 292, and PG 77. 820B, and 912C.

[84] e.g. *Ap. Const.* 2. 35. 2 and 3. 4. 8, SC 320. 258 and SC 329. 128; Basil, *I Shall Knock Down My Barns* 3, in Courtonne, *Homélies*, 23, *On the Wealthy* 2, in Courtonne, *Homélies*, 45; Hilary of Poitiers, *Tractatus on Psalm 118* 14. 9, SC 347. 132 (PL 9. 593); Chrysostom, *Homilies on 2 Corinthians* 19. 3, PG 61. 533; Ambrose, *Commentary on Luke* 2. 90, 5. 57, 5. 65, SC 45. 115, 204, and 206–7; *De Nabuthae* 7. 36, OOSA 6. 156; Jerome, *Ep.* 75. 4, in Labourt, *Lettres*, iv. 36; Gerontius, *Vita Melaniae* 20, SC 90. 171.

[85] Ambrose, *Commentary on Luke* 2. 90, SC 45. 115.

[86] Augustine, *De sermone domini in monte* 2. 24. 80, ed. A. Mutzenbecher, CCSL 35 (Turnhout, 1967), 179; *En. in Ps. CXVIII, serm* 12. 2, CCSL 40. 1701; *De perfectione iustitiae*, PL 44. 299.

[87] This is the reading found e.g., in Eusebius of Vercelli's *Gospel*, ad loc., PL 12. 169; and Hilary of Poitiers's *Commentary on Matthew* 4. 28, SC 254. 148.

## CHRISTIAN GENEROSITY

In book 2 of the *De officiis* Ambrose discussed the 'many different kinds of generosity' (*plurima... genera liberalitatis*).[88] These included the care of orphaned children and provision for their marriage. This, taken out of context, might mean no more than the type of aid to less wealthy relatives, friends, and clients, advocated by Cicero his *De officiis*.[89] But these orphans are more likely to be the very poor, in many cases children of the widows maintained by the Church. And the grant of daily bread is presented as the primary form of *liberalitas*, even though other forms exist. The bishop makes clear that aid to those who were rich but have fallen on hard times is laudable only to the extent it does not drain away funds from this basic and primary form of Christian generosity:

If we are to be praised for keeping our mind unclouded by these things, think how much more impressive it is if you win the people's affection with a generosity that is neither wasted on undeserving claimants nor mean where the poor are concerned! Yet there are many different forms of generosity: not only to provide and distribute food for the poor with a daily supply, but also to advise and help those who are ashamed to display their need in public, so long as the common stock of food for the needy is not exhausted.[90]

Pétré observed Ambrose's linguistic agility in modelling the phrase *liberalitatem facere* on the pattern of *eleemosynam* or *misericordiam facere*.[91] Outside the *De officiis* Ambrose refers to *liberalitas* exercised towards the poor on a number of occasions.[92] In the *De Nabuthae* he presented Joseph opening his granaries to the poor during the long Egyptian famine as an example of *humanitas*.[93]

---

[88] Ambrose, *De officiis* 2. 15. 68–9, in Testard, *Devoirs*, ii. 39.
[89] Ambrose, *De officiis* 2. 72, in Testard, *Devoirs*, ii. 41.
[90] Ibid.
[91] Pétré, *Caritas*, 196, citing *De officiis* 2. 1. 2, PL 16. 103B.
[92] Cf. *De Nabuthae* 9. 41, OOSA 6. 162; *De viduis* 5. 27, OOSA 14/1. 268; *Ep*. 24. 1, OOSA 19. 236; *Ep*. 68. 4, ed. M. Zelzer, *Sancti Ambrosii Epistulae et Acta*, CSEL 82. 2 (Vienna, 1990), 171; and *De paenitentia* 2. 9. 83, ed. O. Faller, in G. Banterle (ed.), *Spiegazione del Credo, I Sacramenti, I Misteri, La Penitenza*, OOSA 17 (Milan and Rome, 1982), 270: 'Neque ego abnuo liberalitatibus in pauperes factis posse minui peccatum; sed si fides commendet expensas. Quid enim prodest conlatio patrimonii sine gratia caritatis?'
[93] *De Nabuthae* 7. 33, OOSA 6. 156.

Ambrose is far from unique in characterizing the donor as generous. The *De Nabuthae* was constructed from two Greek homilies by
Basil of Caesarea, who incorporated almsgiving within the virtue of
*philanthropia*. Ambrose's characterization of Joseph, for example,
is almost certainly taken directly from Basil.[94] In the homily *On
Renunciation* Basil urges his hearers: 'let us, therefore, make up our
minds, beloved, to do something charitable (τι φιλάνθρωπον) where
we are concerned and, if we really wish to do ourselves a favour, let us
share out our burdensome riches among the many, who will both
carry it gladly and secure it in our master's lap, a safe store...'[95] He
goes on to say that we cannot expect to be shown the *philanthropia*
we have not shown others by neglecting the needy.[96]

The Cappadocian father was not the first Christian preacher and
writer to present almsgiving as an expression of generosity. Origen
had certainly linked *philanthropia* and almsgiving in his *Commentary
on Matthew*, although he did so in order to condemn those who gave
alms to display their *philanthropia*.[97] A mid-third century letter of
Pope Cornelius preserved in Eusebius' *Ecclesiastical History* describes
the recipients of Christian alms at Rome as fed by the favour and
*philanthropia* of the Lord.[98] Eusebius himself told how Licinius had
persecuted the churches and decreed that no one was to show
generosity, *philanthropia*, by their gifts of food to prisoners.[99]
In the *Divine Institutes* Lactantius specifically attacked Cicero for
promoting what he regarded as a counterfeit or spurious virtue
of generosity (*humanitas*), wrong precisely because it omitted almsgiving:

the exercise of kindness towards one's fellow man (*humanitatis officium*)
requires that we assist him when in need or danger... So, if in cases of this
sort [of rescue from accidents], it is admitted that help is a part of this
kindness, because they endanger a person's life, what reason is there for

[94] Basil, *I Shall Knock Down My Barns* 2, in Courtonne, *Homélies*, 19.
[95] *On Renunciation* 8, PG 31. 553A.
[96] Ibid., PG 31. 553B.
[97] Origen, *Commentary on Matthew* 11. 15, in *Commentaire sur l'évangile selon
Matthieu*, ed. R. Girod, SC 162 (Paris, 1970), 350 (PG 13. 953). De Labriolle and Pétré
have credited Origen with the adoption of *philanthropia* into a Christian vocabulary,
Pétré, *Caritas*, 209.
[98] Eusebius, *Ecclesiastical History* 6. 43. 11, SC 44. 156.
[99] Eusebius, *Ecclesiastical History* 10. 8. 11, SC 55. 115.

people to think that help is not necessary, if someone is hungry or thirsty or cold?... Be open-handed with the blind, the weak, the crippled, the destitute, who will surely die unless you give to them,... Succour them, and support people's spirits, as far as it is in your power, by your kindness (*humanitate*), lest they perish.[100]

Examples abound from the late fourth and fifth centuries. Augustine advocated this type of generosity in the *De utilitate credendi* and *De bono viduitatis*; and in the first instance it is not only one form of the virtue among others, but is presented as its crowning form or perfection—'generosity that goes so far as to distribute one's family inheritance to the poor' (*liberalitas usque ad patrimonia distributa pauperibus*).[101] In the second text the virtue is set out as an advance over the classical type of generosity, which is vitiated by its entanglement in greed and love of money:

With you love of wealth cools together with love for marriage: the proper use of your possessions is their transfer to spiritual pleasures and your generosity has been put to helping the needy rather than enriching the greedy. It is not the gifts of those who long for more, but the alms for the poor, of great assistance to the widows' prayers, which are dispatched to the heavenly treasury.[102]

Jerome, too, advocates *liberalitas* towards the poor.[103] Paulinus, in praising Pammachius' charitable works, terms them *munera* (as Ambrose also spoke of *munera*) and in contrast attacks expenditure on shows by other members of the Roman elite as characterized by a false generosity, *liberalitas perversa*.[104] Salvian presented the failure to give alms as failure in the virtue of *misericordia* and *humanitas*. He condemned avarice, seen as the opposite of almsgiving, as the 'heartlessness which disowns compassion' (*abdicatrix misericordiae inhumanitas*).[105]

---

[100] Lactantius, *Divine Institutes* 6. 11 in Brandt and Laubmann, *Lactanti Opera*, i. 519–20 and 522.
[101] Augustine, *De utilitate credendi* 17. 35, ed. J. Zycha, CSEL 25 (1891), 45.
[102] Augustine, *De bono viduitatis* 21. 26, ed. J. Zycha, CSEL 41 (1900), 338. Elsewhere Augustine presents almsgiving as part of *largitas* or munificence, cf. *Serm.* 209. 3, PL 38. 1047.
[103] Jerome, *Epp.* 58. 7, 108. 15, and 118. 6, in Labourt, *Lettres*, iii. 82, v. 178, vi. 95.
[104] Paulinus, *Ep.* 13. 15, in CSEL 29. 96.
[105] Salvian, *Four Books* 1. 1 and 2. 11. 52, SC 176. 138 and 222.

It has been said that in John Chrysostom's *Commentary on Matthew* the words *philanthropos* and *philanthropia* appear 'in most of the passages concerning almsgiving and charity to the poor'.[106] Other terms from this constellation of related virtues appear in his homelies on the Gospel. In describing Jesus' entry into Jerusalem, Chrysostom compared the warmth and enthusiasm of the crowds who greeted him with the half-hearted or grudging actions of his congregation in almsgiving, when they saw Christ naked. Were they, he asked, so generous (φιλότιμοι)?[107] He threatened that he would stop preaching on almsgiving, because of their poor response in giving something, but 'not with an open hand'.[108] In another sermon he reminded them that what they thought of as their own possessions were only what God had entrusted to them to give generously to the needy (τῆς εἰς τοὺς δεόμενους φιλοτιμίας).[109]       Elsewhere Chrysostom glossed almsgiving as 'kindness to a fellow human being, generosity towards those in need' (ἡ φιλανθρωπία, ἡ εἰς τοὺς δεομένους φιλοτιμία).[110]

Christian discourse promoted this form of generosity by claiming it was already practised by holy men and women. Gregory Nazianzen's funeral oration for his sister Gorgonia and the oration for his father, the local bishop, both present copious almsgiving as part of *mega-lopsuchia*, 'magnificence' or 'magnanimity'.[111] Of Gorgonia he asked the rhetorical question 'Who was more open-handed to the needy?'[112] While wishing to stress his relatives' excellence in this respect, he nonetheless suggests that such generosity was not uncommon:

When it comes to magnificence with money, someone may have no diffi-culty in finding among other cases, both many where money is wasted on civic and public ambitions, and many where it is loaned to God via the poor, these being the only ones that store up savings for the spenders. But we do not readily find anyone who passes up the glory attached to it.[113]

---

106 Pétré, *Caritas*, 211.
107 Chrysostom, *Homilies on Matthew* 66.3, PG 58. 629.
108 Ibid., PG 58. 630.
109 *Homilies on Matthew* 77. 5, PG 58. 708.
110 *Commentary on the Psalms* 49. 4, PG 55. 228.
111 Gregory Nazianzen, *Or.* 8, PG 35. 804.
112 Ibid., PG 35. 801–2.
113 *Or.* 18. 21, PG 35. 1009.

Gregory presented Basil's poor-relief at Caesarea as expressing *philanthropia* and *megalopsuchia*: 'He did not treat the city in this way, but treat the surrounding country and foreign parts differently. No, when it came to the exercise of philanthropy and magnificence towards the poor, he set a contest for the leaders of the people that was open to all.'[114] Gregory defined *philanthropia* both as a general readiness to assist the weak and a particular devotion to almsgiving: 'Philanthropy is a noble undertaking, both feeding the destitute and coming to the aid of human weakness.'[115] His mother's almsgiving was presented as a similar form of generosity (ἐλευθεριότης).[116] Theodoret of Cyrrhus presented Limnaios, a Syrian monk and ascetic, as displaying *philanthropia* in founding a series of hostels (καταγώγια) for blind beggars where they were provided with food and shelter.[117] The *Acta Archelai* portrayed Marcellus as showing his 'piety and munificence' in ransoming many thousands of captives.[118] Alexander the monk was said to show *megalopsuchia* in the foundation of a *xenodocheion* for the poor at Antioch.[119]

Hilary asserted that the almsgiving practised by his predecessor Honoratus amounted to munificence when the example which the young ascetic had given of his lack of greed in giving away his own wealth made him a channel for the alms of others:

In addition, the wealth at his disposal matched his munificent intentions (*munificentiae animo*) and was put to use with an equal trust. For anyone who had charitably (*misericordiae animo*) determined on making a gift, would hand it over for distribution to one who had readily heard the call to 'Sell all your possessions and give to the poor, and come follow me' (Matt. 19: 21), happily entrusting all their goods to the man whose example they followed in leaving everything.[120]

With whatever accuracy, Hilary has Honoratus ascribe the virtue to himself: 'It is certain that someone is already close by who will provide the wherewithal if we lack anything for our munificence

---

[114] *Or.* 43. 63, SC 384. 264.
[115] Ibid., SC 384. 260.
[116] *Or.* 18. 8, PG 35. 993.
[117] Theodoret, *Historia religiosa*, 22. 7, SC 257. 132
[118] Hegemonius, *Acta Archelai* 1, in Beeson, *Acta*, 2.
[119] *Life of Alexander* 39, PO 6. 688.
[120] Hilary, *Vita Honorati* 20, in Cavallin, *Vitae*, 64.

(*munificentia*)'.[121] He wrote how the charity practised by the young Honoratus and his brother was a lesson in *humanitas* for the bishops who enjoyed the brothers' hospitality.[122] A modern editor of the *Vita*, Fr M.-D. Valentin OP, believes that there may be an echo at this point of a sermon by Quodvultdeus, which also links hospitality with *humanitas*.[123] It is not then surprising to find that Hilary's own biographer, Honoratus of Marseilles, ascribes a like generosity to Hilary, describing him as 'extremely quick to distribute his largesse' (*largitione promptissimus*).[124]

The characterization of the virtuous donor was accompanied by a corresponding representation of the gift as a benefaction (εὐεργεσία) which in some cases was approximated to classical, civic benefactions.[125] Chrysostom urged his congregation to win many who had enjoyed their benefactions of alms (τοὺς εὐεργετουμένους).[126] Basil promised his hearers that the almsgiver would enjoy at the Judgement the honourable titles of 'provider and benefactor' (τροφέα καὶ εὐεργέτην), together with all the other names belonging to charity.[127] In the fictional *Life of Abercius* the saintly bishop of the title claims as a reward from the empress at Rome (for his exorcism of a demon) the construction of a set of baths and a corn dole for the destitute of his native city, Hierapolis. The *siteresion* is 'bestowed' (χορηγούμενον) each year until the Emperor Julian rescinds the favour.[128] In this case almsgiving features alongside one traditional benefaction (the provision of baths) as an adaptation of a second such benefaction: an imperial corn dole for the town's citizens. The verb χορηγέω, with its overtones of public benefaction, recurs a number times in this tale to describe almsgiving: a wealthy matron, Phrygella, after the saint has restored her sight, promises to 'bestow

---

[121] Hitary, *Vita Honorati* 21, in Cavallin, *Vitae*, 64.

[122] Hilary, *Vita Honorati* 9, in Cavallin, *Vitae*, 55.

[123] M.-D. Valentin O P, *Hilaire d'Arles: Vie de saint Honorat*, SC 235 (Paris, 1977), 93 n. 3. The reference is to Quodvultdeus, *Sermo adv. quinque haereses* 4. 9, in R. Braun (ed.), *Opera Quodvultdeo Carthaginiensi Episcopo Tributa*, CCSL 60 (Turnhout, 1976), 269.

[124] Honoratus, *Vita Hilarionis*, 23, SC 404. 142.

[125] e.g. Basil, *In Time of Hunger* 2, PG 31. 309A; Chrysostom, *On Penance*, 7, PG 49. 333.

[126] Chrysostom, *Homilies on 1 Corinthians*, 10. 4, PG 61. 87.

[127] Basil, *I Shall Knock Down My Barns* 3, in Courtonne, *Homélies*, 21.

[128] *Life of Abercius* 65 and 66, in Nissen, *Vita*, 46 and 47.

on the destitute' (τοῖς πτωχοῖς χορηγῆσαι) half her wealth.[129] Bishop Abercius 'provides for the needy' (τοῖς δεομένοις ἐχορήγει).[130] The same verb, the compound ἐπιχορηγέω, and noun χορηγία were frequently used by promoters to describe donations.[131] The *Life of Alexander* portrays its hero as teaching the wealthy in towns along the border with Persia to 'do good deeds' or 'act with beneficence' (ἀγαθοποιεῖν).[132]

## ACCEPTED MEANINGS?

The fictional *Acta Archelai* (briefly described in Chapter 4) open with a figure whose character and actions perfectly display the meanings ascribed to almsgiving by the above promotion. In his obedience to 'what was said about Christ' Marcellus is the ideal listener and reader implied by these texts who is moved to generosity expressed in alms to the needy, above all the widows and orphans, and which wins for him from his fellow-citizens the title of 'amator pauperum', the 'lover of the poor':

There lived in the city a certain man called Marcellus, who was highly famed for his way of life, his pursuits and nobility, as well as his good sense and probity. He commanded great wealth and, most important of all, he feared God devoutly and always heeded reverently what was said about Christ. He lacked nothing truly good. As a result he was held in high honour by the whole city and he himself would frequently reward his city by distributing his largess, giving to the poor, easing the burdens of the afflicted, assisting those in distress.[133]

These fictional superlatives beg the question as to how far the meanings so far set out were accepted in real life. This chapter opened by

---

[129] *Life of Abercius* 20, Nissen, *Vita*, 17.

[130] *Life of Abercius* 19, Nissen, *Vita*, 16.

[131] e.g. Basil, *In Time of Hunger* 7, PG 31. 324A–B; *On Envy* 5, PG 31. 384C; Chrysostom, *On Penance* 7, PG 49. 333; *Ap. Const.* 2.48. 1, 5. 20. 18, and 6. 23. 10, SC 320. 290, 329. 284 and 370.

[132] *Life of Alexander* 33, PO 6. 684. For detailed discussion of examples from sermons of almsgiving presented as a benefaction, cf. De Vinne, *Advocacy*, 96–100.

[133] *Acta Archelai* 1, in Beeson, *Acta*, 1. For his title and care of the widows and orphans, *Acta Archelai* 3, in Beeson, *Acta*, 4.

stating that ascription of meaning by promoters was both a matter of describing a significance already inherent to Christian almsgiving in its social context and constructive of that significance. It might be objected that promoters ascribed meanings which were largely rejected or ignored by those whom they sought to influence.

A number of inscriptions, however, demonstrate how the redescriptions of the donor and his relationship with the recipient found a sufficient degree of public acceptance to feature in epitaphs which celebrated, in terse and conventional terms, a person's acknowledged claim to honours and thus presupposed a common understanding of their import. Marcellus's title, 'amator pauperum', was proudly displayed in an epitaph of 341 recording the burial at Rome of Iunianus by his wife Victoria, who went on to describe herself as 'amatrix pauperum'.[134] The same title has been suggested for an incomplete inscription of 381.[135]

In Roman North Africa a mosaic inscription in the nave of the basilica in the cemetery at Tipasa honours the church's deceased founder, bishop Alexander, as a 'lover of the poor wholly devoted to almsgiving' (*pauperum amator aelemosinae deditus omnis*).[136] Although the construction of the church cannot be dated conclusively, scholarly consensus dates the building to the final years of the fourth century or the early years of the fifth.[137] The church, which marked the burial of earlier saints, perhaps martyrs, contained another large mosaic inscription (2.60 m × 1.15 m), clearly visible to the faithful on entering the basilica, which proclaimed:

> CLAVSVLA IVSTITIAE EST
> MARTYRIUM VOTIS OPTARE
> HABES ET ALIAM SIMILEM
> AELEMOSINAM VIRIBUS FACERE[138]

---

[134] C. Carletti, *Iscrizioni cristiane di Roma* (Florence, 1986), no. 89 = *ICUR* i. 1420 = *ILCV* 2816.

[135] O. Marucchi, *Christian Epigraphy: An Elementary Treatise*, no. 166, tr. J. A. Willis (Cambridge, 1912), 179.

[136] H. Leclercq, 'Tipasa', *DACL* 15 (1953), 2338–2406.

[137] e.g. V. Saxer, *Morts, martyrs, reliques en Afrique chrétienne aux premiers siècles* (Paris, 1980), 303.

[138] Leclercq, 'Tipasa', 2363.

It is part of justice to wish for martyrdom in one's prayers. Yours is another like part: to give alms with your resources.

The text shows how the promotion of almsgiving in sermons as part of justice might be mirrored in the physical environment where that preaching occurred. Its location close to the doors may well reflect the presence of beggars at or near those doors.

An inscription almost identical to that describing bishop Alexander, but adapted for Cresconius, the bishop of Cuicul (Djemila), is found in the choir of the southern basilica in the latter town. Cresconius is honoured as 'pauperum amator elemosin deditus omni'.[139] Scholars have disputed its date: the original editors of the inscription argued for the period shortly after 411;[140] P.-A. Février thought it more likely to date from the mid-sixth century.[141] What is significant here is the scholars' belief that both the Tipasa and Djemila inscriptions were based on a common prototype or pattern, which would suggest widespread use of the honorific title *amator pauperum* by the fifth century. It is in this context that we should note two further instances of the title in tomb inscriptions outside a church at Tabarka.[142] Both apparently honour clerics. Neither may be dated with certainty, though mosaics in the nearby church have been thought to date from the late fourth to fifth century.[143] A marble tablet found near St Paul's Without the Walls at Rome records the burial in 377 of a lector, Cinnamius, similarly described as the 'friend of the poor' (*amicus pauperum*).[144]

Friendship with the poor may be displayed in a fourth-century Sardinian epitaph on what may be either a funerary table in the pagan style, on which food offerings were left for the dead, or a type of 'agape table':

---

[139] *AE* (1922), no. 25 and report by M. Albertini in R. Cagnat, 'Seance de la commission de l'Afrique du nord, Janvier 17', *BCTH* (1922), xxvii–xxxi.

[140] Cagnat, 'Séance, Janvier 17', *BCTH* (1922), xxxi.

[141] P.-A. Février, *Djemila* (Algiers, 1968), 83.

[142] Report by M. Merlin in R. Cagnat, 'Seance de la commission de l'Afrique du nord, Mars 14', *BCTH* (1911), clxxix and clxxxi.

[143] Ibid. clxxii.

[144] I. B. De Rossi and A. Silvagni, *Inscriptiones Christianae Vrbis Romae Septimo Saeculo Antiquiores*, NS (Vatican, 1922–1), ii. 4815.

D(IS) M(ANIBVS)
SPIRITO REQVIESCENTI KARISSIMI
AMICORVM OMNIVM PR(A)ESTATORI BONO
PAVPERVM MANDATIS SERVIENS
VIGE IN OMMNIBVS CHR(IST)I CLEMENTIA BENE
CONIVGET IBIDEM HIS BIXSIT AN(N)IS LXV M(ENSIBVS) III
D(IEBVS) XII R(EQVIEVIT) IN PACE

To the restful spirit of Karissimus, who provided well for all his friends. For serving the demands of the poor, grow strong in them all. May the mercy of Christ here form the bond. He lived 65 years, 3 months, and 12 days. He has gone to rest in peace.[145]

The friends and the poor referred to here may be one and the same. If the monument takes the form of an *agape* table, this suggests the form taken by the deceased's alms and the role of the *agape* in generating these bonds of friendship.[146] The *mandata pauperum* may be both the 'demands (for alms) made by the poor' in the donor's lifetime and 'the prayers of the poor' now offered by recipients on behalf of the deceased.

The epitaph for Pope Siricius in 399 described him, among much else as being 'compassionate and generous' (*misericors largus*).[147] An epitaph in one of the Milanese basilicas remembers the virtues of a woman from the senatorial elite, Manlia Daedalia, plausibly identified as a sister or daughter of Flavius Manlius Theodorus, the consul of 399. This consecrated virgin is proudly described as a mother to the needy (*mater egentvm*), presumably because of her provision of the alms on which they lived.[148]

Inscriptions which do not explicitly refer to the characterization of the generous donor and his or her relationship with the recipient of alms may nonetheless offer an implicit witness to the meanings considered in this chapter simply by recording almsgiving and care of the poor as a matter of honour worthy to find a place on the funerary monument. An inscription from Rome, which Marucchi

---

[145] *ILCV* 3400 = *CIL* 10, 07914 = *AE* (1982), 110, no. 430.
[146] N. Duval, 'Une *mensa* funéraire de Tharros (Sardaigne) et la collection chrétienne du Musée de Cagliari', *Revue des études augustiniennes*, 28 (1982), 284–5.
[147] Marucchi, *Christian Epigraphy*, 420, no. 446.
[148] *CIL* v. 6240 = *ILCV* 1700 = *AE* (1991), 0861.

dated to the mid-fourth century by the style of its lettering, displays the place of almsgiving in the conventional duties of a bishop, Leo: 'I took care to clothe the naked who sought my help and to give out whatever the year had yielded.'[149] An inscription probably from the first half of the fourth century in the Sardinian basilica of S. Gavino in Porto Torres records the praise offered by a husband to his wife and, if the restoration is correct, honours her legacy to the poor: 'CASTA CVSTOS SEDVLA CVNC[TIS PRAEDITA] / MORIBVS EX QVO REM SVAM [PAVPERIBVS] / LINQVIT...' (A chaste and diligent guardian, endowed with all the virtues, in accordance with which she bequeathed her property to the poor).[150] The enumeration of these good works in an epitaph constituted a plea for mercy much as images such as Jonah's deliverance from the whale, the preservation of Noah, and the sparing of Isaac, articulated a silent prayer for the deceased's deliverance.[151]

A second type of evidence for the widespread acceptance of the meanings set out in this chapter is offered by a letter in which the characterization of almsgiving as an act of generosity is not immediately subject to the idealizing or exaggerating conventions of hagiography. Ambrose wrote to a certain Marcellus, a fellow member of the aristocratic elite or *clarissimate*, and almost certainly a fellow bishop, concerning his attempt to provide for his sister in such a way as to leave a considerable portion of the family estates to the Church, with the intention we may presume, of providing income for future almsgiving. The donation was contested by his brother Laetus, and Ambrose, asked to intervene, settled the case in favour of Laetus, but praised Marcellus for his frustrated generosity (*liberalitas*) towards the poor.[152]

Saints' *Lives* have been shown to be rhetorical vehicles for promoting almsgiving. That might appear to make them difficult to cite as direct evidence for the acceptance of promotion, especially where *Lives* may have modelled their protagonists on earlier figures. The *Life of Antony* presents the young man's decision to give away his

---

[149] Marucchi, *Christian Epigraphy*, 197, no. 197.

[150] *AE* (1994), No. 796.

[151] A. Grabar, *Christian Iconography: A Study of its Origins* (London, 1969), 10.

[152] Ambrose, *Ep.* 24, OOSA 19. 237–44. For a reconstruction of the circumstances surrounding the letter, cf. McLynn, *Ambrose*, 270–1.

family wealth and adopt an ascetic life as a response to hearing Matthew 19: 21 recited in church at a time when he was already reflecting on the almsgiving practised by the Jerusalem community in Acts 4: 35–7.[153] There is little reason to doubt Athanasius's veracity, other than our ignorance of his sources and their reliability, but when the *Life of Hypatios* shows the monk ministering to the sick in response to Matthew 25: 34–6, there is some reason to think Callinicus may have been influenced by the earlier example of faithful listening.[154] When Alexander is said to have adopted asceticism and the monastic life on hearing Matthew 19: 21, there may be yet greater reason to think the author of his *Life* was influenced by Antony's example.[155] Life, however, also imitates art, and we cannot presume that Antony's example influenced only the author and not Alexander himself.

The majority of the *Lives* considered in this chapter were written within a short period of the protagonist's death and in many cases by figures close to the protagonist, which increases the reliability of their testimony, while the pressure to conform to accepted images of the holy man or woman militates against promotion of contentious meanings. Dennis Trout has written in this respect of how 'the persuasive power of these new ascetic heroes of the late fourth century was generated as much by their alleged typicality as by their individuality'. And with respect to the former point Trout has observed that, where memories of the holy man or woman were still strong, 'suspected distortions might quickly draw hostile fire'.[156]

The *Vita Honorati* shows how the religious and social meanings of almsgiving interrelated: it is because the young Honoratus and his brother see Christ in the poor that they are prompted to greater generosity in almsgiving and hospitality, indicated first by the language of prodigality and largesse. Honoratus would 'offer with generous compassion' (*miseratione prodigus offerebat*) what was his to dispose of while still a minor and even then thought to 'give away all he possessed once and for all' (*sua simul universa largiri*).[157] The

[153] Athanasius, *Life of Antony* 2, SC 400. 132–4.
[154] Callinicus, *Life of Hypatios* 4. 1–4, SC 177. 84 –6.
[155] *Life of Alexander* 5, PO 6. 661.
[156] Trout, *Paulinus*, 9.
[157] Hilary of Arles, *Vita Honorati* 5 in Cavallin, *Vitae*, 53.

brothers vied to see 'who could give more quickly what came from his possessions . . . who was quicker to welcome the traveller with his tears before dispensing alms, and feed Christ with his love before feeding the stranger with the meal.'[158] They recalled how it was Christ whom they fed in this way. What mattered to them was the christological sense of their actions.

Finally, it is noticeable that *Lives* and other texts do not only describe holy almsgivers as fathers of the poor, but also present them as being so addressed by others. The *Life of Rabbula* reported that the Edessenes mourned him at his death as 'father of the orphans'.[159] Jerome described Florentinus, a man from Aquileia, who was to become a hermit in the East, as 'given the title "father of the poor" by the common people' for his 'great mercy towards the destitute' (*tam misericors in egentes fuit, ut vulgo pater pauperum nominatus sit*).[160]

## THE LANGUAGE OF LEADERSHIP

Readers and listeners were invited to see generous donors as exercising a form of leadership or patronage of those whom they aided by alms. A phrase 'the leadership of the needy' (ἡ προστασία τῶν δεομένων) was a formula used by certain promoters of almsgiving.[161] Gregory Nazianzen portrayed Athanasius not only as a father of the orphans, but as προστάτης of the widows, their 'protector', 'champion', or 'patron': 'Widows will, I think, praise him as their champion, orphans as their father and beggars as one who loved beggars.'[162] Chrysostom urged his congregation to exercise their *prostasia* or leadership in helping their needy neighbours, and promised them that others

---

158 Hilary of Arles, *Vita Honorati* 9, in Cavallin, *Vitae*, 55.

159 *Life of Rabbula*, in Bickell, *Ausgewählte Schriften*, 201.

160 Jerome, *Chronicon*, ad 377, in R. Helm, *Die Chronik des Hieronymus* (Berlin, 1956), 248.

161 Gregory Nazianzen, *Or.* 19, PG 35. 1052A; *Or.* 21. 10, in Mossay, *Discours 20–30*, 130; John Chrysostom, *Homilies on Prayer* 2. 1, PG 63. 586, *Homilies on Romans* 2, PG 60. 402; Anon., *Sermons on Job* 1, PG 56. 565.

162 Gregory Nazianzen, *Or.* 21. 10, PG 35. 1093A.

would praise them for saving the recipients of alms through their *prostasia*.[163] He discussed the bishop's *prostasia* of the enrolled widows.[164] Once again, the Egyptian monk, Isidore of Pelusium, allows us to see this language taken up in local church politics: he complained to a priest, Paul, how clerics responsible for distributing alms had fallen away from their proper task and started to feather their own nests or put private interest over other considerations in how the money is distributed. That initial task is described as the *prostasia* of the *penetes*.[165] The significance of almsgiving for the exercise of a certain sort of leadership is so far taken for granted by Isidore that it stands in as a description of the actual practice.

It is in this context that the language of fatherhood also implied a form of benign authority over the poor in a patriarchal society. Indeed, it was to exercise a god-like spiritual authority, because to be a father of orphans was to be like God as He was praised in the Psalms: 'Father of orphans and protector (*iudex*) of widows is God in his holy habitation.'[166] Gregory Nazianzen may also imply some kind of moral authority when presenting his mother as a παραστάτις of widows and orphans, their 'helper' or 'defender'.[167] Yet, the extent to which this language of leadership is found in the promotion of almsgiving should not be exaggerated. Promoters had far more to say about the meaning of almsgiving as an expression of generosity than as an expression of authority. And the language of benefaction, leadership, and patronage does not necessarily turn the destitute into 'steadfast, unwavering clients' in the traditional sense of that term.[168] Clients have a particular pattern of conduct towards their patrons not adopted by recipients of alms. On the other hand, as the next section will explain, this does not imply that the meanings established here were without significance for the construction of honour and authority in the Christian community.

---

[163] Chrysostom, *Homilies on Matthew* 78. 3, PG 58. 714; *Homilies on 1 Corinthians* 10. 4, PG 61. 88.

[164] *De sacerdotio* 3. 12, SC 272. 201.

[165] Isidore, *Ep.* 1077 = Migne Ep. III. 277, PG 78. 953C.

[166] Ps. 67: 6 (Vulgate and LXX).

[167] Gregory Nazianzen, *Or.* 18. 9, PG 35. 993: Τίς δὲ ὀρφανῶν καὶ χηρῶν ἀμείνων ἐγένετο παραστάτις;

[168] De Vinne, *Advocacy,* 104.

## HONOUR, COMPETITION, AND AUTHORITY

Patlagean has written that the survival of the classical vocabulary of generosity in a Christian context where it was put to new uses is a good example of the progressive change in concepts and social relations.[169] What, then, were the changes in social relations brought about by this adapted generosity as it interacted with the redescription of the poor as intercessors and of their donors as benefactors? Peter Brown has argued recently that the 'notion of "care of the poor" helped to define the place of the Christian church in Roman society. It acted as a discreet control on the clergy. They were to know their place—closer to the poor than to the top of society.'[170] But we shall see that the discourse and practices of Christian almsgiving could be used to exalt clerical status and to act as a discreet control on the laity. Care did not always imply social proximity, and in late antique society those at the top might assert their place in society by how they cared for those at the bottom.

Inscriptions have already shown that generous and assiduous almsgiving on a large scale or over a long period conferred honour on its practitioners. The liberality which Gregory Nazianzen ascribed to his mother is said to be part of an 'inviolable honour'.[171] It might be objected that in this example from an oration we are faced with further promotion open to the charge of falsehood or polemic. Yet, the objection is mistaken: in an *encomium* which sets out to give public honour the passage is as much a performative as a descriptive speech-act: it works by speaking of what is known to be honourable and by so speaking gives honour. It is an illocutionary, not a perlocutionary, act.[172] There is no good reason, then, to doubt Gregory's veracity when he relates that his mother thought giving a small amount in alms to be no better than reminding people of their misery, but that to give alms ($\epsilon\mathring{v}$ $\pi o\iota\epsilon\hat{\iota}\nu$) with greater generosity ($\dot{\epsilon}\lambda\epsilon\upsilon\theta\epsilon\rho\iota\acute{\omega}\tau\epsilon\rho o\nu$) was quite definitely honourable.[173]

---

169 Patalegean, *Pauvreté*, 190.
170 Brown, *Poverty and Leadership*, 31.
171 Gregory Nazianzen, *Or.* 18. 8, PG 35. 993.
172 On speech-acts, cf. A. Cruse, *Meaning in Language* (Oxford, 2000), 331–46.
173 Gregory Nazianzen, *Or.* 18. 8, PG 35. 993.

Jerome's portrait or character assassination in his letter to Eustochium of the Roman matron who doles out coins at St Peter's, but
punches the old woman who returns for a second coin, is evidence of a
more complex type for the honour to be found in generous almsgiving:

> I saw just recently in St. Peter's Basilica one of the noblest Roman women (I
> suppress her name, in case you think this is a satirical attack) who, preceded
> by her eunuchs, was distributing coins one by one to the poor, handing them
> out in person so as to be thought all the more devout. While this was going
> on [as is a well known practice] a certain old woman all enveloped in rags
> and old age, ran up to take another coin. When it came to her turn in line, a
> fist shot out instead of a *denarius*, and blood was spilled to pay for the guilt
> of such a crime.[174]

The noble woman's distribution of alms in person at the *martyrium* is
a practice which she and the readers recognize as a source of honour,
but which Jerome attacks as disreputable, vitiated first by her intention, the desire to win maximum publicity in a premeditated display
of generosity and humility (handing over the coin in person), and
then by the conduct which reveals her true state of mind. The
generosity does not stretch so far as a second *denarius*, while the
blow reveals false humility in the confident assertion of moral and
social superiority.[175] The honour to be won in this way might also be
impugned. It was vulnerable to attack from radical ascetics who saw
it as the figleaf covering the retention of wealth and pursuit of
worldly glory. Jerome wrote to Paulinus in *c*.395 of people 'jealously
guarding former riches under the cloak of almsgiving'.[176] We may
add that the woman's reaction to what she perceives as the hag's
insolence shows the widespread contempt towards the poor which
preachers sought to eradicate, and which is suggested by, for example, Libanius' description of beggars as 'all those who stare at
other people's fingers': the phrase conveys the need to watch for
potential donors and the extent to which this need defined those it
afflicted.[177] Jerome's tale shows how two different attitudes towards

---

[174] Jerome, *Ep.* 22. 32, in Labourt, *Lettres*, i. 147.
[175] For the greater wisdom and virtue thought to accrue to handing out alms in
person, cf. Jerome, *Ep.* 58. 6, in Labourt, *Lettres*, iii. 80–1.
[176] *Ep.* 58. 2 in Labourt, *Lettres*, iii. 75.
[177] Libanius, *Or.* 7. 12, in Foerster, *Opera*, i/2. 376.

the poor, old and new, might inhabit the same breast. What he reveals is the real but limited efficacy of the new Christian rhetoric. It is in this context, where almsgiving gives honour, but the pursuit of honour may itself be impugned as unworthy, that Gregory Nazianzen's account of his father's almsgiving should be understood. Part of his father's virtue was that, although generous in almsgiving as a bishop, he apparently avoided the honour attached to generosity by making his wife the chief vehicle for his charitable works: 'The noblest and greatest aspect was that he attached no desire for honour to his magnificence.'[178] This was of course, as a family and as a bishop, to eat and have one's cake of honour, while the son now honoured his father's disregard for that honour!

According honour to almsgiving was not only a matter of promoting this practice, but of advocating the curtailment of other practices. Basil called on the wealthier members of his congregation to divert their desire for glory from secular pursuits to that to be won from almsgiving: he invited them to take with them to the Lord 'the honour for your good deeds'.[179] Augustine, Ambrose, Paulinus, and others waged a campaign against older expressions of civic generosity of which they disapproved, in particular the provision of games and theatrical shows, and advocated almsgiving as an alternative source of honour from largesse.[180] Money spent in one way was not available to be spent in another, and failure to give alms could be exploited to devalue traditional forms of euergetism. Augustine declaimed: 'he puts on showy games, gives crazy presents to actors, gives nothing to the starving poor: he is unworthy of his riches'.[181] Almsgiving, recast by these leading Christian thinkers as civic euergetism, was meant by them to compete with older expressions of euergetism which fell under Church censure.[182] The timing of the charitable collections by the Roman church set charity in contrast, if not competition, with the largesse distributed at the *Ludi Apollinares* to which the

---

[178] Gregory Nazianzen, *Or.* 18. 21, PG 35. 1009.

[179] Basil, *I Shall Knock Down My Barns* 3, in Courtonne, *Homélies*, 21.

[180] e.g. Paulinus, *Ep.* 13. 15, CSEL 29. 96. Ambrose, *De officiis* 2. 109 in Testard, *Devoirs*, ii. 58–9.

[181] Augustine, *Serm.* 21. 10, CCSL 41. 285–6. Cf also *Ep.* 138. 14, PL 33. 531; *Serm.* 32. 20, CCSL 41. 407; *En. in Ps.* 149. 10, CCSL 40. 2184.

[182] C. Lepelley, *Les Cités de l'Afrique romaine au Bas-Empire*, i (Paris, 1979), 383.

illustrated calendar of 354 alluded in portraying for July heaps of coins from an open sack.[183] The continuing popularity of the traditional *munera*, however, even in cities that were predominantly Christian, shows the short-term failure of this clerical campaign. This is due in large measure to the way in which such *munera* were closely tied into the grant of particular civic honours and titles such as *principalis curiae* and *patronus*.[184] Many Christians adopted almsgiving as an additional form of generosity rather than as a replacement to older forms of euergetism. In this instance, at least, they sewed a new patch onto old wineskins.

Passages discussed in earlier chapters have already suggested how almsgiving featured in the construction and negotiation of spiritual authority in the Christian communities, especially that exercised by the bishop. This can now be studied further. Paulinus's biographer, Uranius, described him as being as generous (*munificus*) as Melchisedech.[185] He told how at the obsequies Christians, pagans, and Jews 'all bewailed the patron, defender, and guardian snatched from them . . . Spurning no one, he gave to all, he bestowed on all . . . He defined gold and silver and the rest in such a way that his liberality claimed them for giving away, not his cupidity for hoarding them.'[186] Uranius, in a metaphor that recalls Christ's impoverishment for humanity's enrichment, stated that Paulinus, in his 'concern for wretched, [and] compassion for the weak . . . alone was a beggar so that he might overflow for all'. There is a conflation here of different types of euergetism, civic patronage, almsgiving, and the foundation of churches. But these coalesce in exalting the status of the bishop.[187]

Spiritual authority brought popular support which might help a bishop to retain his see, whether because recipients of alms might

[183] M. Salzman, *On Roman Time: The Codex-Calendar of 354 and the Rhythms of Urban Life in Late Antiquity* (Berkeley, Los Angeles, and Oxford, 1990), 100–3 and fig. 38.

[184] C. Lepelley, 'Permanences de la cité classique et archaïsmes municipaux en Italie au Bas-Empire', in M. Christol, S. Demougin, Y. Duval, C. Lepelley, and L. Pietri (eds.), *Institutions, société et vie politique*, Collection de l'École Française de Rome, 159 (Rome, 1992), 361.

[185] Uranius, *Vita Paulini* 8, PL 53. 863B.

[186] Ibid. 9, PL 53. 863C-D, tr. Trout, *Paulinus*, 296–7.

[187] On the 'blurred edges of public and private authority in late Roman Italy', cf. Trout, *Paulinus*, 188.

prove loyal agents and defenders of the bishop who provided for them, or because it served to legitimate the bishop's rule over his entire congregation. According to Sozomen, the initial failure to remove Gerontion from the see at Nicomedia in 398 was due to successful popular opposition, and it is significant that those who spoke in Gerontion's favour praised this former Milanese deacon for his use of medical knowledge on behalf of both rich and poor.[188] It is plausible that Gerontion's experience as a deacon aiding Ambrose in his poor-relief had stood the new bishop in good stead. When Eulalios sought to evict Hypatios and his monks from Rouphinianai he sent, among others, the destitute.[189] It is a reasonable conjecture that these were recipients of episcopal alms. The accusations by Ambrose's rivals that he had bribed the crowds to secure their loyalty, to which the Milanese bishop referred in the *Against Auxentius* (33), reflect 'the cynical manipulation by Ambrose's enemies of the bishop's almsgiving'.[190] There was no bribery, only the exercise of a leadership partly constructed and expressed through almsgiving. This suggests that we may detect the hidden value of almsgiving behind other expressions of popular support for threatened bishops, such as the beating administered to two visiting bishops at Emerita in *c*.380 by a crowd loyal to the sitting bishop, Hydatius.[191] The influence occasionally exercised by popular support is seen in Theodoret's account that heckling by the people in the hippodrome finally led the Emperor Constantius II to remove his appointment, Felix, from the bishopric of Rome and restore Liberius to his place.[192] Chrysostom's public stance as a defender of the poor and promoter of almsgiving was certainly one reason for the popular support which for a short time protected him from imperial displeasure.[193]

Almsgiving played a role in how the bishops of Constantinople raised the status of the see in the surrounding region by almsgiving

[188] Sozomen, *Ecclesiastical History* 8. 6, in Bidez and Hansen, *Sozomenus*, 358–9.
[189] Callinicus, *Life of Hypatios* 41. 10, SC 177. 244.
[190] Humphries, *Communities of the Blessed*, 168.
[191] Chadwick, *Priscillian*, 31–2.
[192] Theodoret, *Ecclesiastical History* 2. 17, in Parmentier and Hansen, *Kirchengeschichte*, 137.
[193] Socrates, *Ecclesiastical History* 6. 15–16, in Hansen, *Sokrates*, 336–9, and Sozomen, *Ecclesiastical History* 8. 18, in Bidez and Hansen, *Sozomenus*, 373. Cf. Patlagean, *Pauvreté*, 218.

beyond the city itself. It is known that Atticus at some point before his death in 425 sent 300 gold pieces to the priest at Nicaea for distribution to the hungry in what was probably a food shortage afflicting the community there.[194] A reputation for almsgiving might also help a candidate to become bishop. Socrates related that Sisinnios was chosen to become bishop of Constantinople in late 425 or early 426 with the backing of lay supporters impressed 'above all because he devoted himself to comforting the destitute beyond his means'.[195] In 420 it was the poor (*maxime pauperes*) who were most vociferous in seeking to install Honorius, already a bishop elsewhere in the province, as metropolitan bishop of Caesarea in Mauretania, the position once held by his father.[196] Why the poor were so keen to support the illicit move is perhaps best explained by an allegiance on their part to the father as a generous donor and their hopes that his son would prove equally beneficent.

Hilary described the hospitality and almsgiving practised by Honoratus and his brother on their family estate as episcopal in style: 'even then a form of unofficial episcopacy was to be seen at work in their conduct'. It was, as noted earlier, a lesson to bishops.[197] This suggests that almsgiving was so closely associated with the exercise of episcopal authority by the turn of the fourth century that some forms or practices could become in other hands a means to rival or criticize individual bishops. This is confirmed by other *vitae*: in an urban setting the honourable virtues of monastic almsgiving, exercised in organizing distributions in time of famine or the running of hostels, might amount to, and fuel, competition with the local bishop. It is likely that Callinicus shows Hypatios exercising a typically episcopal form of almsgiving, when he stores food to distribute in a period of scarcity.[198] Monks were often discouraged from storing alms. Hypatios himself rebuked a monk who tried to store clothes which he

---

[194] Socrates, *Ecclesiastical History* 7. 25, in Hansen, *Sokrates*, 373.

[195] Ibid. 7. 26, in Hansen, *Sokrates*, 375. For the date of the election as between Oct. and Feb., cf. G. Dagron, *Naissance d'une capitale: Constantinople et ses institutions de 330 à 451* (Paris, 1974), 492.

[196] Augustine, *Ep.* 22* 7–8, OSA 46b. 354–8. Peter Brown is certain that 'the *pauperes* who supported Honoratus [sic] were not the destitute' but the 'average inhabitants'. Such certainty seems excessive. Brown, *Poverty and Leadership*, 71.

[197] Hilary, *Vita Honorati* 9, in Cavallin, *Vitae*, 55.

[198] Callinicus, *Life of Hypatios*, 31. 3–4, SC 177. 205.

should have redistributed at once.[199] Daily feeding of a great crowd from stores was a bishop's role, and Hypatios was a noted opponent of his own bishop on doctrinal grounds. The detail serves, so to speak, to steal the bishop's clothes. As Eulalios was able to count on the destitute, presumably those whom he fed, so Hypatios was able to defend his monastery with the help of the peasants whom he had fed and kept alive.[200]

Competition between a charismatic monk and bishop is also the context in which Alexander the Akoimetos is presented as persuading the wealthy Christians at Antioch to fund his newly founded *xenodocheion*. His *vita* presents Alexander's monks meeting with hostility from bishop Theodotus, and with expulsion on their first arrival in the city, before re-entering at night and establishing a monastery with perpetual psalmody in a former baths. On recognizing that his preaching had won a sympathetic audience 'and that he enjoyed high renown and honour' Alexander decides to take care of the city's poor and to persuade the rich to finance a *xenodocheion*. The hero's 'great eloquence', which both makes possible his charitable activity and is heightened by that activity, is used 'to criticize both the bishop and the general for their neglect of many things'.[201] Honour is seen to antagonize the clergy whose 'hearts are consumed with envy'. An attempt to have the saint run out of town by the *leticarii* proves unsuccessful in the face of popular support for the hero, until the monks are expelled by the *magister militum*.[202] The story may be false in part. One scholar, who has attempted to correlate what is said of Alexander in his *Life* with the account of his actions in the *Life of Hypatios*, dates Alexander's arrival in Antioch to *c*.404.[203] Yet Theodotus, successor to bishop Alexander and described by Theodoret as a 'pearl of purity',[204] is usually thought to have been bishop from 424 to 428, although these dates cannot be fixed with certainty.[205] But

---

[199] Callinicus, *Life of Hypatios* 34. 4–6, SC 177. 220.
[200] Callinicus, *Life of Hypatios* 31. 5 and 41. 11, SC 177. 206 and 244.
[201] *Life of Alexander*, 38–9, PO 6. 688–9.
[202] *Life of Alexander* 40–1, PO 6. 689–90.
[203] E. Wölfle, 'Der Abt Hypatios von Ruphinianai und der Akoimete Alexander', *Byzantinische Zeitschrift*, 79 (1986), 303.
[204] Theodoret, *Ecclesiastical History* 5. 38, in Parmentier and Hansen, *Kirchengeschichte*, 342.
[205] R. Devreesse, *Le Patriarcat d'Antioche* (Paris, 1945), 117.

this difficulty does not lessen the value of the *Life of Alexander* in showing how conspicuous almsgiving and championship of the poor through fostering almsgiving enabled a charismatic preacher to build up his status in competition with the bishop and protected him for a time from his opponents. If, as may be implied, the care of the poor was one of those matters which the bishop was said to neglect, the duty of almsgiving was also what made the bishop vulnerable to attack.[206]

Competition sharpened through almsgiving, or the perceived threat of competition, could involve others than monks. At Chalcedon, Bassianos, bishop of Ephesus, described how as a young man 'I devoted my life to the destitute and created a hostel ($\pi\tau\omega\chi\epsilon\hat{\iota}o\nu$) for them' which he had furnished with seventy beds for the care of the sick and injured. This, however, had excited the envy of Memnon, then local bishop, on account of the universal popularity Bassianos enjoyed as a result of his almsgiving. Memnon sought to neutralize a rival and remove him from the city in forcibly consecrating him as bishop of another city. When that failed to work, Memnon had him assaulted.[207] Memnon no doubt told a different story, but Bassianos must have thought his account would carry conviction.

On the other hand, more than one factor contributed to the rising status of bishops, including the role of the bishop as an intermediary between the town and the officials of the empire. The value placed on those who could mitigate the violence of imperial government, especially its fiscal exactions, is illustrated by a story in Theodoret's *Historia religiosa*, a gallery of ascetics from the fourth and early fifth century: Abrahames, an ascetic, set up a small monastic community in a pagan village in Lebanon. The villagers' initial hostility was dispelled when he arranged to pay the tax demanded by heavy-handed

---

[206] It will be clear that I disagree with Drake, who has argued that because 'charitable acts were efficacious only if they were offered to God as part of the normal liturgy' and the bishop was thus 'the middleman in such activities' this meant that 'the bishop took on the role of patron of the local Christian community, and moreover that he held the position without fear of potential rivals'. Drake, *Constantine and the Bishops*, 135.

[207] E Schwartz, ed. *Acta Conciliorum Oecumenicorum*, 4 vols. (Berlin, 1914–74), ii/1, part 3, 46 = p. 405 in square brackets. The second city is identified as Evagae in T. E. Gregory, *Vox Populi, Popular Opinion and Violence in the Religious Controversies of the Fifth Century* (Columbus, Ohio, c.1979), 146.

collectors. He borrowed 100 gold pieces to pay the officials (a sign of his wealthy family connections), and the villagers responded by offering to make him their patron (*prostates*).[208] Abrahames remained for some years in the village as its priest and oversaw the building of a local church. He shows how religious and civic leadership might merge.

Similar patterns of convergence can be seen through the career and letters of Synesius. A modern biographer, Bregman, speaks of Synesius having transferred an obligation of service to the *polis* 'as a member of the *boule*, benefactor, ambassador, or magistrate' to the office of bishop.[209] One of Synesius' letters tells how the town of Palaebiscus, earlier in the fourth century, had chosen as its bishop a man with local connections, Siderius, who had served in Valens' army and could act as the town's *prostates* (he was later made bishop of Ptolemaïs by Athanasius).[210] It was not only almsgiving practised within the civic community which facilitated the convergence of religious and civic authority, but the role of the bishop in dealing with the world beyond the *polis*. Nor should this convergence be exaggerated: Augustine in 420 eloquently explained to his fellow bishops Alypius and Peregrinus the need for, and difficulty in obtaining, a *defensor* at Hippo to protect the weaker inhabitants of the city and why the role was unsuited to the bishop himself.[211]

Almsgiving, therefore, had a primary role in the leadership exercised by the bishop over the widows and other recipients of alms, and a significant, but not necessarily a primary, role in the exercise of wider leadership in the Christian community, where the bishop's care for the poor was symbolic of his good government and orthodoxy. In neither case is this leadership to be equated with the classical forms of patronage. Donor and recipient were not bound to the same mutual and exclusive obligations as a traditional patron and client. But nor is this is to say that charity is 'a one-sided relationship between an active benefactor and an essentially passive beneficiary' and therefore

---

[208] Theodoret, *Historia religiosa* 17. 2–3, SC 257. 36–40.

[209] J. Bregman, *Synesius of Cyrene, Philosopher-Bishop* (Berkeley, Los Angeles, and London, 1982), 74.

[210] Synesius, *Ep.* 66 ( = Migne, *Ep.* 67) in A. Garzya (ed.), *Synesii Cyrenensis Epistulae* (Rome, 1979), 108–9.

[211] Augustine, *Ep.* 22* 3–4, OSA 46b. 350–2 and (for the date), 523.

cannot be a form of patronage.[212] For charity had been reconfigured as an exchange of gifts with certain, though untraditional, mutual obligations.

Almsgiving exercised by lay men and women enhanced their claim to honour in the Christian community, and justified, in the eyes of most but not all, their continuing possession of great wealth, while it offered one reason for the respect which they received from church leaders and writers; but any contribution of almsgiving to the exercise of lay leadership proves much harder to characterize. The language of *prostasia* which was directed at (potential) lay donors may work otherwise than as the description of a new and particular form of leadership or patronage available to them. It should be seen in the context of the varied forms of *prostasia* already exercised by lay figures in the civic community, often to the disadvantage of the poor. Isidore of Pelusium insisted to a local bishop, Leontius, in a letter dated by his modern editor, Évieux, to c.420, that bishops must not form alliances with those who used their *prostasia* of the people to fleece the poor.[213] Promoters of almsgiving presented almsgiving as an expression of an existing leadership in order to encourage its practice by those leaders and thereby to mitigate the deleterious effects on the poor of that pre-existing exercise of economic and social power.

## DISTINCTIVE MEANINGS?

Pagan practice and (the rarer) promotion of almsgiving has been noted in Chapters 2 to 4. Were the meanings advanced in the present chapter distinctive to the Christian practice and promotion of almsgiving? Pagans would not see alms as an act of compassion towards Christ himself, but did they understand almsgiving as an expression of particular virtues of justice and generosity or as the articulation of

---

[212] P. Garnsey, *Famine and Food Supply in the Graeco-Roman World* (Cambridge, 1988), 58.

[213] Isidore, *Ep.* 888 = Migne, *Ep.* III. 88, PG 78. 793, and P. Évieux, *Isidore de Péluse*, Théologie historique, 99 (Paris, 1995), 65.

certain mutual relationships between rich and poor? We should not necessarily expect an account of the meanings which pagans ascribed to almsgiving to show the widespread consistency found in the churches, where the concept of an orthodox teaching acted to rule out wide divergences in acceptable meanings.

Gifts to the destitute might be motivated by pity for another human being. Evidence for pity as the predominant motive in pagan gifts to beggars lies in the form taken by such gifts: alms as a response by the individual donor to a plea for help rather than as a premeditated or organized measure of poor-relief associated with religious observance or piety. But did pity for a fellow human being amount to *philanthropia*?

A late antique philosopher, Themistius, who wrote much on *philanthropia*, reveals that the classical virtue belonged to a certain social class, the leisured elite. He observed that it was nothing but 'ridiculous ... to attest to love of mankind in a weaver or a carpenter who has a mean dwelling, and who scarcely leaves his house through weariness and lack of leisure'.[214] Clearly, then, not all gifts of alms prompted by pity could count as expressions of virtue. But another philosophical text gives good reason for believing that no such gifts could count in this way. In the *Definitions* (a Platonic text once wrongly ascribed to Plato himself) *philanthropia* is characterized as a disposition to love a fellow human being so as to assist them as a benefactor: '*philanthropia* is the disposition in which people readily show affection for another human being. It is a disposition to be their benefactor, a state in which one shows gratitude, memory [of kindness received] with kindness [given].'[215] The abstract definition does not explicitly rule out the virtue's expression in almsgiving, but both theoretical and practical difficulties stand in the way of almsgiving as an expression of *philanthropia* defined in this way, namely, the absence on the part of the beggar of any return other than gratitude itself. Plato's virtue exists within a charmed circle of mutual gifts.

D. J. Constantelos has argued that pagan *philanthropia* always included acts of kindness towards the destitute, 'a man's pity for

---

[214] Themistius, *Or. 1.* 83, tr. P. Heather and D. Moncur (eds.), *Politics, Philosophy and Empire in the Fourth Century Select Orations of Themistius* (Liverpool, 2001), 83.
[215] Plato, *Definitions* 412e.

and aid to those in any kind of tribulation'.[216] His use of examples, however, is faulty, when he cites texts from Hesiod's *Works and Days* (390–402), Homer's *Iliad* (8. 546–7, 13. 200–3) and *Odyssey* (22. 490–500), all of which show a practice *assumed* to hold the desired meaning, even though the language of *philanthropia* is absent from the text.[217] The few examples cited by Constantelos which do speak of the virtue must be examined carefully. Xenophon praised Agesilaos, king of Sparta, for his *philanthropia* while on campaign in Asia Minor: Agesilaos prevented the abandonment of young children and elderly prisoners of war when the Greek army moved camp; and he exercised much restraint in the treatment of captured cities.[218] The *Athenian Constitution* praised Peisistratus as φιλάνθρωπος, as well as gentle and ever ready to pardon those who had offended him, lending money to those who had none.[219] In each case the evidence is harder to read than Constantelos allows. The first example may be read as a particular form of royal *philanthropia*, the exercise of clemency towards the defeated and the guilty. It is far removed from the care of beggars. In the second example, it is not clear that we should regard how the tyrant treated the *aporoi* as an expression of this virtue, which is listed among others. But, if the action is presented as an expression of *philanthropia*, we must question the identity of the *aporoi*: they may be poor citizens rather than beggars. Libanius, for example, has much to say about *philanthropia*, but does not suggest that it included gifts to beggars. Susan Holman has noted that only 'in his praise of Theodosius, who ruled at a time when the poor had clearly gained social power in public rhetoric, does Themistius refer to poverty even briefly in defining ideal "philanthropy"'.[220]

Institutional almsgiving was certainly encouraged by Julian as an expression of his *philanthropia*. As noted in Chapter 2, Gregory Nazianzen described Julian as imitating Christians by establishing 'inns...and hostels, holy places, houses of virgins, academies and

---

[216] Constantelos, *Byzantine Philanthropy*, 4–5.

[217] Ibid. 5–6.

[218] Xenophon, *Memorabilia* 2. 1. 28.

[219] *Athenian Constitution* 16.

[220] S. Holman, 'The Entitled Poor: Human Rights Language in the Cappadocians', *Pro Ecclesia*, 9 (2000), 479.

philanthropy for those in need' including letters of recommenda-tion.[221] Sozomen reported that Julian set up hostels 'for the relief of strangers and the poor and for other philanthropic purposes'.[222] What is more telling for our purposes, a letter by Julian himself shows him ordering the establishment of *xenodocheia* and grain distributions as part of a philanthropic programme designed to outshine the Christians.[223] The question is what this reveals: evidence for the ordinary classical virtue, for the classical virtue as interpreted within a particular philosophical tradition, or for its attempted remodelling on Christian lines. Given that the need to initiate such a competitive programme measures the difference between older pagan and Christian practices of almsgiving, it is more likely to be the last of these three—the introduction into the pagan concept of *philanthropia* of a Christian element which was otherwise foreign.[224]

Whether or not almsgiving was understood by pagans as an act of piety and philanthropy, it was not normally seen as an expression of generosity. Wealthy pagans certainly showed generosity (*liberalitas*) by making grain available for citizens at prices well below the current market rate, both during times of shortage and to mark other special occasions. An inscription from Numlulis in North Africa records the *liberalitas* of L. Memmius Pecuarius Marcellinus in restoring the city's temple to Capitoline Jupiter and providing for its rededication gifts (*sportulae*) for the decurions, a gymnasium and banquet for the citizens, and cheap corn.[225] But gifts to citizens are not to be equated with gifts to the destitute, whether citizens or not. Furthermore, gifts of alms to individual beggars were too small to be numbered among the actions of a benefactor. Seneca in the *De beneficiis* had explicitly stated that odd gifts to beggars were too trivial, insignificant, to serve as *beneficia*.[226] They met with no returns, no corresponding expression

[221] Gregory Nazianzen, *Against Julian* 1, PG 35. 648C.

[222] Sozomen, *Ecclesiastical History* 5. 16, in Bidez and Hansen, *Sozomenus*, 218.

[223] Julian, *Ep.* 84a (formerly *ep.* 49). 430B–C, in Bidez and Cumont, *Epistulae et leges*, 114. For Julian's concern to counter the Christian *agapes* cf. *Ep.* 89b. 305D, Bidez and Cumont, 146.

[224] Cf. Pétré, *Caritas*, 211.

[225] *CIL* viii. 26121.

[226] Seneca, *De beneficiis* 4. 29.

of honour. They did not confer dignity on the donor and so failed to contribute to his virtue.

## CONCLUSION

Almsgiving had by the late fourth century acquired specific meanings for Christians which promotion sustained and served to inculcate. Among these meanings, almsgiving as an exchange of gifts altered the relationship between the generous donor and worthy recipient to accord honour to the former which sustained and raised their status within the Christian community, while the latter acquired a new value and place in the community as a reservoir of public and vocal support, both developments with implications for the competitive exercise of power by monks, lay donors, and, above all, bishops. Oswyn Murray's desire 'to know what succeeded the Imperial form of euergetism, and how it developed or was replaced in the early Christian and Byzantine periods' was noted at the end of Chapter 1.[227] The present chapter on the meaning of almsgiving has showed how almsgiving featured in this process as a new form of euergetism alongside the old in the late fourth and early fifth centuries.

Marshall Sahlins has written that

Redistribution by powers-that-be serves two purposes, either of which may be dominant in a given instance. The practical, logistical function—redistribution—sustains the community or community effort in a material sense. At the same time, or alternatively, it has an instrumental function: as a ritual of communion and subordination to central authority, redistribution sustains the corporate structure itself, that is in a social sense. The practical benefits may be critical, but, whatever the practical benefits, chiefly pooling generates the spirit of unity and centricity, codifies the structure, stipulates the centralised organisation and social order and social action.[228]

In the case of almsgiving by bishops, the latter instrumental function was of great importance, but in communities where the bishop

---

[227] Veyne, *Bread and Circuses*, p. xxi.
[228] M. Sahlins, *Stone Age Economics*, 190, cited H. Moxnes, *The Economy of the Kingdom* (Philadelphia, 1988), 38–9.

commanded limited resources, where almsgiving was also enjoined on all, where it might take a great variety of forms or practices, and where some possessed great means at their disposal, the impact was both to exalt and to expose the bishop as a leader. Peter Brown has rightly judged that 'the care of the poor...facilitated a...decisive process by which the bishop became a major urban patron', but that verdict needs to be qualified by recognition of the dangers run in that process.[229] The *Apocalypse of Paul*, reworked if not composed in the late fourth century, and widely read in the first half of the fifth century, above all in monastic circles, contained an extended vision of hell, one figure in which was that of a bishop who was stoned for his twin failures to judge well and to show compassion to the widows and orphans.[230]

This continuing exposure to criticism on the part of the bishop can be seen in Salvian's *Four Books*: 'It remains to say something concerning the clergy and priests, though some of what is said may perhaps be unnecessary! For whatever is said concerning everyone else, applies without a doubt even more to those who are meant to be an example for all and the more they excel others in authority, the more they should excel them by their dedication.'[231]

The claim to honour gave critics the corresponding power to shame. It is significant in this respect that Augustine chose to present himself to the congregation as an ambassador (*legatus*) on the part of the poor, forced by their pleading and the limited resources at his disposal to intercede with the congregation for their alms: 'They have called on me to speak to you and as they see themselves receiving nothing from you, think I achieve nothing among you. They are also looking for something from me...'[232] Augustine here turned to his rhetorical advantage what was potentially damaging criticism of his pastoral care. By humbly presenting himself as a legate, a servant of the poor, he lent his authority to their claims for assistance, a position made possible by the meanings discussed in this chapter

---

[229] Brown, *Power and Persuasion*, 101.
[230] *Apocalypse of Paul* 35, tr. J. K. Elliott, *The Apocryphal New Testament* (Oxford, 1993), 634. For the date of composition and readership, cf. R. P. Casey, 'The Apocalypse of Paul', *JThS* 34 (1933), 1–32.
[231] Salvian, *Four Books* 2. 9. 37, in SC 176. 212 and 214.
[232] Augustine, *Serm.* 61. 13, PL 38. 414.

which recognized in the poor the person of Christ. He thereby hoped to win greater success in promoting almsgiving which would secure his leadership. These complexities in negotiating authority through the meaningful practices of almsgiving are further examined in the next chapter which turns to look in some detail at how almsgiving features in the work of two bishops, Basil of Caesarea and Ambrose of Milan, and one theological polemicist, Jerome.

# 6

## Christian and Classical

I hope to have shown how almsgiving, as repeatedly promoted in Christian discourse and practised in distinctive forms by different church members, acquired significance as a potential expression of generosity which, as such, won for the donor an increased moral and spiritual authority in the eyes of fellow Christians. It has been established that the negotiation of this authority (its acquisition and exercise) by bishops, monks, and lay people was a far from simple matter in a context where almsgiving was a means to competition, but individuals were easily exposed to verbal attack for their supposed ambition or negligence as donors. The authority given by alms was dependent in some circumstances on eloquence, in particular the eloquence with which a bishop preached, and on wider conduct in a given social station such as the self-dispossession of the ascetic. I have scarcely mentioned the non-Christian world beyond the churches except by way of a comparison, necessarily brief, of practices, beliefs, and meanings. The present chapter, however, studies three figures, Basil of Caesarea, Ambrose of Milan, and Jerome to examine finally how this complex pattern of meaningful practice within the Christian communities interacted with the classical, pagan world in which these communities existed, that is to say, how it was both influenced by older patterns of practice in euergetism, how Christian discourse sought to incorporate and reinterpret its classical counterpart in pursuit of its own ends, and how these different patterns of thought and virtue gave rise to controversy within the churches. The first half of the chapter re-examines the issues of competition between donors and of leadership (or patronage). It qualifies what has so far been said by examining the rhetorical and ecclesiastical strategies by which the dangers inherent in competition might be limited or circumvented.

## BASIL OF CAESAREA: ONE PATRON OR MANY?

In 369 the inland towns of Cappadocia experienced a prolonged food shortage that would later be described by Gregory Nazianzen as 'the most severe ever remembered'.[1] Basil recalled for his congregation how cloudless skies from late winter onwards had led to drought and crop failure. The earth was cracked open, springs had dried up, and once deep rivers were reduced to a trickle which even small children could walk through.[2] In a startling reversal of the imagery found at Luke 10: 2, Basil observed that the labourers were many, but the harvest was not even small.[3] Philip Beagon has suggested that in normal times Caesarea would 'have acted as a focus for the redistribution of grain within the province, transmitting it from the cornfields of the west and south-west to the less fertile eastern regions'.[4] Now the city was dependent on the quantities of grain which wealthy farmers and other local traders or householders held in storage.[5] If prices rose sharply, the poor, who could not afford sufficient grain, would quickly exhaust the supplies of other staples or vegetables. For them at least the shortage threatened famine.[6] Basil reminded the

[1] Gregory Nazianzen, *Or.* 43. 34, SC 384. 200. Most historians describe the shortage as occuring within a single year, but differ as to which year. Susan Holman e.g. places the crisis in 368, whereas P. J. Fedwick and Philip Rousseau place it in 369, and Peter Brown favours 370. Cf. Holman, *The Hungry*, 65; P. J. Fedwick, 'A Chronology of the Life and Works of Basil of Caesarea', in his *Basil of Caesarea, Christian, Humanist, Ascetic*, 2 vols. (Toronto, 1981), i. 11; P. Rousseau, *Basil of Caesarea* (Berkeley, Los Angeles, and Oxford, 1994), 136; Brown, *Poverty and Leadership*, 41.

[2] Basil, *In Time of Hunger* 2, PG 31. 305C.

[3] Ibid., PG 31. 308A.

[4] P. Beagon, '*Social and Political Aspects of the Career of St Basil*', D.Phil. (Oxford, 1990), 40.

[5] Basil, *In Time of Hunger* 2, PG 31. 309B.

[6] Famine has been defined as a 'catastrophic food crisis, which is responsible for a dramatic rise in mortality rates in a given population'. Garnsey, *Famine and Food Supply*, p. x. For the view that the local supplies available in Caesarea mean we can speak only of severe shortage not famine, ibid. 23.

congregation of the slow agonizing death that awaited the starving, when the emaciated flesh lay on the bones 'like a cobweb' and the skin turned black.[7]

Two letters show that Basil's presence at Caesarea was considered essential in addressing the crisis, and thereby offer one way to measure its depth. In the midst of the shortage he wrote to Eusebius, bishop of Samosata, to explain why he had cancelled a planned visit. He elaborated the wish, though with little hope, that, 'should the season permit and life still leave time, and should the food shortage not make the journey impossible for me', he might yet realize his desire of visiting Eusebius.[8] A series of verbs in the optative warned Basil's correspondent with all the courtesy due to the bishop that the wished-for visit was unlikely to take place in the near future. A letter to another bishop, Eusebonas, explained why the continuing crisis necessitated that he remain at Caesarea and once again prevented him from travelling: he was to stay either to show 'compassion for the afflicted or because of the distribution to be made'.[9]

What Basil did is relatively well known, in part from the survival of several sermons which he preached in this period, and in part from the accounts given by his brother Gregory of Nyssa and his friend Gregory Nazianzen.[10] The latter's funeral oration for Basil told how the aristocratic priest 'by his words and exhortations opened the

---

[7] Basil, *In Time of Hunger* 7, PG 31. 321B–D.

[8] Εἰ δὲ ὁ καιρὸς ἐνδοίη καὶ τῆς ζωῆς ἡμῖν ἔτι λείποιτο χρόνος καὶ μὴ ἄπορον ἡμῖν τὴν ὁδὸν ὁ λιμὸς ἀπεργάσαιτο, ταχὺ ἂν τύχοιμεν τῆς ἐπιθυμίας... *Ep.* 27, in Courtonne, *Lettres*, i. 65. The letter speaks of a mild winter in the past tense and, according to Basil's sermon *In Time of Hunger* (PG 31. 308C–D), a snowless winter preceded the famine of 369. The letter implies that the food shortage has either already begun or is now grimly expected in the near future. Fedwick, however, dates the letter to the spring of 370. Fedwick, 'Chronology', 11.

[9] *Ep.* 31, Courtonne, *Lettres*, i. 73. Courtonne dates the letter to 369. Marcella Forlin Patrucco, in her *Basilio di Cesarea, Le lettere*, i (Turin, 1983), 385, believes the correspondent cannot be identified. R. Pouchet, in his *Basile le Grand et son univers d'amis d'après sa correspondance: Une stratégie de communion* (Rome, 1992), 190–4, thinks Eusebonas is none other than Eusebius of Samosata.

[10] The sermons concerned are: *In Time of Hunger* (PG 31. 304–28), *God Does Not Cause Evil* (PG 31. 329–53), *I Shall Knock Down My Barns*, and, perhaps, the sermon *On the Wealthy*, the last two edited by Y. Courtonne, *Homélies sur la richesse* (Paris, 1935). Forlin Patrucco includes the last of these four among those preached at this time, although Philip Rousseau does not. Forlin Patrucco, *Lettere*, 367; Rousseau, *Basil*, 136 n. 11.

barns of the wealthy', and then, with the food that was released and resources from his own family, set up a soup kitchen where he and his household servants fed and tended the starving. Gregory wrote of Basil 'collecting together' or 'holding a collection for every kind of food'.[11] The verb suggests a plea for alms in kind from others which Basil then had turned into soup. What is not clear from this account is whether the 'wealthy' gave their alms *gratis*, merely sold their grain to Basil and others at a reduced price, or both.[12] Gregory of Nyssa's account suggests that they sold at least some of their stores to Basil. It makes no mention of any collection, but recalled how Basil 'sold his own belongings and converted the money into food' with which he then proceeded 'to feed for the duration of the crisis those who flooded in from every direction and the city's entire youth providing even the Jewish children with an equal share of his philanthropy'.[13] It appears that Basil acted, therefore, as a cleric in preaching and organizing the collection on behalf of the bishop, but also as a wealthy aristocrat acting independently in redistributing his own wealth. The question is how to understand the full significance of Basil's actions in the dual context of the Christian community and wider cultural life of Caesarea.

The two Gregorys each suggest a particular context in which to view Basil's actions: one in which he acts largely alone; and one in which he co-operates with others in the church. Gregory of Nyssa's account suggests that we should see Basil's acts primarily in the classical context of noble euergetism by a single individual or patron. Among the institutions and practices developed across the centuries by towns in the Graeco-Roman world in order to stave off famine and manage periodic shortages had been the custom of a wealthy patron selling grain at well below the current market price in return for a grant of honour.[14]

Gregory of Nazianzen's account suggests that we should view Basil's actions primarily within the context of church almsgiving where the bishop was supposed to oversee the actions of his clergy.

---

[11] Gregory Nazianzen, *Or.* 43. 35, SC 384. 202–4.

[12] For the view that the other wealthy citizens of Caesarea sold their grain at a reduced price, cf. Forlin Patrucco, *Lettere*, 367.

[13] Gregory of Nyssa, *Oration in Praise of his Brother Basil*, GNO 10/1. 124.

[14] For examples in the late empire, see Garnsey and Humfress, *Evolution*, 117.

This is not only because of what Gregory Nazianzen describes, but of where the description is placed. He states that an earlier quarrel between bishop and presbyter had given way to a second period of co-operation in which Basil acted with the bishop's authority: 'for when he contributed his willing support, he received authority in return'. He became the 'old man's walking stick'.[15] Gregory then presents Basil's care for the poor in general (with reference to the support of hostels for beggars and strangers) and his care for the victims of famine in particular as part of his work as a dutiful church leader.[16] He speaks of Basil's 'leadership of the needy' (προστασίαι τῶν δεομένων) in matters spiritual and physical.[17]

It is theoretically possible that Basil's various actions had different, and discrete, meanings for two different constituencies: the church community and the wider *polis* in which pagans remained a large, and perhaps the largest, group. What one group saw simply as civic patronage, with the use of private wealth for civic ends, the other perceived to be an expression of, or perhaps detraction from, the proper role of the bishop in exhorting donations from others and managing their distribution as alms to the hungry. That seems too simplistic, however, given both the degree of participation by Christians in civic life and what Gregory Nazianzen told elsewhere in his funeral oration of Basil's earlier relations with Caesarea's bishop, Eusebius. Basil had been received by the people of Caesarea on his return from studying in Athens 'as a second founder and protector of the city', but when he had become a presbyter soon afterwards, he had quarrelled with the bishop and withdrawn to the family estates in Pontus.[18] His status at that time as a leading figure in civic life exacerbated tension with a bishop who was himself from the local nobility and whom Basil now served as a priest, all of which makes it highly unlikely that Basil's actions in 369 could be neatly separated into two, separate, spheres of meaning.

Christian and older, classical, practices appear to merge in Caesarea. Though Basil emerges as the major civic donor, there is no

[15] Gregory Nazianzen, *Or.* 43. 33, SC 384. 198.
[16] *Or.* 43. 34–6, SC 384. 200–6.
[17] *Or.* 43. 34, SC 384. 200.
[18] *Or.* 43. 25 and 28, SC 384. 182 and 188.

indication that he followed traditional practice and sold grain at a reduced price. The impact of that shift from sale to outright gift, with the greater expenditure and generosity it thereby entailed, must have struck pagan and Christian contemporaries as unusual, though we should not assume that Basil was the first to act in this way. They would also have been struck by the degree of personal involvement or contact with those in need on the part of the civic donor, that expression of 'sympathy' of which Basil spoke in the letter to Eusebonas. This would both have won admirers and have disturbed competitors for honour. In combining such a sizeable, personal gift with responsibility for the church's alms, Basil appears wholly to have eclipsed his own bishop, of whom he makes no mention in his extant sermons from the period, and to have acquired the mantle of episcopal authority at least a year before his election as bishop. He must also have thrown into the shade any other major donors who contributed either to a collection or who sold grain to him at less than the market price.

The previous chapter should alert us to the dangers which Basil ran in this fashion, the degree to which such behaviour might expose him to criticism. Personal and potentially humiliating contact with the sick and needy offered a limited defence against attack by church members, vitiated to the extent that it trespassed on the bishop's own relations with the poor.[19] We may, therefore, ask whether his conduct shows any other sign of pre-empting or deflecting criticism. Susan Holman has rightly observed with respect to his sermons from the period that '[t]he importance of Basil's references to the civic *tropheus*... rest at their most basic level in the fact that he speaks *as* one himself'.[20] By this she apparently means that the preacher enjoyed a moral authority and eloquence empowered by his own standing and good example. The observation, however, may be pressed further. Basil indeed presents would-be donors as potential patrons: the donor will be acclaimed in the heavenly court as 'provider and benefactor with all the other names belonging to charity'.[21] To that extent they are invited to share in the preacher's standing: a

---

[19] *Or.* 43. 64, SC 384. 264–6.

[20] Holman, *The Hungry*, 82.

[21] Basil, *I Shall Knock Down My Barns* 3, in Courtonne, *Homélies*, 21; Cf. *In Time of Hunger* 7 PG 31. 324A–B.

competitive honour is given a co-operative aspect. This may have been intended to forestall criticism that personal ambition was to be promoted on the back of others' generosity.

Holman has once again rightly noted the unusual prominence in the sermon *In Time of Hunger* which Basil gives to the image of the young child: '[i]n a literary world where infants usually had to be dead before they were mentioned, Basil focuses on newborns who were very much alive'.[22] This insight may lead us to ask who, by contrast, receives less attention in these sermons on almsgiving than might be expected. *In Time of Hunger* contains two references to needy widows and only one passing mention of an orphan. But in only one of the references is the widow a recipient of alms. In the second, the story of the widow of Sidon, she is a donor.[23] Basil's justification of God's providence, *God Does Not Cause Evil*, and his sermon *On the Wealthy* likewise each contain only one mention of needy widows and orphans respectively.[24] The sermon *I Shall Knock Down My Barns* contains the moving portrayal of a father forced into selling one of his children into slavery.[25] It contains no mention of widows and their orphaned children. This pattern cannot be accidental nor insignificant. It is at least possible that Basil avoided speaking explicitly on behalf of those in the Christian community who were perceived to be under the particular care of the bishop, when so speaking for them might be interpreted as a claim to leadership over them.

It is probable that the combination of civic patronage and church almsgiving *both* greatly enhanced Basil's status as a candidate to succeed Eusebius as bishop *and* either made, or armed, opponents to that election, which was to prove contentious. Jean Gribomont has suggested with respect to the two homilies *On the Wealthy* and *I Shall Knock Down My Barns* that they could be interpreted as electoral manifestos at a time when the see was about to become vacant.[26] He

---

[22] Holman, *The Hungry*, 80.

[23] Basil, *In Time of Hunger* 4 and 6, PG 31. 313B and 321A.

[24] *God Does Not Cause Evil* 1, PG 31. 329D; *On the Wealthy* 6, in Courtonne, *Homélies*, 61.

[25] *I Shall Knock Down My Barns*, 4, in Courtonne, *Homélies*, 25–7.

[26] J. Gribomont, 'Un aristocrate révolutionnaire', in *Saint Basile, évangile et église* (Bégrolles-en-Mauges, 1984), i. 70.

has seen a distinction between a radical programme advanced by the episcopal candidate and a later more moderate programme put into practice by the then bishop in his canonical acts of 375. This reading has something to recommend it: the recognition that Basil's display of concern, though made as the bishop's agent, also gave prominence to his own generosity, an episcopal virtue. But Gribomont's contrast between the sermons and canons disregards, or at least underplays, the limits and expectations set by different genres and occasions, while he does not give due weight to the dangers Basil faced through competition in almsgiving and through putting himself forward as a candidate when his bishop was still alive.

The antagonism stirred up by the confusion of classical euergetism and Christian almsgiving may be further glimpsed in Basil's foundation of the charitable complex for the care of the sick, known from an early date as the *Basileiados*, which he had built just outside Caesarea shortly after his elevation to the bishopric. A letter written in 372 by Basil to the local governor, Elias, when construction of the *Basileiados* was about to begin and the necessary materials were being assembled on the site, attempted to rebut criticism from others at Caesarea whose identity remains unspecified and to avoid further antagonizing the governor, who had not reacted well to the charge laid against the bishop, and which, though not specified, centred on whether Basil had exceeded his sphere of competence and independent action in ecclesiastical matters to infringe on matters that were properly the governor's business.[27] Basil denied the charge and claimed imperial sanction for his administration of the churches. Basil presents himself as a 'model of patriotism' whose loyalty is proven by the 'plans for a grandiose building project'.[28] But how did the bishop first incur the charge of disloyalty? Was it by constructing the *Basileiados*, or does Basil turn to this project in order to divert attention from more contentious issues?

Yves Courtonne believed that the new complex was itself to blame.[29] Stephen Mitchell also speaks of Basil seeking support

---

[27] *Ep.* 94, in Courtonne, *Lettres*, i. 206.

[28] T. Kopecek, 'The Cappadocian Fathers and Civic Patriotism', *Church History*, 43 (1974), 303.

[29] Y. Courtonne, *Un témoin du IVe siècle oriental: Saint Basile et son temps d'après sa correspondance* (Paris, 1973), 44.

'against critics of his church-building campaign'.[30] This seems highly probable. It suggests that Basil was exposed to attack by not having sought imperial permission and blessing for his action. This is a measure of the significance attached to his munificence, but also demonstrates that it was yet again an ambiguous act, capable of being 'read' differently by different viewers. That ambiguity may then be connected with the conflation in the *Basileiados* of what Basil authorized and supervised as bishop with what he presumably paid for as a wealthy magnate.

As in the case of Basil's earlier actions during the food shortage, ambiguity is likely to have arisen in large part from the combination of an act of personal and civic euergetism, the construction of a notable building for the city's benefit, and a collective, ecclesiastical, project under Basil's control, though this time as bishop. The way in which the project carried Basil's name from an early date is an important indicator of the status accruing to him as its founder, and suggests that it was built with his money.[31] Gregory presented it as displaying Basil's 'philanthropy and munificence', as mentioned in Chapter 5.[32] But it was meant to attract and spend money donated by others in response to the bishop's preaching. Gregory also presented the complex as the place 'where piety is stock-piled, the deposit-box shared by the wealthy, into which surplus wealth and sometimes, thanks to this man's entreaties, even what people need to live on, is put aside'.[33] It may be that here, too, Basil's channelling of others' alms through his own foundation was seen by some as stolen glory. In describing the *Basileiados* Gregory commented that 'when it came to the exercise of philanthropy and magnificence towards the poor' Basil 'set a contest for the leaders of the people that was open to all'.[34] It is a telling phrase, revealing the inherence of competition and co-operation in a contest which co-ordinated and subordinated other players beneath the leadership of the bishop.[35] Its predominant

---

[30] S. Mitchell, *Anatolia: Land, Men, and Gods in Asia Minor* (Oxford, 1993), ii. 80.
[31] Sozomen, *Ecclesiastical History* 6. 34, in Bidez and Hansen, *Sozomenus*, 291.
[32] Gregory Nazianzen, *Or.* 43. 63, SC 384. 264.
[33] *Or.* 43. 63, SC 384. 262.
[34] *Or.* 43. 63, SC 384. 264.
[35] 'Un corps social, diversifié, hiérarchisé, très loin du nivellement démagogique, domine la vision basilienne et, sans oublier ses origines stoïciennes, s'intègre dans la

metaphor invests Basil with something of the glory due to civic magistrates who provided games. It claims that these new games are open to all civic leaders, but in reality only Christian leaders could participate by donating alms to the centre.

Gregory's oration, perhaps originally delivered on 1 January 382, on the third anniversary of Basil's death, but later reworked for publication,[36] presented Basil as victorious in a competition between Christianity and a paganism slighted and relocated by rhetorical sleight-of-hand to past history: 'In comparison with this work, what is Thebes to me with the seven gates, or Thebes in Egypt, the walls of Babylon, or the Carian tomb of Mausolus, the Pyramids, or vast bronze of the Colossus, the size and beauty of now vanished temples, or whatever else people think wonderful and put in history books?'[37] When Basil built the complex less than a decade had passed since the death of the last pagan emperor; competition between adherents of the different religions of the empire, and between rival versions of Christianity, was still intense.

Gregory urged his readers to 'Go a short distance from the city and set eyes on the new city'.[38] On this basis Liebeschuetz wrote of 'St. Basil's vast new charitable institution outside Caesarea. This was a city in itself, with a church in the centre and around it the house of the bishop, streets of houses for the clergy, hostels for the clergy, and hospitals for the sick.'[39] Liebeschuetz took the 'city' image from Gregory and used it to interpret more detailed information about the plans of the complex given in the letter from Basil to the provincial governor already mentioned (*Ep.* 94). But, while that letter describes a number of buildings around the chapel, there are no streets and some rooms have a dual purpose—they are to be shared by the staff and by the visiting provincial officials. Basil speaks in the plural of 'hostels', but this may mean no more than two: one for the ordinary travellers and another for the diseased and hungry poor.

vision paulinienne du corps du Christ. C'est bien la preuve que, malgré sa conversion révolutionnaire, Basile était resté de bon sang aristocratique et ecclésial.' J. Gribomont, 'Un aristocrate révolutionnaire', 77.

36 Bernardi, SC 384. 27–8.
37 Gregory Nazianzen, *Or.* 43. 63, SC 384. 262.
38 *Or.* 43. 63, SC 384. 260.
39 J. H. W. G. Liebeschuetz, *Antioch* (Oxford, 1972), 240.

There are workplaces. Basil speaks of 'those give nursing care' and 'those who give medical care', all of whom need to be housed, but these may be the same monks or servants of God already mentioned, carrying out their different tasks. And Basil could speak differently of the centre. A letter inviting Bishop Amphilochus to visit the shrine or chapel there in September 374 speaks more modestly of the 'alms-house chapel' (πτωχοτροφείου τὴν μνήμην).[40]

What Liebeschuetz confidently read as a historical description is a theological description. To say that the *Basileiados* was a 'new city' was to allude to the New Jerusalem in Revelation 21. But Gregory's presentation may still shed light on Basil's plans. How cities are set out reveals the play of politics and religion; the social order is inscribed within the civic order as bricks and mortar. The New Jerusalem in Revelation has no temple at its centre, but contains the throne of God. Basil's supposed 'city' is constructed around the martyr's shrine. We should perhaps view the *Basileiados* as a model city, with a model Christian life that centres on the church and is inclusive of the poor and diseased. Gregory invited his audience to go out from the old city to view the new. This is not an invitation to tourism, but to conversion, and Basil's charitable centre stood as a countersign to the older, urban order.

## New wine in old skins

In proclaiming this victory over paganism Gregory's oration drew heavily on classical literature to interweave classical and Christian allusions and registers of speech:

Why turn what I have to say into a tragic speech, when it cannot match the suffering? Yet this man, above all the others, persuaded people, as human beings, not to despise other human beings, nor dishonour Christ, the one head of all, by lack of human kindness towards them. Rather, he persuaded people to serve their own interests when others suffer misfortune by lending to God the pity of which we ourselves stand in need. Therefore, this man of noble birth and ancestry, so highly renowned, did not think it beneath himself to honour the illness with his lips, but rather embraced its sufferers

---

[40] Basil, *Ep.* 176, in Courtonne, *Lettres*, ii. 113.

as brothers, not from vanity, as some may think, ... but as an example in accordance with his own philosophy that people should come into close contact with the bodies of the sick in order to tend them—a telling, yet silent exhortation.[41]

An explicitly signalled echoing of tragedy is matched by allusion to the Gospels, in particular to Luke 12: 33. The phrase 'terrible and pitiful sight' recalls the δεινὸν θέαμα of Euripides' *Medea* (1202). Gregory presents himself as a master of classical rhetoric, but also of a Christian eloquence which surpasses that rhetoric, just as the *Basileiados* surpasses the enumerated wonders of the pagan past. The new wine of Christian eloquence was displayed in the old wineskins of classical culture. The chapter, which has so far examined the interaction of classical and Christian meanings in Basil's almsgiving, next examines how he, too, advanced his cause through incorporating and adapting classical discourse.

## The giver of all good things

Basil repeatedly taught that God as the creator of all is also, thereby, the provider of all good things to his creatures. In his work *On the Holy Spirit* Basil described 'the abundant supply' or 'benefaction' (χορηγία) of goods to us from the Father through the Son', and how the Son apportions these goods 'according to the measure of each one's need'.[42] This supply or expenditure in showering us with gifts is the expression of God's 'munificence' (μεγαλοδωρία).[43] In so acting, God is presented by Basil, who here draws on the Septuagint version of the Psalms, as the great benefactor or εὐεργέτης of the human race.[44] As such, God displays great *philanthropia*.[45] Basil answered

---

[41] Gregory Nazianzen, *Or.* 43. 63, SC 384. 264.

[42] Basil, *On the Holy Spirit* 8. 19. 1–9, PG 32. 100D–101A.

[43] Cf. *Ep.* 183. 1, in Courtonne, *Lettres*, ii. 118; *Hexaemeron* 8. 5. 10 in M. Naldini (ed.), *Basilio di Cesarea, Sulla Genesi* (Milan, 1990), 256; *Homily II on Psalm XIV* 5, PG 29. 277C; *Homily on Psalm CXIV* 5, PG 29. 492B; *On Giving Thanks* 2, PG 31. 221C.

[44] Ps 114(116): 7 (ἐπίστρεψον, ἡ ψυχή μου, εἰς τὴν ἀνάπαυσίν σου, ὅτι Κύριος εὐηργέτησέν σε) in A. Rahlfs (ed.), *Septuaginta*, x (Göttingen, 1931), 283.

[45] Cf. *Hexaemeron* 8. 7. 10, in Naldini, *Sulla Genesi*, 262; *Against Eunomius* PG 29. 524C–D, *Ep.*11 in Courtonne, *Lettres*, i. 41; *On the Holy Spirit* 8. 18. 10, PG 32. 100A; *Long Rules* 10, PG 31. 944C; *Short Rules*, preface, PG 31. 1080A.

those who defended the subordination of the Holy Spirit within the Trinity on the grounds that he acted as our intercessor by retorting that 'it is the height of stupidity to make the benefactor's philanthropy the occasion for ingratitude'.[46]

In this characterization of God as *philanthropos* Basil resembled both ancient writers and a fourth-century orator such as Themistius.[47] The bishop, however, unlike Themistius, turned this classical concept to great advantage in his many exhortations to give alms. By characterizing God as the supreme benefactor Basil suggested what was owed by human beings to God in gratitude, and should happily be given, in terms of a relationship that carried certain expectations for his audience. From what they knew was owed to their patrons and benefactors, or owed to themselves as benefactors, they could appreciate how much more was owed to their Maker:

if we naturally love and are favourably disposed towards our benefactors and patiently take on every hardship in return for what they have first done for us, what adequate account can we give of God's gifts? They are so many in number as to be beyond counting. They are so great in size and of such a kind, that one is enough to require of us that we show the giver every possible favour.[48]

Basil's portrayal of God as the generous benefactor, who requires in return our whole-hearted devotion, is what helps to persuade the rich to redistribute their wealth.

God's initial goodness as a benefactor to the rich must be repaid by their providing a suitable gift in return, where God receives what is given to the poor. When, in the sermon *I Shall Knock Down My Barns*, God is portrayed as the εὐεργέτης, for providing the harvest and enriching the landowner, the landowner's lack of charity is translated into ingratitude, making him seem mean and ignoble: 'What sort of things did the man provide on his side? A harsh demeanour, hatred of his own kind and his tight-fisted inability to share. These are what he showed his benefactor in return. He did not remember our common nature. It did not enter his head that he had

---

[46] *On the Holy Spirit* 19. 50. 9, PG 32. 160B.

[47] Cf. Themistius, *Orationes* 1. 8. in H. Schenkl and G. Downey (eds.), *Themistii Orationes Quae Supersunt* (Leipzig, 1965), 12.

[48] Basil, *Regulae fusius tractatae* 2. 2, PG 31. 912C–913A.

to divide up the surplus among the needy.'[49] The same characterization of God is found in the sermon *In Time of Hunger*. God has
punished the city because people take, but give nothing to others: 'we
give praise for the benefaction ($\tau\dot{\eta}\nu$ $\epsilon\dot{\upsilon}\epsilon\rho\gamma\eta\sigma\dot{\iota}\alpha\nu$), but deprive the
needy of it'.[50] Basil complains in that homily of those who thank
God as their benefactor only when things go well.[51] God is presented
in this way to play on the conventions that give the rich members of
his congregation their identity and status. Ingratitude is the mark of
the base.

Basil exploited the way in which a returned favour should elicit
new and higher favours from the original benefactor. He interpreted
the language of God's grace or favour ($\chi\dot{\alpha}\rho\iota\varsigma$) to refer to either an
initial or responsive gift. In the homily *On Julitta the Martyr* Basil
cites and then gives an answer to the question put by the Psalmist:
'what we can give back to the Lord for his gifts back to us?' (Ps. 116:
10). He picks up on the use in the Septuagint text of a verb saying
that God

in his munificence is not said to have *given* but *given back*, as though he were
not the one who gave the first favour, but was repaying those who had made
the first move. For the gratitude of those who have received gifts counts as a
benefaction. He who has given you money asks for alms from you through
the hand of the poor man. And if he takes what belongs to him, his kindness
to you will lack nothing, as though what he took was yours.[52]

So, the benefactor redoubles his gifts in posing as the one who is
benefited and Basil has interpreted the biblical text in this novel way
specifically to make it refer to God's reward for the almsgiver.

In presenting God as principal benefactor in what should be an
ongoing exchange of gifts the preacher rendered more credible and
gave new force to traditional Judaeo-Christian warnings of the wrath
that falls on those who fail to have pity on the poor, while adding
further grounds to hope in God's promised rewards for the merciful.
In three of the homilies that are likely to have been preached during
the severe food crisis that afflicted Cappadocia in 369 Basil either

---

[49] *I Shall Knock Down My Barns* 1, in Courtonne, *Homélies*, 17.
[50] *In Time of Hunger* 2, PG 31. 309A.
[51] *In Time of Hunger* 5, PG 31. 316C.
[52] *On Julitta the Martyr* 7, PG 31. 253C–D.

included near the end, or concluded with, a vivid, dramatic account, an *ekphrasis*, of how the ungenerous would fare at the Last Judgement: 'how you will shudder and sweat, and what darkness will engulf you, when you hear the sentence'.[53] The longest description is in *On the Wealthy*, where Basil sets up a contrast between how the rich might use their wealth to escape conviction before an earthly judge (with hired advocates, public orators, and a display of status) and their powerlessness to act in this way before Christ's judgement seat.[54]

The concept of God as benefactor is also used to encourage almsgiving by those who otherwise excuse themselves from acting charitably on the grounds of being less well off. *In Time of Hunger* appeals to those who may soon be experiencing shortages. Basil uses the story of the widow of Zarephath (1 Kings 17) to stress the return which God will make for those who are generous with what little they possess:

if you give from what little is left, you too will have a flask of oil brimming over thanks to God's favour and a jar of flour that does not become empty. For God's favour is liberally bestowed on the faithful and follows the pattern of wells that are forever being emptied, but which are never drained and fill twice as fast. Let the man who has nothing lend to God who is wealthy. Put your faith in the one who always marks the gift down on his own account on behalf of the oppressed and returns the favour from his own funds.[55]

Basil explained in a homily against the practice of usury that

whenever you provide for the destitute on account of the Lord, it is both a gift and a loan. It is a gift because you entertain no hope of recovering it, a loan because of our Lord's munificence in paying you back on his behalf, when, having taken a small sum for the poor, he will give you back a vast sum in return. 'For he who takes pity on the poor, lends to God' (Proverbs 19: 17).[56]

It is in this context of God's philanthropic benefactions that we should place Basil's characterization of almsgiving as an expression of *philanthropia*. The bishop draws on the classical appeal to imitate

[53] *I Shall Knock Down My Barns* 8, in Courtonne, *Homélies*, 37.
[54] *On the Wealthy* 6, in Courtonne, *Homélies*, 59–61.
[55] *In Time of Hunger* 6, PG 31. 321A.
[56] *Homily II on Psalm XIV* 5, PG 29. 277C.

God's virtues. He urges his congregation to be 'imitators of God's *philanthropia* by both taking pity and sharing things out and being generous with favours'.[57] That imitation is achieved through imitation in turn of the biblical exemplars of virtue. Thus, in the homily *I Shall Knock Down My Barns* Basil imagines the rich farmer as saying he will throw open his granaries and imitate the Patriarch Joseph 'in advertising the charity available' (τῷ τῆς φιλανθρωπίας κηρύγματι).[58]

## Christian diatribe

Classical philosophers and orators were able by the fourth century to draw on a long rhetorical tradition of attacks upon greed and the insatiability of human desire. This tradition contained both arguments and styles of speech in which to deploy them. Plutarch had expatiated on the unquenchable nature of desire for wealth as opposed to our appetite for food and drink in his essay *On the Love of Wealth*.[59] Dio Chrysostom in his seventeenth discourse had mocked 'some who are ridiculous and disgrace themselves through greed'.[60] This discourse taught self-control, the virtues of leisure dedicated to the goals of philosophy, friendship, and public duty, including generosity towards friends and the civic community. Basil adapted this tradition to urge his flock to practise greater almsgiving.

This adaptation is clearly seen in the use made by the preacher of diatribe in the homily on Luke 12: 16–21, *I Shall Knock Down My Barns*. The characterization of the farmer at Luke 12: 20 as a 'fool' (ἄφρος) opens the way for the preacher to use diatribe in attacking the man's supposed lack of charity as a form of 'folly' (ἀλογία).[61] The opening section in which he discusses together with the congregation the Gospel story soon gives way first to a less reflective and more

[57] Basil (inter dubia), *De Misericordia et Iudicio*, PG 31. 1712C.

[58] *I Shall Knock Down My Barns* 2, in Courtonne, *Homélies*, 19.

[59] Plutarch, *Moralia* 37 in *Plutarchi Moralia*, iii, ed. W. R. Paton, M. Pohlenz, and W. Sieveking (Leipzig, 1972), 332–46.

[60] Dio Chrysostom, *Orationes* 17.: 22, ed. G. de Budé, 2 vols. (Leipzig, 1916 and 1919), ii. 314.

[61] Basil, *I Shall Knock Down My Barns*, 6, in Courtonne, *Homélies*, 31.

impassioned imaginary address to the protagonist: 'Silly man' (ἄνθρωπε). At the beginning of the third section Basil briefly switches to address the congregation individually in the singular: 'Don't let this happen to you.' But he soon returns to the format of diatribe, when he thunders, 'Imitate the land, you silly man' (μίμησαι τὴν γῆν, ἄνθρωπε). Only at the end does Basil once again address the congregation, drawing attention to himself as the preacher and to the choice before his listeners: either to be persuaded or to remain unmoved by his appeal, his final call to alms.

This style has the advantage of licensing a display of anger and mockery against vice in which the congregation are both able to side with the preacher against his imaginary opponent *and* find themselves listening to the preacher as though in the opponent's shoes. When Basil returns to diatribe with the order, 'Imitate the land', it is momentarily ambiguous whether the ensuing diatribe is directed against the protagonist of the parable, against Everyman, or the rich members of the congregation. The first figure stands in some sense for the latter two, and for the archetypal rich or avaricious person. The diatribe enables Basil to place objections almost certainly shared by members of his congregation on his addressee's lips: ' "To whom I am doing an injustice", he asks, "by keeping what is mine?" ' When objections are so placed on the lips of an idiot, they are already at a disadvantage before the preacher gives his riposte.

Likewise, Basil swiftly moves in the homily *On the Wealthy* from talking to the congregation about the man in the Gospel episode to addressing the man himself, but in that speech he can also be heard to address the rich within his congregation. By the third section the preacher has returned to discussing the young man in the third person, and the 'you' addresses what we might term the 'implied hearer'—understood as any rich man overfond of his possessions. The novelty of this adapted diatribe is hard to assess. Bernardi wondered whether the congregation would find it merely conventional, or whether Basil was popularizing a style previously confined to the school.[62] Perhaps what matters most is not whether Basil does this for the first time, but that he does it so well. The performance deserves a generous response on the part of the congregation, the

---

[62] J. Bernardi, *La Prédication des pères Cappadociens* (Marseilles, 1968), 388.

educated members of which might be won over by this confident reworking of classical culture in the service of the Gospel.

## AMBROSE OF MILAN

Where Basil adapted the Greek classical tradition for his Eastern audience, Ambrose adapted the Latin tradition for his Western audience at the imperial capital of Milan, not least by judicious and free translation into Latin of much in Basil's writings on almsgiving. It has long been recognized in particular that the greater part (sections 1–60) of Ambrose's treatise *On Naboth*, which the bishop probably wrote between 386 and 389,[63] borrows heavily from Basil's sermons *I Shall Knock Down My Barns* and *On the Wealthy*. Vincent Vasey, author of the most important modern study of the work, has listed the many stylistic traits which mark Ambrose's adoption of classical diatribe: 'simplicity of style, multiplication of isicola, parallelism, antitheses, varied vocabulary, frequent insertion of commands and admonitions, mordant irony, images drawn from nature, language adorned with reminiscences in the form of classical and scriptural references, anecdotes, examples drawn from history, pithy sayings, *parrhesia*...even to the point of impertinence'.[64] He has also observed Ambrose's citations of or allusions to Vergil, Ovid, and Terence.[65] It is not always recognized, however, just how skilful is Ambrose's adaptation of Basil, and the following paragraphs are intended to supplement Vasey's discussion of the parallels and divergences between the *De Nabuthae* and its Basilian sources.[66]

Ahab featured as one passing example of greed in Basil's sermon *On the Wealthy*.[67] Ambrose turns Ahab into the archetypal rich landowner, and Jezebel is characterized as the epitome and personification

---

[63] V. R. Vasey, *The Social Ideas in the Works of St Ambrose: A Study of the De Nabuthae* (Rome, 1982), 26.

[64] Ibid. 32, and for detailed examples, 35–42.

[65] Ibid. 42.

[66] Ibid. 92–103.

[67] Basil, *On the Wealthy* 5 in Courtonne, *Homélies*, 57.

of greed, the very figure of 'avaritia',[68] so that the Naboth story
becomes an overarching frame leading into the Lukan story of the
rich and foolish farmer. The greed which led Jezebel to plot violence
against a neighbour is identified with the greed that has no mercy on
the poor, and in particular those in debt, who ask for help. Diatribe
and the common charge of madness levelled against Ahab, the
farmer, and the rich in general serve to integrate material derived
from the separate sources in Basil's sermons as well as to persuade the
reader. Neither of the two sermons by Basil opens with a simple
statement followed by a rapid string of rhetorical questions in the
manner of the *On Naboth*. Yet rhetorical questions characteristic of
diatribe feature elsewhere in these sermons, and Ambrose's initial
statement, together with his questions, allow him to make the
Naboth story at once an exemplary instance of a more general
experience:

The story of Naboth may be old, but it is a daily reality. Who among the
wealthy does not daily set their heart on someone else's things? Who among
the richest millionaires does not strive to push out the poor man from his
small-holding and evict the needy man from the boundaries of his family
fields? Who is happy with what is his?[69]

Direct questions, some ninety, abound in the *On Naboth* and contribute to the dramatic impact of the diatribe, as Vincent Vasey has
observed.[70] Most are posed by the figure of Ambrose himself as the
speaker or author. He questions the readers in the above quotation.
He questions the rich landowners as a group.[71] He questions the rich
man, the reader, or perhaps himself, as he asks what he is to say of the
rich man's behaviour, how he is to speak of it.[72] Other questions are
put by characters in the stories which Ambrose relates. The father
asks himself which son he should sell.[73] In accordance with the
Gospel text the rich farmer asks himself what to do with his harvest
and God questions the farmer's soul.[74]

---

[68] Ambrose, *De Nabuthae* 9. 41 and 49, OOSA 6. 162 and 168.
[69] Ibid. 1. 1, OOSA 6. 130.
[70] Vasey, *Social Ideas*, 31.
[71] Ambrose, *De Nabuthae* 1. 2, OOSA 6. 130.
[72] *De Nabuthae* 9. 41, OOSA 6. 162.
[73] *De Nabuthae* 5. 22, OOSA 6. 146.
[74] *De Nabuthae* 6. 29, OOSA 6. 153.

Ambrose's rhetorical questions invite the reader to share a common standard of reason from which the rich man, whom Ambrose supposedly interrogates, appears to have fallen. Ambrose does not simply condemn. He appeals to the reasoning, to the standards of those who hear him, and who therefore are being asked to sign their own condemnation, admit their own folly, to the extent that they, too, fail to give alms. At the same time, Ambrose's questions avoid charges of hostility towards those to be persuaded. Maurice Testard has written of the importance both in the *De officiis* and in the *On Naboth* of avoiding a style or register that would offend and might be dismissed by its rich hearers as inciting envy.[75] These questions with their self-evident answers stand in pathetic contrast to the agonizing and aporetic questions put by the starving father (and which Ambrose borrowed from Basil[76]): "'Whom', he says, "am I to sell first... Whom may I put up? Who will make a good impression on the grain merchant?"'[77]

Ambrose's close dependence on Basil's sermons, as well as his skill in adapting them, is further demonstrated by examining how he belittles Ahab's request for Naboth's vineyard. The shame traditionally attached by the rich to the needy beggar, to scrounging, is attached to Ahab's request. The king's 'Give me your vineyard' (*Da mihi vineam tuam*) is made to sound the same note of dishonour as the 'Give something' (*Da mihi*) of a beggar:

Give me he says. What else does a needy person say, what else does someone say claiming alms for all to see, but Give me? That's to say: 'Give to me, because I'm in need. Give to me, because I can have no other means of staying alive. Give to me, because I have no bread to eat, no coin with which to buy a drink, nothing to pay for a meal, no funds for clothing. Give to me, because the Lord gave you, not me, what you should give away. Give to me, because unless you do, I will not be able to have anything. Give to me, because it is written: 'Give alms' (Luke 11: 41). How debasing, how disgusting these words are! They show no sense of humility, but blaze with greed. But what shamelessness there is in this very debasement.[78]

[75] M. Testard, *Chrétiens latins des premiers siècles* (Paris, 1981), 51.
[76] Basil, *I Shall Knock Down My Barns* 4, in Courtonne, *Homélies*, 25.
[77] Ambrose, *De Nabuthae* 5. 22, OOSA 6. 146.
[78] *De Nabuthae* 2. 8, OOSA 6. 136.

The ploy comes from Basil's attack upon the foolish farmer's self-questioning.[79] Ambrose indeed uses it to make the same attack on the farmer later in the text: ' "What am I to do?" he says. Surely this is a poor man speaking, someone who has nothing on which to live?.... "What am I to do?", he says, "because I have nothing?" The rich man shouts that he has nothing. This is poverty talking. He complains of going without when he is awash with crops.'[80] Yet, Ambrose's borrowing is highly effective when applied to Ahab. The language or eloquence which should articulate the king's dignity instead betrays him, the point underlined by the heavy alliteration in Ambrose's description of the voice as belonging to someone 'claiming alms for all to see' or 'after alms for all to see': 'sti*p*em *p*ublicam *p*ostulantis'. The word *stips*, an alms offering or hand-out, sounds a common note; it does not occur, for example, in Symmachus' erudite and urbane writings, but belongs to a register and social class far beneath him. Now Ahab is found in quite the wrong company. The rich hear their own social prejudices on the lips of the preacher, but directed against one of their own: 'How low, how disgusting this is!' Ahab's ignominy is compounded by the folly of his position in adopting the voice of the have-nots. This is the ignominy which Ambrose will later show Elijah discovering in Ahab (citing 1 Kings 21: 20). Ambrose will there once again pick out the voice of shame: 'The sinner was so depressed in his own mind that he was not even buoyed up by the conceited sense of his royal dignity. So, as though he were base and corrupt, he says "You have found me" '.[81] The same adjective, *vilis*, is found in both passages. And in the first, cutting across the repeated importuning of 'Give me' (*da mihi*), is the authoritative voice of Christ in the Gospels: 'Give alms' (*Date eleemosynam*). Ambrose excels in this intercalation, or interpellation, of Latin scriptural texts and voices.

Both Ambrose and Basil follow the classical tradition of attacking gluttony, but alter that attack to promote the feeding of the hungry.[82] Both attack fasting where the money that is so saved is

---

[79] Basil, *I Shall Knock Down My Barns* 1, in Courtonne, *Homélies*, 17.
[80] Ambrose, *De Nabuthae* 30 and 31, OOSA 6. 154.
[81] *De Nabuthae* 12. 51, OOSA 6. 170.
[82] Basil, *I Shall Knock Down My Barns* 2, in Courtonne, *Homélies*, 19; Ambrose, *De Nabuthae* 5. 19–20, OOSA 6. 142–4.

not distributed in alms.[83] Both allude to the parable of Dives and Lazarus.[84] But, whereas Basil makes the rich man against whom he argues merely another Dives, Ambrose makes the rich worse than Dives: 'Even that rich man, from whose table the poor man Lazarus used to gather up the droppings in the hope of stilling his hunger, was more acceptable.'[85] Ambrose's archetypal rich man is worse than his biblical archetype! And it is Ambrose, not Basil, who in an imperial capital with its attendant bureaucracy and institutional violence writes that Dives' table was financed by wealth exacted from political victims, so that his goblets dripped with blood from the executed. The rich in this startling image literally drain the life-blood of the poor.

The bishop of Milan, when compared with Basil, whose reticence in this respect has been noted above, makes more mention of widows and orphans as worthy recipients of alms.[86] But Ambrose does more than make a traditional appeal for these privileged beneficiaries likely to stir the conscience of his Christian readers. At the opening of the *On Naboth* the plight of the widow is compared with that of the homeless and landless poor, whose fate is found to be worse than the widow's.[87] This points towards another difference between the two authors. While both plead for granaries to be unlocked and food to be given in alms, Ambrose draws on the story of Naboth to place greater emphasis on ending depredation of the poor.

These two authors differ markedly in their use of scriptural citation and allusion. Where Basil cites in *I Shall Knock Down My Barns* from thirteen scriptural passages apart from Luke 12: 16–21, and in *On the Wealthy* cites from fifteen passages apart from Matthew 19: 19–20, Ambrose cites seventy-one verses or sets of verses excepting passages from 1 Kings and Luke 12: 16–21, seventy if passages from Matthew 19: 19–20 are also excepted. If Basil's different citations are added together to total twenty-eight, Ambrose has more than twice as many such citations, and the two authors share only ten such

---

[83] Basil, *On the Wealthy* 3, in Courtonne, *Homélies*, 49; Ambrose, *De Nabuthae* 5. 19, OOSA 6. 142.

[84] Basil, *On the Wealthy* 9, in Courtonne, *Homélies*, 69; Ambrose, *De Nabuthae* 5. 19 and 12. 52, OOSA 6. 142 and 172.

[85] Ambrose, *De Nabuthae* 5. 19, OOSA 6. 142.

[86] *De Nabuthae* 7. 36, 7. 37, 8. 39, 13. 57, OOSA 6. 158, 160, and 176.

[87] *De Nabuthae* 1. 1, OOSA 6. 130.

citations outside the passages which may in some sense be regarded as their common subjects.

The greater frequency of Ambrose's citations derive in part from his inclusion within the work of a commentary on Psalm 76, but also represent a concern to confirm his assertions by appeal to the unquestionable authority of scripture. The appeal is itself artful. For example, in refuting the excuse that the poor should receive no aid because their poverty is a God-sent condition or 'curse', Ambrose apparently cites from the Beatitudes: 'inasmuch as it is written "Blessed are the poor, for theirs is the kingdom of heaven"'.[88] Ambrose has either quoted from Matthew 5: 3 while omitting the qualifying 'in spirit', or recast Luke 6: 20 from an address in the second person ('Blessed are you, poor') to one in the third. Each of the original passages allowed for the objection that Jesus was not speaking of the poor in general, while the quiet conflation leaves no such gap. The 1781 edition of Ambrose's works prints 'Beati pauperes spiritu' (Blessed are the poor in spirit), which suggests that some later copyists thought to correct this as a slip![89] Ambrose can then cap his argument by turning the tables on his imagined objector by citing the warning in Proverbs 11: 26 that 'the man who seizes control over the price of grain will be cursed'. This citation he found in Basil, but he excises the mention there that this curse was from the people.[90] Ambrose so edited and placed the verse that the rich appear to be threatened by *God's* curse.

Ambrose uses frequent citation to display his command over the scriptures and his interpretative authority as bishop. Classical and Christian strands of argument are closely interwoven. This can be seen, for example, in how various texts, especially other biblical texts, are used to make sense of a given verse. After citing Psalm 41: 1, 'Blessed is he who considers the poor and the needy' (*Beatus est qui intelligit super egenum et pauperum*), he asks 'Who is it who has this understanding?' with regard to the poor and the needy.[91] His answer draws in part on classical philosophy: it is the one who sees the poor

[88] *De Nabuthae* 8. 40, OOSA 6. 160.
[89] *Sancti Ambrosii Mediolanensis Episcopi Opera*, ii (Venice, 1781), 47.
[90] Basil, *I Shall Knock Down My Barns* 3, in Courtonne, *Homélies*, 23.
[91] Ambrose, *De Nabuthae* 8. 40, OOSA 6. 160.

person as a fellow human being, 'who recognizes him as sharing the same nature', but this is then glossed as the knowledge 'that the Lord has made both rich and poor' (*quod et divitem et pauperem fecit dominus*), which echoes Proverbs 22: 2, 'The rich and the poor man are to meet together, for God has made them both' (*Dives et pauper occurrerent sibi, fecit autem ambos Dominus*).[92] If Franco Gori is correct, Ambrose continues with a further allusion to Sirach 35: 11. The claim to wisdom given in this way forms a sharp contrast to the ignorance of which the rich stand accused. The shameful charge of ignorance—'you do not know', 'he did not know' (*nescis, non novit*)—is repeatedly levelled at them.[93] Basil had likewise berated the ignorance of the rich, but Ambrose is more vehement and makes the point more often.[94] The right kind of knowledge turns out to be an awareness of a common humanity that in turn makes for pity and poor-relief. Classical commonplaces may be used to castigate the vices of the rich, but in *On Naboth* wisdom with respect to the poor and the virtuous behaviour towards them which it enjoins come principally from the Christian scriptures.

The difference between the use of scripture by each author is further seen if we consider the use of Matthew 19: 21 made by Ambrose in *On Naboth* and by Basil in *On the Wealthy*: Ambrose cites the verse once, Basil cites it there four times.[95] This is one element in Ambrose's decision to pass over the Gospel story which forms the primary text on which Basil based his sermon. That decision may partly be pragmatic in a text which already has two stories to narrate, but it also downplays and effectively removes any strand in the Greek sermon of radical and ascetic self-dispossession. It belongs with the decision not to follow Basil in using Proverbs 22: 1 ('Better a good name than great wealth'). These changes orientate the text towards a readership whose worldly status is not itself being questioned, but who are to be persuaded forcefully to make a different use of their power and wealth.

[92] The verse is given here in the form cited by Augustine in *Serm.* 85. 7, PL 38. 523.

[93] Ambrose, *De Nabothae* 2. 4, 6. 29, 7. 33, 7. 36, 8. 38, 13. 57, 14. 60, 15. 63, OOSA 6. 134, 152, 156, 158, 178, 180, and 184.

[94] Cf. Basil, *I Shall Knock Down My Barns* 2 and 6, in Courtonne, *Homélies*, 19 and 31.

[95] *On the Wealthy* 1, 3, 4, and 7, in Courtonne, *Homélies*, 41, 49, 53, and 63; Ambrose, *De Nabuthae* 14. 58, OOSA 6. 178.

## Rewriting Cicero

The previous chapter observed that book 2 of Ambrose's *De officiis* incorporated almsgiving within an account of *liberalitas*. It did not discuss in any detail how Ambrose adapted the virtue which he found in the Ciceronian *De officiis*, the model for his moral treatise, how he altered the older virtue not only with respect to those who benefit from it, but with respect to those who practise it, the motives which are to govern its use, and its relationship with the opposing vices of excessive and niggardly giving, a transformation in which Cicero's vocabulary is heavily reused, but in which its descriptive terms for poverty, need, and those who suffer want now latch onto far different social conditions and people.

The recipients are easily identified. Ambrose, like Cicero, allows for the exercise of generosity towards close relatives: 'That generosity (*liberalitas*) is also to be approved which ensures that you do not neglect your close relatives if you learn that they are in need.'[96] Yet, this is not the area in which Ambrose first describes the exercise of this virtue, nor the primary form of the virtue, for the enriching of family members is not to claim the resources that belong to the poor: relatives are not to be helped 'out of a wish on their part to grow rich on what you are able to give to the needy'.[97] The extreme want and low social status of those labelled needy are then indicated by the bishop's identification of generosity towards them with redemptive almsgiving: God has given wealth to some that they may gain eternal life by employing it to atone for their sins: 'so that you may redeem your sins for the price of compassion' (*ut... pretio miserationis peccata redimas tua*). Ambrose's words here may echo the scriptures. In one of the *Veteres Latinae*, the Latin translations of the Bible which preceded the Vulgate, Daniel bids Nebuchadnezzar: 'redeem your sins with alms and your injustices with acts of compassion towards the poor' (*peccata tua eleemosynis redime et iniustitias tuas miserationibus pauperum*).[98] The exercise of *liberalitas* is to be seen in the

---

[96] Ambrose, *De officiis* 1. 30. 150 in Testard, *Devoirs*, i. 168.

[97] Ibid.

[98] Daniel 4: 24, in the version cited by Cyprian, *De opere et eleemosynis* 5, SC 440. 88.

gift of alms before it is seen in generosity to one's own kin. And how far this represents a change from the classical practice may further be measured by Ambrose's concern to pre-empt or defuse hostile comment by family members who consider themselves cheated of gifts.[99]

As mentioned in Chapter 2, Ambrose argues in the *De officiis* that generosity is most fully, though not exclusively, shown in good works for fellow Christians in need, whom he describes in Pauline terms (Galatians 6: 10) as the 'household members' (*domesticos fidei*).[100] The deserving poor are first the Christian poor. Ambrose then picks out different types of worthy recipient in stressing the blame that attaches to neglect by the rich:

It is a grave fault if one of the faithful is in want, even though you know that they lack money, put up with hunger, experience distress, in particular one ashamed to be in need—if it turns out that their family has been seized or they have been falsely accused and you do not help, if they are in prison, punished and cruelly tortured despite their innocence, on account of some debt—for though pity should be shown to all, it should be shown all the more to the innocent . . .

What Ambrose regards as the primary form of *liberalitas* is not, however, what he advocates as the height of generosity, which expresses itself in the ransom of prisoners.[101] And where Cicero had in mind the ransom from pirates of one individual by another, whether friend or relative, Ambrose also has in view 'those ransomed by the churches' from the Goths. His defence of selling church plate for the purpose has already been noted in Chapter 2.[102] The importance of ransoming prisoners is also evident in a passage of Ambrose's work against usury, the *De Tobia*. When he copies from Basil of Caesarea a description of the rich man's inflexible refusal to show pity towards a suppliant he adds in a reference to the plight of those 'whom the barbarian sells as prisoners'.[103]

Where Cicero excluded from *liberalitas* the kind of giving that exhausts the *patrimonium* or family wealth, Ambrose rejects wastage

[99] Ambrose, *De officiis* 1. 30. 150 in Testard, *Devoirs*, i. 168.
[100] Ambrose, *De officiis* 1. 30. 148 in Testard, *Devoirs*, i. 166–7.
[101] Ambrose, *De officiis* 2. 15. 70 in Testard, *Devoirs*, ii. 40.
[102] Ambrose, *De officiis* 2. 28. 136–43 in Testard, *Devoirs*, ii. 70–4.
[103] *De Tobia* 3. 9, OOSA 6. 204.

of the *patrimonium* on public shows in a passage close to his Ciceronian model,[104] but explicitly makes allowance for such radical dispossession in the cause of almsgiving: Christ gave a rule 'to be followed so that there is a good reason for depleting one's patrimony, if someone has banished the hunger of the poor and relieved their need'.[105] At the other end of the social scale, Ambrose insists that *liberalitas* is a virtue which the poor themselves may exercise. The point of the widow's mite, as he notes in a number of places outside the *De officiis*, is that generosity is measured by the intention it expresses, not the amount spent.[106] The classical virtue has been redefined to include a wide range of charitable behaviour, including behaviour among the elite which disrupts the *status quo* by allowing those who so choose to renounce their wealth and with it their place and duties in the social order.

The virtue which Ambrose presents, although the generosity of particular individuals, is mediated through the practices of the institutional Church. Ambrose imparts much advice intended for the clerics in discharging their duties with respect to almsgiving: they are to sift the genuine from the fraudulent by means of their enquiries; the priests are to exercise restraint and not capitalize on their display of bounty, 'so that they distribute [alms] not in order to boast about it but as a matter of justice', a remark suggestive of the troubled links between almsgiving and status.[107] They are not to deny alms to the needy who are in some sense cut off from the church (*ab Ecclesia relegatis*), perhaps as penitents.[108] The moderation exercised by the clergy inspires others to confide to them further alms for distribution.[109] Moderation on the part of the bishop in distributing alms is integral to the wise division of resources between expenditure on alms for the poor, for travellers, on buildings, and on gifts to the clergy who, it appears, are to be kept from devoting themselves to

---

[104] *De officiis* 2. 21. 109 in Testard, *Devoirs*, ii. 58–9.

[105] *De officiis* 1. 30. 151 in Testard, *Devoirs*, ii. 169.

[106] Ambrose, *De viduis* 27, OOSA 14/1. 268–70; *Ep.* 68. 4 in Zelzer, *Epistulae*, 170–1.

[107] *De officiis* 2. 16. 76 in Testard, *Devoirs*, ii. 42. Cf. *De officiis* 2. 21. 110 in Testard, *Devoirs*, ii. 59.

[108] *De officiis* 2. 16. 77 in Testard, *Devoirs*, ii. 43.

[109] *De officiis* 2. 16. 78 in Testard, *Devoirs*, ii. 44.

commerce.[110] In all of this Ambrose carefully and laboriously adapted his Ciceronian model. It is necessary to ask why his ethical treatise was carved from this earlier text. The answer to be given here has several parts. First, as Cicero's *De officiis* had been presented as a gift for his son Marcus to further his education, so the bishop sought to educate his chosen 'sons', the clergy of the diocese who had received the 'grace of sacred ministry',[111] in particular those whom Ambrose had himself ordained and so 'begotten' for the service of the Gospel.[112] The work's classical title and source, its parentage, so to speak, serve to strengthen Ambrose's quasi-paternal authority over the Milanese clergy.[113] Christian discourse on almsgiving and ethics in general here adapts a pagan past for purposes of internal, Christian, discipline.

Cicero's work of moral philosophy was intended for a wide, cultured, readership and had come to occupy an honoured place in the education of the elite among those works which Ammianus Marcellinus, for example, thought should have improved the 'somewhat crude nature' of the Augustus Valens, unpolished by 'texts even of the slightest antiquity'. That historian gave pride of place among the orators to Cicero (*excellentissimus omnium Cicero*).[114] It seems that Ambrose's work aimed to give clerical and wider Christian formation a polish equal to that offered by Cicero to future magistrates. The training of young clerks to serve in the Church as men were formerly trained for civic service is, as Testard has suggested, to set up an analogy between the two careers in which the cleric may approximate to or appropriate something of the magistrate's dignity.[115] The clergy are kept in place, but that place is given a new honour. Furthermore,

---

[110] *De officiis* 2. 21. 111 in Testard, *Devoirs*, ii. 59.

[111] *De officiis* 1. 50. 249 in Testard, *Devoirs*, i. 216.

[112] *De officiis* 1. 24 in Testard, *Devoirs*, i. 106. Ambrose may be referring to his *deacons* in particular. Towards the close of book 2 he distinguishes between a bishop's *clerici* and his *ministri* 'qui sunt vere filii' (2. 134). Testard, *Devoirs*, ii. 186, translates *ministri* as 'diacres' with reference to (*a*) the citation by Ambrose of 1 Tim. 3: 1–10 at 1. 246 and (*b*) R. Gryson, *Le Prêtre selon saint Ambroise* (Louvain, 1968), 142–4.

[113] Testard, *Devoirs*, i. 49–52, has argued convincingly that the long title *De officiis ministrorum* is not original.

[114] Ammianus Marcellinus, *Res gestae* 30. 4. 2 and 30. 4. 7 in G. Sabbah and L. Angliviel de la Beaumelle (eds.), *Ammien Marcellin, Histoire*, vi (Paris, 1999), 66 and 68.

[115] Testard, *Devoirs*, i. 30.

the rewriting of Cicero's *De officiis* belongs in the context of Ambrose's presentation of Christianity as comparable with, and better than, the classical tradition, which is thereby transmuted into a heritage available to Christianity. All three figures whose writings on almsgiving have been examined so far in this chapter, Basil, Gregory Nazianzen, and Ambrose, incorporate classical discourse not only for its persuasive eloquence and connotations of high education, but in seeking to relegate a competing pattern of virtue to history.

## JEROME: RESISTANCE TO CHANGE AND INTERNAL CONFLICT

Competing patterns of virtue had not, of course, disappeared into history and would not simply vanish. The difficult interaction of Christian generosity in almsgiving with classical culture which is evident in Basil's writings also finds a parallel in those of Ambrose. His letter to Marcellus, mentioned in the previous chapter, may now be examined in this context. The Milanese bishop was asked to adjudicate in a family dispute concerning the wish of another bishop, Marcellus, who apparently came from a senatorial background, to divest himself of his family wealth or patrimony and give his estates to the Church, motivated by generosity towards the poor (*in pauperes liberalitatis voluntas*).[116] Marcellus had made provision for his widowed sister to enjoy part of the income from the estate in her lifetime, but a brother, Laetus, a *vir consularis* or man of consular status, objected to the plan. Ambrose awarded the property to Laetus in return for an annual gift of produce to support the sister. Selling one's belongings and giving the proceeds to the poor in accordance with the dominical command was frustrated in this instance by stiff, family opposition. Ambrose's teaching sanctioned the loss of patrimony in generous almsgiving, but prudential concerns prevented the Milanese bishop from advocating its practice in this instance.

---

[116] Ambrose, *Ep.* 24, OOSA 19. 236.

It is not known whether Marcellus' brother was Christian or pagan. It is quite likely that he was Christian. Classical patterns of thought and virtue interacted with the meaningful practices of almsgiving not only in Christian dealings with non-Christians, but within the churches, where that interaction gave rise to conflict. Indeed, it may be helpful to see the controversy in the late fourth and early fifth centuries over the proper place of asceticism in the Christian life as fuelled in large part by the tension between different versions of generosity, by resistance, especially, to that version outlined by Ambrose in the *De officiis* which sanctioned the loss of patrimony in almsgiving, and by questions over the proper scope of this virtue—whether, for example, it was required of a bishop and of a consecrated virgin.

Newly elected bishops from wealthy backgrounds were clearly pulled between different expectations. Jerome might record with admiration in the *De viris illustribus* that Cyprian at baptism 'gave away all his wealth to the poor'.[117] He might praise Bishop Exuperius of Toulouse because he charitably 'gave away all his wealth for Christ's flesh and blood'.[118] But it was not always possible to live up to this high ideal. Cyprian himself had probably failed to give everything away at his consecration.[119] Ambrose's actions with regard to his own family estate have been discussed in Chapter 2.

Jill Harries has detailed the extent to which wealthy Roman ascetics were careful not to alienate estates from their families.[120] Jerome was ferocious in verbally attacking virgins who sought to retain considerable family wealth. He told Eustochium in what amounts to a public letter to 'avoid the sin of avarice' not only by refraining from theft, but more importantly 'in not keeping your own property, which does not really belong to you'.[121] The attack was intended to strike at what was common practice. Eustochium must

---

[117] Jerome, *De viris illustribus* 67, in A. Ceresa-Gastaldo (ed.), *Gerolamo, Gli uomini illustri* (Florence, 1988), 172.

[118] *Ep.* 125. 20, in Labourt, *Lettres*, vii. 133.

[119] See comments by A. A. R. Bastiaensen in C. Mohrman, *et al.*, *Vita*, 252 n. 25, and C. A. Bobertz, *Cyprian of Carthage as Patron: A Social Historical Study of the Role of Bishop in the Ancient Christian Community of North Africa* (Ann Arbor, 1993), 127 n. 87.

[120] Harries, 'Treasure in Heaven', 59–62.

[121] *Ep.* 22. 31 in Labourt, *Lettres*, i. 146.

not 'say: "this one and that one enjoys her own possessions, is honoured by people and receives visits from her brothers and sisters. Surely she has not stopped being a virgin?" '[122] Jerome rebuts such thoughts by doubting whether such a woman is really a virgin at all, by distinguishing between a physical and spiritual virginity.

Jerome was taking a radical position within an old debate about the possession of wealth by consecrated virgins. Cyprian in his *De habitu virginum* replied to those rich virgins who claimed they should retain and use their wealth, that they must use it only in accordance with God's commands and give it to the poor in alms: 'You say that you are rich and wealthy, and think that you should use those things which God has willed that you own. Use them, then, but for good purposes... Let the poor know you are rich; let the needy know you are wealthy.'[123] And Ambrose, in the *De virginibus*, which he began in 377, presented the virginal life characterized by almsgiving as an escape from greedy desire: 'What a joy it is for you to be enflamed by no lust for ownership? The poor man demands what you have, has no call for what you lack. The fruit of your work is a treasure for the person in need, and two coins, if that is all there is, qualifies as the wealth of a generous donor (*census est largientis*).'[124] Ambrose, that is, identifies the virgin with the poor widow of Mark 12: 42 and Luke 21: 2 who places her last two coins in the Temple treasury.

Jerome followed Cyprian and Ambrose by insisting on the virtue of almsgiving in the life of consecrated virgins, but implicitly questioned the validity of Ambrose's confident association of the virgin with the poor widow. When the letter to Eustochium is compared with Ambrose's *De virginibus* it is clear that Jerome places greater emphasis on the renunciation of family wealth. He imagines Eustochium raising the objection that, if she gives too much away, she will have nothing on which to live in her old age. He insists that she need

---

[122] *Ep.* 22. 38 in Labourt, *Lettres*, i. 154.
[123] Cyprian, *De habitu virginum* 11, in G. Hartel (ed.), *S. Thasci Caeli Cypriani Opera Omnia*, CSEL 3/1 (Vienna, 1868), 195: 'Locupletem te dicis et divitem et utendum putas his quae possidere te Deus voluit. utere, sed ad res salutares... divitem te sentiant pauperes, locupletem te sentiant indigentes.'
[124] Ambrose, *De virginibus* 1. 54, OOSA 14/1. 154.

not fear; she should rely on God's providence.[125] While Ambrose recognizes in the *De virginibus* that a girl who defies her parents' wishes to become a consecrated virgin may lose her 'patrimonium',[126] he presents a story in which the relative who had objected most vociferously to the girl's decision to become a virgin suddenly died, so that her 'virginity did not bring with it the loss of income due to her'.[127]

It is instructive to compare Jerome's letter to Eustochium with a letter of 414, some thirty years later, to another young woman and heiress from the senatorial class embarking on the life of consecrated virginity, Demetrias, the grand-daughter of Proba, one of the powerful Anicii. The tone adopted in the second letter is quieter, more deferential. Jerome, who makes it clear that Demetrias had only just escaped a marriage arranged by her mother and grandmother,[128] is careful not to alienate the family, and praises the relatives for giving Demetrias the intended dowry.[129] In the very act of disclaiming such a warning, Jerome warns the virgin against moral compromise: 'It is quite unnecessary to warn you against avarice, when you come from a family that both has and spurns riches and the Apostle teaches avarice to be a worship of idols.' He then proceeds to cite Matthew 19: 21, and to discourse on the moral perfection to be found in giving not something but everything away, not to close relatives but those in need. And, while Jerome asserts that Demetrias is not to disobey her mother and grandmother, his talk of what she owes them in their lifetime leads to what she should do after their death, and he repeats what he had previously said to Eustochium, that her belongings are not truly hers, are hers only in as much they have come to be the property of Christ, who is to be fed and clothed in the poor:

Ever since that time when you were consecrated to perpetual virginity, your possessions have not been your own. Rather, they are really yours, because they have come to belong to Christ, to be distributed with the consent either of your grandmother or mother during their lifetime. But when they are dead and enjoy the restful sleep of the saints . . . you will do what seems right

---

[125] Jerome, *Ep.* 22. 31, in Labourt, *Lettres*, i. 146.
[126] Ambrose, *De virginibus* 1. 64, OOSA 14/1. 160.
[127] *De virginibus* 1. 66, OOSA 14/1. 164.
[128] Jerome, *Ep.* 130. 5, in Labourt, *Lettres*, vii. 170.
[129] *Ep.* 130. 7, in Labourt, *Lettres*, vii. 173.

to you. Or, rather, you will do what God commands, knowing that you will have nothing, except what will have been given away in good works.[130]

Jerome was by no means the only author who argued against the continued possession of family wealth by virgins. Palladius included in his *Lausiac History* a tale of a miserly virgin 'who was exceedingly rich but never gave an obol to a stranger, virgin, church, or poor man'. She even adopts a niece as her heir. Palladius denounces her: the devil leads people 'into greed under the excuse of loving one's relatives'.[131]

Jerome appears to have thought that only complete self-dispossession of wealth to be given away in alms, the most extreme form of Christian generosity, was free from danger. He explored the dangers of compromise in his *Life of Malchus the Captive Monk*. The protagonist, after spending some years as a monk in the region of Chalcis, as Jerome himself had done, thinks of returning to his widowed mother with the intention of selling the family property after her death. He plans to give part to the poor, part to the monasteries, but to keep a third part for his own comfort. It is a compromise that he confesses with hindsight to have been a moral weakness and act of infidelity.[132] In the *Commentary on Hosea* Jerome criticized those clerics who thought to atone for their sins by almsgiving while still enmeshed in those sins.[133] It is significant that Jerome's consolatory epistle for Bishop Heliodorus on the death of his nephew Nepotianus, with its customary eulogy, is nonetheless marked by Jerome's explicit unhappiness with the period of Nepotianus's life in which he was giving alms while pursuing a military or administrative career: 'I dislike these delays that belong to an imperfect service of Christ.'[134]

Others disagreed with Jerome's extremism. Palladius defended both total immediate self-dispossession for the sake of almsgiving and a long-term investment and distribution of wealth for the care of the poor with another tale in the *Lausiac History*, where each position is adopted by one of two brothers, Paesius and Isaias, whose relative

---

[130] *Ep.* 130. 14, in Labourt, *Lettres*, vii. 185.

[131] Palladius, *Lausiac History* 6. 1 and 6. 2, ed. Bartelink, *Palladio*, 32.

[132] Jerome, *Life of Malchus* 3, PL 23. 55.

[133] *Commentary on Hosea* 1 ad 5. 6–7 in *Commentarii in Prophetas Minores*, ed. M. Adriaen, CCSL 76 (Turnhout, 1969), 54.

[134] *Ep.* 60. 9, in Labourt, *Lettres*, iii. 97.

virtues are hotly contested by others until a vision reveals both men enjoying equal glory before God.[135] Some argued that Jerome's call to immediate and complete renunciation of property by the wealthy was a disservice to the poor. Jerome attributes to Vigilantius the argument that 'those who put their possessions to work and gradually distribute to the poor the profits from their holdings behave better than those who sell their possessions and give it away once and for all'.[136] The debate is echoed by an anonymous sermon, once falsely ascribed to Ambrose, which was listed in Chapter 3, *Sermon Against Those Who Say that Possessions are Not to be Dispersed, But Their Fruits Used for Almsgiving.*[137]

Jerome characteristically met such objections by citing certain authoritative examples in the scriptures: the immediate action of Cornelius in seeking baptism; the fate of Ananias and Sapphira, who had held back part of their fortune (Acts 5: 1–5);[138] the virtue of the apostles, who had at once left their nets and ships to follow Christ (Matthew 4: 18–22); the call of Christ to the rich young man to sell all (and not merely some of) his possessions and give the money to the poor (Matthew 19: 21);[139] and the widow who had put her entire wealth, those two brass coins, into the temple treasury (Luke 21: 1–4).[140] These examples did not so much answer the objection as turn the focus away from the external and uncertain consequences of a person's acts to the internal or spiritual surrender of the ascetic's life to God expressed through those same acts.

It is in this context of the interaction between differing patterns of generosity in the classical and Christian traditions that we must examine Jerome's reference to Cicero's *De officiis* in a letter to Paulinus of Nola. He urges Paulinus not to keep money back like Ananias and Saphira in Acts. However, they are not to pour out Christ's wealth (*Christi substantiam*) carelessly (*imprudenter*), and destroy

---

[135] Palladius, *Lausiac History* 14, in Bartelink, *Palladio*, 58–62.

[136] *Against Vigilantius* 14, PL 23. 350–1.

[137] Sermo 2 ex cod. Sessoriano, PL 18. 119A–122A. Its date is not known.

[138] Jerome, *Epp.* 66. 8 and 130. 14, in Labourt, *Lettres*, iii. 174 and vii. 185; *Life of Hilarion*, 3, PL 23. 30; *Commentary on Matthew*, 3 ad 19. 21, in *Commentariorum in Matheum Libri IV*, ed. D Hurst and M Adriaen, CCSL 77 (Turnhout, 1969), 170.

[139] *Against Vigilantius* 14, PL 23. 351; *Ep.* 66. 8, in Labourt, *Lettres*, iii. 174.

[140] *Epp.* 53. 11, 71. 3, and 118. 5, in Labourt, *Lettres*, iii. 24, iv. 11, and vi. 94.

generosity with generosity as that 'most careful man' (*prudentissimus*) Cicero had warned. Perrin has noted that Lactantius had cited Cicero in this respect only to reject a moderation which kept back one's patrimony. Perrin then reads Jerome as approving of Cicero's stance, but this is to misread Jerome at this point. Jerome cites the phrase of Cicero with approval, but twists the application of that phrase in a quite different direction to that intended by Cicero.[141] For what is careless is not lack of moderation, but to give to others 'with an ill-measured judgement' (*immoderato iudicio*) what belongs to the poor.[142]

It is also in this context that we should study Jerome's portrayal of the large-scale almsgiving practised by Pammachius after the death of his wife in a letter to the aristocrat intended for a wide readership in elite circles (*Ep.* 66). The letter contains an unusually graphic description of the recipients of alms: the cripple 'using his whole body to drag himself along'; someone so swollen with dropsy he is said to be on the point of giving birth to death; a mute; and someone whose living body is already rotting away. The images are startling, forcing their attention on readers who would not expect to be confronted by them. Where one might instead expect standard abstract references to the poor, needy, widows, and orphans, the blind man who 'puts out his hand and shouts, often when no one's there' is said to be Paulina's 'heir' and Pammachius' 'co-heir'.[143] Jerome aims to shock by yoking together opposites: the elite and the dregs whose 'squalor whitens' Pammachius, who in making this radical decision to dispense so much wealth, is said to be ministering to Christ. Jerome aims to elicit pity, as well as to give the maximum praise where he believes it due. But Jerome's desire to give praise should not be read as flattery: in all of this he may be rescuing Pammachius from charges of family and civic betrayal.

It is significant that Jerome raises the possibility of family betrayal only to deny it: 'the mother of such a daughter delights in her heir. She is not grieved that her wealth has passed to another, when she

[141] M. Perrin, 'Jérôme lecteur de Lactance', in Y.-M. Duval (ed.), *Jérôme entre l'Occident et l'Orient: Actes du colloque de Chantilly (septembre 1986)* (Paris, 1988), 113.

[142] Jerome, *Ep.* 58. 7, in Labourt, *Lettres*, iii. 82.

[143] *Ep.* 66. 5, in Labourt, *Lettres*, iii. 171.

sees that wealth bestowed on the same people as she had wanted ... For it is not a lessening of their wealth but a change of staff.'[144] The charge is read in order for the defendant to be acquitted. Jerome states that Pammachius is the 'public sponsor of the poor and the candidate of the needy' (*munerarius pauperum, egentium candidatus*),[145] the candidate for office who sponsors their games. In this way Jerome seeks to redefine what counts as truly honourable conduct for the elite in Roman society, to confer the status which had traditionally accrued to political advancement on a way of life that involved a renunciation of political ambitions. We do well to imagine this revisionary account as set against charges of deserting civic duty.

Jerome's description later in the same letter and his praise of Pammachius' foundation at Portus of a hostel or hospice (*xenodochium*) holds out a new vision of what for Christians should count as truly glorious euergetism.[146] To this end Jerome uses an elaborate mixture of classical and biblical allusions to add lustre to the scheme: Pammachius had 'planted a twig from Abraham's tree on the Ausonian shore'. The oak at Mamre has been transplanted into Virgilian soil. Indeed, Pammachius has outdone Aeneas, for where the hero had once been reduced to eating tranches of bread, Pammachius has built a house where the needy are fed, in what Jerome, playing with the etymology of Bethlehem, calls a house of bread. Allusion to Pythagoras is set beside an interpretation of *Genesis* 23 in which Pammachius is another Abraham constructing a mausoleum (*monumentum*) for his wife. The hospice is presented as Paulina's funerary monument, which may suggest the role of the poor in winning her salvation. It is to stand beside a 'city-state of letters' (*civitas litterarum*).

The interaction in Pammachius' gifts of classical and Christian patterns of conduct are, thus, complex. The tradition of civic euergetism in the form of building projects probably influenced Pammachius' decision about how to aid the poor, as it had influenced Basil in constructing the *Basileiados*, and had influenced earlier generations of aristocrats to build churches and *martyria* in which they

[144] *Ep.* 66. 5, in Labourt, *Lettres*, iii. 172.
[145] *Ep.* 66. 5, in Labourt, *Lettres*, iii. 171.
[146] *Ep.* 66. 11, in Labourt, *Lettres*, iii. 177–8.

would be buried. But the interaction of classical and Christian views regarding the dispersal of substantial wealth created the potential for family conflict and elite censure. Finally, Jerome's interaction of classical and Christian allusion in the description of Pammachius' acts deflects criticism to allow Pammachius his triumph. Classical letters have their value in building the distinctively Christian city.

## CONCLUSION

The meaningful practices of Christian almsgiving did not exist in communities sealed off from the wider culture. Classical patterns of conduct and virtue influenced how donors acted and how their actions were interpreted by others. Basil's actions at Caesarea during the famine and his foundation of the *Basileiados* confused the characteristic behaviour of the civic patron and Christian bishop in ways which generated criticism as well as praise. This is not to say that Basil's acts or those like them turned a bishop into a civic patron, though they disturbed an older pattern of patronage. Pammachius' actions at Portus show a similar influence of the old on the new. Classical ideas concerning patrimony did not disappear, and fed controversy within the churches, so that there was far from complete agreement on the proper shape of Christian generosity towards the poor on the part of wealthy bishops, virgins, and lay men and women. On the other hand, Ambrose's close adaptation of Basil's writings in the late fourth century suggest the absence of any divide in this matter between Eastern and Western churches. Partly in response to controversy, Christian writers such as Basil, Ambrose, and Jerome reworked classical discourse in their sermons, treatises, and letters to promote a Christian moral philosophy, which could be seen to answer critics. This involved them in emphasizing co-operation rather than competition in almsgiving, offering a shared patronage or leadership of the poor under the co-ordinating authority of the bishop, and the presentation of classical culture as history capped by the advent of Christian almsgiving.

# 7

## Concluding Remarks

The mid-third century *Life of Cyprian* related how under that bishop's direction the Christian community at Carthage had cared for the poor and the sick during an epidemic that had brought many deaths.[1] When the city had first been struck, the citizens in their fear had thought only of themselves and the risk of infection. Cyprian, it was claimed, had called together the populace (the *plebs*) and preached to them: 'in the first place he taught the assembled populace about the good works of mercy and taught them with examples from Holy Scripture how much the duties of religion serve to win God's favour'.[2] As a result the 'Christian populace' (*Christiana plebs*) had devoted themselves to the task:

Help was given out continuously according to people's social rank and circumstances. Many who could not put up money thanks to their poverty, put up more than money, making up for it with their own labour, a treasure of greater value than all riches. And who would not be quick to find some post in such an army, by which they might please God the Father, Christ the Judge and, here and now, their bishop? So, through the generosity of such abundant charitable works, the good which was done helped not only those who belonged to the household of faith; they achieved more than is attested as accomplished through Tobit's peerless devotion.[3]

Pontius portrayed a Christian community, in contrast to the wider urban community whose leaders remain invisible, co-operating harmoniously together in almsgiving and poor-relief inspired by the preaching, and under the saintly leadership, of its bishop. At

---

[1] Pontius, *Life of Cyprian* 9. 1, in Mohrmann *et al.*, *Vita*, 22.
[2] *Life of Cyprian* 9. 6, in Mohrmann *et al.*, *Vita*, 24.
[3] *Life of Cyprian* 10. 2–4 in Mohrmann *et al.*, *Vita*, 26.

Cyprian's instigation they together display an exemplary and distinctive generosity in which all play a part, but in which the bishop's authority under God gains new emphasis. That generosity is articulated in care first and foremost for fellow Christians, the 'domesticos fidei', but is by no means limited to them. Pontius presents Cyprian, through his undisputed leadership of the *Christiana plebs*, reaching out to leadership of the whole *plebs* in the wider city. Pontius sets out a clear ideal of the interaction between Christian discourse and practice in almsgiving, in which the meaning of the latter practice among Christians is also significant for those who do not yet share their faith. It was an idealized account much read and admired in the fourth and fifth centuries.

I have examined whether and to what extent Christian discourse and practices in the fourth and early fifth centuries lived up to this ideal to reveal both what Pontius chose not to portray and what he could not portray, because in the mid-third century its development still lay in the future. Christian communities did co-operate in almsgiving undertaken by the bishop and his assistants through church collections, both regular collections and others for special occasions. Though it proved impossible to detect a single standard pattern of regular giving beneath the biblical language in which gifts were variously described, it is likely that in most places there was a regular weekly collection and by the fifth century a chest or area in the church reserved for alms and known as the *corban* or *gazophylacium*. Episcopal alms did not draw on regular or obligatory offerings of tithes and first fruits distinct from the general offerings made by the faithful, but the language of tithes and first fruits was applied to those offerings, a share of which went towards the bishop's almsgiving. After the accession of the first Christian emperors, funds for episcopal charity were swelled by revenues derived either from imperial subventions or properties, the donation of which to the church was now legal. Yet, the costs of building, enlarging, decorating, and maintaining churches, together with the support of their poorer clergy, bit deeply into those revenues and limited the numbers who could be assisted on a regular basis. Numbers varied from city to city. The principal beneficiaries of episcopal alms were the enrolled widows and their children, for whom a low but relatively secure dole ensured their survival without falling into utter destitution. What remained benefited the very poorest in the Christian community and, if there was anything left over after that, the non-Christians. To those in particular who were not citizens of the cities in which they begged, it is likely that this help was crucial to their survival.

This episcopal charity, though it was an important element in the construction of the bishop's spiritual authority, required eloquence on his part in raising funds and overcoming opposition to the sale of church treasures. It required his supervision and church legislation to secure effective co-operation from the diocesan clergy, whose share in the honour accorded to this form of almsgiving could also turn priests and deacons into competitors for status with the bishop. Church canons also reveal the need to defend bishops from criticism of maladministration and fraud to which they were exposed by their responsibility for almsgiving. The latter further involved the bishop in publicizing the generosity of the wealthy who made large individual donations, and whose standing was enhanced alongside the bishop's.

Hans-Georg Gadamer warned that 'the interpreter of history always runs the risk of hypostasizing the sequence of events when he sees their significance as that intended by actors and planners'.[4] Pontius presented Cyprian as exercising his leadership through almsgiving in a way that impressed an entire city, but the impact of episcopal almsgiving in the fourth and fifth centuries was neither so pronounced nor so simple. The bishop's generous care for the poor, by exemplifying the virtues characteristic of episcopal office, was constructive of his leadership over them and over the wider Christian community, though this leadership was not patronage in the classical sense. The leadership generated through almsgiving probably gave some, though limited, support to beleaguered bishops during the long period of upheaval caused by christological and Trinitarian controversies. Popular support could secure a bishop for a time from expulsion by imperial officials. Even an unpopular bishop in a metropolis bitterly contested between Arian and Nicene Christians could give vivid testimony to a bond constructed in part through alms: Ammianus Marcellinus described George the

---

[4] H.-G. Gadamer, *Truth and Method*, 2nd edn. Eng tr. ed. G. Barden and J. Cumming (London, 1975), 334.

Cappadocian, the luckless Arian bishop of Alexandria (who would be murdered by a mob just one month later) as moving through the city in 361 'surrounded as usual by a dense crowd of people'.[5] But authority was also constructed from many things other than almsgiving, and almsgiving was exercised to great effect by others than the bishops. Nothing has demonstrated that Nicene and Arian Christians differed in their approach to almsgiving. But each side saw and presented their own episcopal charity as a marker of orthodoxy, and sought to blacken the reputation of their opponents by accusing them of fraud or violence towards the poor.

It is in this context that the historian should set the story told in exile by Eusebius of Vercelli to his Nicene supporters in Italy of the persecution he suffered at the hands of the Arian bishop, Patrophilus, after his banishment in 355 to Scythopolis. Eusebius had been lodged with his senior clergy in a hostel or 'hospitium' but was twice forcibly removed. His letter told how on his return the first time with his clergy 'we began once again with the Lord's blessing to care for the needy'. This, however, his enemies found intolerable: 'their cruelty (*inhumanitas*) would not put up with this'. The Arians again evicted him from the hostel and destroyed 'everything that had been collected together either to live on or for the poor'. Eusebius was isolated from his fellow clerics.[6]

It is not clear whether Eusebius' hostel was a traditional guesthouse for visitors or a hostel for the very poor and sick, but by caring for the poor there he was reasserting his episcopal authority. The hostel had become a centre for Nicene Christians, and almsgiving was an integral element in the running of this rival church community. Eusebius had entered into competition with Patrophilus for the loyalty of the needy and so for leadership over them, while his actions implicitly gave credit to his own orthodoxy and impugned that of his rival. Hence Patrophilus' repeated actions to break up this rival institution. This in turn allowed Eusebius to capitalize on his persecution in the propaganda he sent to Italy, in which he could portray

---

[5] Ammianus Marcellinus, *Res gestae* 22. 11. 7, in J. Fontaine, E. Frézouls and J.-D. Berger (eds.), *Ammien Marcellin, Histoire*, iii (Paris, 1996), 125.

[6] Eusebius of Vercelli, *Ep.* 2. 6. 2–3, in V. Bulhart (ed.), *Eusebii Vercellensis Episcopi Quae Supersunt*, CCSL 9 (Turnhout, 1957), 107.

himself as the virtuous almsgiver and his opponent as the agent of cruelty and the very opposite of episcopal generosity. He was able to exploit in this way to the full the complex position of episcopal almsgiving established here, where co-operation, competition, honour, and scandal, the discourse and practice of generosity, interact in a field of possibilities and pitfalls which Jerome once summarized in these telling lines: 'it is the glory of a bishop to provide for the needs of the poor. To devote oneself to amassing private wealth brings shame on all priests.'[7]

Episcopal charity was only one, distinct, form of almsgiving among others. Almsgiving by monastic communities grew in importance throughout the period, while ascetics caught the popular imagination by seeking to divest themselves of all they possessed and giving it away in alms in accordance with the Lord's command at Matthew 19: 21. They, even more than others, were encouraged where possible to give alms in person. The difficulties which they encountered first because of family ties are evident in the account which Theodoret of Cyrrhus gave of the ascetic Zeno in his *Religious History*.[8] When Zeno came to embrace asceticism in the late fourth century, he kept back 'both money and items of property' which he owned jointly with his two younger brothers, then minors. He remained afraid to sell his third even at a much later date in case the buyer would harass the brothers or nephews (the manuscripts vary at this point) who now held the other two shares. He chose not to sell until he could sell to another family member. Religious ideals and family duties were not easily reconciled. Even after this sale had been completed, Zeno found it impossible to distribute himself all the proceeds to the poor. When he fell gravely ill, he was forced to summon bishop Alexander of Antioch (*c*.411–18) and bid him act as the 'best distributor of this money'. The damage that might otherwise have befallen his reputation is evident in what Jerome related to Eustochium about one of the monks at Nitria, whose cell had been found, at his death, to contain a considerable quantity of money which he had made from weaving. The monks had debated what to

---

[7] Jerome, *Ep.* 52. 6, in Labourt, *Lettres*, ii. 180–1. Some MSS read 'pauperum inopiae providere'.

[8] Theodoret, *Historia religiosa* 12. 7, SC 234. 470–2.

do with the hoard of one hundred coins. 'Some said that the coins ought to be distributed to the poor', but more senior monks insisted that the money be buried with him together with the words of St Peter to Simon Magus: 'may your money perish with you' (Acts 8: 10). Jerome certainly quoted the decision to bury the coins in the grave with approval, and asserted the deterrent effect of the decision: since that time it had been thought wicked to leave so much as one *solidus*.[9] Zeno risked posthumous conviction on charges of greed.

In a development not anticipated by Pontius, bishops, monks, and wealthy lay men and women began to build hostels and hospices for the poor where almsgiving took on a new institutional character. This adaptation of classical euergetism spread quickly in the East and slowly developed in the West. Foundations frequently depended on private wealth, whether that of a bishop or lay Christians, while their management often depended on deacons or monks. This combination of factors made them sources of particular honour and led them to feature often in disputes for control, which legislation at Chalcedon attempted to secure for the local bishops.

Beggars continued to crowd around church doors and martyrs' shrines in the hope of alms from individual Christians, who were routinely encouraged to give alms. Pontius portrayed Cyprian assembling and inspiring the entire Christian community with 'examples from Holy Scripture'. While attendance at the *synaxis* and other church services in the fourth and fifth centuries was often patchy, there was sustained promotion by preachers and writers across the empire, which reached both the general congregation and those groups within the congregation whom it particularly concerned: catechumens and neophytes, virgins, widows, monks, and members of the cultured elite. This promotion sought to shape and sustained the distinctive practices of Christian almsgiving. Conventional exhortation in sermons encouraged greater almsgiving by individuals especially at Lent and Easter, or during the winter cold, when the poor were more vulnerable. Indirect promotion in, for example, the valorization of almsgiving undertaken by biblical characters, was arguably as important as direct exhortation. The ethical teaching contained in the scriptures, perceived as divinely inspired,

---

[9] Jerome, *Ep.* 22. 33 in Labourt, *Lettres*, i. 148–9.

was rehearsed in liturgy, both as read to the congregations and sung by them, before also being interpreted and applied by preachers to the conduct of the faithful. Augustine began a sermon with a reminder to his congregation of the words they had just sung together and the Gospel they had just heard: 'while singing to God, we said to him, "Blessed is the man whom you train, Lord, and whom you teach from your law" (Ps. 94: 12). So then the Gospel resounded, Zacchaeus gave alms. Learn! For what better law of God is there than the holy Gospel?'[10] The preacher made explicit what in the Gospel text was implicit, and turned description to prescription. People did learn. But the literate also learnt from popular, hagiographic, literature, of which Pontius' *Life of Cyprian* remained a notable example. Much which had been composed in this vein before the mid-fourth century, such as apocryphal *Acta*, continued to be widely read and admired for the moral exempla contained therein. Christian discourse was pluriform to an extent that Pontius did not envisage.

Pontius suggests the way in which preachers encouraged almsgiving as a means of winning God's blessing, their appeal to self-interest, and the crucial description of almsgiving as an expression of generosity, but not the degree to which the different voices of Christian discourse in the fourth and fifth centuries would redescribe the poor as brethren, friends, and fellow servants, whose prayers now constituted a valuable return for alms received. Almsgiving was incorporated into a moral theology of the virtues, in particular as an expression of *philanthropia, liberalitas, humanitas,* and *iustitia.* These virtues brought to almsgiving a new honour and status for practitioners. The promotion examined in Chapter 4 was not a matter of hawking contentious ideas, a sales-pitch before the sceptical and disinterested public. It was the welcome articulation on behalf of the church community of a traditional ethic by recognized authorities, whose task it was to goad and persuade. That task of persuasion need not be seen only or primarily as an index of resistance to the practices of almsgiving, as Krause would believe, but as the way in which those practices were valorized as acts of moral conversion, Christian commitment, and virtue. Preachers such as Chrysostom attacked alms proffered with contempt and the hard

---

[10] Augustine, *Serm.* 25. 1, CCSL 41. 335.

hearts of the faithful, but while this is one measure of resistance to the promotion discussed it may also be another means of inscribing value, where '[e]xperiential meanings are defined in fields of contrast, as words are in semantic fields'.[11]

Such promotion, in appealing to scripture and adapting the classical language of the virtues, took a form which both allowed Christians to set themselves apart from non-believers and at the same time to find an advantageous place for themselves in the common discourse and power-politics of generosity. Their Christian identity was affirmed by service of Christ in the person of the poor and in particular duties towards fellow Christians in need, while poor-relief brought not only spiritual goods, but also an honour colouring present relationships. The lever of change was a means of insertion into the life of the late Roman cities. The complexity of this insertion has been seen in the context first of one late Roman city, Cappadocian Caesarea. Classical and Christian patterns of generosity merged in Basil's aid for the victims of the food shortage and in his establishment of the *Basileiados*. This merger led to an increase in status and in the risk of criticism. Christian discourse on alms was not simply a matter of exhortation which automatically raised the status of the bishop into a leading civic patron, but was an essential instrument in the sometimes fraught negotiation of authority amongst competitors. The writings of Basil, Gregory, Ambrose, and Jerome drew on classical and Christian sources in part to deflect criticism of different practices of almsgiving. They show how different versions of generosity within the Christian community, one more strongly influenced by classical tradition and one more opposed to it, led to controversies surrounding the proper conduct of bishops and virgins with respect to their *patrimonium*. Christian discourse was polyphonic to an extent that Pontius did not portray.

In the urban communities of the later Roman Empire monks and bishops, pagan and Christian notables, all competed for status. Almsgiving increasingly figured in that competitive arena, in conflicts between monks and bishops, but also in raising the bishops' status and in the contest between Christianity and paganism, where

---

[11] Charles Taylor, 'Interpretation and the Sciences of Man', in F. Dallmayr and T. McCarthy (eds.), *Understanding and Social Inquiry* (Notre Dame, 1977), 110.

Christians appealed to almsgiving as a measure of their moral superiority. At the same time, episcopal almsgiving offered the possibility of co-operation among members of the Christian community, a participation in shared honours. Michael De Vinne's contrast between local elites seeking to 'turn Christian charity into pagan euergetism' and bishops striving 'to transmute pagan euergetism into Christian charity' must be rejected as a simplistic and false opposition.[12] Beyond the boundaries of the churches traditional forms of euergetism, shows, games, races, the repair of buildings, and the heating of public baths, all of which had long been associated with civic prominence or magistracies, continued to flourish in the period under review, often despite Christian discourse opposed to their continuance. All three of these factors, competition between almsgivers, the co-operative dimension of episcopal almsgiving, and the continuing vitality of classical euergetism, should be seen as a significant limit on the ability of generous almsgiving to elevate bishops to civic leadership as supreme patrons. Contrary to De Vinne's view, there was no 'monopolization of almsgiving' by the bishops in this period, nor as a result of their almsgiving did they emerge as 'the megapatrons of their communities'.[13]

Several major questions remain concerning Christian almsgiving in the late empire. The religious competition in which almsgiving featured was not a two-horse race between Christians and pagans. It is highly probable that Christian and Jewish discourse on almsgiving in this period interacted, and that the respective practices, never really separable from discourse as this thesis has shown, also interacted. The difficulty lies in specifying the nature of the interaction. It is comparatively easy to understand the nature of the interaction between Jewish and Christian discourse at a much earlier period. Chapter 1 noted how book 2 of the *Sibylline Oracles*, which scholars reckon is a Christian redaction or reworking of an original Jewish work to be 'dated no later than A.D. 150',[14] incorporates a passage from a Hellenistic Jewish text, the *Sentences of Pseudo-Phocylides*, containing lines on alms for the destitute. Christians in the second

---

[12] De Vinne, *Advocacy*, 118.
[13] Ibid., p. iv.
[14] J. H. Charlesworth, *The Old Testament Pseudepigrapha* (London, 1983), i. 332.

century borrowed heavily from Jewish educational and catechetical materials in this respect. But what happened in the late empire?

A late rabbinic text, *Kallah*, tells how Rabbi Tarphon asked Rabbi Akiba to buy on his behalf one or two cities with a vast sum of money. Akiba gave the money to the poor. To explain what he had done, Akiba took Tarphon to the 'House of Study' where they read the Psalms until reaching Psalm 112: 9 ('he has distributed funds, he has given to the poor; his justice lasts forever'). Akiba then said to Rabbi Tarphon: 'This is the city I bought for you.'[15] The story bears a structural resemblance to the tale recounted by Ambrose of how St Lawrence shortly before his martyrdom tricked the Roman persecutor who had demanded from him the fabulous treasures of the Roman church. Lawrence gave the wealth to the poor and presented them to his antagonist with the words: 'these are the Church's treasures'.[16] What we cannot tell is how and when the two stories may have influenced each other. Joel Gereboff, who has studied the traditions concerning Tarphon, has compared the rabbinic story in *Kallah* with four similar versions, in which some or all of the money is given to those studying the Torah. He has concluded that this version is the 'most embellished' and one of the latest.[17] This raises the suspicion that whereas in the second century the interaction was predominantly one of Christian adaptation of Jewish discourse, the traffic in ideas may have been more various in later centuries.

One of two controversial Greek inscriptions from a synagogue at Aphrodisias has been reconstructed by scholars as referring to the foundation there of a soup-kitchen for the destitute and for 'the relief of suffering in the community'.[18] The inscription honours those who financed the project. The likely date of the inscription has been the subject of much dispute, but recent scholarship has favoured a date in the fifth century.[19] How did Christian and Jewish practice interact?

---

[15] *Kallah* 21, cited in J. Gereboff, *Rabbi Tarfon: The Tradition, the Man, and Early Rabbinic Judaism* (Misoula, 1979), 273–4.

[16] Ambrose, *De officiis* 2. 28. 140 in Testard, *Devoirs*, ii. 72.

[17] Gereboff, *Rabbi Tarfon*, 275.

[18] J. Reynolds and R. Tannenbaum, *Jews and God-Fearers at Aphrodisias* (Cambridge, 1987), 41.

[19] M. Palmer Bonz, 'The Jewish Donor Inscriptions from Aphrodisias: Are they Both Third-century, and Who are the *Theosebeis*?', *Harvard Studies in Classical Philology*, 96 (1994), 287–90.

It seems that we should at least conjecture that by sharing a similar pattern of honouring donors and of adapting monumental euergetism to include centres of poor-relief, Jews and Christians reinforced this pattern of meaningful behaviour in their respective communities and gave greater prominence to this attitude in the late antique city. It is also likely that Jewish and Christian donors were rivals in this form of euergetism, so that care of the poor entered into the political competition for status among citizens and the religious competition between Jews and Christians for converts from paganism. The opening phrase of the inscription has been shown to borrow from Christian usage.[20] This at least suggests we should not try to isolate Jewish and Christian practices.

It has been evident on occasion that pagans such as Julian and Libanius in the later empire were forced to engage with the Christian discourse and practices of almsgiving. How far that engagement went, and its nature, has not been tackled here. Nor has there been space to examine how Christian discourse and practices in this period influenced later Christians in the Byzantine world of John the Almsgiver or the post-imperial world of Western Europe, where Caesarius copied and adapted Augustine's sermons, and where almsgiving came to feature among the characteristic acts of royalty.

In all of the above it is apparent how the historical evaluation of Christian promotion and practice of almsgiving has suffered in the past from a separation by which the first has been treated largely by theologians, who have until recently neglected moral matters in pursuit of doctrine, and the second has been treated by historians, who have shown greater interest in trying (and failing) to measure practices in terms of their economic impact than in seeking to understand the meaning of those practices. Only by proper appreciation of the discourse surrounding practice, with attention to that discourse's rhetorical structure and the many different things which authors do with their words, does the meaning of the practice become clear, where 'the language by which we describe our goals, feelings, desires is also a definition of the meaning things have for us'.[21] A history of events cannot be established in isolation from the history of ideas.

---

[20] Ibid. 290.     [21] Taylor, 'Interpretation', 108.

# Bibliography

**Primary literature**

Classical and late antique authors and works by those authors are cited by their common English name and title, except where the Latin or transliterated Greek remains customary among English readers.

*Acta conciliorum oecumenicorum*, ed E. Schwartz, 4 vols. (Berlin, 1914–74).

*Acts of Phileas*, ed. and tr. H. Musurillo *The Acts of the Christian Martyrs* (Oxford: Clarendon Press, 1972), 328–44.

*Acts of Shmona, Guria and Habbib*, ed. F. C. Burkitt, *Euphemia and the Goth with the Acts of the Martyrdom of the Confessors of Edessa* (Oxford, 1913).

Aelius Herodianus, *On Universal Prosody*, in *Herodiani Technici Reliquiae*, ed. A. Lentz (Leipzig, 1867).

Ambrose, *De excessu fratris*, ed. O. Faller, in G. Banterle, *Le orazioni funebri*, OOSA 18 (Milan: Biblioteca Ambrosiana, and Rome: Città Nuova Editrice, 1985), 24–158.

—— *De Nabuthae*, ed. F. Gori, *Elia e il digiuno, Naboth, Tobia*, OOSA 6 (Milan: Biblioteca Ambrosiana, and Rome: Città Nuova Editrice, 1985), 130–94.

—— *De Helia*, ed. F. Gori, *Elia e il digiuno, Naboth, Tobia*, OOSA 6 (Milan: Biblioteca Ambrosiana, and Rome: Città Nuova Editrice, 1985), 44–126.

—— *De officiis*, ed. M. Testard, *Les Devoirs*, 2 vols. (Paris: Les Belles Lettres, 1984 and 1992).

—— *De paenitentia*, ed. O. Faller, in G. Banterle, *Spiegazione del credo, i sacramenti, i misteri, la penitenza*, OOSA 17 (Milan: Biblioteca Ambrosiana, and Rome: Città Nuova Editrice, 1982), 172–282.

—— *De viduis*, in F. Gori (ed.), *Verginità e vedovanza*, 2 vols., OOSA 14/1 and 2 (Milan: Biblioteca Ambrosiana, and Rome: Città Nuova Editrice, 1989), i. 244–318.

—— *De virginibus*, in F. Gori (ed.), *Verginità e vedovanza*, 2 vols., OOSA 14/1 and 2 (Milan: Biblioteca Ambrosiana, and Rome: Città Nuova Editrice, 1989), i. 100–240.

—— *Commentary on Luke's Gospel*, ed. G. Tissot, *Traité sur l'évangile de S. Luc*, SC 45 and 52, 2 vols. (Paris: Éditions du Cerf, 1956 and 1958).

Ambrose, *Letters*, 1–35, ed. O. Faller, in G. Banterle, *Lettere*, i, OOSA 19 (Milan: Biblioteca Ambrosiana, and Rome: Città Nuova Editrice, 1988).

—— *Letters*, 36–69, ed. M. Zelzer, *Sancti Ambrosi Opera, Epistularum Libri VII–VIII*, CSEL 82/2 (Vienna, Verlag der Österreichischen Akademie der Wissenschaften, 1990).

—— *Letters*, 70–7, ed. M. Zelzer, in G. Banterle, *Lettere*, iii, OOSA 21 (Milan: Biblioteca Ambrosiana, and Rome: Città Nuova Editrice, 1988).

Ammianus Marcellinus, *Res gestae* 22 in J. Fontaine, E. Frézouls and J.-D. Berger (eds.), *Ammien Marcellin, Histoire*, iii (Paris: Les Belles Lettres, 1996).

—— *Res gestae* 30, in G. Sabbah and L. Angliviel de la Beaumelle (eds.), *Ammien Marcellin, Histoire*, vi (Paris: Les Belles Lettres, 1999).

Aphrahat, *Demonstrations*, ed. M.-J. Pierre, *Aphraate le sage persan: Les Exposés*, SC 349 and 359 (Paris: Éditions du Cerf, 1988 and 1989).

*The Apocalypse of Paul*, tr. J. K. Elliott, *The Apocryphal New Testament* (Oxford: Clarendon Press, 1993), 619–44.

*Apocryphal Acts of John*, in R. A. Lipsius and M. Bonnet (eds.), *Acta Apostolorum Apocrypha*, ii (Leipzig, 1898), 151–216.

*Apocryphal Acts of Peter*, in R. A. Lipsius and M. Bonnet (eds.), *Acta Apostolorum Apocrypha*, i (Leipzig, 1891), 45–103. Also, L. Vouaux (ed.), *Les Actes de Pierre* (Paris: Letouzey & Ané, 1922).

*Apocryphal Acts of Paul and Thecla*, in R. A. Lipsius and M. Bonnet (eds.), *Acta Apostolorum Apocrypha*, i (Leipzig, 1891), 235–72.

*Apocryphal Acts of Thomas*, in M. Bonnet (ed.) *Acta Philippi et Acta Thomae accedunt Acta Barnabae* (Leipzig, 1903), 99–291.

*Apophthegmata Patrum*, PG 65. 71–440.

*Apostolic Church Order*, ed. J. W. Bickell, *Geschichte des Kirchenrechts* (Frankfurt, 1843), 107–32.

*Apostolic Church Order* (Latin tr.), in E. Tidner (ed.), *Didascaliae Apostolorum Canonum Ecclesiasticorum Traditionis Apostolicae Versiones Latinae*, Texte und Untersuchungen, 75 (Berlin: Akademie-Verlag, 1963).

*Apostolic Constitutions*, ed. M. Metzger, *Les Constitutions apostoliques*, SC 320, 329, 336 (Paris: Éditions du Cerf, 1985–7).

'Asterius', *Two Easter Homilies*, ed. J. Liébaert, *Deux Homélies anoméenes pour l'octave de Paques*, SC 146 (Paris: Éditions du Cerf, 1969).

Athanasius, *Apologia de fuga sua*, ed. J-M. Szymusiak, *Apologie à l'empereur Constance, Apologie pour sa fuite*, SC 56 (Paris: Éditions du Cerf, 1958).

—— *Apologia secunda (contra Arianos)*, in H.-G. Opitz (ed.), *Athanasius Werke*, ii/1 (Berlin and Leipzig, 1935), 87–168.

—— *Festal Letters*, PG 26. 1360–1444.

—— *Historia Arianorum*, in H.-G. Opitz (ed.), *Athanasius Werke*, ii/1 (Berlin and Leipzig: De Gruyter, 1935), 183–230.

—— *Life of Antony*, ed. G. Bartelink, *Vie d'Antoine*, SC 400 (Paris: Éditions du Cerf, 1994).

Augustine, *Contra Faustum*, ed. J. Zycha, CSEL 25 (Prague: Tempsky, 1891).

—— *City of God*, ed. B. Dombart and A. Kalb, *Sancti Aurelii Augustini De Civitate Dei*, CCSL 47 and 48 (Turnhout: Brepols, 1955).

—— *Confessions*, ed. J. J. O'Donnell, 3 vols. (Oxford: Clarendon Press, 1992).

—— *De bono viduitatis*, ed. J. Zycha, CSEL 41 (Vienna: Tempsky, 1900).

—— *De gestis Pelagii*, in C. F. Urba and J. Zycha (eds.), *Sancti Aurelii Augustini Opera*, 8/2, CSEL 42 (Prague: Tempsky, 1902), 51–122.

—— *De sermone Domini in monte*, ed. A. Mutzenbecher, CCSL 35 (Turnhout: Brepols, 1967).

—— *De perfectione iustitiae*, PL 44. 291–318.

—— *De utilitate credendi*, ed. J. Zycha, CSEL 25 (Vienna: Tempsky, 1891).

—— *Enarrationes in Psalmos* i–l, ed. D. Dekkers and J. Fraipont, CCSL 38, (Turnhout: Brepols, 1956).

—— *Enarrationes in Psalmos* li–c, ed. D. Dekkers and J. Fraipont, CCSL 39 (Turnhout: Brepols, 1956).

—— *Enarrationes in Psalmos* ci–cl, ed. D. Dekkers and J. Fraipont, CCSL 40 (Turnhout: Brepols, 1956).

—— *In Iohannis Evangelium tractatus*, ed D. Willems, CCSL 36 (Turnhout: Brepols, 1954).

—— *Letters*, ed. A. Goldbacher, *S. Aurelii Augustini Hipponensis Episcopi Epistulae*, 5 vols., CSEL 34 (1–2), 44, 57, and 58 (Prague: Tempsky, 1895–1923).

—— *Letters* 1*–29*, ed. J. Divjak, *Lettres* 1*–29*, Œuvres de saint Augustin, 46b (Paris: Études augustiniennes, 1987).

—— *On Christian Instruction*, in J. Martin (ed.), *Sancti Aurelii Augustini De Doctrina Christiana*, CCSL 32 (Turnhout: Brepols, 1962).

—— *Quaestiones Evangeliorum*, ed. A. Mutzenbecher, CCSL 44B (Turnhout: Brepols, 1980)

—— *Sermons on the Old Testament* i–l, ed. C. Lambot, *Sancti Aurelii Augustini Sermones de Vetere Testamento*, CCSL 41 (Turnhout: Brepols, 1961).

—— *Sermons* 15A, 68, 72A, 97A, 104, 217, 299D, 301A, 305A, 306B, 339, 358A, ed. G. Morin, *Sermones post Maurinos reperti*, Miscelleanea Augustiniana, 1 (Rome: Tipografia Poliglotta Vaticana, 1930).

—— *Sermon* 56, ed. P. Verbraken, *RB* 68 (1958), 26–40.

—— *Sermon* 58, ed. P. P. Verbraken, *Ecclesia Orans*, 1 (1984), 119–32.

Augustine, *Sermon* 107A, *RB* 49 (1937), 271–8.

—— *Sermon* 204A, ed. R. Étaix, *RB* 98 (1988), 12.

—— *Sermon* 229Z, in C. Lambot (ed.), 'Une série pascale de sermons de saint Augustin sur les jours de la création', *RB* 79 (1969), 206–14.

—— *Serm* on 343, ed. C. Lambot, *RB* 66 (1956), 28–38.

—— *Sermon* 356, in C. Lambot (ed.), *S. Augustini Aurelii Sermones Selecti Duodeviginti* (Utrecht: In aedibus Spectrum, 1950), 132–43.

—— *Sermon* 359A, *RB* 49 (1937), 258–70.

—— *Sermon* 389, ed. C. Lambot, *RB* 58 (1948), 43–52.

—— *Speculum*, ed F. Weihrich, CSEL 12 (Vienna: Tempsky, 1887).

—— *Vingt-Six Sermons au peuple d'Afrique*, ed. F. Dolbeau, the 'Dolbeau Sermons' (Paris: Institut d'études augustiniennes, 1996).

—— *The Works of Saint Augustine: A Translation for the 21st Century*, part 3, *Sermons*, tr. E. Hill O P, i–xi (New York: New City Press, 1990–7).

—— Other sermons by Augustine cited here are to be found in PL 38 and 39.

Aulus Gellius, *Noctes Atticae*, ed. P. K. Marshall, 2 vols. (Oxford: Clarendon Press, 1990).

Basil of Caesarea, *Against Eunomius*, PG 29. 497–773.

—— *Hexaemeron*, ed. M. Naldini, *Basilio di Cesarea, Sulla Genesi* (Milan: Fondazione Lorenzo Valla, Mondadori, 1990). Also, ed. S. Giet, *Basile de Césarée, Homélies sur l'Hexaéméron*, SC 26 (Paris: Éditions du Cerf, 1950).

—— *Letters*, ed. Y. Courtonne, *Saint Basile, Lettres*, 3 vols. (Paris: Les Belles Lettres, 1957–66). Also, ed. Marcella Forlin Patrucco, *Basilio di Cesarea, Le lettere*, i (Turin: Società Editrice Internazionale, 1983).

—— *On the Holy Spirit*, PG 32. 68–217.

—— *Regulae fusius tractatae*, PG 31. 889–1052.

—— *Regulae brevius tractatae*, PG 31. 1079–1306.

## Basil of Caesarea: Sermons

To avoid confusion, Basil's sermons are given by an English title, followed where helpful by their Latin title, their number in the Clauis patrum Graecorum (CPG), their old sermon number, and new sermon number. Where a critical edition exists this follows. The reference in Migne's *Patrologia* is given in each case.

—— *God Does Not Cause Evil* (*Quod Deus non est auctor malorum*), CPG 2853, *serm.* old 9 = new 336, PG 31. 329–53.

—— *Homily I on Psalm XIV*, CPG 2853, *serm.* new 346, PG 29. 249–64.

—— *Homily II on Psalm XIV*, CPG 2853, *serm.* new 347, PG 29. 264–80.

—— *Homily on Psalm CXIV*, CPG 2853, *serm.* new 357, PG 29. 484–93.

—— *Homily on Psalm LXI*, CPG 2853, *serm.* new 356, PG 29. 469–84.

—— *I Shall Knock Down My Barns* (*Destruam horrea mea*) CPG 2850, *serm.* old 6 = new 322, in *Saint Basile: Homélies sur la richesse*, ed. Y. Courtonne (Paris, 1935), 15–37. PG 31. 261–77.

—— *In Time of Hunger* (*In tempore famis et siccitatis*), CPG 2852, *serm.* old 8 = new 325, PG 31. 304–28.

—— *Look to Yourself* (*Attende tibi*), CPG 2847, *serm.* old 3 = new 319, in *L'Homélie de Basile de Césarée sur le mot 'observe-toi toi-même'*, ed. S. Y. Rudberg (Stockholm: Almqvist & Wiksell, 1962). PG 31. 197–217.

—— *On Giving Thanks*, CPG 2848, *serm.* old 4 = new 328, PG 31. 217–37.

—— *On Julitta the Martyr*, CPG 2849, *serm.* old 5 = new 334, PG 31. 237–61.

—— *On Renunciation* (*Quod rebus mundanis adhaerendum non sit*), CPG 2866, *serm.* old 21 = new 339, PG 31. 540–64.

—— *On the Forty Martyrs*, CPG 2863, *serm.* old 19 = new 338, PG 31. 508–25.

—— *On the Martyr Gordius*, CPG 2862, *serm.* old 18 = new 327, PG 31. 489–508.

—— *On the Wealthy*, CPG 2851, *serm.* old 7 = new 323, in *Saint Basile: Homélies sur la richesse*, ed. Y. Courtonne (Paris, 1935), 40–71; PG 31. 277–304.

Basil (inter dubia), *De misericordia et iudicio*, PG 31. 1705–14.

*The Bohairic Life of Pachomius* in L. T. Lefort, *Les Vies coptes de saint Pachôme et de ses premiers successeurs* (Louvain: Bureaux du Muséon, 1943).

Caesarius of Arles, *Sermons*, ed. D. Morin, *S. Caesarii Arelatensis Sermones*, CCSL 103 (Turnhout: Brepols, 1953).

Callinicus, *Life of Hypatios*, ed. G. Bartelink, *Vie d'Hypatios*, SC 177 (Paris: Éditions du Cerf, 1971).

*The Canons of Athanasius of Alexandria*, ed. W. Riedel and W. E. Crum (London 1904).

*Les Canons d'Hippolyte*, ed. R.-G. Coquin, PO 31/2 (Paris, 1966).

*The Canons of Antioch, Carthage, Chalcedon*, etc. in P.-P. Joannou (ed.), *Discipline générale antique*, 2 vols. (Rome: Tipografia Italo-Orientale S. Nilo, 1962–3).

Cassian, *The Conferences*, ed. E. Pichery, *Jean Cassien, Conférences*, 3 vols., SC 42, 54, 64 (Paris: Éditions du Cerf, 1955–9); Eng. version by B. Ramsey OP, *The Conferences* (New York: Paulist Press, 1997).

Chromatius, *Sermons*, in R. Étaix and J. Lemarié (eds.), *Chromatii Aquileiensis Opera*, CCSL 9A (Turnhout: Brepols, 1974), 3–180.

—— *Tractatus on Matthew*, in R. Étaix and J. Lemarié (eds.), *Chromatii Aquileiensis Opera*, CCSL 9A (Turnhout: Brepols, 1974), 185–498.

*Chronicon paschale*, PG 92. 69–1028. Eng. tr. by Michael Whitby and Mary Whitby, *Chronicon Paschale 284–628 AD* (Liverpool: Liverpool University Press, 1989).

Clement, *Quis dives salvetur?*, ed. O. Stählin, *Clemens Alexandrinus*, iii (Leipzig: Heinrich, Akademie Verlag, 1909), 159–91.

Commodian, *Instructions*, in J. Martin (ed.), *Commodiani Carmina*, CCSL 128 (Turnhout: Brepols, 1960), 3–70.

Constantius of Lyons, *Life of Germanus*, in R. Borius (ed.), *Vie de saint Germain d'Auxerre*, SC 112 (Paris: Éditions du Cerf, 1965).

*Consultationes Zacchaei et Apollonii*, in J. L. Feiertag and W Steinmann (eds.), *Questions d'un païen à un Chrétien*, 2 vols., SC 401 and 402 (Paris: Éditions du Cerf, 1994).

Cyprian, *De ecclesiae catholicae unitate*, ed. M Bévenot S J, *Cyprian, De Lapsis* and *De Ecclesiae Catholicae Unitate* (Oxford: Clarendon Press, 1971).

—— *De habitu virginum*, ed. W. Hartel, *S. Thasci Caecili Cypriani Opera Omnia*, CSEL 3/1 (Vienna: Tempsky, 1868), 187–205.

—— *De opere et eleemosynis*, ed. M. Poirier, *Cyprien de Carthage, La Bienfaisance et les aumônes*, SC 440 (Paris: Éditions du Cerf, 1999).

—— *Letters*, ed. G. F. Diercks (ed.), *Sancti Cypriani Episcopi Epistulae*, CCSL 3B–D, 3 vols. (Turnhout: Brepols, 1994, 1996, and 1999). Eng. tr. in G. W. Clarke, *The Letters of St. Cyprian of Carthage*, 4 vols. (New York: Newman Press, 1984).

—— *Testimonia ad Quirinum*, ed. R. Weber, *Sancti Cypriani Episcopi Opera*, i, CCSL 3 (Turnhout: Brepols, 1972), 1–179.

Cyril of Alexandria, *Festal Letters*, PG 77. 401–981, and i–xvii, ed. W. H. Burns, *Cyrille d'Alexandre, Lettres festales*, SC 372, 392, 434, 3 vols. (Paris: Éditions du Cerf, 1991–8).

*Dialogue between a Montanist and an Orthodox*, ed. A. M. Berruto Martone, *Dialogo tra un Montanista e un Ortodosso* (Bologna: EDB, 1999).

*The Didache*, ed. W. Rordorf and A. Tuilier, *La Doctrine des douze Apôtres (Didachè)*, SC 248bis (Paris: Éditions du Cerf, 1998). Also, ed. J. P. Audet, *La Didachè, Instructions des Apôtres* (Paris: Gabalda, 1958).

*Didascalia Apostolorum*, ed. F. X. Funk, *Didascalia et Constitutiones Apostolorum*, 2 vols. (Paderborn, 1905).

Dio Chrysostom, *Orations*, ed. G. de Budé, 2 vols. (Leipzig, 1916 and 1919).

Diogenes Laertius, *Vitae Philosophorum*, ed. M. Marcovich, *Diogenis Laertii Vitae Philosophorum*, 3 vols. (Stuttgart and Leipzig: Teubner, 1999–2002).

Epictetus, *Discourses*, ed. J. Souihlé, *Épictète, Entretiens*, 4 vols. (Paris: Les Belles Lettres, 1943–65).

Epiphanius of Salamis, *Panarion*, ed. K. Holl, *Epiphanius, Panarion, 34–64*, GCS (Berlin: Akademie-Verlag, 1980) and *Epiphanius, Panarion, 65–80*, GCS (Berlin: Akademie-Verlag, 1985).

Eugippius, *Vita Severini*, ed. P. Régerat, *Eugippe, Vie de saint Séverin*, SC 374 (Paris: Éditions du Cerf, 1991).

Eusebius of Caesarea, *Ecclesiastical History*, ed. G. Bardy, *Eusèbe de Césarée: Histoire ecclesiastique*, 4 vols., SC 31, 41, 55, and 73 (Paris: Éditions du Cerf, 1952–60).

—— *The Life of Constantine*, ed. F. Winkelmann, *Über das Leben des Kaisers Konstantin*, Eusebius Werke, i/1, 2nd edn. (Berlin: Akademie-Verlag, 1991). Eng. version and commentary, A. Cameron and S. Hall, *Eusebius: Life of Constantine* (Oxford: Clarendon Press, 1999).

—— *On the Martyrs of Palestine*, ed. E. Schwartz, *Über die Märtyrer in Palaestina*, Eusebius Werke, ii/2, GCS 6/2 (Berlin 1999), 907–50.

Eusebius of Vercelli, *Letters*, in V. Bulhart (ed.), *Eusebii Vercellensis Episcopi Quae Supersunt*, CCSL 9 (Turnhout: Brepols, 1957), 103–10.

—— *Evangelium*, PL 12. 141–838.

*Four Martyrdoms from the Pierpoint Morgan Coptic Codices*, ed. E. A. E. Reymond and J. W. B. Barns (Oxford: Clarendon Press, 1973).

Gaudentius, *Life of Filastrius*, in A. Glueck (ed.), *S. Gaudentii Episcopi Brixensis Tractatus*, CSEL 68 (Vienna and Leipzig: Hoelder-Pichler-Tempsky, 1936), 184–9.

—— *Sermons*, ed. A. Glueck, *S. Gaudentii Episcopi Brixensis Tractatus*, CSEL 68 (Vienna and Leipzig: Hoelder-Pichler-Tempsky, 1936).

Gennadius, *De viris illustribus*, in W. Herding (ed.), *Hieronymi De Viris Inlustribus Liber* (Leipzig, 1924), 67–112.

Gerontius, *The Life of Melania the Younger*, ed. Denys Gorce, *Vie de sainte Mélanie*, SC 90 (Paris: Éditions du Cerf, 1962); English tr. E. A. Clark, *The Life of Melania the Younger, Introduction, Translation, and Commentary*, Studies in Women and Religion, 14 (New York and Toronto: Edwin Mellen Press, 1984).

*Gesta apud Zenophilum consularem*, in J.-L. Maier (ed.), *Le Dossier de Donatisme*, 2 vols. (Berlin: Akademie-Verlag, 1987 and 1989), i. 211–39.

Gregory Nazianzen, [Oration 4] *Against Julian I*, in J. Bernardi (ed.), *Grégoire de Nazianze, Discours 4–5*, SC 309 (Paris: Éditions du Cerf, 1983), 86–293.

—— *Oration 8*, PG 35. 789–817.

—— [Oration 14] *On the Love We Owe the Poor*, PG 35. 857–910.

—— [Oration 16] *In patrem tacentem propter plagam grandinis*, PG 35. 933–64.

—— *Oration 18*, PG 35. 985–1044.

Gregory Nazianzen, *Oration 19*, PG 35. 1043–64.

—— *Oration 21*, in J. Mossay (ed.), *Grégoire de Naziance, Discours 20–30*, SC 270 (Paris: Éditions du Cerf, 1980), 110–92.

—— [Oration 43] *In Praise of Basil*, in J. Bernardi, *Grégoire de Naziance, Discours 42–43*, SC 384 (Paris: Éditions du Cerf, 1992), 116–307.

Gregory of Nyssa, *Against Eunomius*, ed. W. Jaeger, GNO 1 (Leiden: Brill, 1960), 3–409.

—— *Against Usurers*, ed. E. Gebhardt, GNO 9 (Leiden: Brill, 1967), 195–207.

—— *De pauperibus amandis* i, ed. A. Van Heck, GNO 9 (Leiden: Brill, 1967), 93–108.

—— *De pauperibus amandis* ii, ed. A. van Heck, GNO 9 (Leiden: Brill, 1967), 111–27.

—— *Life of Gregory Thaumaturgus*, ed. G. Heil, GNO 10/1 (Leiden: Brill, 1990), 3–57.

—— *Life of Macrina*, GNO 8/1, ed. W. Jaeger, J. Cavarnos, and V. Woods Callahan (Leiden: Brill, 1952), 370–414.

—— *Oration in Praise of his Brother Basil*, ed. O. Lendle in G. Heil, J. P. Cavarnos, O. Lendle, and F. Mann (eds.), GNO 10/1 (Leiden: Brill, 1990), 109–34.

Hegemonius, *Acta Archelai*, ed. C. H. Beeson (Leipzig: J. C. Hinrichs'sche buchhandlung, 1906).

Hilary of Arles, *Life of Honoratus*, in S. Cavallin (ed.), *Vitae Sanctorum Honorati et Hilarii Episcoporum Arelatensium* (Lund: Gleerup, 1952), 47–78. Also, ed. M.-D. Valentin OP, *Hilaire d'Arles: Vie de saint Honorat*, SC 235 (Paris: Éditions du Cerf, 1977).

Hilary of Poitiers, *Commentary on Matthew*, ed. J. Doignon, *Hilaire de Poitiers, sur Matthieu*, SC 254 and 258, 2 vols. (Paris: Éditions du Cerf, 1978 and 1979).

—— *Tractatus in Psalmum CXVIII*, ed. M. Milhau, *Hilaire de Poitiers, Commentaire sur le psaume 118*, SC 344 and 347 (Paris: Éditions du Cerf, 1988).

*Historia monachorum in Aegypto* (Greek version), ed. A.J. Festugière OP (Brussels: Société des Bollandistes, 1971).

—— (Latin version) ed. E. Schulz-Flügel, *Tyrannius Rufinus: Historia Monachorum sive De Vita Sanctorum Patrum* (Berlin: Walter de Gruyter, 1990).

Honoratus, *Vita Hilarionis*, in P.-A. Jacob (ed.), *Honorat de Marseille: La Vie d'Hilaire d'Arles*, SC 404 (Paris: Éditions du Cerf, 1995). Also, in S. Cavallin (ed.), *Vitae Sanctorum Honorati et Hilarii Episcoporum Arelatensium* (Lund: Gleerup, 1952), 81–109.

Irenaeus, *Adversus Haereses* 4 in A. Rousseau, B. Hemmerdinger, L. Doutreleau and C. Mercier (eds.), *Irénée de Lyons: Contre les hérésies, Livre IV*
(SC 100), 2 vols. (Paris: Éditions du Cerf, 1965).

Isaiah, Abba, *Logoi*, ed. the monks of Solesmes, *Abbé Isaïe: Recueil ascétique*,
Spiritualité Orientale, 7 (Bégrolles: Abbaye de Bellefontaine, 1970).

Isidore of Pelusium, *Letters*, PG 78. 177–1646, ed. P. Évieux, *Lettres*, i, SC 422
(Paris: Éditions du Cerf, 1997), letters 1214–1413.

*Itinerarium Burdigalense*, ed. P. Geyer and O. Cuntz, *Itineraria et alia
geographica*, CCSL 175 (Turnhout: Brepols, 1965).

Jerome, *Against Vigilantius*, PL 23. 339–52.

—— *Chronicon*, ed. R. Helm, *Die Chronik des Hieronymus* (Berlin: Akademie-Verlag, 1956).

—— *Commentary on Hosea*, in *Commentarii in Prophetas Minores*, ed.
M. Adriaen, CCSL 76 (Turnhout: Brepols, 1969).

—— *Commentary on Isaiah, Books 12–18*, ed. M. Adriaen, *Commentariorum
in Esaiam* xii–xviii, CCSL 73A (Turnhout: Brepols, 1963).

—— *Commentary on Jeremiah*, ed. S. Reiter, *Sancti Hieronymi Presbyteri
Opera: In Hieremiam Prophetam Libri Sex*, CCSL 74 (Turnhout: Brepols,
1960).

—— *Commentary on Malachi*, ed M. Adriaen, *S. Hieronymi Presbyteri
Opera*, i/6, CCSL 76A (Turnhout: Brepols, 1970).

—— *Commentary on Matthew*, ed. D. Hurst and M. Adriaen, in *S. Hieronymi Prebyteri Opera, Commentarium in Matheum Libri IV*, CCSL 77
(Turnhout: Brepols 1969).

—— *De viris illustribus*, ed. A. Ceresa-Gastaldo, *Gerolamo, Gli uomini illustri* (Florence: Nardini Editore, 1988).

—— *Letters*, ed. J. Labourt, *Saint Jérôme, Lettres*, 8 vols. (Paris, 1949–63).
I. Hilberg (ed.) *Sancti Hieronymi Epistulae*, 3 vols., CSEL 54–6, 2nd edn.
(Vienna: Verlag der Österreichischen Akademie der Wissenschaften,
1996).

—— *Life of Hilarion*, PL 23. 29–54.

—— *Life of Malchus*, PL 23. 53–60.

—— *Tractatus in Psalmos*, ed. D. Morin, CCSL 78 (Turnhout: Brepols,
1958).

John Chrysostom, *Ad Stagirum a daemone vexatum*, PG 47. 423–94.

—— *Catechetical Sermons*, 1–8, ed. A. Wenger, *Jean Chrysostome, Huit
catéchèses baptismales*, SC 50 (Paris: Éditions du Cerf, 1957).

—— *Catechetical Sermons*, 9–11, ed. A. Piédagnel and L. Doutreleau, *Jean
Chrysostome, Trois catéchèses baptismales*, SC 366 (Paris: Éditions du Cerf,
1990). For an Eng. tr. of the catechetical sermons, P. W. Harkins, *St John
Chrysostom, Baptismal Instructions* (London: Newman Press, 1963).

John Chrysostom, *Commentary on the Psalms*, PG 55. 35–528. Eng. tr. in R. C. Hill, *St John Chrysostom, Commentary on the Psalms* (Brookline, Mass.: Holy Cross Orthodox Press, 1998).

—— *Homilies on Matthew*, PG 57. 13–PG 58. 794.

—— *Homilies on 1 Corinthians*, PG 61. 11–382.

—— *Homilies on 2 Corinthians*, PG 61. 381–610.

—— *Homilies on Ephesians*, PG 62. 9–176.

—— *Homilies on Philippians*, PG 62. 177–298.

—— *Homilies on Thessalonians*, PG 62. 391–500.

—— *Homilies on 2 Thessalonians*, PG 62. 467–500.

—— *Homilies on 1 Timothy*, PG 62. 503–600.

—— *Homilies on 2 Timothy*, PG 62. 599–662.

—— *Homilies on Hebrews*, PG 63. 13–236.

—— *Homilies to the People of Antioch on the Statues*, PG 49. 15–240.

—— *On Elijah and the Widow* 1, PG 51. 337–48.

—— *On Almsgiving*, PG 51. 261–72.

—— *On the Priesthood (De sacerdotio)*, ed. A.-M. Malingrey, *Jean Chrysostome, Sur le sacerdoce*, SC 272 (Paris: Éditions du Cerf, 1980).

—— *On the Ten Virgins and Almsgiving*, PG 49. 291–300.

Julian, *Letters*, ed. J. Bidez and F. Cumont, *Iuliani Imperatoris epistulae et leges* (Paris and London: Les Belles Lettres and Oxford University Press, 1922).

Justin Martyr, *First Apology*, in M. Marcovich (ed.), *Iustini Martyris Apologiae Pro Christianis* (Berlin and New York: De Gruyter, 1994).

Lactantius, *Divine Institutes*, in S. Brandt and G. Laubmann (eds.), *L. Caeli Firmiani Lactanti Opera Omnia*, CSEL 19 and 27, 2 vols. (Prague: Tempsky, 1890), i. 1–672. Eng. tr. by A. Bowen and P. Garnsey, *Divine Institutes* (Liverpool: Liverpool University Press, 2003).

Leo, *Letters*, PL 54. 593–1218.

—— *Sermons*, ed R. Dolle, *Léon le grand, Sermons*, 4 vols., SC 22bis, 49bis, 74, 200 (Paris: Éditions du Cerf, 1964–73).

Libanius, *Orations*, ed. R. Foerster, *Libanii Opera*, 12 vols. (Leipzig, 1903–23).

*The Life of Abba Apphou*, in F. Rossi, *I papiri copti del Museo Egizio di Torino*, in *Memorie delle Reale Accademia delle Scienze di Torino, 37* (1886). Italian tr. in T. Orlandi, *Vite di Monaci Copti* (Rome: Città nuova editrice, 1984), 55–65.

*The Life of Abercius*, ed. T. Nissen, *S. Abercii Vita* (Leipzig, 1912).

*Life of Alexander*, ed. E. De Stoop, *Vie d'Alexandre l'Acémète*, PO 6 (Paris, 1911), 641–705.

*Life of Longinus*, in T. Orlandi and A. Campagnano (eds.), *Vite dei monaci Phif e Longino* (Milan: Cisalpino-Goliardica, 1975).

*The Life of the Man of God*, ed. A. Amiaud, *La Légende syriaque de saint Alexis l'homme de dieu*, Bibliothèque de l'École des Hautes Études, 79 (Paris, 1889).

*Life of Olympias*, in A.-M. Malingrey (ed.), *Jean Chrysostome, Lettres à Olympias, Vie anonyme d'Olympias*, SC 13bis (Paris: Éditions du Cerf, 1968), 393–449.

*The Life of Rabbula*, tr. G. Bickell, *Ausgewählte Schriften der syrischen Kirchenväter Aphraates, Rabbula und Isaak v. Ninivie* (Kempten, 1874), 155–211.

*Life of Simeon Stylites* (Greek), tr. A. J. Festugière O P, *Antioche païenne et chrétienne* (Paris: E. de Boccard, 1959).

*Life of Simeon Stylites* (Syriac), tr. F. Lent, *JAOS* 35 (1915), 103–98.

*Life of Syncletica*, Eng. tr. in E. Castelli, 'Pseudo-Athanasius, The Life and Activity of the Holy and Blessed Teacher Syncletica', in V. I. Wimbush (ed.), *Ascetic Behavior in Greco-Roman Antiquity* (Minneapolis: Fortress Press, 1990), 265–311.

*Life of Thecla*, in G. Dagron (ed.), *Vie et miracles de sainte Thècle* (Brussels: Société des Bollandistes, 1978).

Mark the Deacon, *Life of Porphyry*, in *Marc le Diacre, Vie de Porphyre, évêque de Gaza*, ed. H. Grégoire and M.-A. Kugener (Paris: Les Belles Lettres, 1930),

Maximus of Turin, *Sermons*, in A. Mutzenbecher (ed.), *Maximi Episcopi Taurinensis Sermones*, CCSL 23 (Turnhout: Brepols, 1962).

Optatus, *Against the Donatists*, ed. M. Labrousse, *Optat de Milève, Traité contre les Donatistes*, 2 vols., SC 412 and 413 (Paris: Éditions du Cerf, 1995 and 1996).

Origen, *Contra Celsum*, ed. M. Borret, *Origène, Contre Celse*, 5 vols., SC 132, 136, 147, 150, 227 (Paris: Éditions du Cerf, 1967–76).

—— *Commentary on John*, ed. C. Blanc, *Origène, Commentaire sur S. Jean*, iv, SC 290 (Paris: Éditions du Cerf, 1982).

—— *Commentary on Matthew's Gospel*, ed. E. Klostermann, *Origenes Matthäuserklärung*, GCS 40 (Leipzig: Akademie-Verlag, 1935). Also, ed. R. Girod, *Commentaire sur l'évangile selon Matthieu*, SC 162 (Paris: Éditions du Cerf, 1970).

Pacianus, *Sermo de Paenitentibus*, in *Pacien de Barcelone: Écrits*, ed. C. Granado, tr. C. Épitalon and M. Lestienne, SC 410 (Paris: Éditions du Cerf, 1995).

Palladius, *Lausiac History*, ed. G. Bartelink, *Palladio, La storia Lausiaca* (Milan: Fondazione Lorenzo Valla, A. Mondadori, 1974).

Palladius, *Life of John Chrysostom*, ed. P. Coleman-Norton, *Palladii dialogus de vita s. Joannis Chrysostomi* (Cambridge: Cambridge University Press, 1928).

Paphnutius, *Histories of the Monks of Upper Egypt*, ed. T. Vivian, *Histories of the Monks of Upper Egypt and the Life of Onnophrius by Paphnutius* (Kalamazoo: Cistercian Publications, 1993).

—— *Life of Omnophrius*, ed. T. Vivian, *Histories of the Monks of Upper Egypt and the Life of Onnophrius by Paphnutius* (Kalamazoo: Cistercian Publications, 1993).

Paulinus of Milan, *Life of Ambrose*, ed. M. Pellegrino, *Vita di S. Ambrogio* (Rome: Editrice Studium, 1961).

Paulinus of Nola, *Letters* (including *De Gazophylacio*), ed. W. Hartel, *Sancti Pontii Meropii Paulini Nolani Epistulae*, CSEL 29 (Vienna: Tempsky, 1894).

Pelagius, *On the Christian Life*, PL 40. 1031–46.

Peter Chrysologus, *Sermons*, ed. A. Olivar, *Sancti Petri Chrsyologi Collectio Sermonum*, CCSL 24 (Turnhout: Brepols, 1975).

Photius, *Library*, ed. R. Henry, *Photius, Bibliothèque*, 9 vols. (Paris: Les Belles Lettres, 1959–91).

Plato, *Definitions*, tr. D. S. Hutchinson, in *Plato: Complete Works*, ed. J. M. Cooper (Indianapolis: Hackett, 1997), 1678–86.

Plutarch, *Moralia* 37 in *Plutarchi Moralia*, iii, ed. W. R. Paton, M. Pohlenz, and W. Sieveking (Leipzig: Teubner, 1972).

Pontius, *Life of Cyprian*, ed. A. A. R. Bastiaensen, in C. Mohrmann, A. A. R. Bastiaensen, L. Canali, and C. Carena (eds.), *Vita di Cipriano, Vita di Ambrogio, Vita di Agostino* (Milan: Fondazione Lorenzo Valla, A. Mondadori, 1975), 4–48.

Possidius, *Life of Augustine*, ed. A. A. R. Bastiaensen, in C. Mohrmann, A. A. R. Bastiaensen, L. Canali, and C. Carena (eds.), *Vita di Cipriano, Vita di Ambrogio, Vita di Agostino* (Milan: Fondazione Lorenzo Valla, A. Mondadori, 1975), 130–240.

Priscillian, *Works*, in G. Schepss, *Priscilliani quae supersunt*, CSEL 18 (Vienna: apud C. Geroldi Filium, 1889).

Prudentius, *Peristefanon*, ed. M. P. Cunningham, *Aurelii Prudenti Clementis Carmina*, CCSL 126 (Turnhout: Brepols, 1966), 251–389.

—— *Psychomachia*, ed. M. P. Cunningham, *Aurelii Prudenti Clementis Carmina*, CCSL 126 (Turnhout: Brepols, 1966), 149–81.

Pseudo-Athanasius, *Against Arius* 28. PG 28. 440–501.

Pseudo-Chrysostom, *On Matthew* 6: 13, PG 59. 571–4.

—— *De eleemosyna*, PG 60. 747–52.

Pseudo-Rufinus, *On the Psalms*, PL 21. 651–960.

Quodvultdeus, *Sermons*, in R. Braun (ed.), *Opera Quodvultdeo Carthaginiensi Episcopo Tributa*, CCSL 60 (Turnhout: Brepols, 1976).

Rufinus, *Preface to the Sentences of Sextus*, in M. Simonetti (ed.), *Tyrannii Rufini Opera*, CCSL 20 (Turnhout: Brepols, 1961).

Salvian, *Four Books of Timothy to the Church*, ed. G. Lagarrigue, *Salvien de Marseille, Œuvres*, SC 176 and 220 (Paris: Éditions du Cerf, 1971 and 1975).

Seneca, *De vita beata*, ed. L. D. Reynolds, *L. Annaei Senecae Dialogorum Libri Duodecim* (Oxford: Clarendon Press, 1977).

*The Sentences of Sextus*, ed. H Chadwick, *The Sentences of Sextus: A Contribution to the History of Early Christian Ethics* (Cambridge: Cambridge University Press, 1959).

*Septuagint, Deuteronomy*, ed. J. W. Wevers, *Septuaginta*, iii/2 (Göttingen: Vandenhoeck & Ruprecht, 1977).

*Septuagint, Leviticus*, ed. J. W. Wevers, *Septuaginta*, ii/2 (Göttingen: Vandenhoeck & Ruprecht, 1986).

*Septuagint, Psalms*, ed., A. Rahlfs, *Septuaginta*, X (Göttingen: Vandenhoeck & Ruprecht, 1931).

*Sibylline Oracles*, ed. J. Geffcken, *Die Oracula Sibyllina*, GCS 8 (Leipzig 1902).

Socrates, *Ecclesiastical History*, in G. Hansen (ed.), *Sokrates Kirchengeschichte* (Berlin: Akademie Verlag, 1995). PG 67. 33–841.

Sozomen, *Ecclesiastical History*, ed. J. Bidez and G. Hansen, *Sozomenus Kirchengeschichte*, 2nd edn. (Berlin: Akademie Verlag, 1995).

*Statuta ecclesiae antiqua*, in C. Munier (ed.), *Concilia Galliae A. 314–A. 506*, CCSL 148 (Turnhout: Brepols, 1963).

Sulpicius Severus, *Life of Martin*, ed. J. Fontaine, *Sulpice Sévère, Vie de saint Martin*, SC 133, 134, 135 (Paris: Éditions du Cerf, 1967–9).

Symmachus, *Letters*, in Symmache, *Lettres*, ed., tr., and commented by J. P. Callu, i (books 1–2) ii (books 3–5), iii (books 3–5) (Paris: Les Belles Lettres, 1972, 1982, 1995).

—— *Orations*, in Symmachus, *Reden*, ed., tr., and commented by A. Pabst (Darmstadt: Wissenschaftliche Buchgesellschaft, 1989).

Synesius, *Letters*, in A. Garzya (ed.), *Synesii Cyrenensis Epistulae* (Rome: Typis Officinae Polygraphicae, 1979).

Tertullian, *Apologeticum*, in *Tertulliani Opera*, ed. D. Dekkers, CCSL 1 (Turnhout: Brepols, 1954).

—— *De patientia*, ed. J.-C. Fredouille, *De la patience*, SC 310 (Paris 1984).

Themistius, *Orations*, ed. H. Schenkl and G. Downey, *Themistii orationes quae supersunt* (Leipzig: Teubner, 1965).

Theodoret, *Ecclesiastical History,* ed. L. Parmentier and G. Hansen, *Theodoret Kirchengeschichte,* 3rd edn. (Berlin: Akademie Verlag, 1998).

—— *Historia Religiosa,* ed. P. Canivet and A. Leroy-Molinghen, *Théodoret de Cyr, Histoire des moines de Syrie,* 2 vols., SC 234 and 257 (Paris: Éditions du Cerf, 1977 and 1979).

Theophanes, *Chronicle,* ed. C. De Boor (Leipzig, 1883). Eng. tr. C. Mango and R. Scott, *The Chronicle of Theophanes Confessor* (Oxford: Clarendon Press, 1997).

Uranius, *De obitu Paulini,* PL 53. 859–66.

*Vulgate,* ed. R. Gryson, B. Fischer, J. Gribomont, H.F.D. Sparks, W. Thiele, and R. Weber, *Biblia Sacra Iuxta Vulgatam Versionem* (Stuttgart: Deutsche Bibelgesellschaft, 1994).

Zeno, *De iustitia,* ed. B. Löfstedt, *Zenonis Veronensis Tratatus,* CCSL 22 (Turnhout: Brepols, 1971), 145–50.

**Secondary literature**

Aldama, J. A. de, *Repertorium Pseudochrysostomicum* (Paris: Centre national de la recherche scientifique, 1965).

Allen, P., and Mayer, W., 'Chrysostom and the Preaching of Homilies in Series: A Re-examination of the Fifteen Homilies *In Epistulam ad Philippenses* (CPG 4432)', *Vigiliae Christianae,* 49 (1995), 270–89.

Amand de Mendieta, E., 'L'Authenticité des lettres ascétiques 42 à 45 de la correspondance de saint Basile de Césarée', *Recherches de science religieuse,* 56/2 (1968), 241–64.

Aubineau, M., 'Un extrait retrouvé, chez Cosmas Indicopleustès, d'un *Discours sur l'aumône* de Jean Chrysostome (PL 49, 293)', *Bulletin de littérature ecclésiastique,* 80 (1979), 213–18.

Augé, C., 'Les Monnaies antiques de Gaza', in J.-B. Humbert (ed.), *Gaza méditerranéenne: Histoire et archéologie en Palestine* (Paris: Errance, 2000).

Badewien, J., *Geschichtstheologie und Sozialkritik im Werk Salvians von Marseille* (Göttingen: Vandenhoeck & Ruprecht, 1980).

Bagnall, R., *Egypt in Late Antiquity* (Princeton: Princeton University Press, 1993).

Baldovin, J. F., *The Urban Character of Christian Worship: The Origins, Development, and Meaning of Stational Liturgy* (Rome: Pontificium Institutum Studiorum Orientalium, 1987).

Bardy, G., *Recherches sur saint Lucien d'Antioche et son école* (Paris: Beauchesne, 1936).

Barnes, T. D., 'Constantine and Christianity: Ancient Evidence and Modern Interpretations', ZAC 2 (1998), 274–94.

—— *Constantine and Eusebius* (Cambridge, Mass.: Harvard University Press, 1981).

Barns, J., and Chadwick, H., 'A Letter Ascribed to Peter of Alexandria', *JThS* (Oct. 1973), 443–55.

Bastiaensen, A. A. R., 'Jérôme hagiographe', in G. Philippart (ed.), *Hagiographes*, 2 vols. (Turnhout: Brepols, 1994 and 1996), i. 97–123.

Bauer, C., *John Chrysostom and his Time* (London: Sands, 1959).

Beagon, P., 'Social and Political Aspects of the Career of St Basil', D.Phil. thesis (Oxford, 1990).

Bernardi, J., *La Prédication des pères Cappadociens* (Marseilles: Presses universitaires de France, 1968).

Bobertz, C. A., *Cyprian of Carthage as Patron: A Social Historical Study of the Role of Bishop in the Ancient Christian Community of North Africa* (Ann Arbor: UMI, 1993).

Bolkestein, H., *Wohltätigkeit und Armenpflege im Vorchristlichen Altertum* (Utrecht: A. Oosthoek Verlag, 1939).

Boyarin, D., *Dying for God* (Stanford, Calif.: Stanford University Press, 1999).

Bradshaw, P. F., 'Ancient Church Orders: A Continuing Enigma', in G. Austin OP (ed.), *Fountain of Life* (Washington, DC: Pastoral Press, 1991), 3–22.

—— *The Search for the Origins of Early Christian Worship* (London: SPCK, 1992).

Brakke, D., *Athanasius and the Politics of Asceticism* (Oxford: Clarendon Press, 1995).

Bregman, J., *Synesius of Cyrene, Philosopher-Bishop* (Berkeley, Los Angeles, and London: University of California Press, 1982).

Bridge, S. L., 'To Give or Not to Give? Deciphering the Saying of Didache 1. 6', *JECS* 5 (1997), 555–68.

Brock, S., 'Ephrem's letter to Publius', *Le Muséon*, 89 (1976), 262–305.

—— 'From Antagonism to Assimiliation: Syrian Attitudes to Greek Learning', in N. Garsoïan, T. Mathews, and R. Thompson (eds.), *East of Byzantium: Syria and Armenia in the Formative Period* (Washington, DC: Dumbarton Oaks, 1982), 17–34.

Brottier, L., 'Le Prédicateur, émule du prophète ou rival de l'acteur? Jean Chrysostome: Un pasteur déchiré entre ses auditeurs et son Dieu', *Connaissance des Pères de l'Église*, 74 (1999), 2–19.

Brown, P., *Poverty and Leadership in the Later Roman Empire* (Hanover, NH and London: University Press of New England, 2002).

Brown, P., *Power and Persuasion in Late Antiquity: Towards a Christian Ethic* (Madison, Wis.: University of Wisconsin Press, 1992).

Brown, P., *The Cult of the Saints: Its Rise and Function in Latin Christianity* (London: SCM, 1981).

Bundy, D., 'The *Life of Abercius*: Its Significance for Early Syriac Christianity', *The Second Century*, 7 (1989–90), 163–76.

Burnett, A., Amandry, M., and Carradice, I., *Roman Provincial Coinage*, ii/1 (London and Paris: British Museum Press and Bibliothèque nationale, 1999).

Buytaert, E. M., *L'Héritage littéraire d'Eusèbe d'Émèse*, Bibliothèque du Muséon, 24 (Louvain: Bureaux du Muséon, 1949).

Cagnat, R., 'Seance de la commission de l'Afrique du nord, Janvier 17', *BCTH* (1922), xxii–xxxiii.

—— 'Seance de la commission de l'Afrique du nord, Mars 14', *BCTH* (1911), clxx–clxxxiv.

Caillet, J.-P., *L'Évergétisme monumental chrétien en Italie et à ses marges* (Rome: École française de Rome, 1993).

Cameron, Averil, *Christianity and the Rhetoric of Empire* (Berkeley, Calif.: University of California Press, 1991).

—— *The Later Roman Empire* (London: Fontana Press, 1993).

Carletti, C., *Iscrizioni cristiane di Roma* (Florence: Nardini Editore, 1986).

Casey, R. P., 'The Apocalypse of Paul', *JThS* 34 (1933), 1–32.

Castelli, E., 'Pseudo-Athanasius, The Life and Activity of the Holy and Blessed Teacher Syncletica', in V. I. Wimbush (ed.), *Ascetic Behavior in Greco-Roman Antiquity* (Minneapolis: Fortress Press, 1990), 265–311.

Chadwick, H., *Priscillian of Avila: The Occult and the Charismatic in the Early Church* (Oxford: Clarendon Press, 1976).

Chastagnol, A., 'Observations sur le consulat suffect et la preture du Bas-Empire', *Revue historique*, 219 (1958), 221–53.

Chastel, E., *Études historiques sur l'influence de la charité* (Paris, 1853).

Cheal, D., *The Gift Economy* (London and New York: Routledge, 1988).

Chitty, D., *The Desert a City* (London and Oxford: Basil Blackwell, 1966).

Clark, E. A., *Jerome, Chrysostom and Friends* (New York and Toronto: Edwin Mellen Press, 1979).

—— 'Piety, Propaganda, and Politics in the *Life of Melania the Younger*', *Studia Patristica* 18/2 (1983), 167–83.

—— *Reading Renunciation: Asceticism and Scripture in Early Christianity* (Princeton: Princeton University Presss, 1999).

Claussen, M., 'Pagan Rebellion and Christian Apologetics in Fourth Century Rome: The *Consultationes Zacchaei et Apollonii*', *JEH* 46 (1995), 589–614.

Coleman-Norton, P. R., *Roman State and Christian Church: A Collection of Legal Documents to A.D. 535*, 3 vols. (London: SPCK, 1966).

Constantelos, D. J., *Byzantine Philanthropy and Social Welfare* (New Brunswick, NJ: Rutgers University Press, 1968).

Countryman, L. W., *The Rich Christian in the Church of the Early Empire: Contradictions and Accommodations* (New York: Edwin Mellen Press, 1980).

Courtonne, Y., *Un témoin du IVe siècle oriental: Saint Basile et son temps d'après sa correspondance* (Paris: Les Belles Lettres, 1973).

Cox Miller, P., *Biography in Late Antiquity: A Quest for the Holy Man* (Berkeley, Los Angeles, and London: University of California Press, 1983).

—— 'Strategies of Representation in Collective Biography: Constructing the Subject as Holy', in T. Hägg and P. Rousseau (eds.), *Greek Biography and Panegyric in Late Antiquity* (Berkeley, Los Angeles, and London: University of California Press, 2000), 209–54.

Cruse, A., *Meaning in Language* (Oxford: Oxford University Press, 2000).

Cunningham, A., 'Women and Preaching in the Patristic Age', in D. G. Hunter (ed.), *Preaching in the Patristic Age: Studies in Honor of Walter J. Burghardt, S.J.* (New York: Paulist Press, 1989), 53–72.

Dagron, G. 'Les Moines et la ville: Le Monachisme à Constantinople jusqu'au Concile de Chalcédoine (451)', *Travaux et mémoires*, 4 (1970), 229–76.

—— *Naissance d'une capitale: Constantinople et ses institutions de 330 à 451* (Paris: Presses universitaires de France, 1974).

Davis, S. J., *The Cult of Saint Thecla: A Tradition of Women's Piety in Late Antiquity* (Oxford: Oxford University Press, 2001).

Delehaye, H., *Les Origines du culte des martyrs* (Brussels, 1912).

Delmaire, R., *Largesses sacrées et res privata: L'Aerarium impérial et son administration du IVe au VIe siècle* (Rome: École française de Rome, 1989).

De Rossi, I. B., *Inscriptiones Christianae Urbis Romae* (Rome, 1861).

—— and Silvagni, A., *Inscriptiones Christianae Urbis Romae Septimo Saeculo Antiquiores*, NS (Vatican, 1922– ).

De Ste. Croix, G. E. M., 'Aspects of the "Great" Persecution', *HTR* 47 (1954), 75–113.

De Vinne, M., 'The Advocacy of Empty Bellies: Episcopal Representation of the Poor in the Late Roman Empire', Ph.D. thesis (Stanford, 1995).

Devreesse, R., *Le Patriarcat d'Antioche* (Paris: Gabalda, 1945).

Di Berardino, A. (ed.), *Patrology* (Westminster, Md.: Christian Classics, 1986).

Doignon, J., 'Le Retentissement d'un exemple de la survie de Lactance', in J. Fontaine and M. Perrin (eds.), *Lactance et son temps, recherches actuelles* (Paris: Beauchesne, 1978), 297–306.

Döpp, S., and Geerlings, W. (eds.), *Dictionary of Early Christian Literature*, tr. M. O'Connell (New York: Crossroad, 2000).

Drake, H. A., *Constantine and the Bishops: The Politics of Intolerance* (Baltimore and London: Johns Hopkins University Press, 2000).

Drijvers, H. J. W., 'The Man of God of Edessa, Bishop Rabbula, and the Urban Poor: Church and Society in the Fifth Century', *JECS* 4 (1996), 235–48.

Dümler, B., 'Paulinus of Milan', in S. Döpp and W. Geerlings (eds.), *Dictionary of Early Christian Literature*, tr. M. O'Connell (New York: Crossroad, 2000), 468.

Duval, N., 'Une *mensa* funéraire de Tharros (Sardaigne) et la collection chrétienne du Musée de Cagliari', *Revue des études Augustiniennes*, 28 (1982), 281–7.

Duval, Y.-M., 'L'ecriture au service de la catéchèse', in J. Fontaine and C. Pietri (eds.), *Le Monde latin antique et la Bible* (Paris: Beauchesne, 1985), 261–87.

Elm, S.,'*Virgins of God': The Making of Asceticism in Late Antiquity* (Oxford: Clarendon Press, 1994).

Évieux, P., *Isidore de Péluse*, Théologie historique, 99 (Paris: Beauchesne, 1995).

Fedwick, P. J., 'A Chronology of the Life and Works of Basil of Caesarea', in his *Basil of Caesarea, Christian, Humanist, Ascetic*, 2 vols. (Toronto: Pontifical Institute of Mediaeval Studies, 1981).

Février, P.-A., *Djemila* (Algiers, 1968).

Frend, W. H. C., 'Town and Countryside in Early Christianity', in D. Baker (ed.), *Studies in Church History*, 16 (Oxford: Blackwell, 1979), 25–42.

—— 'The Winning of the Countryside', *JEH* 18 (London, 1967), 1–14

Gadamer, H.-G., *Truth and Method*, 2nd edn., Eng. tr. ed G. Barden and J. Cumming (London: Sheed & Ward, 1975).

Garnsey, P., *Famine and Food Supply in the Graeco-Roman World* (Cambridge: Cambridge University Press, 1988).

—— 'Lactantius and Augustine', *Proceedings of the British Academy*, 114 (2002), 153–79.

—— and Humfress, C., *The Evolution of the Late Antique World* (Cambridge: Orchard Academic, 2001).

Garrison, R., *Redemptive Almsgiving in Early Christianity* (Sheffield: JSOT Press, 1993).

Gaudemet, J., *L'Église dans l'empire romain (IVe–Ve siècle), histoire du droit et des institutions de l'Église en Occident*, ed. G. Le Bras and J. Gaudemet, iii (Paris: Sirey, 1958).

Gereboff, J., *Rabbi Tarfon: The Tradition, the Man, and Early Rabbinic Judaism* (Misoula, Mont.: Scholars Press, 1979).

Glaser, F., *Frühes Christentum im Alpenraum* (Regensburg: Friedrich Pustet, 1997).

Goehring, J. E., *Letter of Ammon and Pachomian Monasticism* (Berlin: De Gruyter, 1986).

—— 'New Frontiers in Pachomian Studies,' in B. A. Pearson and J. E. Goehring, *The Roots of Egyptian Christianity* (Philadelphia: Fortress Press, 1986), 236–57.

—— 'The World Engaged: The Social and Economic World of Early Egyptian Monasticism', in J. Goehring, C. W. Hedrick, J. T. Sanders, and H. D. Betz (eds.), *Gnosticism and the Early Christian World* (Sonoma, Calif.: Polebridge Press, 1990), 134–44.

Gordon, A. E., *Album of Dated Latin Inscriptions* (Berkeley and Los Angeles: University of California Press, 1965).

Grabar, A., *Christian Iconography: A Study of its Origins* (London: Routledge & Kegan Paul, 1969).

Gregory, T. E., *Vox Populi, Popular Opinion and Violence in the Religious Controversies of the Fifth Century* (Columbus, Ohio: Ohio State University Press, c.1979).

Gribomont, J., 'Un aristocrate révolutionnaire', in *Saint Basile évangile et église* (Bégrolles-en-Mauges: Abbaye de Bellefontaine, 1984), i. 65–77.

Gryson, R., *Le Prêtre selon saint Ambroise* (Louvain: Édition orientaliste, 1968).

Haas, C., 'The Arians of Alexandria', *VC* 47 (1993), 234–45.

Hamel, G., *Poverty and Charity in Roman Palestine: First Three Centuries C.E.* (Berkeley, Calif., and Oxford: University of California Press, 1990).

Hamm, U., 'Gennadius of Marseilles', in S. Döpp and W. Geerlings (eds.), *Dictionary*, tr. M. O'Connell (New York: Crossroad, 2000), 248–9.

Hands, A. R., *Charities and Social Aid in Greece and Rome* (London: Thames & Hudson, 1968).

Harries, J., '*Treasure in Heaven*: Property and Inheritance among Senators of Late Rome', in E. M. Craik (ed.), *Marriage and Property* (Aberdeen: Aberdeen University Press, 1984), 54–70.

Hatzfeld, J. , 'Inscriptions de Lagina en Carie', *BCH* 44 (1920), 70–100.

—— 'Inscriptions de Panamara', *BCH* 51 (1927), 57–122.

Head, T., *Medieval Hagiography: An Anthology* (New York and London: Routledge, 2001).

Heather, P. J., and Moncur, D., *Politics, Philosophy and Empire in the Fourth Century Select Orations of Themistius* (Liverpool: Liverpool University Press, 2001).

Herrin, J., 'Ideals of Charity, Realities of Welfare: The Philanthropic Activity of the Byzantine Church', in R. Morris (ed.), *Church and People in Byzantium* (Birmingham: University of Birmingham, 1986), 151–64.

Hill, G. F., *Catalogue of the Greek Coins of Palestine (Galilee, Samaria, and Judaea)* (London, 1914).

Hock, R. F., 'Homer in Greco-Roman Education', in D. R. MacDonald (ed.), *Mimesis and Intertextuality in Antiquity and Christianity* (Harrisburg, Pa.: Trinity Press International, 2001), 56–77.

Holman, S. R., *The Hungry are Dying: Beggars and Bishops in Roman Cappadocia* (Oxford: Oxford University Press, 2001).

—— 'The Entitled Poor: Human Rights Language in the Cappadocians', *Pro Ecclesia*, 9 (2000), 476–89.

Hopkins, K., 'Early Christian Number and its Implications', *JECS* 6 (1998), 185–226.

Humphries, M., *Communities of the Blessed* (Oxford: Oxford University Press, 1999).

Hunt, D., 'Christianising the Roman Empire: The Evidence of the Code', in J. Harries and I. Wood, *The Theodosian Code, Studies in the Imperial Law of Late Antiquity* (London: Duckworth, 1993), 143–58.

Jacopi, G., 'Esplorazioni e studi in Paflagonia e Cappadocia', *Bollettino del Reale Istituto di Archeologia e Storia dell'Arte*, 8 (Rome, 1938), 3–43.

Jaffé, P., and Wattenbach, W., *Regesta Pontificum Romanorum*, 2nd edn. (Leipzig, 1885).

Janes, D., *God and Gold in Late Antiquity* (Cambridge: Cambridge University Press, 1998).

Jones, A. H. M., *The Decline of the Ancient World* (London and New York: Longman, 1966).

—— Martindale, J. R., and Morris, J. (eds.), *The Prosopography of the Later Roman Empire*, i (Cambridge: Cambridge University Press, 1971).

Kelly, J. N. D., *Jerome, His Life, Writings, and Controversies* (London: Duckworth, 1975).

Kopecek, T., 'The Cappadocian Fathers and Civic Patriotism', *Church History*, 43 (1974), 293–303.

Krause, J.-U. 'La Prise en charge des veuves par l'église dans l'antiquité tardive', in C. Lepelley (ed.), *La Fin de la cité antique et le début de la cité médiévale* (Bari: Edipuglia, 1996), 115–26.

—— *Witwen und Waisen im Römischen Reich*, 4 vols. (Stuttgart: F. Steiner, 1994–5).

La Bonnardière, A. M., 'Pénitence et réconciliation des pénitents, d'après saint Augustin—I', *Revue des études augustiniennes*, 13 (1967), 31–53.

Lalleman, P. J., *The Acts of John* (Leuven: Peeters, 1998).

Leclercq, H., 'Dîme', in *DACL* iv (Paris, 1921), 995–1003.

—— 'Tipasa', in *DACL* xv (Paris, 1953,) 2338–2406.

Lepelley, C., *Les Cités de l'Afrique romaine au Bas-Empire*, 2 vols. (Paris: Études augustiniennes, 1979 and 1981).

—— 'Permanences de la cité classique et archaïsmes municipaux en Italie au Bas-Empire' in M. Christol, S. Demougin, Y. Duval, C. Lepelley and L. Pietri (eds.), *Institutions, société et vie politique*, Collection de l'École Française de Rome, 159 (Rome: École Française de Rome, 1992), 353–71.

—— 'Saint Leon le Grand et la cité romaine', *Revue des sciences religieuses*, 35 (1961) 130–50.

Leyerle, B., 'John Chrysostom on Almsgiving and the Use of Money', *HTR* 87 (1994), 29–47.

Liebeschuetz, J. H. W. G., *Antioch* (Oxford: Clarendon Press, 1972).

—— *Barbarians and Bishops* (Oxford: Clarendon Press, 1990).

Lienhard, J. T., 'Origen as Homilist', in D. G. Hunter (ed.), *Preaching in the Patristic Age: Studies in Honor of Walter J. Burghardt, S.J.* (New York: Paulist Press, 1989), 36–52.

Lieu, S. N. C., 'Fact and Fiction in the *Acta Archelai*', in Peter Bryder (ed.), *Manichaean Studies*, i (Lund: Plus Ultra, 1988), 69–88.

Lizzi, R., *Vescovi e strutture ecclesiastiche nella città tardoantica (L' Italia annonaria nel IV–V secolo d.C.)* (Como: Edizioni New Press, 1989).

McCabe OP, H., *Law, Love and Language* (London and Sydney: Sheed & Ward, 1968).

McLynn, N., *Ambrose of Milan: Church and Court in a Christian Capital* (Berkeley, Los Angeles, and London: University of California Press, 1994).

MacMullen, R., *Christianity and Paganism in the Fourth to Eighth Centuries* (New Haven, Conn., and London: Yale University Press, 1997).

Maier, H. O., 'Religious Dissent, Heresy and Households in Late Antiquity', *VC* 49 (1995), 49–63.

Maier, J.-L., *Le Dossier de Donatisme*, 2 vols. (Berlin: Akademie-Verlag, 1987 and 1989).

Markus, R., *The End of Ancient Christianity* (Cambridge: Cambridge University Press, 1990).

Marucchi, O., *Christian Epigraphy: An Elementary Treatise* (Cambridge: Cambridge University Press, 1912).

Martin, A., *Athanase d'Alexandrie et l'Église d'Égypte au IVe siècle (328–373)* (Rome: École française de Rome, 1996).

Mattingly, D. J., *Tripolitania* (London: Batsford, 1995).

Mayer, W., 'Female Participation and the Late Fourth-Century Preacher's Audience', *Augustinianum*, 39/1 (1999), 139–47.

—— 'John Chrysostom: Extraordinary Preacher, Ordinary Audience', in M. B. Cunningham and P. Allen (eds.), *Preacher and Audience: Studies in Early Christian and Byzantine Homiletics* (Leiden: Brill, 1998), 105–37.

Mazzarino, S., *Storia sociale del vescovo Ambrogio* (Rome: 'L'Erma' di Bretschneider, 1989).

Millar, F., *The Roman Near East, 31 BC–AD 337* (Cambridge, Mass., and London: Harvard University Press, 1993).

Miller, T., *The Birth of the Hospital in the Byzantine Empire*, 2nd edn. (Baltimore and London: Johns Hopkins University Press, 1997).

Misset-Van de Weg, M., 'The Purpose of the Wondrous Works and Deeds in the *Acts of Peter*', in J. Bremmer (ed.), *The Apocryphal Acts of Peter* (Leuven: Peeters, 1998), 97–110.

Mitchell, S., *Anatolia: Land, Men, and Gods in Asia Minor* (Oxford: Clarendon Press, 1993).

Mollat, M., 'Les Problèmes de la pauvreté', in M. Mollat (ed.), *Études sur l'histoire de la pauvreté*, 2 vols. (Paris: Publications de la Sorbonne, 1974), i. 11–30.

Morgan, T., *Literate Education in the Hellenistic and Roman Worlds* (Cambridge: Cambridge University Press, 1998).

Moxnes, H., *The Economy of the Kingdom* (Philadelphia: Fortress Press, 1988).

Munch-Labacher, G., 'Cyril of Alexandria', in S. Döpp and W. Geerlings (eds.), *Dictionary of Early Christian Literature* (New York: Crossroad, 2000), 153–7.

Neri, V., *I marginali nell'occidente tardoantico* (Bari: Edipuglia, 1998).

Norman, A. F., *Antioch as a Centre of Hellenic Culture as Observed by Libanius* (Liverpool: Liverpool University Press, 2000).

Ogilvie, R. M., *The Library of Lactantius* (Oxford: Clarendon Press, 1978).

Olivar, A., 'Reflections on Problems Raised by Early Christian Preaching', in M. B. Cunningham and P. Allen (eds.), *Preacher and Audience: Studies in Early Christian and Byzantine Homiletics* (Leiden: Brill, 1998), 21–32.

Orlandi, T., 'Letteratura copta e cristianesimo nazionale egiziano', in A. Camplani (ed.), *L'Egitto cristiano: Aspetti e problemi in età tardo-antica* (Rome: Institutum patristicum Augustinianum, 1997), 39–120.

—— *Vite di monaci copti* (Rome: Città nuova editrice, 1984).

Osborn, E., *Tertullian, First Theologian of the West* (Cambridge: Cambridge University Press, 1997).

Osiek, C., 'The Widow as Altar: The Rise and Fall of a Symbol', *The Second Century*, 3 (1983), 159–69.

Palmer, A.-M., *Prudentius on the Martyrs* (Oxford: Clarendon Press, 1989).

Palmer Bonz, M., 'The Jewish Donor Inscriptions from Aphrodisias: Are they Both Third-Century, and Who are the *Theosebeis*?', *Harvard Studies in Classical Philology*, 96 (1994), 281–99.

Parkin, A., 'Poverty in the Early Roman Empire: Ancient and Modern Conceptions and Constructs', Ph.D. thesis (Cambridge, 2001).

Patlagean, E., *Pauvreté économique et pauvreté sociale à Byzance 4e–7e siècles* (Paris: Mouton,1977).

Pearson, B., and Vivian, T., *Two Coptic Homilies Attributed to Saint Peter of Alexandria: On Riches, On the Epiphany* (Rome: CIM, 1993).

Pellegrino, M., 'General Introduction', tr. M. J. O'Connell, in J. Rotelle OSA (ed.), *The Works of Saint Augustine, A Translation for the 21st Century*, part 3, *Sermons*, tr. E. Hill OP, i (New York: New City Press, 1990), 13–137.

Perrin, M., 'Jérôme lecteur de Lactance', in Y.-M. Duval (ed.), in *Jérôme entre l'Occident et l'Orient: Actes du colloque de Chantilly (septembre 1986)* (Paris: Études augustiniennes, 1988), 99–114.

Petit, P., *Libanius et la vie municipale à Antioche au IVe siècle après Jésus-Christ* (Paris: Geuthner, 1955).

Pétré, H., *Caritas: Étude sur le vocabulaire latin de la charité chrétienne* (Louvain: Spicilegium Sacrum Lovaniense, 1948).

Pietri, C., 'Donateurs et pieux établissements d'après le légendier romain (Ve–VIIe s.)', in E. Patlagean and P. Riché (eds.), *Hagiographie, cultures et sociétés IVe–XIIe siècles* (Paris: Études augustiniennes, 1981), 435–53.

—— 'Evergétisme et richesses ecclésiastiques dans l'Italie du IVe à la fin du Ve siècle: L'Exemple romain', *Ktema*, 3 (1978), 317–37.

—— 'Les Pauvres et la pauvreté dans l'Italie de l'empire chrétien (IVe siècle)', in *Miscellanea Historiae Ecclesiasticae*, vi, Bibliothèque de la *Revue d'histoire ecclésiastique* 67 (Brussels: Publications universitaires de Louvain, 1983), 267–300.

—— *Roma christiana: Recherches sur l'Église de Rome, son organisation, sa politique, son idéologie de Miltiade à Sixte III (311–440)*, 2 vols. (Rome: École française de Rome, 1976).

—— and Pietri, L., *Prosopographie chrétienne du Bas-Empire*, ii. *Prosopographie de l'Italie chrétienne (313–604)*, 1 (Rome: École française de Rome diff. de Boccard, 1999).

Pouchet, R., *Basile le Grand et son univers d'amis d'après sa correspondance: Une stratégie de communion* (Rome: Institutum Patristicum 'Augustinianum', 1992).

Poupon, G., 'L'Origine africaine des *Acta Vercellenses*', in J. Bremmer (ed.), *The Apocryphal Acts of Peter* (Leuven: Peeters, 1998), 192–9.

Prell, M., *Sozialökonomische Untersuchungen zur Armut in antiken Rom: Von den Gracchen bis Kaiser Diokletian* (Stuttgart: F. Steiner, 1997).

Rahlfs, A., 'The Canons of Athanasius of Alexandria by W. Riedel and W. E. Crum', off print of the *Göttingischen gelehrten Anzeigen* (Berlin, 1905).

Ramsey OP, B., 'Almsgiving in the Latin Church: The Late Fourth and Early Fifth Centuries', *TS* 43 (1982), 226–59.

——*Ambrose* (London and New York: Routledge, 1997).

Rea, J. (ed.), *The Oxyrhynchus Papyri*, xl (London: Published for the British Academy by the Egypt Exploration Society, 1972).

Rees, B. R., *Pelagius, Life and Letters* (Woodbridge: Boydell Press, 1998).

Reynolds, J., and Tannenbaum, R., *Jews and God-Fearers at Aphrodisias* (Cambridge: Cambridge Philological Society, 1987).

Rist, J., *Human Value* (Leiden: Brill, 1982).

Roberts, C., *Manuscript, Society and Belief in Early Christian Egypt* (London: Oxford University Press, 1977).

Rondeau, M.-J., *Les Commentaires patristiques du Psautier (IIIe–Ve siècle)*, 2 vols, OCA 219 and 220 (Rome: Pont. Institutum Studiorum Orientalium, 1982 and 1985).

Rousseau, P., *Basil of Caesarea* (Berkeley, Los Angeles, and Oxford: University of California Press, 1994).

——*Pachomius: The Making of a Community in Fourth-Century Egypt* (Berkeley, Calif., and London: University of California Press, 1985).

Russell, N., *Cyril of Alexandria* (London and New York: Routledge, 2000).

Saller, R. P., *Patriarchy, Property and Death in the Roman Family* (Cambridge: Cambridge University Press, 1994).

Salzman, M., *On Roman Time: The Codex-Calendar of 354 and the Rhythms of Urban Life in Late Antiquity* (Berkeley, Los Angeles, and Oxford: University of California Press, 1990).

Sarre, F., and Herzfeld, E., *Archäologische Reise im Euphrat-und-Tigris-Gebiet*, ii (Berlin: D. Reimer, 1920).

Savon, H., 'Ambroise prédicateur', *Connaissance des Pères de l'Église*, 74 (1999), 33–45.

Saxer, V., *Morts, martyrs, reliques en Afrique chrétienne aux premiers siècles* (Paris: Beauchesne, 1980).

Schneemelcher, W. (ed.), *New Testament Apocrypha*, 2 vols. (Cambridge and Louisville: Clarke, 1990 and 1992).

Segal, J. B., *Edessa: 'The Blessed City'* (Oxford: Clarendon Press, 1970).

Suberbiola Martinez, J., *Nuevos concilios Hispano-Romanos de los siglos III y IV: La coleccion de Elvira* (Malaga: Universidad de Málaga, 1987).

Taylor, C., *Human Agency and Language, Philosophical Papers*, i (Cambridge: Cambridge University Press, 1985).

—— 'Interpretation and the Sciences of Man', in F. Dallmayr and T. McCarthy (eds.), *Understanding and Social Inquiry* (Notre Dame: University of Notre Dame Press, 1977).

Testard, M., *Chrétiens latins des premiers siècles* (Paris: Les Belles Lettres, 1981).

Trapé, A., *St. Augustine; Man, Pastor, Mystic*, tr. M. J. O'Connell (New York: Catholic Book Publishing Co, 1986).

Trout, D., *Paulinus of Nola* (Berkeley, Los Angeles, and London: University of California Press, 1999).

Truzzi, C., *Zeno, Gaudenzio e Cromazio: Testi e contenuti della predicazione cristiana per le chiese di Verona, Brescia e Aquileia (360–410 ca.)* (Brescia: Paideia, 1985).

Uhlhorn, G., *Christian Charity in the Ancient Church*, tr. S. Taylor (Edinburgh, 1883).

Uthemann, K.-H., 'Eine christliche Diatribe über Armut und Reichtum (CPG 4969): Handschriftliche Überlieferung und kritische Edition', *VC* 48 (1994).

Van Dam, R., 'From Paganism to Christianity at Late Antique Gaza', *Viator*, 16 (1985), 1–20.

Van de Paverd, F., *St John Chrysostom, The Homilies on the Statues: An Introduction*, OCA 197 (Rome: Pont. Institutum Studiorum Orientalium, 1991).

Vasey, V. R., *The Social Ideas in the Works of St Ambrose: A Study of the De Nabuthae* (Rome: Institutum Patristicum 'Augustinianum', 1982).

Veyne, P., *Bread and Circuses*, abridged O. Murray and tr. B. Pearce (London: Allen Lane, 1990).

Vööbus, A., *History of Asceticism in the Syrian Orient*, 3 vols. (Louvain: Secrétariat du Corpus scriptorum Christianorum Orientalium, 1958–88).

White, C., *Christian Friendship in the Fourth Century* (Cambridge: Cambridge University Press, 1992).

Whittaker, J., 'Christianity and Morality in the Roman Empire', *VC* 33 (1979), 209–25.

Wickham, L., *Hilary of Poitiers, Conflicts of Conscience in the Fourth-Century Church* (Liverpool: Liverpool University Press, 1997).

Wilkinson, J., *Egeria's Travels* (Warminster: Aris & Phillips, 1999).

Wilson, S. G., *Related Strangers: Jews and Christians, 70–170 CE* (Minneapolis: Fortress Press, 1995).

Wipszycka, E., *Les Ressources et les activités économiques des églises en Égypte* (Brussels: Fondation Égyptologique Reine Élisabeth, 1972).

Wölfle, E., 'Der Abt Hypatios von Ruphinianai und der Akoimete Alexander', *Byzantinische Zeitschrift*, 79 (1986), 302–9.

Wyrka, D., 'Clement of Alexandria' in S. Döpp and W. Geerlings (eds.), *Dictionary of Early Christian Literature* (New York: Crossroad, 2000), 130–3.

# Index